PAINTING CULTURE, PAINTING NATURE

PAINTING CULTURE, PAINTING NATURE

Stephen Mopope, Oscar Jacobson, and the Development of Indian Art in Oklahoma

Gunlög Fur

UNIVERSITY OF OKLAHOMA PRESS: NORMAN

Library of Congress Cataloging-in-Publication Data
Names: Fur, Gunlög Maria, author.
Title: Painting culture, painting nature : Stephen Mopope, Oscar Jacobson, and the development of Indian art in Oklahoma / Gunlög Fur.
Description: Norman : University of Oklahoma Press, [2019] | Includes bibliographical references and index.
Identifiers: LCCN 2018036568 | ISBN 978-0-8061-6287-4 (hardcover : alk paper)
Subjects: LCSH: Mopope, Stephen, 1898–1974. | Jacobson, Oscar Brousse, 1882–1966. | Art—Study and teaching (Higher)—Oklahoma—History—20th century. | Kiowa Five (Group of artists)
Classification: LCC ND237.M694 F87 2019 | DDC 709.2/2—dc23
LC record available at https://lccn.loc.gov/2018036568

The paper in this book meets the guidelines for permanence and durability of the Committee on Production Guidelines for Book Longevity of the Council on Library Resources, Inc. ∞

1 2 3 4 5 6 7 8 9 10

Contents

Illustrations

FIGURES

PLATES

MAPS

ACKNOWLEDGMENTS

ON A HUMID AUGUST night more than thirty years ago I arrived in Oklahoma to take up graduate studies. A few months later my host and I traveled to the Indian fair in Anadarko and walked among the artists' booths, where I paused at the friendly face of a woman named Vanessa Paukeigope Jennings, who displayed exquisite beadwork. She invited me to a conversation; she was curious of my foreignness and as a Swede I was spellbound by my fascination with American Indians. Over the years I would return to Anadarko, and slowly we built a friendship that has lasted more than a quarter of a century. As I would later learn, however, it was not the first time a Swede and a Kiowa became acquainted. As a Swedish teacher on a scholarship to study American Indian history at the University of Oklahoma in the mid-1980s I was intrigued to find that one of the university's buildings was named Jacobson Hall. My maternal grandfather's name was Sigfrid Jacobsson, and he had emigrated to the United States in 1903 but returned to Sweden to raise a family in Småland. He died before I was old enough to know what questions to ask him about his time as an emigrant. Norman's Jacobson Hall honored another Swede who had emigrated from the Småland region, Oscar Jacobson. He had become fascinated with American Indians, which seemed to mirror my own experience. Serendipity had placed me in the way of Jennings, the granddaughter of Stephen Mopope who belonged to the group of Kiowa artists whom Oscar Jacobson mentored. She and others in the Mopope family have maintained and retained knowledge of what transpired in ways that have allowed me to create a history of the Mopope-Jacobson entanglement that testifies to its significance. Our conversations inspired this book, but the direction it took is my responsibility alone. Mopope descendants and their neighbors in Redstone and around Anadarko have given generously of their time. They have hosted me as I visited Anadarko, their homes, and the Kiowa Black Legs Ceremonial over the years. I thank them deeply for sharing their memories and stories and for their friendship. I am also grateful for permission to use family photographs to illustrate this book. The Indian Hall of Fame in Anadarko became the venue for many long conversations with Vanessa Paukeigope Jennings, Carl Jennings, and Dorothy Whitehorse. Lee TsaToke sat with me an entire afternoon and gave me valuable suggestions for the manuscript.

I have also benefited from discussions with other scholars, beginning with fellow graduate students Sally Bradstreet and Linda Reese; Sally's interest in the public works art in Oklahoma and Linda's insights into Oklahoma history have helped me enormously. Jenny Tone-Pah-Hote shared her knowledge in delightful conversations about Kiowa art and material culture and about Jacobson and the Kiowa artists, and she graciously read parts of the manuscript. More than anyone, Karen V. Hansen has provided support, encouragement, and astute comments, and I am greatly in her debt for reading my work, talking and walking through its various stages, and believing in it. Dag Blanck and Angela Hoffman read parts of the manuscript and have been immensely helpful and generous with their knowledge of Swedish immigrants in America.

Many others have provided hospitality and enjoyable exchanges over the years. I thank Juliana Barr, Gurminder Bhambra, Diana Brydon, Ann McGrath, all my colleagues at the Concurrences Centre at Linnaeus University, especially Margareta Petersson and Emilie Wellfelt, and Stefan Amirell Eklöf for his help with illustrations.

Scholarship is not possible without dedicated and knowledgeable archivists. I thank the staff at Oklahoma History Center and the Dickinson Research Center at the Western Heritage Museum both in Oklahoma City, the Western History Collections at the University of Oklahoma, the Jacobson House in Norman (especially its former director Russ Tall Chief), and the Birger Sandzén Memorial Gallery in Lindsborg. I greatly appreciated the trip Ron Michael and Cori North treated me to around Lindsborg, when we visited the Jacobson homestead, the cemetery, and went to the Coronado Heights for the view.

John Hennessey assisted me in getting the manuscript in shape and provided insightful comments and tenacious effort in collecting images and permissions. I could not have asked for more. His friend Minchao Wu made the maps to my specifications, for which I am most grateful.

Toward the end of the project I finally made contact with descendants of Oscar and Sophie Jacobson. I thank Mark White at the Fred Jones Jr. Museum of Art in Norman for facilitating that contact. I have appreciated immensely email correspondence with Jacobson grandchildren Sophie and Sim Sheppard and Bob and Peter Harris. I thank Sophie Sheppard and Karen Logback Graham for permission to use family photographs, and for traveling more than the extra mile to scan them in the proper format.

My own family have shown tremendous patience and support. My in-laws, Paula and Duane Jones, offered room and board and company on my countless research trips to Oklahoma. My sister-in-law Jeannie Mullendore Jones drove several times to Anadarko to help me with illustrations. My wife, Cheryl Jones Fur, has read the book through and through and is my most honest critic and my greatest inspiration. My mother, Ulla Fur, taught me to love to read and write.

My editor at University of Oklahoma Press, Alessandra Jacobi Tamulevich, has shown great confidence in this project from the first tentative ideas I presented to her and has guided it with skill and discernment through a demanding review process. Emily J. Schuster welcomed me at the Press and ably guided the procedure with proofs including some deft long-distance instructions. I also thank the readers for their astute, sometimes critical, but essentially productive comments. Together they have helped make this a better book, and they should not be blamed for any of its shortcomings. Those are mine, and mine alone.

The research for this book has been made possible through generous financial support from the Swedish Research Foundation (Vetenskapsrådet) and from Linnaeus University.

Arrell M. and Rosemary Gibson took me in when I came to Norman, offered me guidance and imparted their love for Oklahoma's checkered past to me. They are no longer here to see this project come to fruition, but I am so grateful for the events that placed me in their way.

PAINTING CULTURE, PAINTING NATURE

Introduction

An Indian and an Immigrant in the Land of the Red Earth

IN THE LATE 1920S six young Kiowa Indians crossed boundaries of race and culture for the love of art. In pursuing art studies at the University of Oklahoma, they came in contact with and found a promoter in the professor of fine arts, Oscar Jacobson. Together they forged a spectacular moment in the emergence of a national and international interest in "Indian art." Was it really possible that American Indians had produced such works of beauty? Czechoslovakian president Tomas Masaryk posed this question to Jacobson as the novelty of the Kiowa paintings echoed across the Atlantic to Europe. For a brief period, the combination of immigrants and disenfranchised Indigenous people transformed Oklahoma into the center of an exciting new art development.

This growth of a movement for and interest in American Indian art coincided with the renewal and reshaping of Indian dance, which demonstrated the bold determination of American Indians to mold a central element of culture and religion to challenge government bans, develop pan-Indian connections, serve as entertainment, and provide a much needed income, while protecting some of its sacral meaning. The Kiowas who began to paint for a large multicultural audience in the late 1920s also stood at the center of the effort to retain and remodel dances. In the Kiowas' encounter with Oscar Jacobson, the American Indian struggle to redefine their place in America intersected with Swedish immigrants' homemaking in the new world. For some Swedish immigrants the contact with Native America provided an opportunity to forge a specific position as both separate from and part of modern America.

In *Painting Culture, Painting Nature* this encounter is narrated and interpreted through the experiences of two men, Oscar Brousse Jacobson and Stephen Mopope. The aim is to develop the anatomy of an encounter rather than straightforward biographies. Coming out of two radically different, yet in some small way comparable forms of diaspora, the dispossessed Kiowas and the Swedish immigrant and his French wife together participated in creating a specific place for Oklahoma, for American Indian art, and for the West in the life of the American nation. This is an account of concurrent places and movements that became entangled, intersected, and coproduced a new space that changed Oklahoma. Like many others, Jacobson and Mopope were locked into preassigned oppositional roles, structured in a discourse that presumed a fundamental difference between "primitive" and "modern." Yet each tried to transcend these strictures.

In 1907 while an art student at Yale University, a young Oscar Jacobson performed the role of Mistonkah, an Indian chief, in the play *Sunset* at the Foy Auditorium in New Haven. He enacted his part wearing a feathered headdress described as "the genuine article," which had been "obtained under great danger."[1] This was not the first time Jacobson tried on a costume, one might call it an identity, but it turned out to be one that followed him throughout the rest of his life. Only a few years later, sixteen hundred miles to the southwest, Stephen Mopope, still in his teens, was given a challenging task by his great-uncles Oheltoint and Silver Horn, as they decided to repaint a hallowed battle tipi. Young Stephen drew a series depicting three stories on the large ceremonial tipi and later stated that being asked to do this represented the greatest honor of his life. It proved a pivotal moment for the young man, as he was encouraged to use his gift for drawing and painting to participate in the creation of Kiowa cultural expressions. The two episodes set the stage for an encounter that would draw on imaginary representations of American Indians, on memories of war and loss, and on the rebuilding of lives on a frontier. Open warfare now lay in the past, but the ravages of life on a reservation, encroaching settlements of white people, and the establishment of Oklahoma as a new state in 1907 dramatically affected Kiowa economy and social life, along with the landscape itself.

The unexpected conjunction of the Kiowa artists Spencer Asah, James Auchiah, Lois Bougetah Smoky, Jack Hokeah, Stephen Mopope, Monroe Tsatoke and the Swedish art professor Oscar Jacobson helped create a new phase for American Indian art and culture in Oklahoma and the West. At times, Jacobson's and Mopope's pursuits intersected, the direction of their lives contingent upon the other, whether concretely, such as when Jacobson offered the Kiowas guidance on how to interpret legal contracts, or representationally, as in photographs of Jacobson together with the Indians, which allowed him to mold himself as a westerner. Most of the time they appeared to be hierarchically linked—with Jacobson as the helper, provider, promoter, and Mopope and the other Kiowas as the protégés, recipients, and preservers. Yet, they were also friends who played a meaningful role in each other's separate lives. They were bound by mutual need. Jacobson needed the Indians in order for himself to become the revitalizer of a Native art movement, which in the first part of the twentieth century became known as the Oklahoma or Bacone style of painting. His link to the Kiowas helped him become the westerner that he made himself into. In turn, Mopope and the other Kiowas needed support and guidance in order to traverse the boundary of the reservation and negotiate the commercial art world.

CONCURRENCES AND DIASPORAS

In examining concurrences and diasporas, a number of questions arise. How was it possible that the Kiowa artists and their heirs and followers produced such works of exquisite beauty, living as they were under a heavy yoke of assimilation policies? How did a Swede come to assume a significant role in this process, and what did it mean for his life to get to know the Kiowas? How did he depend upon the Kiowas for his own work and career? How was it possible for Stephen Mopope to shape a career as an artist?

A love of art brought these two men together, but the primary purpose in this book is not to narrate the lives of two artists so much as to investigate a relationship that cut across a social, cultural, and racial divide. A fundamental assumption is that these two men did not inhabit the same world. In one sense they did, of course—the physical location known as Oklahoma at the beginning of the twentieth century. But as a Kiowa Indian and a Swedish immigrant, they navigated within worlds much separated one from another, inflected by separate languages, moral and spiritual systems, cultural practices, and social organizations. Kiowas were not simply absorbed into American and (white) Oklahoman society after statehood in 1907, and neither were Swedish immigrants, who continued to arrive in the United States in large numbers up until the 1920s. Many realities shaped by different cultural expectations and power dynamics, challenge historians to craft narratives that do not assume the convergence of all these into one unified time and form of development. The relationship between Stephen Mopope and the other Kiowa artists and their families and Oscar Jacobson and his family and circle of contacts can be understood as a story of concurrences. Interpreting their worlds as concurrent offers a contribution to the scholarly work to conceive of diversity and conflicting claims. Concurrences arise out of the multiplicity of simultaneous worlds and suggest that we take care to listen to their complementary or contradictory claims. This account, then, is an attempt to present aspects of the concurrent lives of immigrants and Indians in Oklahoma as they touched one another around points of visual culture, arguing that these tangents reveal significant aspects of the development of American history.[2]

While the multiplicity of worlds may seem like a commonplace observation for most people, we are nonetheless trained to think of these worlds as uneven and bestowed with varying degrees of importance and range. In such thinking, "American history" forms a naturally overarching category of history that may contain a subset of "immigration history" or "American Indian history." Different groups, such as immigrants, ethnic minorities, and Indigenous peoples are arranged according to their position in relation to general trends of the nation, like modernity. What if modernity was not so much a characteristic of the nation but emerged as a consequence of the interaction between separate and entangled worlds?

My argument in this study is that, rather than being linked hierarchically, concurrent histories influence one another through their entanglements and thus bring about a world different from all their origins. Concurrences point to disparate spheres of existence and meaning that are interlinked, but that do not necessarily overlap and are not organized hierarchically—even though asymmetrical power relations will influence these relations. The terrible and exciting upheavals of diaspora, in this study signified by the opposing but comparable processes of relocation to reservation life and emigration, threw margins together in a way that created something entirely new and, for a moment in time, marvelous—the success of the Kiowa artists and the emerging fascination with American Indian art. Focusing on Oscar Jacobson and Stephen Mopope allows us to catch sight of a larger process—namely, that of how American Indians and immigrants in different circumstances and localities forged alliances and collaborative partnerships in order to protect and advance both cultural distinctiveness and political inclusion. However, it must never be forgotten that structures of huge inequality inflected every facet of their interaction.

Treating the life trajectories of Jacobson and Mopope as parallel may seem to downplay the very real disparities that colored their experiences in a thoroughly unequal society. Swedish immigrants became intricately involved in a process of settler colonialism that ultimately dispossessed American Indian peoples of land, culture, and language. Postcolonial scholarship recognizes that, although colonialism fundamentally reshaped relations in the world, there is need to "confront the power behind European expansion without assuming it was all-determining and to probe the clash of different forms of social organization without treating them as self-contained and autonomous."[3] Focusing on the concurrent lives and experiences as they emerge out of the different archives and materials consulted informs a historical narrative that goes beyond the binary of colonizer and colonized. To recognize these concurrent systems is to take seriously their claims of validity within their orienting systems of value *and* to look for how they entwined and shaped shared, but not necessarily equal, conditions.

Diaspora, as employed here, is not a given for studies of either American Indians on reservations or Scandinavian immigrants. It does, however, reveal distinct meanings for both experiences. Ruth B. Phillips suggests that European immigrant and exiled artists related to American Indigenous artists in a specific way, inflected by experiences of dislocation. "*Both* the stranger-artist *and* the indigenous artist are de-territorialised, although in different ways—the stranger as immigrant or exile and the native through colonial histories of displacement. *Both* desire, furthermore, to affirm their belonging in terms of a relationship to the land." White European immigrants certainly were complicit with the denial of Indigenous presence in their new land, but Phillips finds that "the arrival of a stranger armed with a modernist European openness to the primitive has repeatedly initiated artistic movements which ran counter to such erasures."[4]

The use of a diasporic perspective places the focus on mobility (and its restriction) and loss, both aspects that deeply affected the lives of Kiowas forced onto the reservation and Swedish American immigrants establishing new homes on American territory taken from American Indians. I do not suggest that American Indians and white immigrants share the same form of diaspora. On the contrary, different historical experiences of interactions with the American state and different requirements and opportunities shaped their relations with American society. They did not suffer similarly from diasporic upheavals, but the experience of dislocation marked their lives, and as Phillips suggests, this enabled a form of triangulation that shaped the unfolding of the events retold in this book and the participation of both men in the formulation of American art and life.

Such an investigation requires a concurrent methodology. By looking at different archives, divergent voices and claims, and competing perspectives of time and place, I seek a way of approaching these encounters from circuitous directions so as to catch sight of multiple meanings and relationships. I wish to tell stories of concurrences, of human lives lived—individually and collectively—in separate but interconnected time lines, following their own rhythms, dancing to their own drums, but by necessity drumming in step with, or in contest with, those other drumbeats, strong and weak, coming from other spaces. Likewise, Karen V. Hansen writes of entangled and controversial histories that require "a concurrent method that goes beyond triangulation. It needs to locate subjects in space, chronicle change over time, and incorporate a multiplicity of voices that speak from contrasting perspectives on different structural levels."[5]

Difference and asymmetry deeply marked the lives of these men. Jacobson and his wife, while at times struggling with experiences of inferiority in relation to a dominant Anglo-American society, nonetheless benefited enormously from the privilege of being white and deriving from northwestern Europe. His gender and his education and position as a university professor underscored authority and power that the dominant society denied to Kiowa men and most women of all ethnicities both legally and culturally. Class and gender played an enormous part in structuring the possibilities and interactions of the people involved in developing the art of the Kiowas. Still, a relationship emerged between Jacobson and Mopope, not because their life conditions were equal but because the relationship mattered to both of them.

A focus on friendship runs the risk of stressing complementarity at the expense of inequality and conflict. As recent studies demonstrate, such relationships were never unidirectional, nor always hostile. Colonial expropriation of Indian land and resources and the policies of indoctrination that accompanied that intrusion placed different people in close proximity to one another and inspired actions and feelings of mutuality and companionship, however strained. People of different races entered into many forms of relationships. Investigating friendship is a way to expose both possibilities and restrictions in a colonial contact zone. Elizabeth Hutchinson in her book *The Indian Craze* suggests that it "is not enough to identify the negative effects of racialist beliefs; we must also come up with new paradigms of analysis that permit new kind [*sic*] of questions about ethnicity and culture."[6]

INDIANS AND IMMIGRANTS

What can a book about one immigrant and one American Indian tell us that has not already been said over and over again? Their entanglement exists in a larger context of encounters between American Indians and immigrants, occurring all across the zones of American expansion. The massive waves of immigration coincided with American Indian experiences of dispossession. In this book I argue for the importance of viewing these two processes, one of migration and one of dispossession, as being interlinked and interdependent. Jacobson and Mopope's interaction is one example of larger processes, and the serendipitous conjunction of Swedes and Kiowas in Oklahoma allows us a rare occasion to glimpse encounters and entanglements from within different but concurrent histories.

From the 1840s until the end of the 1920s, nearly one and a half million people migrated from Sweden to North America. Of course, over such an extended period of time, causes for leaving home to settle in a new world differed—from religious persecution and hunger to perceived opportunities and hopes for a better life. Many of the Swedes ended up in the Midwest and Upper Midwest, attracted by the promise of available agricultural land or by opportunities in the fast-growing cities. The conventional story tells of emigrants leaving an impoverished rural Sweden for land that was granted almost for free on the American prairies. Countless books and articles have been written on the topic of Swedish and Scandinavian emigration to North America, yet not even a handful of these deal with interactions—voluntary or not—between Swedish or Scandinavian immigrants and American Indians.[7]

Similarly, histories written concerning different American Indian peoples rarely recognize the encounter with specific immigrant groups. Instead, cross-cultural relations focus on representatives of American or Canadian government authority or military, even though immigrant settlers constituted the vehicle for colonial westward expansion. When immigrants enter into the picture, they are often lumped together as "white settlers." While understandable, and at times founded in theoretical assumptions about the nature of settler colonialism, it is nonetheless problematic to assume that "settlers" consisted of a homogenous group, just as it is erroneous to describe all Indians as similar, specifically in studies that seek to deal with conflicts and entanglements. The separation of immigrant and Indian histories depends on their relation to dominant constructions of national narratives and on the fictive notion that Indigenous Americans and newcomers inhabited different times and places, each of little or no consequence for the other.[8]

In this book I challenge the separation of immigrant and Indigenous experiences, arguing that for the developments described, it mattered that Oscar Jacobson was a Swedish immigrant and Stephen Mopope a Kiowa. At the time when they met, the dominant discourse held that Indian and white societies represented diverging positions on a scale from primitive to modern. Yet, as historian Phil Deloria argues, Indians were not exempt from change, nor were they simply victims of it. Instead, the stunning explosion of technology and communication taking place in the young American nation was intrinsically connected to and grounded in the land of Indigenous peoples. Deloria identifies a persistent American account that describes how "Indian people, corralled on isolated and impoverished reservations, missed out on modernity—indeed, almost dropped out of history itself." In contrast to this narrative, he argues that the "world we inhabit is the shared creation of all peoples, though the costs and benefits have been parceled out with astonishing inequality, as have the notions about who has been active in that creation and who has been acted on." Thus, a study of where Indians are allowed to be placed, where Indians assert their presence, and how time and space structure relationships between Indians and non-Indians promises to reveal how Indians "have always participated in the *production* of modern discourse—and of modernity itself."[9]

Around the turn of the twentieth century, the American West constituted a significant and symbolically loaded space for forging perceptions of the American nation, at the same time as it contributed essential natural resources for the development of industries and trade and the growth of economic wealth. In this process, non-English immigrants constituted a major force, at the same time as they, as newcomers, vied for recognition and place. On both sides of the Atlantic, white people desired to forge connections to land, culture, and masculine values through romantic notions of American Indians. Several scholars have identified the allure of "playing Indians and cowboys" (as the expression was in Sweden). One strong motivation for this performance lies in a desire to belong to the new land. Immigrant groups sought to establish relations to the land they settled, and for some, the link to American Indians provided such an opportunity. Confronting the two—Mopope and Jacobson—thus offers an opportunity to study how the discursive dichotomy of primitive and civilized played into the lives of both American Indians and immigrants as they strove to secure a place in American society, thereby also shaping it.[10]

Some previous studies demonstrate that attention to the context of displacement and encounters has had a profound impact on how uneasily joined historical experiences have unfolded. An example of such processes is found in *Women of Oklahoma*, Linda W. Reese's pioneering interethnic study of how American Indian, African American, and white women negotiated life on the Oklahoma frontier. While not identifying non-Anglophone immigrant women as specific agents, she nonetheless opened up "exploration of relationships among and between women of different races, and between women and men" that "provides insight into the daily negotiation of life in a multicultural setting." Joan M. Jensen's magisterial *Calling This Place Home* interweaves stories of Native and Newcomer women on the Wisconsin frontier from the time of large influxes of German, Polish, and Scandinavian settlers from the 1850s up through the early twentieth century. Her poignant aim in linking these stories is that "Native people were displaced—not replaced." They were always there, in photographs and in reminiscences, and through their labor, adjustments, beliefs, and political activism Indigenous women and immigrant women "shaped the landscapes, mental and material, we now travel through." In *Encounter on the Great Plains,* Karen V. Hansen lays out how the federal process of settling the Spirit Lake Dakota Reservation in North Dakota made impoverished Scandinavians the tools of expansion and placed them in uneasy and entangled proximity to displaced and destitute Dakota Indians. By employing a perspective of entanglements rooted in land between wary neighbors, Hansen demonstrates that Dakotas and Scandinavians were not only victims and oppressors in a history shaped by inequalities and a racial-ethnic divide but also profoundly enmeshed in ways that led to enduring interconnections.[11]

In *Wild Men* Douglas Cazaux Sackman explores the relationship between Ishi, the Yahi Indian who became world famous as "the last wild Indian," and the eminent anthropologist Alfred Kroeber, a son of German immigrants. Their friendship invoked the intimate tension between wilderness and modernity in the early twentieth century. Sackman's wish to write a multiperspectival history of the West and his cautious and sensitive approach to conveying different viewpoints served as encouragement even as this study took a different route. Sackman downplays Kroeber's immigrant heritage but shows how he needed Ishi to establish his own position. Sackman argues that "each man made tracks on the other; each man made a name for the other."[12] Arguing for concurrent histories, I seek to respect the claim that immigration history and American Indian history are valid in their own right but nonetheless inextricably intertwined. In this book I aim to interrogate relations of wariness, enclaves of entanglement, and the mutual tracks that shaped conditions for both Indigenous peoples and immigrants in the molding of the modern West in the United States.

OKLAHOMA

The setting for this encounter is itself a conundrum. In the early 1900s Oklahoma represented the frontier in the American union, its famous land run signaling the opening of the last available free land in the scramble for dividing the prairie into square parcels. Not long before, the region had been envisioned as a haven for Indigenous peoples, displaced from other parts of the United States, perhaps even an Indian state in the union. Its sizable American Indian population came to resemble a veritable United Nations, as émigrés and displaced groups arrived from as far away as Idaho, Oregon, and New York to join Cherokees, Chickasaws, Choctaws, Creeks, and Seminoles, whom the United States government had forced from their homes in the Southeast onto land in eastern Indian Territory after President Jackson signed the Indian Removal Act in 1830.[13]

Long before this exodus began, Kiowas and Wichitas lived in Oklahoma, and Comanches and Kiowa-Apaches had joined them in making the vast rolling grassy plains their home. In white America's imagination it was a wild land, one not easily defined. It did not belong to the South, at least it had not formally been a part of the Confederacy, yet the last Confederate general to lay down his arms was Stand Watie, an Oklahoma Cherokee who himself, like many other American Indians in the territory, owned slaves. After the Civil War, great numbers of freedmen entered Oklahoma territory and established black towns, uneasily balancing poor economic conditions and white encroachment. The predominantly white leaders of the new state after 1907 anxiously sought to make it into a worthy member of a civilized, white, and Christian union, yet the population was mixed, poverty was excruciating, and divisions between its various constituencies were potentially explosive. The Jacobsons arrived in 1915 with a mission to civilize Oklahoma—or at least the small part of it that was its new university's art department—and prominent Scandinavian immigrants were hired to take on that task.[14]

Oklahoma defies simple categorization and therefore serves well to question some of the most pervasive binaries often used to describe American society and culture. East and West, North and South appear to converge in Oklahoma, creating an indefinable mix that eludes and baffles visitors and inhabitants alike. "Primitive" and "modern"—terms eminently popular in the early part of the century to describe the difference between Indians and Americans—collapse in the face of Oklahoma social relations. Not West, not South, not Midwest, not white, not red, not black, but all of these. At odds with the nations' politics, Oklahomans elected a governor on a socialist platform in 1923 yet established some of the first and harshest Jim Crow laws. Grueling poverty afflicted all, whether red, white, or black, memorialized not least in John Steinbeck's haunting description of the Dust Bowl (even though he famously misplaced it). However, it was also the site of some of the most spectacular affluence in American history, as oil was discovered on Osage Reservation lands in northern Oklahoma, briefly turning the two thousand or so Osages into some of the world's wealthiest individuals.[15]

Historian Linda W. Reese describes frontier Oklahoma as "a virtual laboratory of cross-cultural contacts."[16] She aptly cites Oklahoma doyen historian Angie Debo who wrote that, in Oklahoma, the "dim facets of the American character stand more clearly revealed. For in Oklahoma all the experiences that went into the making of the nation have been speeded up. Here all the American traits have been intensified."[17] For Debo, one of these traits was despoliation of Indigenous peoples, their land, and rights. "Such treatment of an independent people by a great imperial power would have aroused international condemnation," she wrote in 1940, "but these Indian republics were—to quote John Marshall's famous opinion—'domestic dependent nations,' and the destruction of their autonomy was a matter of internal policy."[18] American Indians were an indelible part of this new state, but its creation built on strategies of their annihilation—the Trail of Tears, the land run, the Dawes Act—and the white elite of the newborn state struggled hard to scrub off the Indian taint, even as the flag bore visible witness to their presence. Such encompassing rejection has continued to characterize the state's racial relations. In 2002, "The Guardian," a massive bronze statue sculpted by Seminole artist and state senator Enoch Kelly Haney, was placed on top of the capitol building in Oklahoma City, which became the first state capitol to exhibit an American Indian as a symbolic adornment, while racial lines still fragment the social and economic landscape.[19]

Race, class, and gender—classic components of social history analysis—thus characterized the encounter between Kiowa Indians and Swedish and French immigrants in ways specific to Oklahoma. Their association took place in the long shadows of General Philip Sheridan's cruel winter campaign against the tribal nations on the Southern Plains in 1874–75, and the incarceration of Kiowas, Comanches, and Cheyennes at Fort Marion. It followed on the aftermath of one of the worst race riots in American history, when a white mob reduced Tulsa's black Greenwood community to smoldering ruins; it was colored by Jim Crow legislation, reservation policies banning Indian dances and religious expressions, and Klan activity.[20] To forge friendships of whatever kind under such conditions must be deemed truly remarkable.

COLONIAL ARCHIVES, RECORDS, AND RECORDINGS

I am a tracker; I follow footsteps that have crossed the terrain I wish to cover before me. I follow these footsteps of lives that I see not as parallel but as concurrent. "Parallel" brings to mind surveyors' maps, tracts, and sections, a movement in unison along separate but identical lines. That is not what I have in mind here. No, the Kiowas and the immigrants lived concurrent histories, existing in the same time and place but moving to different steps, unsynchronized but at times intersecting and touching, jostling these different movements into change and digressions that could only have emerged out of these particular encounters.

Such a project depends on a wide collection of sources of different kinds. All studies are structured by certain sets of assumptions. American Indian history—but also to some extent immigrant history—requires recognizing what I think of as "silent archives," silent only in the sense that they have not been properly acknowledged as reservoirs of information and knowledge. An uncertainty pertaining to oral sources still haunts much historic scholarship. In societies where writing has not provided the dominant vehicle for containing and transmitting information, oral forms of socially recognized collections of facts and interpretations are passed from generation to generation according to specific methods, containing evidence of such things as historic events and processes, law, and religion. The past decades of postcolonial scholarship have seen an ongoing effort to define and resist the dominance of "colonial archives" in the interpretation of histories of colonial entanglements and to examine the relationship between oral and written remnants and memories of the past.[21]

For this study I have consulted a number of official archives housing written documents, photographs, and moving images; I have listened to interviews; and I have conducted interviews myself. Official records of the Kiowa Agency, kept at the Oklahoma History Center, offer perspectives on the life on the reservation, its economy and social conditions, while newspaper articles testify to the interest in the Kiowa art students. I am particularly indebted to the Arthur and Shifra Silberman Native American Art Collection at the Dickinson Research Center in Oklahoma City. This collection contains correspondence, clippings, photographic materials, and research notes, in addition to extensive interviews carried out from the 1970s to the 1990s pertaining to the Kiowa artists. These include interviews with Lois Smoky, James Auchiah, Stephen Mopope's daughter LaQuinta Mopope, and Oscar Jacobson's daughter Yolande Sheppard. In this project, I have also had invaluable access to Vanessa Paukeigope Jennings's memories, stories, and collected papers. The granddaughter of Stephen Mopope and an accomplished artist herself, she has power as a descendant and as an informed history keeper. Jennings is a historian of Kiowa history. From early on in life she practiced patience and endurance to listen and record in memory, and it is her passion and obligation to pass on the information she has gathered and kept. She has emphasized to me, time and again, that hers is just one voice and one perspective, but through her it has been possible to glimpse in greater detail the life of one of the Kiowa artists who came into contact with Oscar Jacobson, a rare opportunity in most contact studies involving immigrants and American Indians. Jennings's informed account and Stephen Mopope's own papers, left unorganized in large plastic boxes on the allotment in western Oklahoma, allows for a unique possibility to narrate aspects of his life that rarely emerge in general accounts of the Kiowa artists. At the same time, this approach limits the study in significant ways. I have interviewed a few other Kiowas, and I have consulted the interviews collected by Arthur Silberman, which in various ways throw a light on Mopope as an artist, dancer, and person, but it has never been my agenda to generally survey members of the Kiowa nation. This is not a history of the entire Kiowa people but, hopefully, one contribution to Kiowa history. I, as the author, take full responsibility for the choice of materials and the interpretations made from them. Throughout our conversations, Vanessa Jennings repeatedly voiced a concern that "There is so much you need to know, I don't know if I am telling it right." She combined this concern for my ignorance with an awareness of her own bias. Vanessa Jennings's awareness of the boundedness of her discourse is relevant to the topic of concurrent voices. She does not claim to speak for all Kiowas, nor that I, as a listener, should restrict myself to only her account. Yet, it is not only her individual story that she shares with me. It is also a history placed in a specific time and place—that of the Kiowa-Comanche-Apache Reservation where the context of the determination of the Kiowa inhabitants of the Redstone Valley to preserve culture and beliefs produced the artists who entered into a relationship with Oscar Jacobson. Vanessa Jennings describes the process when she writes that "culture is a conscious, consistent, deliberate passing on of knowledge taught every day by an older generation to the next generation." History is thus passed on in a context of relationships.[22]

For the Jacobson family, a new beginning awaited them in Lindsborg, Kansas, where they arrived in 1890. "It was over his vehement protest that Oscar came to the new country," wrote his wife in her memoir over their life together. He was eight years old and had his birthday on the ship crossing the Atlantic. He had grown up by the seaside and remained homesick for the ocean, "until his father gave him a horse that was to become his inseparable companion and friend. Together they roamed until, little by little, Oscar transferred some of his love of the sea to the long horizons of the Plains." Jeanne d'Ucel (the pen name used by Oscar Jacobson's wife, Sophie Brousse) wrote several manuscripts recounting their life together. They are dated to the 1960s but presumably built on notes kept for many years.[23] Her writing is the major source to access Oscar Jacobson's work, inspiration, and thoughts. Because of the importance of her writings I have chosen to refer to her primarily under her pen name. Jacobson apparently did not preserve any personal papers, and it is therefore through his wife's writings and through some of his own newspaper and journal articles that his voice emerges. His scrapbooks, preserved at the Oklahoma History Center, also attest to significant connections and themes in his life. At the same time, as is the case with Mopope, the reliance on a relative's reminiscences provides both depth and limits. D'Ucel's writings are clearly crafted as a tribute to Jacobson's life and achievements and must be approached with some caution. Yet, they provide a deeper insight into the contacts with the Kiowa students than any other source.

Immigrant history, too, often survives in an oral context. Joan Jensen writes: "Family histories are the legacy of the poor, the foreign born, and the disenfranchised; as such they are important to the story of any region." I do not wish to overstate the similarity between oral histories surviving (only) in a family context, enfolded in a culture of standardized written history, and the predominantly oral and pictorial body of knowledge protected and preserved among Indigenous peoples. They are both what Andrew Newman calls "communities of history and memory." Indigenous peoples share family histories, and their collective history contains internal differences and hierarchies. However, they also have to contend with a colonial power matrix that relegates Indigenous versions of history to the realm of myths and stories, thus making them appear less relevant to accounting for the truth of the past. In this book my hope is, again borrowing from Joan Jensen, that telling a history of immigrants and American Indians in some small way enables both "to be a part of our shared vision of the past and their descendants to share in the shaping of the future."[24]

By placing discordant and complementary voices, claims as it were, in dialog with one another regarding a number of themes, I seek to illuminate the intersections of the times of which they speak, as well as the limitations of their claims. I understand making claims as a way to attempt to control the form and direction of historic interpretation. "Beneath these personal stories," writes Randall Jimerson, "simmers an ongoing contest over what America is and means and who gets to define it."[25] In appropriate places I have therefore included the voices and words of my sources, not because I do not wish to take responsibility for the account forged here but, rather, because I wish to invoke the cadence and rhythm of different voices expressing experiences and claims on this historical terrain. In referring to sources in Swedish, I have kept the original spelling and made translations closely following the original text.

A NOTE ON ART

While this is a book that centers on artistic work, it is not focused on the objects of art themselves but on the artists and their locations. I am indebted to art historians for recognizing the centrality of art for investigating issues of identification and for interpreting cross-cultural encounters. They have critically investigated the intersection between artistic expression, representation, and social policy in the relationships between American Indians and white audiences, patrons, and administrators. Janet C. Berlo and Ruth B. Phillips, Jennifer McLerran, and Elizabeth Hutchinson make explicit the role of art in negotiating colonial encounters and how these colonial relations insisted on rendering Indians as primitive and static even as they were expected to participate in the economy of a capitalist market. In this way, Native art came to play a very specific role in the construction of an American national identity. Indigenous people responded to these developments, both taking opportunities and resisting the roles this conjunction of art and identity placed them in. Laura E. Smith's work on the Kiowa photographer Horace Poolaw, a contemporary of Stephen Mopope, offers an important perspective on how Kiowas experienced and managed strictures and emerging opportunities in the early 1900s.[26]

Surprisingly few studies have focused on the Oklahoma Indian artists and on Jacobson, while several fine works deal with the earlier generation of artists coming out of imprisonment at Fort Marion. Bridging the gap between these and the present study, Jenny Tone-Pah-Hote's dissertation "Envisioning Nationhood" specifically deals with the Kiowa artists and emphasizes the significance of women's expressive culture. The recent catalog of the Fred Jones Jr. Museum of Art's special exhibition of Oscar Brousse Jacobson's art, *A World Unconquered*, edited by Mark A. White, has been especially helpful. In an anthology chapter, Ruth B. Phillips poignantly identifies needs and bonds between what she calls stranger-artists and Indigenous artists and how the resulting relationship affects the work of both. She briefly discusses Jacobson and the Kiowa artists in useful ways. A play by Russ Tall Chief, former director of the Jacobson House Native Art Center, of Jacobson's entanglement with the artists builds significantly on Kiowa voices in representing history.[27]

Art offers clues to means of engaging with uniquely human social and spiritual conditions. It constitutes an ideal site for investigating both the expanse and the limits of individual imagination and for observing those patterns as concurrent and entangled. "Art and aesthetics are essential ways in which contemporary Native people express their senses of identity . . . it encompasses the ideas of traditional images and relationships with the earth, the impact of historical change, and the notion of what constitutes Indian identity," write Clara Sue Kidwell and Alan Velie. For immigrants too, art formed points of material connections to both the new land and the one they had left behind. The late Mary Towley Swanson identified among Swedish Americans a particularly strong network of artistic patronage that was available for Swedish emigrant artists arriving in America between 1880 and 1920. She found that the visual arts helped Swedish assimilation into American society, while at the same time affirming the bonds with Sweden.[28]

Dancing was—and is—closely tied to visual arts in Kiowa society. Clyde Ellis charts the changing dance culture and evolution of the modern powwow on the Southern Plains and argues that Indian people "used dancing to negotiate new social and cultural realities and protect tribal and community values." But immigrants danced too, as did American-born whites. Dance as an expression of culture and a vehicle for nation formation through multicultural performances featured prominently in the many ethnic and folk festivals emerging in the early part of the twentieth century. In *Staging Tradition*, Michael Ann Williams details the folk festivals emerging in the 1930s and their originator, Sarah

Gertrude Knott. Knott expressed her ambition behind organizing the National Folk Festival as a desire to collect and display the "songs and dances that bind us all to this country which is now home."[29]

Dance and art are manifestations of claims and sites of colonial contestation. Through attention to art and dance, then, we may catch glimpses of how people of different ethnic collectives expressed their understanding of their origins and belonging, and how their encounter with the American nation restricted and challenged these understandings.

OVERVIEW OF THE BOOK

This book is structured to reflect the notion of concurrent developments, as well as the movements of diaspora. Purposefully, some chapters describe parallel movements or entanglements, while others diverge between Kiowas and immigrants. There is an overt risk connected to this narrative structure. Changing perspectives in the different chapters, see-sawing between Jacobson and Mopope as it were, threatens the cohesion of the text. The purpose is to reflect the necessity of taking both sets of experiences into account, but without downplaying the real differences between them. The Swedish immigrant community may have viewed itself as disadvantaged in relation to the Anglo elite, yet they as a collective and Jacobson as an individual were never perceived with the denigration and paternalism that met American Indians in early twentieth-century American society. Nor did Swedish immigrants express an awareness of their own role in the dispossession of American Indians in parts of America where Swedish settlements depended on the denial of Native title. There are more abundant sources regarding Jacobson's experiences and that of Swedish immigrant communities than those pertaining to Kiowas and Mopope's family and kin. In addition, I speak Swedish but not Kiowa and that severely limits what I am able to narrate. I humbly ask readers to keep this in mind.

The first chapter provides a setting for the two disparate forms of displacement experienced by Swedish emigrants and Kiowa Indians around the turn of the twentieth century. The next two chapters diverge as they describe the years before the Kiowa students arrived in Norman. The second chapter follows Oscar Jacobson as his family emigrated from the island of Västra Eknö on the southeastern coast of Sweden to settle in Lindsborg, Kansas, where Oscar grew up and discovered the West. The third chapter illuminates the conditions of Stephen Mopope's youth and education in the Redstone Valley of Oklahoma.

The August 1927 issue of *My Oklahoma* reported that "Mopope and three other boy artists from the Kiowa tribe" had entered the art department as students of Oscar Brousse Jacobson. "In no time," the article stated, "the four boys were one of the sensations of the campus." Bringing the threads together suggesting a common arrival in a new setting, Chapters 4 and 5 pause at the time when in fact six young Kiowas came to study art at University of Oklahoma. The focus is on the period that laid the foundation for a lifelong relationship between Mopope and Jacobson. These chapters are devoted to the University of Oklahoma's development of art education for Native students, and to the ways in which the Kiowas and the Jacobsons negotiated over the meaning and content of art, as well as on practical aspects of accommodations and work in Norman.

"In the tapestry of our life," wrote Jeanne d'Ucel in her memoir of her life together with Oscar Jacobson, "some of the brightest threads represent our contacts with interesting people, whether for a brief hour, or for long, matured friendships." Chapter 6 is centered primarily on the Jacobsons and their many relations, concerning friendships and cross-cultural ties and also investigating the conflicts that emerged among white patrons of Indian artists and dancers regarding their own role in the development of Kiowa art and culture. Chapter 7 focuses on Stephen Mopope and his family and connections. Based on his preserved personal papers, this chapter chronicles how he strove tirelessly to make this development possible—by forever being alert to contacts who might be interested in purchasing art or by writing to galleries and collectors. He came to function as a chief organizer for dance troupes, as individuals and organizations contacted him to ask Indians to participate in private events and local and national exhibitions long after his close collaboration with Jacobson had ended.

Chapter 8 brings the narrative to a close through an analysis of the meanings conveyed in visual representations. Oscar Jacobson painted landscapes of the West. He followed a tradition of painting nature as it was supposed to be, uninfluenced by human activity. He sought nature just "as it was created." Stephen Mopope, in contrast, painted history as well as contemporary culture. His paintings represented Kiowa life as he knew it, and as it had been told to him, and painting it thus was part of a moral way of being human. Both Jacobson and Mopope were modern men who through their joint actions and diverging motives made Oklahoma—and America—the unique place that it is.

The concurrent streams of Jacobson's and Mopope's lives flowed together in the early twentieth century. Focusing on only one of these men would not capture the magnitude of their joint creation of appreciation and acceptance of American Indian aesthetic expression as fine art. They reached across the gulf that divided Indians and whites in Oklahoma to forge something qualitatively new. That this group of artists emerged and engaged such interest is remarkable, and even more so considering the time and place. It did not happen by itself; it was not the work of one element (promoters, Indian service, Kiowas, teachers, and so on) but required the collaboration of all. Such collaboration was often marred by friction, jealousies, and competition yet also developed into friendships and support. This history demonstrates the tenacity and sacrifices such a venture demanded, plus the disappointments and frustrations, and ultimately the huge significance for a continuation and change in Kiowa culture, for American Indian and western art in Oklahoma and the nation as a whole, and for enduring cross-cultural relations.

PART I

DIASPORAS

CHAPTER 1

DIASPORAS, 1860S–1910S

FOR SOME PEOPLE the past is distinctly divided into a before and an after. That holds true for both Indigenous peoples and for immigrants. Reminiscences as well as records from the past identify a break, when that which had until then been normal, recognizable, and true was altered forever. For the Kiowas and their Indigenous neighbors on the Southern Plains, this time came in the middle decades of the nineteenth century, when a dramatic loss of independence in terms of subsistence and social organization forced them into a limited existence on a reservation—in effect, an unwilling diaspora in their own country. For thousands of Swedes who emigrated from the 1840s and into the early twentieth century, this period too signified a form of diaspora. Most people left Sweden voluntarily and with hopes of a better and brighter future; some returned or traveled back and forth. Migration for many nonetheless represented a break that led to hardship and loss and threw into question issues of identity and belonging. Dislocated, but with dramatically different perspectives, by the end of the century Kiowas and Swedes struggled with how to re-create structures of belonging under new and unfamiliar conditions. For Swedish emigrants, locations shifted through a distance of more than four thousand miles, across an ocean and often farther to the interior of a vast continent, while for the Kiowas the most dominant feature of their situation was the contraction of mobility through imposed boundaries. For both groups, culture in the form of art, dancing, music, and stories became a crucial vehicle for expressing and asserting identity and meaning.

Anthropologist James Clifford defines the term "diaspora" as "a history of dispersal, myths/memories of the homeland, alienation in the host country, desire for eventual return, ongoing support of the homeland, and a collective identity importantly defined by this relationship."[1]

Such a definition identifies specific temporal and spatial ruptures that give structure to this chapter. There is a "before" to which people look backward, an arrival in a new place, and a subsequent struggle to identify borders and formulate one's belongings.

Focusing on the experience of European migration as diaspora is not the most common, nor perhaps seemingly relevant, context for referring to the vast and prolonged chain of migrants crossing the Atlantic in response to perceived opportunities and escaping strictures in their home countries. Previous scholarship on Scandinavian emigration has focused more on opportunities and on the back-and-forth flow of migration networks that helped blunt ruptures and sharp breaks. Nor is it immediately apparent how diaspora can be an appropriate reference for American Indians, whose dispossession and loss often occurred in the very regions they considered home.

My argument is that diaspora provides an instrument for revealing the ambiguities that infused the lives of both American Indians and immigrants, such as the urgent search for new roots and the ambivalent meanings of belongings. The term "diaspora" resonates with scholars of colonialism because it serves to illuminate how regimes of colonial power structured relations not only within specific communities but also in encounters between communities. Colonialism gave the patterns of migration a particular shape in the United States. "Immigration and ethnic identity in U.S. history," writes historian Paul Spickard, "have been intimately tied to race and slavery, on the one hand, and to colonial expansion across the continent, on the other." Paying attention to transnational linkages enables "us to examine the flow of ideas and cultures across natural and politically constructed borders," as historian Gregory Smithers argues. "This [helps scholars] understand how the larger structures of colonialism impacted the ways in which indigenous people envisioned, heard, and experienced the world around them, [and how] they endured as indigenous peoples through creative and adaptive processes."[2]

Immigrants were part of that flow of cultures, and focusing on their experiences serves two purposes. Like American Indians, they were embroiled in colonialism's reshuffling of human collectives and its hierarchies of race and culture. Their diaspora turned them inward, to focus on their own loss and subsequent need for reclamation, which insulated them from their own role in the dispossession of Indigenous peoples.

Education scholar Celia Haig-Brown argues that the "very construction of a diasporic discourse in the U.S. holds a certain irony when it fails to see the oppression of Native Americans as integral to the formation of both the nation and inextricably related to the many Diasporas now there."[3]

Another advantage of including both Swedes and Kiowas in the experiences of diaspora is that it enables recognition of the significance of aesthetic expressions. Anthropologists Pnina Werbner and Mattia Fumanti argue that people in diaspora shape "'a multisensory ambiance,' a space of multiple sensorial experiences that enrich their sense of self." According to Werbner, this space includes "collective literary genres, symbolic representations, historical narratives of loss and redemption, and practical forms of political alliance and lobbying that are uniquely theirs." These forms, which certainly must include visual art, are actively asserted through embodied communal celebrations. Communities collectively emphasized their links to a common past through stories and reminiscences. Practices such as dancing, public celebrations, and commemorations established diasporic communities' claims on the present, and through organized political and religious institutions and alliances people sought to build a future as self-identified collectives.[4]

The following sections ("Before," "Arrival," and "Belonging") purposefully weave back and forth between Kiowa country and Sweden so as to create a context for both the Kiowas' loss of independence and the Swedish emigration to rural America—along with its role in the dispossession of Indigenous peoples, which framed the conditions of the encounter between Stephen Mopope and Oscar Jacobson. These sections also form a metaphorical link emphasizing the connection between past, present, and future in the individual and collective search for identification among both Kiowas and Swedes.

BEFORE

LIFE BEFORE THE RESERVATION

Kiowas relayed history as part of a vast and varied body of stories, retold and reenacted in camps and gatherings and passed on between generations. Kiowa anthropologist Gus Palmer Jr. describes these stories as "the best ideas Kiowas have of themselves. They are acts of the imagination and memory. They tell of time immemorial. By means of these stories Kiowas are able to remember people and relive events important in tribal history and culture."[5] Stories placed the Kiowas in the world. At the center of the world there was a pool of water. Whoever dared jump into the pool would get to live there. But sharp points, like cattails, stuck out of the water, frightening the contestants. Finally, a Kiowa ran up, shouted, and jumped in, and he was not harmed. Instead he went through the roots of the sharp growths and came out on the other side. All assembled "heard a voice saying that the Kiowa had won the reward—to live in the centre of the world, all the others were to live around him, none could harm him or chase him away. So this is his land. The voice said again that after the life of the Kiowa ended there would be no more life on this earth. When the Indian race and language come to an end, there will be no more life on this earth."[6]

This story, written down by anthropologist Elsie Clews Parsons when she was visiting among Stephen Mopope's family members in the early 1920s, describes how the Kiowas became prominent in the world. Yet, they too had migrated. Once, they had lived in the Rocky Mountains around the headwaters of the Yellowstone and Missouri Rivers, forming an enduring alliance with the Crow Nation. In the early nineteenth century, conflicts with the Cheyennes and Sioux forced the Kiowas to migrate south into the region between the North Platte and Arkansas Rivers and eventually to cross the Cimarron River and establish council fires south of the Washita River. There they had to contend with the powerful Comanche empire that initially threatened their existence.[7]

The new country, a dry and undulating land surrounding the rocky outcroppings of the Wichita Mountains, caught their imagination; it was filled with bison and other animals that provided plenty of sustenance for them. Kiowa author N. Scott Momaday describes the enchantment of this country: "Loneliness is an aspect of the land. All things in the plain are isolated; there is no confusion of objects in the eye, but one hill or one tree or one man. To look upon that landscape in the early morning, with the sun at your back, is to lose the sense of proportion. Your imagination comes to life, and this, you think, is where Creation was begun."[8]

Kiowas had already acquired horses in the early eighteenth century, possibly traded from the Wichitas and Caddos in the south, and they became mounted buffalo hunters. Horses changed the Indigenous social structures of the plains, shaping a hierarchical leadership fusing independent bands into political entities united by shared ceremonies and prominent men's societies that gathered members from across bands. Societies became more stratified, and individuals found opportunities to augment their personal status and that of their families. Families owning the best-trained buffalo horses and the largest herds began forming high-ranking groups, and this was particularly true for the Kiowas, who developed distinct social categories for horse-owning elites. These high-ranking families often also possessed powerful and expensive medicine bundles.[9]

In the early decades of the nineteenth century the Kiowas sought peace with the powerful Comanchería empire. The alliance forged between 1790 and 1806 turned out to be the strongest and most enduring on the Southern Plains and allowed the less populous Kiowas and their even smaller allies, the Naishans (or Kiowa-Apaches), access to fertile grazing land and a more accommodating climate on the upper Canadian and Red Rivers at the northern edge of Comanche territory. The alliance between Kiowas and Comanches primarily involved commerce, and the Kiowas served as middlemen in the trade. Importantly, this exchange also included customs and beliefs. The Comanches participated in the Kiowa Sun Dance, eventually developing their own version of the ceremony. Historian Pekka Hämäläinen describes the Comanche empire as a large kinship network: "Affinity was the medium through which Comanches organized exchange across boundaries, and their trading empire can be seen as a vast kinship circle where ritual exchanges of words, food, gifts, and spouses stabilized intersocial spaces, creating a high threshold for intergroup violence." The Kiowas who had come into its orbit found it a "safe place to live."[10]

The Kiowas constituted a formidable presence on the Southern Plains, fanning out from their central location around the Wichita Mountains. Their foundational stories contained narratives of migration as well as the establishment of significant relations with enemies and new neighbors. Mary Buffalo described how her people came to Oklahoma from the Black Hills in South Dakota, traveling on horses with tipi poles tied on them to transport their household belongings. "That was our only way of traveling in those days—before the white man came."[11] Other stories describe the sharing of rituals and the acquisition of powerful medicine that could heal war wounds and disease and could be used to both predict the future and influence its outcome. One of these stories testifies to the dramatic change brought by the acquisition of the horse, equating the power of the horse to that of the tornado. The Kiowas heard stories of an animal that could run great distances and was "brave enough to face a charging buffalo bull." They had never seen a horse but decided to try to make one out of earth and their own medicine. "The beast's head was created a monstrous size. But it was so strong and powerful that the Kiowas and their Medicine Men were not able to stay close enough to finish making four legs and hooves. It moved about with incredible speed and power on the prairie on only one leg!" The "power in that single ominous hoof" confounded the Kiowas and it broke "free from its heavy buffalo ropes, throwing the handlers and the Medicine Men to the ground as it roared off, away from the camp, destroying the brush and trees and blinding everyone with the dust on the Great Southern Plains."[12]

The story demonstrates the uncontainable nature of power and the unpredictable consequences of human actions. Living in such an environment required order, system, and respect. Kinship shaped social ties that structured Kiowa society through band, social rank, and tribal nation. Extended family groups formed bands, comprising between twelve and fifty tipis. A generally complementary division of labor characterized women's and men's contributions to society. For example, women constructed and owned the tipis and were dependent on men's skills as hunters. Girls and boys were socialized into their roles and responsibilities through different social organizations. Military societies, which cut across families and bands, performed duties in connection with the Sun Dance but also had social and economic functions. Kiowas recognized four named ranks that striated society, forming around horse ownership and war honors.[13]

Many stories related war deeds. One referred to Stephen Mopope's paternal grandfather, Ghoulayee. The Kiowas and Comanches attacked a Spanish wagon train crossing through northern Texas. The wagon train's leader fought valiantly, but the Kiowa warriors observed him making a movement with his hand behind him. They decided to let the man live because of his bravery. But the Comanches did not honor their decision and killed all the Spaniards. When the victors looked behind the wagon, they found a small boy. The Kiowas claimed him and adopted him, naming him Little Colt ("Ghoulay" means "colt," and the "–ee" is a diminutive). Ghoulayee grew up to become a Kiowa warrior, earning a war name in a horse-stealing raid, and came to be known as Pokeitay (meaning "He Ropes His Enemy"). He died fairly young leaving two small children: Maigoday (known as George Mopope) and Sendemah (also known as Sindy Keahbone).[14]

During the early decades of the nineteenth century Kiowas established peace accords with various neighbors on the Southern Plains, and such relations included receiving and sharing dances, medicine, and warrior societies. Vanessa Paukeigope Jennings recounts what she has learned about the exchanges of the important Sun Dance. The Sun Dance began in Kiowa country and then spread to the Comanches, who took it to their allies and relatives the Shoshones. They in turn carried it to the Crows, and from the Crows the Sun Dance made its way to the Sioux, and from there it began to move south again. Other accounts, however, suggest that the Sun Dance was a gift to the Kiowas from the Crows, who also gave them the dominant sacred object of this ceremony, the *Taime* effigy.[15]

One of the most powerful gifts was that of the Buffalo Medicine. One account attributes it to a young Kiowa woman who was captured by Pawnees and destined for sacrifice. She managed to escape and hid from her captors inside a buffalo carcass. While she was lying there, the buffalo spoke to her and gave her instructions on how to make a medicine that could heal battle injuries and gunshot wounds. The girl made her way back to her people, and she married a Kiowa man. She asked him to bring her a piece of hide from a buffalo's neck and also a piece of deer hide. With this she constructed a shield, which her husband carried in battle. The couple adopted two orphaned boys, to whom they passed on the gift of the Buffalo Medicine. Through stories and dances, Kiowas made the Southern Plains their home and imbued the land with meaning, naming their connection to its places. The Wichita Mountains became the center of their world, in particular as it held the spirit of the buffalo, which sustained their society.[16]

Being allies with the Comanches allowed the Kiowas a certain insulation from interaction with Americans, as Comanche diplomats conducted foreign affairs for both nations. Kiowas only came into direct contact with representatives of the US government in the summer of 1834, when some ninety Kiowas attended a council held in a Wichita village located on the North Fork of the Red River. Three years later the tribe signed its first treaty with the United States, which also established peace between the Kiowas and the Osages and the Creeks and guaranteed all signatories equal rights to hunting on the Southern Plains in exchange for allowing US citizens free passage across the Plains region. In 1840, however, the Kiowas and Comanches concluded a peace with the Cheyennes, and together the accords between Kiowas, Kiowa-Apaches, Comanches, and Cheyennes effectively barred white access along the southern overland trails.[17]

In the aftermath of the Civil War, US military resources were deployed to break down Indigenous resistance to white encroachment on the Southern Plains. Two treaties, on the Little Arkansas in 1865 and at Medicine Lodge in 1867, established a joint reservation for the Comanches and the Kiowas west of the ninety-eighth meridian and stretching from the Washita River in the north down to the North Fork of the Red River in the south. Although prominent Kiowa chiefs—Dohausan and Satanta among them—signed the treaties, the treaty minutes make clear that they in no way intended to accept confinement on a reservation, and the US commissioners had to agree to let them "hunt on any lands south of the Arkansas River so long as the buffalo may range thereon in such numbers as to justify the chase." In the decade that followed, Kiowas continued to hunt and carry out attacks against cattle drives and settlements south of the border in Texas.[18]

By the mid-nineteenth century, despite increasing numbers of white settlers passing through their country, Kiowas still expected the continuation of the way of life they had built around the buffalo. Bison provided sustenance and enabled them to perform the Sun Dance and other central ceremonies. The provisions of the Medicine Lodge Treaty assured them the right to continue to hunt wherever necessary. That very provision, however, also handed white authorities a strategy for subduing the peoples on the plains. The United States increased the pressure on Kiowas and began employing rations to induce them to accept the reservation boundaries. Conditions on the reservation led to starvation, aggravated by the government's use of rations as a means to "domesticating and disciplining Indian bodies" through new diets and subsistence activities. Withholding rations became a way through which US officials sought to control the movements and the cultural and economic practices of Indian people.[19]

In the late 1860s, the government authorized an all-out war against the tribes on the Southern Plains in order to force Comanches, Kiowas, and Cheyennes to accept the reservation provisions stipulated in treaties. During 1868–76, US Army Lieutenant General Phil Sheridan was given wide latitude to pursue Indians and punish them as he deemed fit, wherever they tried to hide or escape. Meanwhile, a thriving business in buffalo hides led to an aggressive depletion of the bison herds on the Kansas plains. The US Army watched without interfering and even hired hunters to diminish the enormous herds of buffalo leading to what a Kiowa historian, Old Lady Horse, called the "war between the buffalo and the white men." She described how "the white men hired hunters to do nothing but kill the buffalo. Up and down the plains those men ranged, shooting sometimes as many as a hundred buffalo a day. Behind them came the skinners with their wagons. They piled the hides and bones into the wagons until they were full, and then took their loads to the new railroad stations that were being built, to be shipped east to the market. . . . The buffalo saw that their day was over. They could protect their people no longer."[20]

Kiowas watched as their livelihood and the plains ecosystem was rapidly and deliberately destroyed, forcing them into an alien system of remote markets attached to their home through the unrelenting tentacles of the railroad. The government did little to uphold the protection of the borders agreed upon in the Medicine Lodge Treaty and failed to provide the rations and annuities stipulated in the treaty. Young Kiowa men struggled to provide sustenance for their people through hunting and raiding beyond the confines of the reservation. Government officials pressured Kiowa leaders to control their young men who were described as "renegades" carrying out "depredations," and the US Army relentlessly pursued those who left the reservation. In 1874 Colonel Randall Mackenzie chased fleeing Kiowas, Comanches, and Cheyennes into Palo Duro Canyon in the Staked Plains. Torching abandoned camps and rounding up and killing more than a thousand horses, the soldiers forced warriors, women, and children to attempt escape on foot toward the south, where they were surprised by inclement weather and suffered from lack of provisions during blizzards and ice storms. In 1875, starving and destitute, Kiowas reported to Fort Sill where they were imprisoned, awaiting decisions about their future at the hands of the American authorities.[21]

LIFE BEFORE EMIGRATION

Sweden, with a population of some 2.4 million people in 1815, faced a century of dramatic transformations. Reductions in infant mortality, traditionally credited to "the peace, the vaccine, and the potato," led to a rapid population increase, which by 1910 had reached 5.5 million.[22] New agricultural methods demanded a restructuring of farmland and pastures, and several enclosure initiatives led to the consolidation of holdings but also to the expulsion of cottagers and the loss of viability on small farm holdings. Work opportunities emerging in connection with developing industrialization attracted some of the landless people to towns and growing cities, but the population was overwhelmingly agrarian well into the twentieth century.

In the middle of the century, during the years 1867–69, parts of the country experienced a particularly devastating period of crop failure due to inclement weather conditions. The northern half of the country suffered most heavily, but the province of Småland (the small countries) in southern Sweden (see map 1)—where Oscar Jacobson's family lived—was severely affected as well. Family stories relate how women collected scrapings from cutting boards to boil into a watery soup. Following the drought and famine of the late 1860s conditions in Småland were similar to those pertaining to the country at large, although there were comparatively fewer estate owners of greater means. The number of cottagers and crofters, and young men with no prospects of owning their own farms, had grown exponentially in the first half of the century, although the number of farm laborers remained relatively low, most likely on account of the lack of large estates. The fishing industry remained less developed than in the country in general, despite a long coastline on the Baltic Sea. In contrast to the rest of the country, Småland experienced a decline in population during the second half of the nineteenth century, a development that according to historian Olle Larsson was primarily due to emigration, internal as well as external. In terms of emigration to America in relation to the population, the three districts that made up Småland placed second, fourth, and fifth in Sweden.[23]

Emigration from Småland to North America began modestly in the 1840s, but the first great wave followed on the years of crop failures in the 1860s. During the 1870s interest in leaving Sweden receded following

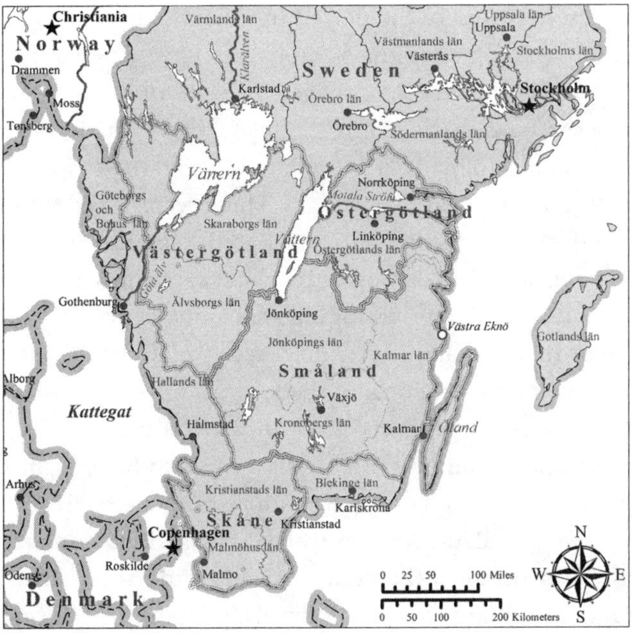

MAP 1. Map of the southern third of Sweden in 1900 showing the region of Småland and the location of the island of Västra Eknö on the Baltic (eastern) coast.

economic recovery. But in the 1880s and 1890s more people than ever emigrated and between 1879 and 1930 more than half a million Swedes left for North America, the aggregate number for the three Småland districts equaling nearly two hundred thousand.[24]

Perhaps it was the hardships and the meager soil studded with rocks emerging out of the ground after each thaw that made people from Småland cautious and conservative. Perhaps it was the lack of a landed aristocracy that bred a comparatively egalitarian approach to community, or perhaps it was a history of opposition to the dictates from Crown and Church that made them suspicious of both authorities and innovations. Ethnographers have identified these as traits that were prevalent in the region, along with such demographic specificities as a lower incidence of reported suicides and children born out of wedlock than in the rest of the country. In small rural villages people established inclusive support networks, which also exercised a high level of social control.[25]

Large parts of Småland were swept up in recurring religious revivals over the course of the nineteenth century. These evolved in opposition to the omnipresent power of Sweden's Lutheran State Church, which held the monopoly on religious rituals and expressions as well as the mandate to check on each citizen's knowledge of the central tenets of the faith. The local vicar held yearly examinations in each parish and noted the parishioners' ability to read, write, and understand the scripture, as well as births, deaths, baptisms, and marriages. These records laid the foundation for a detailed census system, dating back to the seventeenth century. The church thus registered all demographic data regarding citizens and issued passports, which were required for internal as well as foreign travel.[26]

A royal ordinance, the Conventicle Act of 1726 aimed at curbing the influence from pietistic beliefs, forbade privately held prayer meetings. However, in the nineteenth century the law was primarily used against various revivalist movements. Methodists came to Sweden in the 1830s, and Baptists in the middle of the century, influenced largely by sailors returning from the United States where they had encountered the new movement. Even more influential in challenging the teachings of the state church were many localized revivals, including the visionary experiences of lay people. These movements had many followers in Småland, in particular in the northern Jönköpings län, who defied the Conventicle Act, continued to hold prayer meetings and share communion in their homes, and joined together to build chapels. Along the northern coast of Kalmar län a sectarian form of Methodism attracted many converts. Harsh punishments forced some of the revivalist leaders to emigrate and inspired some of the earliest Swedish migration to America. The Christian revival in Småland had a concrete influence on the social life of communities. Alcohol consumption, which had been a major social problem, was reduced drastically as the converted took vows of temperance. Local congregations formed, organized meetings, and helped members in need. Most revival leaders and the "awakened" lacked formal education, but they scrutinized the Bible for answers to pressing issues regarding the nature of sin and salvation, which incidentally strengthened their ability to read and write. For many, this world was only a waiting room to the next, and spiritual awakening was a step in the direction of heavenly salvation. The year 1898 was a particularly intense year for religious sentiment. It had been prophesied that Christ would return on Easter Day, and people dressed in their best clothes and went out on the roads, looking skyward in anticipation.[27]

Oscar Jacobson was born in 1882 on the island of Västra Eknö on the east coast of Småland, the son of Anna Lena Olofsdotter and Nils Petter Jacobsson. The island is hilly, with a broken coastline, close to the open Baltic ocean. The name suggests its prevalent vegetation (it is an island of oaks), a common name for islands along the Swedish east coast. It housed two estates, which combined farming with fishing. In 1800 the farms were enclosed and divided into upper and lower farmsteads (Oppgård and Nergård). In the 1880s documents show that the farms paid part of their taxes in pike, herring, cod, and eel. It became increasingly difficult for the meager soil on the island to feed the large number of children in the families, and emigration became a solution for many young people. However, not all of them went to America. One young returnee from Australia set up the island's first general store in the 1930s.[28]

Anna Lena Olofsdotter grew up on the island of Västra Eknö, and after her marriage in 1866 the couple settled near her family home, eventually moving in with her mother at Oppgården, where they lived until they emigrated to America in 1890. Nils Petter was a fisherman and a farmer, and Anna Lena managed the household and worked in the fields as well. Fresh catch was transported to the mainland and sold, while herring and cod were preserved in salt brine and dried. In the wintertime, salted dried fish were hauled on sleds across the ice and sold. The family had cows that grazed during summers on a nearby island, to which family members traveled by boat to do the milking. They kept a hayfield for the winterfeed for the cows and planted rye for grain.[29]

In her memoirs Jeanne d'Ucel relays stories of a life on the island that appeared easy and bountiful. Early on the children learned to become expert fishermen. The family had a sheltered beach to themselves where they played and swam. "There were delicious wild berries in the woods, birds, toads, bugs to watch, rocks to climb and to play hide and seek around; and, when they returned home, a big kitchen redolent with the exquisite odors of those heavenly cakes and cookies the women were forever baking." Living on a farm the family had their own milk, cream, butter, eggs, and meat. A kitchen garden provided vegetables, and there were "juicy apples and pears on trees around the house, for the picking." They grew flax, which they used to weave their own linens, and "they sheared their own sheep to make blankets." Surplus production of beef, grain, and potatoes were sold on the mainland or traded for coffee, sugar, and rice.[30]

The description of the easy life on the island is likely to be a later construction, painting a nostalgic picture of a lost paradise. But it was a life of basic self-subsistence, common to most peasant households in Sweden. There is no recollection of want or poverty; it appears the family was quite well-off. There was much work to do on the farm, particularly for the women of the household. "Mother Jacobson, a little wisp of a woman, electric with energy, managed, with the help of a servant or two, later that of her growing daughter, to keep her big house immaculate, to cook in the great Swedish tradition, to spin and weave and sew. She even found time for making delicate embroideries." Nils Petter enjoyed hunting and loved woodworking. "He spent on cabinet making all the time he could spare from the care of his farm."[31]

There were no schools on the island before 1890. Perhaps lessons were organized in a temporary location in order for children on the island to attend school, as all children were required to do, according to the Charter of 1842. D'Ucel describes Oscar's vivid memories of book illustrations from his first school. In his home there were books, but none with pictures. Nor did he remember newspapers or magazines, although such publications had become increasingly available and common by the end of the century.[32]

Oscar may have remembered a comfortable life on the island, but his parents found it difficult to cater to the needs of a growing family. Emigration offered a solution. The Jacobson family did not flee religious oppression or imminent poverty. Instead, like so many other emigrants, they chafed against unpopular restrictions in Sweden and felt the pull of superior opportunities in America. According to the Jacobson family history, compiled by Delbert Jacobson in 1996, Nils Petter desired to keep his sons out of conscripted military training. By the early 1880s, a number of young men from the island had already emigrated and the advertisements from steamship companies promised "large acreages of land . . . available for homesteading or for a very reasonable price."[33] In 1885 the oldest son, Emil, sailed for the United States, eventually arriving in the Swedish community of Lindsborg, in Kansas. He wrote glowingly of the possibilities in the region fairly recently opened for settlement. He already had his eye on a good stock farm and urged his father to buy it. In 1890 his parents and siblings followed.[34]

Letters collected for a Royal Commission of Inquiries into the causes and conditions of emigration (*Emigrationsutredningen*) describe how emigrants perceived Sweden and detail their reasons for leaving. One young man, the son of a skipper from the Kalmar district to which Västra Eknö belonged, emigrated in 1870. He described beginning school at the age of six, in a one-room school on top of which lived the teacher. His teachers, one after the other, died from tuberculosis and the conditions in the cramped schoolhouse contributed to spreading the disease. "I don't wonder, that so many of the children caught the same disease, because we were expected to sweep the barn twice a week and then the dust swirled like on a well-worn country road in a dry summer." Classes consisted of "reading the catechism, the testament, the hymnbook, biblical history and a small excerpt of Swedish history and Swedish grammar for those who could afford to buy the books. Arithmetic and writing we had twice a week."[35] The young man desired to study, but neither his class position nor his environment allowed him to do so. After a long life as a sailor and traveler, he ended up in Tennessee owning a small farm. Yet, he loved Sweden and ended his letter with expressions of commonly voiced grievances with nineteenth-century Swedish society. "When you give your children the right to vote (because it is at the ballot that class differences evaporate), when you cut the bonds between church and state, when you modernize some of your ancient laws and take away education from the prelates, then I will liquidate all my assets and travel home to rest in your soil."[36]

ARRIVAL

RESERVATION LIFE EARLY IN THE TWENTIETH CENTURY

While living under hugely different circumstances, by the end of the nineteenth century Kiowas and Swedish immigrants both had to struggle with new surroundings and new sets of circumstances. For the Kiowas in Oklahoma Territory these novel conditions meant the threat of complete erasure of culture and society. White officials and observers expected them to at least fade into oblivion, if not vanish for good. During the last frenzy of the Buffalo Wars in the mid-1870s, newspapers speculated in ever more exaggerated terms about the need for a final settlement to the problem of "hostile Indians," ranging from banishment from Indian Territory to extermination. Washington politicians argued more cautiously, but they also favored some form of removal and incarceration, as did military officers. By 1875 Kiowa and their allies' resistance had been broken. As a forceful punctuation to their claims of freedom to move across the territory which they regarded as home, more than seventy Cheyenne, Comanche, Kiowa, and Apache men were imprisoned and sent to Fort Marion in St. Augustine, Florida.[37]

There, under the watchful eye and tutorship of Lieutenant Richard Henry Pratt, the incarcerated men (and at least one woman) became part of an experiment intended to transform them into ambassadors of civilization upon their eventual release three years later. As part of Pratt's progressive pedagogy and to alleviate the boredom of their heavily regimented lives, the prisoners were given ledger book paper and pencils, and some of them eagerly availed themselves of the opportunity to document past and present experiences. Twenty-six of the men produced several hundred illustrations, transferring traditional illustrations on tipi covers, shields, and calendars to paper. They featured war deeds, camp life, councils, and dancing. The images portrayed everyday life, historic events, comic moments, and stories. Pratt began a practice of selling these paintings to the surrounding white community.[38]

Sequestered far away from home, the prisoners drew and enacted links with their kin and with their past that would have lasting consequences. Scratched into the sandstone walls of the cells are images of an Apache Fire Dancer and of a Kiowa Sun Dance, testifying to someone's deep yearning for communion with his community. The men expressed their longing for connection, their historical consciousness, and asserted their sense of cultural identity through their art. One of the incarcerated men was Oheltoint, whose sister Keintaddle became grandmother to Stephen Mopope and whose brother Silver Horn was a preeminent painter and illustrator among the Kiowas.[39]

Literary scholar Birgit Brander Rasmussen suggests that the drawings from Fort Marion show that the captives over time began to view themselves not just as defeated men but as "individuals with the capacity to perform feats of the kind that affirmed (and constituted) masculine identity on the Plains." Perfecting drawings on paper with ink and pencil thus represented not only a way of remembering and preserving past and present deeds and visions but also expressed male valor and achievement. Paintings on paper connected with earlier practices of young men to express spirit power through painting signs on their bodies, animals, shields, and hides. Decorating one's horse, shield, or tipi signaled a spiritual connection between humans and the other-than-human world. This constituted power, actualized through responsibilities toward the community, values of discipline and balance, and readiness to exert physical strength in a manner befitting a proper warrior.[40]

Back on the reservation, people similarly struggled with the loss of livelihood and a sense of having been abandoned by the buffalo who had so richly sustained the people in the past. Old Lady Horse relayed a haunting story of how the war between the buffalo and the white men ended. Early one morning a young woman watched from a camp on the north side of Mount Scott. Through the morning haze the last buffalo herd appeared before her eyes "like a spirit dream." The line of buffaloes, cows, calves, and a few young males who had survived the slaughter, walked straight toward Mount Scott and a doorway opened into the mountain. Curious, the young woman followed. Inside the mountain "the world was green and fresh, as it had been when she was a small girl. The rivers ran clear, not red. The wild plums were in blossom, chasing the red buds up the inside slopes. Inside this world of beauty the buffalo walked, never to be seen again."[41] Life as buffalo hunters had ceased, the giant animals had retreated into the heart of the large Kiowa, Comanche, and Apache (KCA) Reservation. Piecing together a new life bounded by an imposed reservation presented the Kiowas with formidable challenges. They had been cast out, despite the reservation's location in a territory they recognized as their own. The past held glories; but also the most devastating violence, the scourge of recurring epidemics, and starvation. The future appeared to promise only the elimination of all that they recognized as familiar, including language, customs, and beliefs.[42]

Living conditions on the reservation were bleak. Government policies of herding together different tribes in bounded enclosures also aggravated tensions among peoples who had a history of enmity. In 1878 the Indian agencies administrating the Kiowas and the Wichitas were consolidated, and Kiowas came to share a reservation with American Indian nations from the region of Texas, such as the Caddos, Wichitas, Hasinais, and Tonkawas, as well as with tribes with origins in the East, like the Delawares. Jennings describes the reservation as a gigantic "open air prison camp." No wonder it turned into a witches' brew of hostility, with its tentacles of resentment reaching into the present day. It is not hard to imagine what US policies of restriction would do to a small society, where anonymity was practically denied, movement restricted (even the most innocuous visit required permission from agency officials), and the most basic exercising of rights or subsistence depended upon the rules of regulations of the Indian Office.[43]

Hunger haunted the reservation. A white woman, Mrs. W. C. Jarboe, described the pitiful conditions of the Kiowas and Apaches amid what she perceived as an abundant and glorious landscape. In 1891 her family, passing through Fort Sill on their way west, happened on the twice-monthly distribution of annuity cattle and watched as men on horseback shot down about fifty animals using mostly bows and arrows. She found the practice barbaric and described "a very disgusting incident" when "a bunch of Indians" began "eating greedily of the intrails" of the butchered animals, along with "five dogs eating ravenously from the hind-quarters." Her account conformed with racial stereotypes prevalent in her time and glossed over the specter of starvation plaguing the people on the reservation. Mrs. Jarboe ended her observation with their departure from Fort Sill, and in stark contrast to her characterization of the reservation, the family "enjoyed every minute of our camp life. Fish were very plentiful in all the beautiful little streams. There was also plenty of wild game."[44]

Kiowa descriptions and Indian agent reports confirm the hunger and humiliation hidden in Jarboe's observation. Jennings recalls being told that "people were reduced to fighting over rabbits. I mean these are powerful Kiowas, with this beautiful culture and they're fighting over rodents." The intention of the government was to transform Kiowas, Comanches, and Apaches into sedentary farmers, but the climatic conditions in the region as much as their subsistence culture worked against this ambition. In 1882 Indian agent P. B. Hunt lamented the "disastrous results of the drought of the last few years and the complete failure of crops and the loss of their year's labor will deter them from again engaging in farming operations." Between 1893 and 1895 conditions were particularly excruciating, and the Baptist missionary Isabel Campbell declared that the "Indians know more about starvation than any other people on the earth." In 1896 the agent Frank D. Baldwin described the situation in his report: "For thirty-four consecutive days during that part of the season when the crops needed rain the thermometer registered an average of 107 degrees and more each day, with little or no rain, and hot winds prevailing most of the time."[45]

Health problems followed on the deplorable conditions on the reservation. An epidemic of measles that spread across the reservation in 1892 took the lives of more than two hundred people, mostly children. Agent Ernest Blecker wrote in his report in 1910 that tuberculosis "is very common. Trachoma in varying stages exists in at least 75% of all eyes about 10% of which is in severe form. During the year epidemics of measles, German measles, and whooping-cough occurred. Broncho-pneumonia as a complication of each caused a number of deaths among children." Health concerns remained central in the reports of agents and matrons well into the 1920s.[46]

The mixture of different peoples all placed on the same reservation caused problems. Jennings describes how "the Delaware are brought from New York and Pennsylvania and New Jersey, and they're brought here 'cause nobody wants them. Texas wanted to get rid of all of their Indians, so they brought everyone up here, except for the Kickapoo. Somehow the Kickapoo got away from them. The Caddos they brought here, and the Government didn't care that there were peaceful, farming tribes that were in the middle of the most barbaric warriors that ever existed." The Kiowas considered the Tonkawas the most frightening of all enemy peoples and related fear-filled stories of their supposedly cannibalistic practices. Sometimes the Kiowas feared each other, too. In 1891 the agent reported trouble "with a bad and unprincipled Kiowa Medicine man." For years, he "held a rod of terror over the Kiowas." He demanded from them "horses, cattle and other of their possessions," and if they refused he threatened them with "the use of his evil power." Outside the reservation, stories circulated regarding the cruelty of Kiowas, contributing to strengthening stereotypes among white Americans regarding the uncivilized manner of Indians and serving as an excuse for continued control over their lives. The Baptist reverend Herman Clouse described the past of one of his converts in a Christmas letter in 1914. Jack Wolf had been "trained for the warpath and participated in all its atrocities. He was great in the war and sundance, danced for four days and nights without anything to eat or drink, cutting flesh from his body and holding it up as he prayed to the sun to help him kill the white man."[47]

The tract set aside for the Kiowas, Comanches, and Kiowa-Apaches in the Medicine Lodge Treaty comprised almost 3.0 million acres, and north of them the Cheyenne-Arapahoe reservation was even larger, covering

4.3 million acres. By the 1880s land available for white homesteading had become scarce, and many agitators were attracted to what they argued were the vast stretches of unused land contained in Indian reservations. These Boomers clamored for opening surplus Indian land to settlement by white homesteaders. The Dawes Severalty Act of 1887, named for its instigator Senator Henry Dawes, responded to these demands with a proposal to allot Indian land serving the dual purpose of enabling American Indian assimilation into the United States based on individual landownership and freeing up land for homesteading. The implementation of the act took more than a decade. The Cherokee (or Jerome) Commission—set up by Congress in 1889 to negotiate allotment in Oklahoma—arrived on the reservation in 1892 and found 1,104 Kiowas, 1,531 Comanches, and 241 Apaches mostly living in tipis in large multigenerational households, wearing Indian clothing with braided hair, and participating in peyote ceremonies. David H. Jerome, the commission's chief representative, informed the tribes that they had more land than they could use and offered them to "sell to the great father all the land that you can not use for homes for his white children." In addition, he made clear that Indians could not own land in the same way as white farmers, "they could not sell an acre of the reservation nor lease any of it to cattlemen without government permission."[48]

The Kiowa spokesmen who appeared before the Jerome Commission almost unanimously expressed doubts and disaffection with several parts of the process. Their protests were to no avail, however, since in 1901, after allotting some 450,000 acres to individual Indians, a presidential proclamation opened 2 million acres for white settlement on the KCA Reservation. Lone Wolf, principal chief of the Kiowas, continued to protest and brought suit in a federal court to stop the process. In 1903 the Supreme Court's verdict in *Lone Wolf v. Hitchcock* brought an end to the Kiowas' attempt to reverse allotment, and the Court confirmed that Congress had the "plenary authority over the tribal relations of the Indian." By this assertion Indians across the continent were firmly established as wards of the government. The Jerome Commission illustrates better than perhaps any other example the dubious manner in which the US government asserted its dominance over the territory of the Kiowas and their neighbors, even after these tribes had been confined to reservations and in the face of almost unanimous Indian opposition.[49]

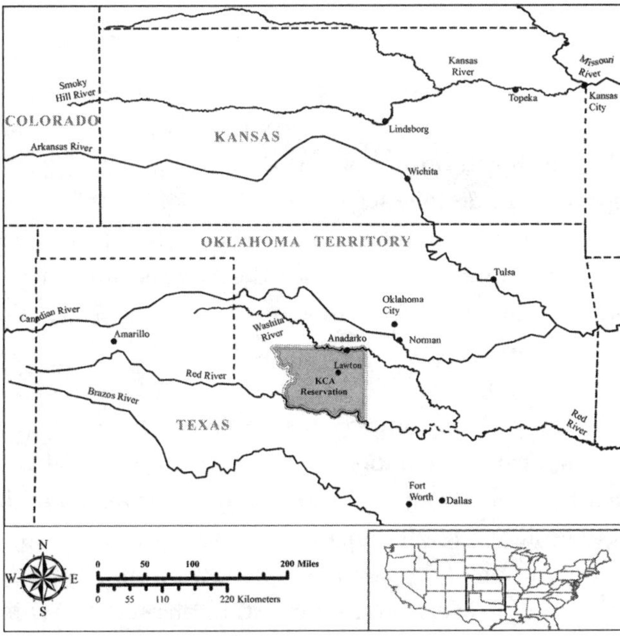

MAP 2. Map of Kansas and Oklahoma, 1900, showing the location of the KCA Reservation as well as Lindsborg, Kansas.

Beginning in July 1900, the inhabitants of the reservation selected allotments. Kiowas and Apaches generally favored locations north of the Wichita Mountains, while Comanches congregated to the south. The enormous pressure from prospective homesteaders in anticipation of the opening of the reservation on August 6, 1901, moved the president to decide to sell surplus land by lottery. In less than a month, over 165,000 people registered for the lottery of 13,000 homesteads. Over 10,000 people camped out in a tent city near Anadarko (see map 2), awaiting the outcome, and another 10,000 camped near Lawton. Overnight the Kiowas, Comanches, and Apaches were reduced to a small minority on the reservation, constituting less than 10 percent of the population. They immediately experienced encroachment from boomers attempting to stake out mineral rights on allotted land. For years following the opening of the reservation, the Kiowas and their American Indian neighbors suffered harassment from white settlers and squatters. In addition, Congress reduced beef issues and rations, and people often went hungry. Leasing allotted land to cattlemen and farmers turned into a vital source of income.[50]

SETTLING IN SWEDISH AMERICA

At least one Swedish immigrant was among the white settlers who leased land on the KCA Reservation.[51] However, most Swedish rural settlements emerged farther north on the plains. Despite the hardships of emigration, prospects were definitely less bleak for most of the Scandinavians who crossed the ocean to make a new home in North America around the turn of the century than it was for the Kiowas and other American Indians on reservations. One commentator wrote in 1927, "The Swedes in general bring to their new homes the love of what their native land represents and a desire to give their best in quality to the new land which offers opportunity." Many immigrants would not have recognized their lives in this upbeat presentation, but it appeared true that for many Swedes their new home offered possibilities for improvement. The story of Swedish immigration and diaspora harbors within it both affirmation of hope and recognition of despair, but in contrast to the Kiowa struggle, it entered the twentieth century on a more triumphant note. While Swedish authorities and academics worried about the harmful effects of the population drain, Swedes who settled in America could safely hope for relative success. After initial difficulties, most of them managed to improve their conditions, learned English, and the Anglo-Saxon elite of the country generally viewed Swedes as easily assimilable strangers. Swedish Americans agreed. Already in 1880, E. Johnson and C. F. Peterson wrote about the large Swedish population in Illinois that, while "Americans and English associate as cousins, the association between Americans and Swedes is like brothers. . . . That the Swedes in Illinois—and in all of America for that matter—in time will merge with the Anglo-American people, cannot be doubted and should, in our opinion, not be lamented."[52]

Yet, these were optimistic claims made by ethnic leaders who participated in fashioning "homemaking myths." Such mythmaking assured them of "a status clearly above that of so many other groups and on a virtual par with 'old stock' Americans," as historian Jørn Brøndal describes. The earliest Swedish arrivals consisted of groups, some of them religious dissidents, who during the 1840s and 1850s founded settlements in western Illinois and Iowa, central Texas, southern Minnesota, and western Wisconsin. Succeeding decades saw mostly family migration to rural areas and urban centers in the Midwest and Upper Midwest, following established migration chains and often attracted by the availability of land after the Homestead Act of 1862. Some ventured farther west, attracted by the mining and logging industry. After the Civil War, Swedish settlers moved west onto the plains, and in 1870 the bulk of Swedish immigrants resided in Illinois, Minnesota, Kansas, Wisconsin, and Nebraska. Toward the turn of the century, settlement in cities and industrial regions increased, and young single men and women dominated the migration flows. While land had seemed plentiful during the middle decades of the century, toward the end it became scarce. The opening up of so-called surplus land on Indian reservations for white settlers also presented Scandinavians with opportunities. There, however, they often shared conditions of extreme poverty with their American Indian neighbors.[53]

Nils Petter Jacobsson and Anna Lena Olofsdotter's oldest son, Emil, obtained a permit to leave Västra Eknö and began his journey to America in August 1885. Emil arrived in New York in September and proceeded to the Swedish Agricultural Company in Chicago (one of many immigrant institutions formed to aid their specific community), which placed young arrivals on Swedish-owned farms throughout the states. Emil was sent to Kansas where he found work on a farm in the Galva–New Gottland area. Two years later his younger brother Karl arrived. In 1890 the rest of the family followed—Nils Petter and Anna Lena, their daughter, Amanda Matilda, and three other sons, Gustav Adolph, Johan Hjalmar, and Anders Oskar.[54] They were among the thirty-four thousand Swedes who emigrated that year.[55]

In certain aspects, the migration of non-English speaking peoples to the United States required a reshaping of culture and customs that paralleled that of Indigenous Americans on the reservations. The first point of entry for the family of emigrants after crossing the Atlantic was at the Barge Office Immigration Center in New York. There, new arrivals received screening to determine their desirability as immigrants and their health status was checked. Nils Petter and Anna Lena and their children passed inspection, but at the center the family adopted Nils Petter's patronym as their family name. Previously they had all been known by the name of their father, with the addition of *–son* or *–dotter* (daughter) to that name. Now the whole family became identified as "Jakobson," spelled with only one "*–s*." This may seem like a small change, but it nonetheless heralded their new identity as immigrants and one that was not entirely self-chosen.[56]

Scholarship on Swedish immigration shows that Swedes, like many others, tended to marry within the group and preserve a strong connection to other Swedish immigrants well into the twentieth century, and when they began marrying outside their own cohort, they primarily chose mates from among the other Scandinavian groups. In urban environments where large numbers of Swedes settled, such as Chicago and Rockford, Illinois, and Worcester, Massachusetts, Swedes often sparred against Irish and Italian Catholics. Historian Dag Blanck argues that the Swedish immigration experience, in contrast to the Irish Catholic, was one characterized by general success. By aligning themselves with "Yankees" and adopting an anti-Catholic rhetoric in the Swedish American press, Swedes positioned themselves as "good Christians, trustworthy, and freedom-loving," and Blanck finds that, although "Swedes did suffer from stereotyping and discrimination, it is also clear that by the end of the nineteenth century, they both embraced and were being embraced by . . . Anglo-Saxon American society." Karen V. Hansen, whose study focuses on impoverished homesteaders on marginal soils rather than on the ethnic elite among immigrants, points out that early twentieth-century immigration policies, notably the American Indian Citizenship Act and the Johnson-Reed Immigration Act, both of 1924, "redefined the terms and contours of social and political engagement along and across the boundaries of race-ethnicity and, in the process, defined the United States as a white country." Scandinavian immigrants, rich or poor, thus benefited, and by the turn of the century the claim that they "were the fairest among the so-called white races" appeared indisputable. Generally of Protestant affiliations and arriving with some means that often allowed them to take advantage of the opening of land in the West through the Homestead Act also positioned them near the top of the racial hierarchy. The Johnson-Reed Immigration Act enforcing quotas from sending countries severely curbed the arrival of Scandinavians, but their numbers did not plummet nearly as much as those from southern and eastern Europe.[57]

For the Jacobson family, a new beginning awaited them in Lindsborg in midwestern Kansas, a Swedish enclave on the vast American prairie. A handbook for emigrants published around the time that the Jacobsons arrived described the transformation of the region. "In previous times practically all open soil within the state was covered with so called buffalo grass, thus the state also brimmed with bison, deer and other game and constituted a veritable paradise for the Indian tribes, which inhabited this entire area. But after the Indians had been expelled from there, all

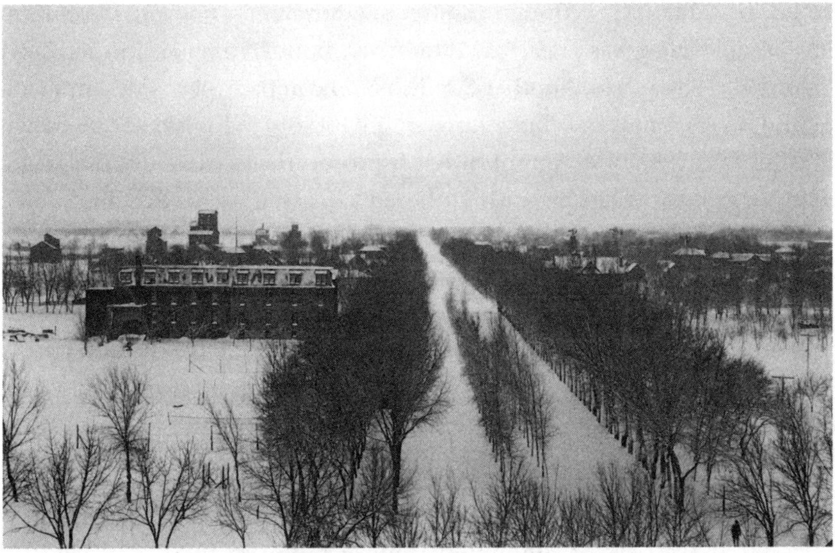

FIGURE 1. Winter view from Lindsborg, Kansas, 1880s. Photo taken around the time of the arrival of the Jacobson family to the town. Courtesy of the Sandzén Archives, SGA.

the big game have been exterminated by invading white settlers, who instead have spread enormous herds of cattle, horses and sheep across the grazing land, where the bison formerly roamed." A history of Lindsborg, published in Swedish in 1909, began its account with the Louisiana Purchase of 1803, at which time Kansas was inhabited by tribes, "among which the Osage, Pawnee, Kansas, and Paduca tribes are believed to have lived here the longest." In 1866, nine young Swedish men took up claims in the Smoky River valley, south of Salina. They found fertile land in the valley where the bluestem grass grew over six feet tall. They built dugouts as their first abodes and when they finished the first one, a couple of Indians appeared to look in on the project. A frightened Swede pulled a gun and was about to shoot when the Indian said in English, "Friend to white man."[58] In Lindsborg, as elsewhere where European immigrants took up settlements, guidebooks, memoirs, and histories glossed over the erasure of Indigenous settlements and made no connection between their own arrival and American Indian removal.

In 1868 Swedish immigrants in Chicago formed the First Swedish Agricultural Company (later the Swedish Agricultural Institute), aiming to buy up land and encourage Swedes to cultivate it. They settled on Kansas because land was cheap and the newly built Kansas-Pacific Railroad afforded ready access. Another Swedish land company, the Galesburg Colonization Company in Illinois, also bought up land in Kansas and the stage was set for a steady stream of Swedish prospective settlers. In 1869 Olof Olsson, a pastor of the Swedish Lutheran Church but with dissident views, arrived together with eighty families, and they all settled in Lindsborg. In the following years more Swedes came, and the settlement prospered after initial difficulties. From 1879 a branchline of the Union-Pacific Railroad passed through the town, and south of it ran the Missouri Pacific Line.[59]

BELONGING

SURVIVANCE ON THE KCA

Both Kiowas on the reservation and Swedish immigrants in Kansas found that novel restrictions and opportunities required of them that they rework notions of belonging and re-create structures of social cohesion. This meant vastly different things in the two locations but involved assertions of cultural identification and autonomy. In 1876 twenty-two Kiowas identified as chiefs joined in authorizing a letter to be sent to the president of the United States, asking for the release of the prisoners at Fort Marion. They described the dilemma that faced Kiowas in the aftermath of war. "For generations it has been our custom to live upon the plains; each generation has educated the succeeding one in the ways peculiar to our race, ignorant of white man's laws and governed only by our own, we have regarded as worthy of commendation many of the acts, which white man's laws visit with punishment." The chiefs recognized that they must accept changes and get "our children to go to school, many of them are now reading in the white man's books and will soon obtain a knowledge of his laws and ways." Some of their people had "voluntarily, and others forced by circumstances, beyond their control" been "placed in a hostile position to the laws of the Government," and now the letter writers waited and watched for the return of their relatives from imprisonment with "feelings of attachment as strong as those of the white man for his kindred." The secretary of war, J. D. Cameron, responded that he strongly advised against the release of any prisoners. In light of the battle at Little Bighorn in June 1876 at which General George Armstrong Custer's regiment had been annihilated by combined Lakota and Cheyenne forces,

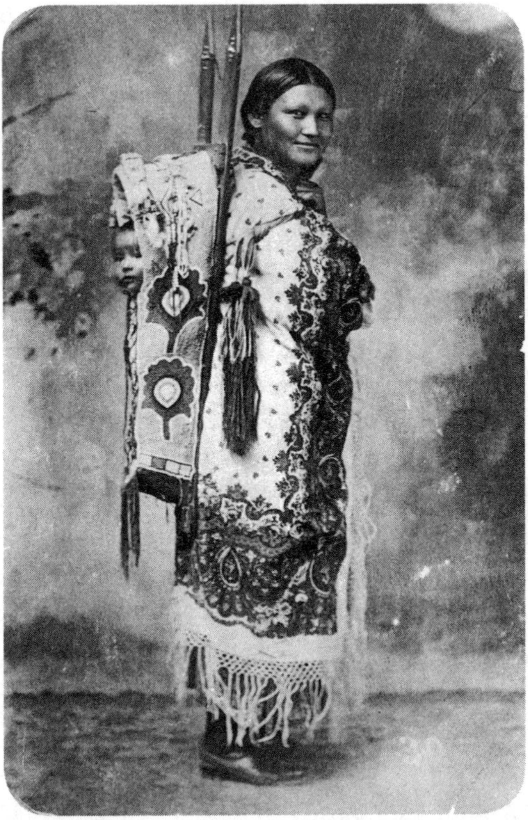

FIGURE 2. Stephen Mopope in a cradleboard with his mother, Paukeigope, ca. 1898. She and her mother, Keintaddle, were both skilled at beadwork and had made the cradleboard together for Paukeigope's firstborn. For many years, the cradleboard was lost to the family, but it reemerged in the late twentieth century as part of a collection at Colorado Springs Fine Arts Center. Courtesy of the Museum of the Great Plains, Sam Devenney Collection 754.

the secretary feared a second war in Comanche country. The Kiowas had to wait another two years for the prisoners to return.[60]

As the letter explained, the Kiowas had come to realize that many of their practices that had been passed down through generations could not coexist with American laws. They were forced to make adaptations, but the extent of these became a matter of deep contention in the years that followed. The trauma of warfare, reservation policies, and allotment haunted all aspects of Plains Indian life toward the end of the nineteenth century and lingered on in generations to come. Yet, this was also a period when Kiowas refashioned culture and community, which fascinated and frightened both neighbors and enemies alike. Jacki T. Rand observes that "Kiowas found ways to respond to their dire circumstances, but their capacity to adapt does not make the appropriation system of the late nineteenth century any less disgraceful." They adopted sacred as well as social dances from their neighbors, forged military societies that maintained honor and discipline among their members, protected ancient medical knowledge, and performed ceremonies and prayers of healing and hope. They adorned their tipis with depictions of their greatest deeds and with meaningful symbols, even though the material was now canvas and not animal hides. They carried their children in intricately decorated cradleboards and danced in magnificently beaded regalia.[61]

Joy Porter has described the incredible efforts required of Indigenous peoples to resist obliteration as cultures and peoples during the Progressive Era at the beginning of the twentieth century. Indian persistence, she argues, "required survival first and the maintenance, often against terrific odds, of the web of social, familial, political, and cultural platforms that make such resistance possible. This was work done by women as much as by men," and she urges scholars to "look afresh at what it meant to rebuild Indian culture at the darkest point before what we can now see, with hindsight, was a new indigenous dawn."[62]

Such resistance and rebuilding required the utilization of all available channels. While many cultural and religious expressions were banned on the reservation, visual arts appeared to be an inoffensive product, in the view of reservation agents. Just as men adapted to painting on paper, women found new materials through which to express both communal values and individual status. Women among the Kiowas owned and oversaw the construction of their lodges; they learned and passed on invaluable knowledge regarding herbal medicinal properties and how to derive and prepare food from plants. They processed hides, primarily from bison but also from other animals such as deer, bobcats, and mountain lions. As bison became scarce, women continued to prepare leather from other origins, primarily from cattle, although it was a poor substitute. From hides and from canvas and cotton materials, women fashioned tipi covers, clothing, and a range of other household items, such as cradleboards, which they decorated with expressive signs and patterns. By the end of the nineteenth century, these patterns began to be transferred to items for sale to tourists, which were channeled through local traders and could be used to settle debts and augment the household's income. Items such as pouches, belts, watch fobs, and medallions quickly became highly sought after among tourists, despite being produced from cheap materials and with simple designs. "Beginning in the reservation, allotment, and post-allotment periods," writes Rand, "Kiowa women thus held the dual roles of earning household income and preserving material culture production."[63]

One of the returning prisoners from Fort Marion was Oheltoint (also known as Charley Buffalo), Stephen Mopope's uncle. Oheltoint's brother Haungooah (Silver Horn) may well have been the most prolific of all the Plains Indian artists and left more than a thousand drawings as well as paintings on buffalo robes and tipi linings. Lined ledger books and pencils, primarily intended for financial accounting, became increasingly available, and Plains Indian artists found that pictorial drawings previously made on other materials could be transferred to paper, requiring a minimum of alteration in shape and form. With the near obliteration of the bison, this new medium became nearly the only one obtainable for drawings. In many cases Indians worked ardently with visiting anthropologists to transfer calendars and other images from sensitive hides to paper.[64]

At the same time as military commanders feared the outbreak of more hostility on the frontier, other whites were busy taking advantage of the allure of the vanishing West. Reservation agents received multiple requests from private collectors as well as government officials for Indian objects of various kinds. Such was the attraction of these objects that Indian allotments were illegally searched. Even the anthropologist James Mooney, who maintained friendly relations with people on the reservation, was not above trickery to access a "most interesting piece of Indian sacred paraphernalia." Indian-derived objects became collectables, and with the expectation that Indian cultures would soon cease to exist private collectors, government employees, and anthropologists rushed to preserve as much as possible before it was gone. In the process, they ever more firmly established through scholarship and policies that Indian cultures were static, definable, and incapable of change. Ironically, the commodification of Indian objects created a small but significant space for reservation residents to make an income by creating new kinds of products, such as the previously mentioned beadwork, for this market.[65]

The frantic desire to collect objects at the end of the century included collecting Indians themselves. In 1880 H. Caruthers wrote all the way from Tarrytown, New York, to Agent P. B. Hunt wanting "savages to try and tame." At the same time as prisoners were sent in chains to St. Augustine, Indian fairs and Wild West shows emerged that combined an interest in the material culture and practices of the vanquished Indians with entertainment, and the allure of western romance provided both opportunities and hazards. In 1887 Indian commissioner John Atkins admonished the KCA agent to "keep a close watch over your Indians, with a view to preventing unauthorized persons from inducing them to leave their reservation" and instructed him to "remove any and all persons, from the reservation under your charge, who may be found there with this object in view." The commissioner worried that Indians, who were enticed to leave the reservation and participate in shows, would be left destitute by "irresponsible persons." But the Wild West shows were unstoppable, attracting audiences all across America and in Europe. Local county fairs and expositions followed suit. The Bureau of Indian Affairs soon realized that they could not hinder Indians from dancing, but they could demand that they receive reasonable wages for their participation, and so-called Show Indians could earn from twenty-five to ninety dollars a month, making performances in western shows much more lucrative than farming allotments.[66]

Kiowas made use of these novel opportunities and contributed to shaping them. Native communities became adept at managing sometimes very deep-seated and painful dissonances such as these, and this ability was no doubt borne out of necessity in the constrained conditions on the reservation. This in no way glosses over the very real tragedies and institutional and personal violence visited upon and carried out among individuals living there, and their legacies into the present. Anishinaabe author and poet Gerald Vizenor has coined the term "survivance" to encompass this "action, condition, quality, and sentiments of the verb survive." Native survivance is a testament to the perseverance and creative desire of American Indian peoples such as Kiowas in upholding community and pride in their culture, and their survivance stories renounce "dominance, tragedy, and victimry."[67]

IMMIGRANT HOME-MAKING CLAIMS

Swedish immigrants, too, sought ways to connect with the past and retain links with their land of origin, while reshaping institutions and practices in America. As for Kiowas, culture became a powerful tool in this process. Albin Widén was one of many scholars who, in the early part of the twentieth century, attempted to understand the massive Swedish migration not just as a demographic and economic phenomenon but also as a psychological one. People left Sweden to evade military service, taxes, failed harvests, oppressive clergy, and unemployment, but many people were simply in the grips of "America fever." Emigration spawned its own legend of romance. Not only did emigrants write home with larger-than-life success stories of gold and bounty, but the mythologizing lived also in the conviction that Swedes had contributed to building the land of the future through their diligent and disciplined labor, driven by their desire to find that "in the great mass of people they would be left alone with their own eccentric selves in a different way than in the small homeland, which censured each and every person." Writing in the 1930s Widén recognized in this dream of the Promised Land a universal human "nostalgia of the soul" for a lost Eden, one that in time took shape in Swedish American imagination as a fusion of the old and the new homeland. The second Swedish language newspaper established in America was named *Hemlandet, Det Gamla och Det Nya* (The homeland, the old and the new), and during the nineteenth century, patriotic Swedish poetry emerged, along with other expressions of identification, that praised the ties between the character of the place that was left behind and the possibilities of the new home.[68]

Swedish settlers established a number of institutions devoted to maintaining and developing a distinct cultural identity, such as newspapers, schools and colleges, churches, lodges, and social institutions. Headquartered in Rock Island, Illinois, the Augustana Synod to which the Lindsborg settlement was intimately connected remained the dominant force in the formulation and practice of a Swedish American identity, but this force was not uncontested nor did it represent all of the voices of Swedes in America. Many of the predominant Swedish American ethnic leaders were connected to Augustana and its affiliated churches and organizations. They belonged to a literate middle class, which attempted to shape a specific form of ethnic identity. Within Augustana's fold, literary and artistic expressions emerged that built on and molded specific notions of what it meant to be Swedish in America and of the Swedish contributions to the greatness of the nation. The Swedish American cultural elite were particularly eager to support and promote the arts, especially the visual arts and music. Bethany College, established in Lindsborg in 1881, took part in this endeavor through its music and arts programs.[69]

Initially, however, early settlers in the agricultural community of Lindsborg worried mostly about the challenges from the natural environment and from other contenders for the territory. In a memoir of his early years as a settler in the Smoky valley, Johan Augustin Pihl remarked that, "We had no knowledge of the country's language, laws, culture and organization, climate, weather, wind, thunder, cyclones, grasshoppers, prairie fires, Texas cattle herds, and Indians." To the settlers, Indigenous people simply constituted one of the landscape's many obstacles. The hardships that were endured in the new community on the Kansas plains had a leveling influence. In order to break the soil, the settlers needed oxen, and in the beginning two or three of them would buy a team together and help each other plow. "Great helpfulness prevailed. One shared willingly the little one had. All were in about the same position in terms of property." Life "was simple and poor" for several years. "Rattle snakes visited in the dugouts, and 'skunks' looked in on the church during morning service."[70]

During the first decade, most of the men were employed working on the railroad and thus became witnesses to the massive campaigns to reshape the plains territory that had such devastating consequences for the Kiowas. Pihl describes taking part in a small company of Swedish men and women who in the summer of 1872 worked on the Santa Fe Railroad. "It was somewhat of a bold adventure to go out among the wilds, the buffaloes, and the Indians." He wondered at the large herds of buffalo. "We had buffalo meat almost every day. But it was sad to see how they were hunted and shot down. In some places the air was putrid from the dead animals." Some of the settlers recognized, albeit obliquely, that this destruction formed a prerequisite for their success. Olof Olsson, who became the leader of the Lindsborg colony, wrote in 1869 to a friend in Sweden: "You should see our settlement out here. It is a unique view. Prairie and still more prairie. . . . It has been wonderful to see this summer the large planted fields, which a few years ago belonged to buffalo and Indian."[71]

Struggles with both wild animals and indigenes formed part of emigration lore, and in Albin Widén's summation, Swedish immigrants had performed a remarkable feat, despite severe labor and insecurities. Over the course of the nineteenth century, through an unfathomable collective effort, they had broken ten million acres of previously unplowed land in the United States alone, which equaled more than the entire cultivated acreage in Sweden. "The labor of the Swedish pioneers in America is the largest conquest ever made by Swedes and the glory is not diminished by the fact that this is a matter of peaceful and not warlike exploits," Widén asserted.[72] It was a compelling and attractive trope, and one that was readily adopted both in America and in Sweden after the world wars. By then, any ambiguity of land taking had ceased to lead to questions such as the one raised by Augustana synod pastor Eric Norelius in the aftermath of the Dakota war in 1862. Have "the white men, who call themselves Christian and civilized, discharged their duty toward [the Indians]?" he asked. "We have reason to dread the day when the reckoning will be made."[73]

In Sweden, authoritative textbooks and popular publications in magazines and books established a space for Swedish emigrants in America in the emptied swathes of fertile land awaiting their labor of cultivation. Sweden enjoyed a very high literacy rate, and peasants and laborers too were able to read and write to some extent. A growing bourgeoisie created a market for cheap publications, and over the course of the nineteenth century an increasing number of magazines emerged targeting the "reading family." While books were likely to be less available, many homes had access to monthly periodicals. In addition, a large volume of publications appeared geared toward offering emigrants advice and guidance. Already before leaving Sweden, people thus possessed certain preformed notions of what awaited them. In *Läsebok för folkskolan* (Reader for elementary school), children could learn about the great transformation of the United States. The reader described the inevitable nature of the relationship between emigrants and Indigenous peoples. "Settlers in the new land" could not avoid contact with the "original inhabitants" and often violent bloodshed followed "before the settlers were successful in pushing the Indians away from their old hunting grounds, where cultivation now proceeded." Eventually, however, the settlers "naturally gained the advantage," and they "cleared and burned, cultivated the land and erected their abodes; their numbers increased, and new hosts arrived endlessly from the east; the rivers became passageways for trade, and villages and towns grew with astonishing haste; the redskins, who did not wish to give up the customs of their fathers, were compelled to move further and further to the west and north."[74] Such histories normalized the eviction of Indigenous people from their land, and passive language, understatements, and the framing of the scenario as "natural" created the illusion that settlers had little part in this process. It was, if anything, a consequence of the Indians' unwillingness "to give up the customs of their fathers."

Many, if not most, emigrating Swedes arrived with notions of American Indians shaped through "Indian books," which as a genre became immensely successful in Sweden. By the 1880s Swedish children were familiar enough with American Indians to incorporate popular images of them in their games, and in 1900 one-fifth of all books published for children and young adults contained "Indian stories." These images, although romantic and alluring, also cast the relationship between emigrants and Indians in a specific mold. An old rhyme in Swedish America chanted:

> Behind the Indian's birch canoe
> Propelled boats come trotting
> And surveyed plots laid out
> On top of Indian graves.[75]

To Swedes, this seemingly harmless and playful representation masked the sinister consequences of settlement and the complicity of Swedish settlers. Widén cites it to demonstrate that Swedes too took part in colonizing the vast continent as part of a great civilizing mission, but without attaching to it any of the blame that Swedish commentators levied at Anglo-Americans for waging a race war against American Indians. Generic "Indians" as tropes of entertainment and adventure conveniently enabled immigrants to ignore their own role in the dispossession of American Indian land.[76]

The fictional and representational "Indian" was thus well established in Swedish perceptions of America. But what happened when Swedish immigrants encountered actual Indigenous individuals and groups? What were the circumstances that converged in the meeting of Oscar Jacobson and Kiowa artists in Oklahoma in the 1920s? Jacobson's formative years contained a mixture of perceptions brought along from Sweden and experiences in Lindsborg.

The Smoky River valley in central Kansas that became the Jacobson family's new home held a long history of Indigenous presence. The settlers identified the Kaws as their immediate predecessors and neighbors. But pinpointing abandoned or temporary tribal villages along the bend of the river where Lindsborg lay obscured a difference in land use and territorial claims. Several Indigenous nations had settled or utilized the valley. Arapahoes, Pawnees, and Osages hunted there. Kaw (or Kansa), Omaha, and Ponca villages lined the waterways. For all of them, the Smoky River valley comprised a much larger area through which their contacts and movements extended, but this did not mean they were "roving" or "nomadic" as white settlers often contended. Permanent white settlements in the valley dealt them a severe blow, but these peoples had been under pressure since the 1820s from increased competition for the bison chase and from migrants, such as the Kiowas, coming from the Northern Plains. The rivalry over hunting increased dramatically and led to overhunting. Immediately to the north, the Kaws faced conflict with the Pawnees who had formed an alliance with the Omahas and Poncas. In 1846 the Kaws ceded two million acres to the United States and settled on a reservation just east of where Lindsborg would be established. By 1873 pressure from white settlers wanting land increased dramatically, and the government pressured the Kaws to remove to Indian Territory. Pawnees ceded land in 1857 and settled on a small reservation in Nebraska. They built a significant part of their subsistence economy around agriculture and suffered the same hardships as European immigrants did when grasshoppers and droughts in the 1860s destroyed their crops. In the 1870s they, too, were forced to remove to Indian Territory.[77]

All through the 1860s and 1870s, Swedes in the Smoky River valley expressed fear and unease in their contacts with Indigenous people in the region. "It did not look so promising to build a secure home on these naked plains," wrote Johan Augustin Pihl. "Everything seemed so wild. Indians roved about and even came to us in our houses. Their appearance alone was enough to terrorize our women and children and they were not too friendly towards the newcomers." Another account, in Bergin's history of Lindsborg, both minimized the enmity between Kaw Indians and newcomers and underlined the immigrants' initial insecurity.

"The Indians who lived here, or now and then crisscrossed the territory, belonged to the Kaw-tribe and were not hostile to the white people. The only trouble one had with them was, that they begged and stole a little. During one of their visits Spångberg got angry with an Indian, who had stolen, and was about to shoot him, but was stopped by Johnson. If he had not stopped him, it may be that the history of the Swedes in the Smoky Valley would have been entirely different, as down by the river there lay more than four hundred redskins, who soon could have finished off the few Swedes."[78] These stories commonly placed the Swedish settlers in a position as fearful and weak, while the Indians were framed as dangerous and threatening. From a Kaw perspective the roles would most certainly have been reversed, as Swedish settlers arrived backed with the might of the expanding United States.

Fifty years after the founding of Lindsborg, Bergin's history of the town contained these ambiguous sentiments in a section headlined "Adventures among Indians," which recorded some violent and fear-filled encounters. In May 1869, three Swedes camped by Spillman Creek, located some seventy miles northwest of Lindsborg, found themselves surrounded by Sioux warriors who began shooting at their wagon. The Swedes took refuge in a dugout and shot at the circling Indians through the window. On the following day they were rescued by a party of six men on horses, who informed them that the whole region had been under attack, "13 white people killed in the most brutal manner," and three women and a child had been taken prisoners. The eight-day-old child had been killed when "one Indian took and beat it against a log, so that it died." The contrast between the descriptions of the most distressing violence, the rage of the settlers and the headline promising "adventures," says something about the awkward mixture of emotions that beset the early settlers. Locating danger and violence farther to the west, as these stories did, also served to reinforce the notion of relatively peaceful interactions between Swedish settlers and Indians in the immediate vicinity of Lindsborg. In 1909 Indians in the Smoky River valley belonged to the realm of the past and came into focus only as objects of pity or amusement, but the memories of conflict and fear were real enough, and the immigrants' contemplation of their settlement on Indian land filled with contradictions.[79]

In 1881 just southwest of Lindsborg along a tributary to the Smoky River, Professor Johan August Udden found the ruins of an old Indian village, containing fifteen mounds. He excavated them thoroughly and donated the "valuable relics" to Bethany College, where they were incorporated into the collections of the college. The collection consisted of arrowheads, knives, axes, awls, and other tools made out of flint, bone, antlers, and mussel shell, along with clubs, millstones, and whetstones. A piece of a chain mail, possibly Spanish, was also found in these graves.[80] Lindsborg was now well established, and its previous Indigenous population could be relegated to the realm of antiquities. From then on, by consigning Indians to the past the Swedes could place themselves seamlessly as inheritors of the valley. Emory Lindquist, president of Bethany College, looked back on nearly a century of Swedish occupation when he wrote of the "silent history of the centuries before the coming of Europeans" when "native Indians roamed freely in the area." Not entirely silent, however, the Indians had according to tradition given the valley its name. "When the Indians scanned the horizon from elevated points on eastern, western, and southern approaches, they saw a broad valley through which wound lazily a narrow river seeking the inevitable destiny of a faraway ocean. Intense veneration resulted while viewing this valley over which a mystic haze hung low in autumn and spring, and so they called it Smoky Valley, believing it endowed with some unusual quality." But the Indians' "camp numbering more inhabitants than early Lindsborg" had been supplanted by "the adventurous descendants of the Vikings."[81] The Swedes built their castle of linden trees and made the valley of the sacred smoke their own.

Thus, by the time the Jacobsons arrived in Lindsborg, Indians had been safely relegated to the museum. Swedish settlers faced other challenges, problems that they to some extent shared with the Indigenous peoples who had not so much vanished as been put out of sight and mind. A new generation had grown up for whom the early days of settlement were merely an adventure story. They, said the older generation of emigrants about the youngsters of the early twentieth century, "did not know what it was like to be poor, hungry or in any way deny oneself anything one would like to have." The first generation of settlers had lived apart, shielded by their language, but in the first decades of the twentieth century their community had increasingly been drawn into contact and competition with the nation's various peoples. The Swedes in Lindsborg, as in so many other Swedish settlements in the greater Midwest, asked urgent questions: "Will we be able to keep anything of that which is valuable and dear to us as a Swedish and Lutheran people? Or should we let all that is our own go and be content to carry wood and water for this country's other tribes?"[82]

LOOKING FORWARD OR LOOKING BACK?

Kiowas and Swedish immigrants in Lindsborg met the new century with different experiences of displacement. Choosing diaspora as the framework for these histories places the emphasis on ruptures, on the need to refashion cultures and identities in an alien setting. Social historians have argued for greater continuity between the Old World and the New, and emphasized how the back-and-forth flow of migration networks helped blunt sharp breaks.[83] By describing both migration and the consignment to a reservation as diaspora, I wish to train the searchlight on the collective identity work that each group found necessary in order to shape links between the present and a remembered past in a different place, and how this implicated cultural and aesthetic expressions. When Kiowas looked back into the past from the point of view of the early twentieth century, they could still see a world of relative plenty, in which changes in economy (the acquisition of the horse, increased reliance on the bison, trade), culture (adoption of new ceremonies, dances, and songs), living space (Southern Plains, Wichita Mountains), and demographics (population growth, assimilation of captives) had held the promise of opportunity and progress. If not a golden age, their recent past held stories of bounty and optimism, which gradually eroded with the pressures from white settlers, the depletion of the bison herds, and the wars of the 1870s. Swedes, on the other hand, and particularly those from the province of the small lands (Småland) experienced decline and strained against the strictures of state, church, and environment. For those like the Jacobson family who could afford it, transoceanic migration involved the promise of something better. This would have led to profoundly different relationships with the memories of the past and practices of history. The Swedes traveled toward tomorrow with the past safely behind them, with it emerging primarily as nostalgic reminiscences of individual significance. But for the Kiowas, a history of a life of self-determination and collective pride was one of the few possessions they could carry with them into the reservation and life on restricted allotments.

CHAPTER 2

A Westerner at Yale, an Easterner in Pullman, and a Swede in Between, 1890–1920s

THERE IS A PIVOTAL MOMENT in Delbert Jacobson's family history of the Jacobsons' long trek from the Baltic coast in Sweden to the middle of Kansas. After weeks on wagons, trains, and ships, a harrowing passage through customs in New York, and a tiresome train ride to Chicago, they finally embarked on the last leg of their journey. On Friday, May 30, 1890, at midnight, twenty-five days after the family had left Västra Eknö, they boarded the train bound for McPherson, Kansas. "Sleeping on the train was almost impossible. Everyone was becoming more excited as the night wore on and daybreak arrived." The train chugged along through Illinois, across the corner of Missouri, and then into Kansas. "Everyone kept looking for Indians, cowboys and buffaloes. Many times they had heard these stories in Sweden that the plains of Kansas were covered with Indians, cowboys and buffaloes." Finally, the train pulled into McPherson station to the waiting brothers, Emil and Karl (now called Charley). "With memories of the Motherland, Sweden, still lingering, they all joined hands and the Jacobson Odyssey continued as a new adventure had just begun."[1] Thus, Delbert Jacobson imagines the moment when the two eldest sons greeted their parents and younger siblings as the family disembarked after their long voyage.

The quintessential characterization of the Wild West as one of "Indians, cowboys and buffaloes" came to the Jacobsons through books, magazine stories, and images published in ever-increasing numbers in Sweden from the middle decades of the nineteenth century. Thus, in the midst of the stark reality of ultimate change and irreversible loss was this

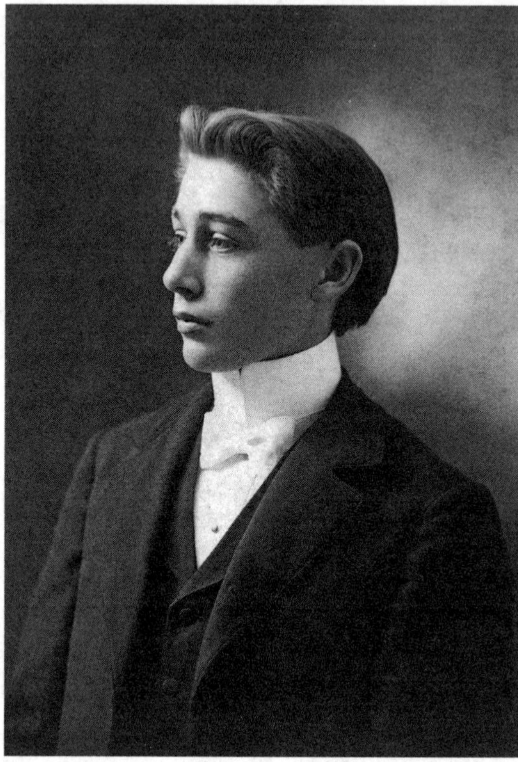

FIGURE 3. Oscar Jacobson as a young man, probably a high school graduation photograph. Photo taken in 1900 by B. G. Gröndal, a local Lindsborg photographer who was also an immigrant from Sweden. From the private collection of Delbert Jacobson, Oscar's nephew. Courtesy of Karen Logback Graham.

sense of adventure, strengthened no doubt by the fact that this move was voluntary. After some initial trepidation, Oscar appears to have taken to it when he received his first pony.[2]

Of all the seven children Oscar was the only one who did not remain in the Lindsborg region, and his peregrinations arched from the West in the United States across to Europe and North Africa. His restlessness set him apart from his siblings, and it started early. He and his brother Ernst preferred roaming around the countryside on their ponies to farm duties. Working on the family's stock farm without pay did not suit Oscar. In addition, his fascination with drawing was cause for concern. His father worried that "Oscar sat around and drew pictures of horses rather than doing his chores on the farm," and his older brothers thought it "a terrible waste of time." According to his wife's memoir, their "bossiness" may have contributed to Oscar's decision—at the age of only thirteen—to take odd jobs on other farms in the area, such as working on threshing crews and rounding up cattle, "sometimes sleeping in the soft, new straw stacks under the starry skies."[3]

He went to school and learned English, and already at the age of thirteen he enrolled in classes in painting and drawing at Bethany College in Lindsborg. These lessons were most likely offered through the Bethany Academy for younger students, rather than actual college instruction.[4] In 1900, at the age of eighteen, Oscar began taking regular college classes. His summer earnings as a ranch hand put him through college. He graduated in 1903 with honors, and his first degree was in business and accounting, but he soon changed course to concentrate on art.[5]

At Bethany, Oscar met the Swedish American artist Birger Sandzén, who was impressed by the younger man's talent. Sandzén had arrived in Lindsborg in 1894, the year before Jacobson began taking art classes, and he would stay on as a teacher for over fifty years. Despite Sandzén being Jacobson's senior by eleven years, the two men "went together hunting and sketching. Thus began a beautiful friendship that was to unite these two artists for their whole lifetime." The pair would remain in contact, correspond, and share in joint exhibitions. Sandzén was a gifted teacher and envisioned an association of western artists, which he labored assiduously to initiate and shape. Through Sandzén, Jacobson would become part of a vibrant and nurturing network of Swedish American artists, which would be of vital importance to his career.[6]

The first years of the new century also saw Oscar busy establishing his western credentials. While he did work as a cowboy, his western activities also involved role-play and impersonation. Donning costumes and engaging in cultural playacting would be activities he enjoyed through much of his life. Oscar's favorite horse was a mustang named Brady, and together with friends he organized a riding group known as the Crazy Ridge Wild West Riders, patterned on Theodore Roosevelt's Rough Riders. In 1902, the *Lindsborg Record* reported that the town was busy preparing for the Fourth of July parade: "One of the leading features will undoubtedly be the wild west section commanded by Oskar Jakobson. Don't fail to be here in time to see it." The next edition specified that "Jakobson's Rough

Riders" would be accompanied by another set of actors "Chief Umpolosogoelah with his band of picturesque Indian warriors in full dress uniform."[7] This was neither the first nor the last time that Jacobson and his friends would engage in Indian impersonations. In October 1903, newspapers reported that a group of young men and women had laid "aside all worries and college cares" for a few days on an outing "to the wilds and beauties of the natural scenery in Ellsworth county." The party brought tents and camping equipment and stayed out over a long weekend. Ten Swedish American Lindsborg women and men constituted the group and "traveled incognito under the following names: Heap Good White Squaw, Sunset, Scalp, Heap Big Eyes, Pine Ridge Pete, Pocahontas, Mustang Jake, Kiote Son, Buck, Papoose, Leather Stocking." All of these names made references to western and Indian lore, and "Mustang Jake," of course, was Jacobson's moniker, while among the others were his good friends (Victor) Oscar Freeburg and Harry Larson.[8]

Young Oscar came of age just at the time when "the West" captured the imagination of the world, and it is perhaps not surprising that he shaped quite a conventional role for himself as a westerner. Open-range cattle drives had already ceased by the time the Jacobsons arrived in Kansas, but the cowboy remained a representation of freedom, masculine honor, and adventure. Oscar's youthful admiration for Theodore Roosevelt directly influenced his staging of the West and his role-play and may well have nurtured his sense of the West as the quintessential America. He had the means, both social capital in his standing in the community and to some extent monetary capital, to pursue an education and maintain his public persona. He was not encumbered by government restrictions or policies, despite the fact that he was not an American citizen, and appears to have been well on the way to becoming a model of Roosevelt's assimilated immigrant. Yet, assimilation was more complicated than that. Jacobson, as many other immigrants, would continue to relate to different contexts and assert the right to a hyphenated identity.[9]

ST. LOUIS CENTENNIAL EXPOSITION

In 1903—thanks to the intervention of powerful patrons, among them the founder of Bethany College, Reverend Carl A. Swensson—Oscar managed to secure a position in the Jefferson Guards during the preparations for the Centennial Exposition in St. Louis. Once the fair opened,

Oscar exchanged the uniform for an appointment as the custodian of the Fine Arts Building of the Swedish display, while at night he doubled as a rider in the "Wild West Show"—a show that also saw the appearance of a young Will Rogers, only a few years older than Jacobson.[10] The *Bethany Messenger* reported that, at the end of the fair, Oscar would be in charge of crating all the paintings to send back to Sweden. "Mr. Jakobson is a very talented young man, and the fact that the Swedish government has placed so great a trust in his care speaks very highly for him."[11]

A letter to his friend and mentor Sandzén, written on Jacobson's twenty-second birthday in 1904 demonstrates this convoluted nature of the lure of the West and Swedishness. On May 15, when working at the St. Louis world's fair, Oscar—or "Jake" as he was known then to Sandzén—wrote a long letter describing the day's events. What is striking is that of the few letters from Jacobson retained in the Sandzén collection, this is the only one written entirely in Swedish. Otherwise the two appear to have communicated in English. This letter shows how the English language had infiltrated into his Swedish vernacular, demonstrated in the quote below by words within quotation marks. He describes how he "celebrätade" (making a Swedish word of "celebrated") together with his friend Harry Larson.

> At 5 o'clock we "started" to walk on Broadway dressed in our most sacred Cowboy costumes. We almost stopped traffic for a while. Then we took "dinner" at one of the finest hotels. We made some purchases but it seemed that business in the big "department stores" were at a very "low ebb" while we were there.
>
> The Salvation Army were singing and making noise on 6th street. We stopped to listen "at a respectable distance" but it did not take long before we attracted the less delicate audience away from the preachers and that was of course not as it should. So we left for the Exhibition Very pleased with ourselves and with people's "appreciation" of us. . . . Yes we took "in" 6 shows during that night but paid we certainly did not. No! No! We got in for free in every single place and no one so much as sneezed at us. Yes it was great fun. It was the first craziness I have been part of in a long time and now I guess I'll have to "behave" again.[12]

Oscar later related an incident to his wife from his stint in St. Louis, which demonstrates again how he consciously framed himself as a westerner. His dual occupations as attaché to the Swedish commission and as Wild West rider at night drew the attention of the Swedish Royal Commissioner, Dr. Nils Lagerstedt, who had visited the entertainment section one evening in the company of friends and noted the resemblance of one of the riders to Jacobson, asking the young man about the coincidence the next morning. "Oscar kept a straight face as he replied 'Oh! I guess that's the Western type; we all grow that same way out West.'"[13] Another episode further emphasized the distance between "old Sweden" and Jacobson's new world of the West. While Oscar was helping the Swedish landscape painter Anshelm Schultzberg unpack his paintings, the latter asked Jacobson if it was safe to travel further west than St. Louis—a concern he ridiculed in a letter to Sandzén.[14]

At the same time, Jacobson's letters to Sandzén reveal his investment in the world of Swedish America. Lindsborg strove to rival Augustana College, situated in Rock Island, Illinois, as a center of Swedishness in America. The Swedish pavilion at the Exposition in St. Louis eventually found a home in Lindsborg, where it served as art studio, among other things. While first disparaging of the pavilion—Jacobson compares it unfavorably with the palaces of France and England and even remarks that the "obscure nations of South America beat us ten times over in style and size"—he nonetheless thinks it is a good idea to move the building to Lindsborg, if for no other reason than to beat Augustana.[15]

The St. Louis World's Fair, officially named the Louisiana Purchase Exposition, turned out to be a formative experience for the young man. In particular, he grew in his appreciation for art, as he had ample opportunities to study the different contributions as he helped to unpack paintings that were submitted to the fine arts jury. He delighted in the artwork from France. "Oh! The French art is glorious. They are the leaders all right!" He particularly noticed a piece by Albert Bernard, and describing it to Sandzén he reverted to Swedish: "Den är så vacker så en kann bli sjuk!"[16] Taking care of the artwork sent from "Old Sweden" that came through the Swedish pavilion strengthened his links to Swedish art. He particularly appreciated Anders Zorn's work. Zorn had been one of Sandzén's teachers in Sweden. In a long article to the *Lindsborg Record*, Jacobson described what he had seen under the headline "Swedish Art at the World's Fair." It is possible that this is the first piece of writing he ever published, and he demonstrated pride in his country of origin, as well as considerable writing skills. He described Swedish art with an argument that would follow him throughout his working career: "Where, however, Sweden not only takes a leading place but rivals, if not to say outclasses, almost all the nations of the world is in her Fine Arts Exhibition." Sweden's art, he argued, "possesses a national character; it is more positive and full of atmosphere than any other country's represented [*sic*]." He described in detail the ten paintings by Anders Zorn "who is not only well known but greatly honored and admired all over the world." The contributions of Carl Larsson—one of the best known and most loved Swedish artists of this period—failed to excite Jacobson in equal measure, but he did commend them for their original style. He was clearly more impressed with Bruno Liljefors's paintings of nature and animals. In describing *The Wood Grouse*, he anticipated his own later assertion of what it was that he wished to do with his art: "Here perched high on a branch in the deep spruce woods sits a grouse just within 'gun shot.' The picture gives one a feeling of being miles and miles away from human habitation, way into the realms of the animal kingdom where birds and animals live, undisturbed by man." He clearly valued the landscape painters, and in his description of Anshelm Schultzberg's works he wrote: "his work shows a large grasp of complicated whole, is consistently composed and painted with a vigorous and joyous touch that compels a unity in pictorial quality and brings immediate conviction of artistic purpose. While he realizes the form of the landscape as it lies back under the sky, the richness of texture and wealth of color in the foreground he leads back into the distance of delicate and subtle tenderness in color value. The drawing, the tone and harmony of color gives one a feeling of rare completeness of his work."[17]

Jacobson's stretch as attaché had certainly given the young artist a crash course in art, not just from Sweden, and strengthened his sense of commitment to painting. His work even included helping the judges in the jury of the fine arts competition. He wrote to Birger Sandzén: "For the last 4 weeks I have done nothing but handled and seen painting of all nationalities, sizes and kinds. I have seen so much art that my eyes are sore." He also learned of the workings of the art market, and although he was "not at all ashamed of our little school, of course location is against us. Almost all the good work comes from the East."[18]

The St. Louis Fair opened up the world for him. The multitude of peoples and cultures represented at the fair attracted the curious young man, who took every opportunity to explore its diversity. He most certainly saw Geronimo, the Mescalero Apache chief who was living out his life as a prisoner of war at Fort Sill in Indian Territory and who was one of the main attractions at the fair. Oscar had met him already as a teenager and owned his autographed photograph. One day while on duty with the Jefferson Guards, he encountered a man both dejected and hungry, who did not speak much English. Jacobson offered him food and found him some temporary work until the fair opened, when the man would work in the concessions. The man turned out to be a "sword dancer" from Egypt, and he brought with him a "troupe of Oriental Belly dancers" who "scandalized the ladies of Oscar's party." It appears that the most exotic encounter was with a delegation from the Philippines. He described it in a letter to Sandzén: "There are about 400 brand new Phillipenos [*sic*] here. Some of the tribe (Igerroties) don't wear much in the line of clothes about all the men wear is a breach cloth about 3 inches wide dangling loose. Its quite a novelty to see them dance and play their native Instruments. All the 'bow-wows' in the neighborhood are chained up for fear of being cooked, they always want more dog meat." He also met dervishes and bedouins from the Middle East and concluded in his letter that "I'm glad I'm here, it is a chance indeed to see the world on a small scale."[19]

As the presence of these Filipinos testifies, the world he saw was one distinctly shaped by American imperialism. Theodore Roosevelt opened the St. Louis Fair. The anthropological exhibits were the most extensive ever put on display and included a forty-seven-acre-sized "Philippine Reservation," which housed nearly twelve hundred people. The exhibit was designed to impress visitors strolling along the L-shaped midway, called the Pike, with the world's progress in stages, and Philippine Day celebrated the surrender of Manila to American troops as "a great step in the diffusion of freedom over the globe." Placed side by side, American Indians and Filipinos both showcased the dominance and progress of the United States. What differed, argued John W. Hanson in the official history of the fair, "is that the Indian is of a disappearing race, while the Filipino appears to be just on the eve of a substantial and lasting development." Anthropologists did not agree, and the enormous size of the exhibits of human cultures was a testament to their dawning realization that the Indigenous peoples of America, who had appeared doomed only a decade before, were not vanishing.[20] As he wandered the exhibits, young Oscar no doubt took part in this debate and came to share in these ambiguous sentiments.

A STUDENT AT YALE

The exposure to the world of art through the St. Louis Fair strengthened Jacobson in his resolve to pursue his own career, and in 1905 he enrolled in art classes at Yale University. The Fine Arts School at Yale originated in 1869, and at the time Jacobson attended it ranked as one of the nation's finest art education institutions. Through its connection to the Augustana College, Bethany College appears to have had links to Yale, and Jacobson was not the only student from Lindsborg. A list of students from Bethany College studying at Yale in 1905 included Victor Oscar Freeburg, Carl Ostrum, and Luther Anderson. Tuition was steep, and Jacobson's parents living on an eighty-acre farm in Kansas could not afford to put him through art school, but Jacobson solved the problem by winning scholarships and doing different odd jobs to pay for room and board. He worked as a cashier for a fancy club for wealthier students and clerked in a bookstore to pay for his supplies. He was an usher at the football field and landed a job at the Shubert Theater, which enabled him to see several hundred plays with many distinguished actors during the three years he spent at Yale.[21]

He shared an apartment with two other Swedish students, also alumni from Bethany. Despite being short of funds, the trio reveled in all kinds of antics to liven up their student years. They sailed around Long Island and almost perished in an unexpected storm; later Jacobson paddled a canoe alone across Long Island Sound. They liked to stage performances and costume play. Parties re-created settings from history or from other parts of the world. In January 1905, a brief notice in the *New Haven Leader* described them enacting a scene from the seventeenth century when English Lord Protector Cromwell received four foreign diplomats, a "French couple, Oscar Freeburg and Mrs. A. C. Bristol; Spanish, Oscar Jakobson and Ruth Thrasher; Swedish, Dr. Ed. Thorstenberg and Elizabeth Patton; Netherlands, Dr. Heyke and Anna Peterson."[22] At other times their pranks were viewed with less amusement, such as when they cleared out their college rooms by throwing out glassware and crockery on the street—a common practice in the neighborhood. The *New Haven Union* reported that "numerous cyclists have been caused expense and annoyance by cut tires in that vicinity."[23]

The trio—joined by another Swede, Jack Anderson—formed "The Anderson Dramatic company." Together with non-Swedish Yale students, including Sinclair Lewis, the future Nobel laureate and author of *Babbitt* and *Elmer Gantry*, they spent much of their time acting in plays authored by Victor Freeburg. The plays were almost exclusively set in the West; the young men all considered themselves westerners and in addition owned a fair amount of paraphernalia that suited such a location, including boots, sombreros, war bonnets, and revolvers.[24]

In *Sunset*, the most notable of these plays, Jacobson again acted the part of an Indian. According to Jeanne d'Ucel's memoir he "nearly shocked New England because he insisted on wearing the Indian costume in its natural scantiness; but he darkened his flesh so well it went over." *Sunset*, written by Victor Freeburg and set in Kansas in 1877, centered on the rivalry between two ranch foremen for the hand of an Indian princess. The staging of the play as well as its story line and attire placed it firmly in an imagined West, staged so as to give it an aura of authenticity. The *New Haven Union* described the plot and noted that the play was "given out of doors and although the stage was rather poorly lighted, the production was quite realistic and successful. An extra flavor was added by the fact that most of the actors are Westerners, and are thoroughly acquainted with the life they acted." The play was successful enough to be put on stage at the Foy Auditorium in December 1907 and received generous reviews in New Haven newspapers. The *Saturday Chronicle*, for example, began its two-page well-illustrated spread with the assertion: "Western life is always interesting to easterners, and a true picture of western ranch life will be seen . . . when the amateur performance, 'Sunset' is to be given by several college men and their friends."[25]

Reviews commented on the realism of Oscar's portrait of "Mustango" or "Mustonkah," Pawnee chief and father of "Sunset." The *New Haven Leader* wrote: "'Mistonkah,' chief of the Pawnee Indians, is played by Oscar Jacobson of Kansas. He is a wonderful Indian impersonator and his Indian effects were all obtained by himself from an Indian reservation near his home. His chief's head gear is the genuine article and was obtained under great danger." The *Saturday Chronicle* headlined its review "Real Indian Togs" and apostrophized "Interesting Things Gathered from the Plains to be Used in 'Sunset,'" among them a Sioux war bonnet and General Nelson A. Miles's pistol. It recounts in fanciful detail how

Oscar Jacobson came to own "a real Indian war bonnet," which had "once belonged to the son of a Sioux chief." According to the newspaper Jacobson had visited the Rosebud reservation in South Dakota and attempted to buy the war bonnet, but the owner refused to sell. He then disguised himself as an Indian and during the middle of the night crept into the man's tipi and stole the bonnet. His moccasins "were made for him by Dayethe, a princess of the Ponca tribe in Indian Territory," his Navajo blanket was a gift to him by an Indian in New Mexico, and a peace pipe came from the Redstone quarry in Minnesota. On the clipping, which he pasted in his scrapbook, Jacobson noted in pencil beside the story of his alleged theft of the war bonnet "Of course not!" and "*Liar!*"[26]

The reference to the "real" was played up in advertisements of the play. On a poster from what must have been one of the first performances in August 1907, *Sunset* is described as "A real western play produced by real westerners. Men who have lived the life they act." "Mustango," the character Jacobson played, sports "the only complete Indian Chief's Costume East of the Mississippi." Reviews consistently emphasized the realistic nature of Jacobson's portrayal of the Pawnee chief. The appeal of the play rested more on its claims to authenticity than on originality or the quality of acting. "The quest for such an authentic Other," writes Philip J. Deloria, "is a characteristically modern phenomenon, one that has often been played out in the contradictions surrounding America's long and ambivalent engagement with Indianness." The lure of the authentic caught the imagination of white Anglo-Saxon Americans who worried about "the character development of immigrants and the next generation of American children." They were concerned with what they viewed as the threat of deterioration of a frontier mentality of rugged individualism and hardworking ethics that followed the supposed decadence of modern life. Authentic displays fundamentally structured the concept underlying the demonstration of global cultures in St. Louis, and Jacobson had ample opportunities to observe this during his time with the Exposition.[27]

In the play, Freeburg formulated ideas about the nature of relationships between white settlers and Indigenous peoples. His characters experienced the tension between East and West in America, with references to Freeburg's own life. He borrowed names and places from his background in Lindsborg. He set the play in New Haven, Connecticut, and Crazy

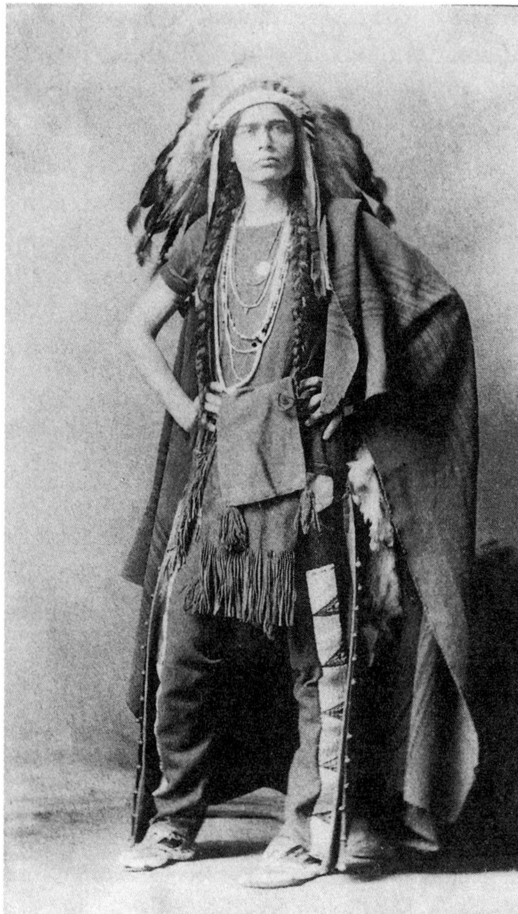

FIGURE 4. Oscar Jacobson as "Mustango, chief of the Pawnee Indians" in the play *Sunset* written by Victor Oscar Freeburg and performed in New Haven in 1907. Courtesy of Sophie Sheppard.

Ridge, Kansas. Freeburg had been a member of Jacobson's Crazy Ridge Wild West Riders during his earlier youth. "Sunset" appeared on the list of pseudonyms for the group of youngsters who took a camping trip in 1903, and another member of that gang was "Kiote Son." I have not been able to identify the pseudonyms with the exception of Jacobson's "Mustang Jake," but it is apparent that the names carried meaning all the way to Yale, as the young men formed their reputation as westerners. Relating to Indians was part and parcel of that character. In a conversation between

Tom Horn "of Crazy Ridge" and his New England college friend Gil, Tom reveals his fondness for Sunset, as they look at her picture:

> Tom—(firmly but not angrily) That's no savage, Gil.
>
> Gil—It isn't, eh (another look at picture). Well—what is it then?
>
> Tom—(proudly) That's an American princess, only daughter of Mustonkah, chief of the Pawnees, and her mother called her Sunset.
>
> Gil—(astonished) Oh,—but I didn't suppose you people mingled social with the red-skins.
>
> Tom—Well, we don't usually, but Sunset is an exception. Everybody knows Sunset and everybody likes her. She's as free as the sunshine, and as cunning as a coyote. She's as pure as the first breeze after an April thunderstorm. She's as bright as a sunbeam, and as sweet as a wild rose.

Tom confesses to having a crush on Sunset, but after he went to college and "got a larger view of things" he realized he "wanted a girl with education and culture and all that goes with it." Sunset, he told Gil, remained a friend, and he expected "to have lots of good times with" her when he visited his family's ranch in Kansas. Read against the background of white male sexual harassment and violence directed at Indigenous women, Tom's reference to "good times" is discomforting. However, Gil responds with a different concern: "I should advise you to keep this Sunset business on the quiet. Might shock conventional society, you know." Tom reacts strongly to this: "Convention. What's that? A lot of Tommy rot! Don't you think I know what's right and wrong without convention telling me? Why, man, I come from a country where there is no convention and no law. Why? Because we don't need it, that's why."[28]

This dialog connected to a discourse of natural law and authentic lives, presumed to have been lost in the overcivilized East but which still lingered in the West. Indians were most poignantly perceived to possess this quality. The westerner placed himself as a link between the East of conventionality and the West of nature and authenticity. It is noteworthy that Freeburg chose Anglo-American names for his white characters. Tom Horn, Brian Guilbert, Dave Scott—none of the names indicated a connection to the immigrant backgrounds of almost all the actors. Yet, both Freeburg's and Jacobson's later careers demonstrate that Sweden was never far from their minds. Around the turn of the century, immigrants, as Deloria points out, were seen as a threat to the American character, just as much as Indians were, and it is possible that Freeburg realized immigrants could not serve as mediators between the raw nature of the West and the overcomplicated constructions of the East.[29]

In the play, as Gil and Tom discuss Sunset in New Haven, violence brews in Kansas. Conflicts between Pawnees and cattle drives threaten the last of the Indian holdings. Sunset's father, Mustango, is unable and unwilling to prevent the oncoming war. He cannot let go of his anger. Sunset is afraid for her father's life and asks him to reconsider. Mustango turns to his daughter and in a long oratory explains the greed of the white man, the Pawnee's losses, and their inevitable passing. The monologue, filled with conventional white American tropes about American Indians, blames "the pale face" for the imminent destruction of "the Red man," through invading their land and forcing them to freeze and starve to death, stealing their horses and using them to plow up the land. Finally, after unleashing all this violence on Indians and their land, the white man asks the chief: "Why are you not happy? I want to be your friend. Let us bury the hatchet." But the war will come to be, the division between white and red is a chasm that cannot be spanned. One of the cowboys enters, intoxicated, and accidentally kills Sunset with a gunshot aimed at Mustango.[30]

Commonly, dramatizations of the frontier myth around the turn of the century often ended in a literal union of Eastern civilization and Western savagery through the marriage of a heroic white male hero, representing the savage West, and an educated white female, who stands for the values of civilization. *Sunset* does not quite follow that script and demonstrates, I believe, that the young men from Lindsborg were grappling with these tropes. While Tom found in the East that he wanted a girl with education and culture "and all that goes with it," he never marries one. Although sharing many of the features of white constructions of Indian identities, such as the "noble savage" and the "Indian princess," the play differs in others. While Sunset dies, Mustango does not, and there is no resolution to the play in which the white protagonists occupy the space of the "vanishing Indian." Mustango's oratory may be read as a serious indictment of white American actions and policies toward American Indians and an exposure of the hypocrisy entailed in the request of friendship once the Indians had been conquered. Yet, that is not how it was received. It is striking that none of the thirty-plus newspaper articles and items describing the play that are collected in scrapbooks by Jacobson and Freeburg specifically comments on this oratory. The only time it is mentioned is in connection with praise of Jacobson in his performance of the role as Mustango. One item describes it as a "denunciation scene," while one lauds Jacobson for his professional acting and thorough familiarity with his character. "His story of the red men held the audience spellbound, and he was obliged to respond to several curtain calls."[31] Thus, any potential for critique of American expansion and policies of dispossessing Indigenous peoples was averted and replaced with a focus on Jacobson as an actor and Indian impersonator.

While filled with stereotypical representations of both Indians and cowboys, typical for the period, one central facet of this play is its role in establishing the participants as westerners. The nucleus of the group consisted of the three roommates from Lindsborg, and most of their companions were also Swedish Lindsborg settlers. But in their performances at Yale and in the local newspapers their Swedishness is clearly undercommunicated in favor of their connection to the American West. In fact, not a single newspaper item mentions that they are immigrants, but all describe them as westerners. The fact that they preferred to be known as westerners may not be all that surprising.

As Deloria has shown, tapping the "Indian" was a way for white Americans to establish their claims to the country. In her study of Swedish immigrant letters Jennifer Eastman Attebery argues for the elaborate blending and mixing of identities that characterized the immigrant condition. "Western regional identity," she suggests, "is a mixed identity created by the immigrants as well as the Easterners who moved westward. Westering was a process in which the Swedes and other European immigrants were equal partners with the 'Americans.'" "Going native" was just one way in which these young men asserted their claim to being "not just an American but an indigenous Westerner, transformed by the region into a rugged individual who is at home in the new region."[32] By stressing that they were from and inhabited the West, these young men who may have felt disadvantaged and marginalized at Yale announced a superior claim to America. It does, however, appear in striking contrast to Jacobson's clear and definite connection to Swedish America and his defense of Swedish culture elsewhere.

Oscar Jacobson, Victor Freeburg, and Carl Ostrum (later they were joined by Harry Larson) rented an apartment, which they fashioned into a manifestation of their western origins. It was known as the "Kawraw Kiotes' Den," with "Kawraw" probably being a play on the name of the Kaw tribe that had originally settled the Smoky River valley in which Lindsborg was situated. The *Saturday Chronicle* devoted a full page to their rooms in an article in 1906:

> The rooms of these quondam ranchers is a veritable museum, and are said to contain the largest private collection of Indian relics east of the Mississippi. Among these curios is to be found a genuine Sioux chief's war bonnet. This striking piece of head-wear is made of selected eagle feathers and is worth a little fortune in itself. Other articles are Navajo blankets, beaded leggins [*sic*], moccasins, arrows, strings of wampum, war clubs, etc. A special object of pride is a peace pipe direct from "the great red pipe-stone quarry," mentioned in Longfellow's Hiawatha. Besides these things, the "Kiotes" have several original Indian photographs procured personally from such characters as Geronimo, Handsome Elk, etc., and, in a place of honor, a real little "Silver Heels" from the Ponca tribe in Indian Territory.[33]

In addition, the rooms held several revolvers, hats, photographs, and posters, but what most impressed the journalist was "the genuineness of everything exhibited." Everything had "its own little story and it takes the 'Kiotes' to tell it." At the same time, the rooms were more than a museum, and the "Kiotes" organized frequent teas and social gatherings emphasizing that "Our latch string always hangs out."[34]

Their "Indian corner" showed that the Lindsborg students were keyed into the latest trend of the day, that of decorating one's home with American Indian objects. Typically a display of objects, photographs, arts, and crafts relating to American Indians and the West placed in a den, porch, or living room, the Indian corner addressed anxieties emerging at the turn of the century about how industrialized production, urbanization, and international trade threatened American culture. The corner signaled a connection to an "'authentic' primitive life" that was distinctly American in origin, in contrast to foreign-made fashion. It did so by "appropriating the material culture of subjugated indigenous people as an expression of national aesthetics," writes Elizabeth Hutchinson. Indian corners emphasized the illusion that American Indian art and crafts were products of a world predating, and entirely detached from, modern society. But, as Hutchinson argues, "both the consumption and the production of Native American art of this time was quintessentially modern." The "Kawraw Kiotes' Den" shows Oscar Jacobson and his roommates as coproducers of that modernity which enabled artistic exchanges between eastern artists and collectors and American Indian producers of craft and provides a background to Jacobson's later evaluation of both arts and crafts as essential Indigenous aesthetic expressions.[35] It also demonstrates, as did *Sunset*, how comfortably Jacobson took on the role of interpreter of American Indians and the West to eastern audiences. It offered him both standing and reputation in the Yale community, although it came at a price of the undercommunication of his Swedish heritage.

Jacobson, thus, most certainly learned of theories of primitivism in art when he attended Yale. Ruth B. Phillips argues that the "peculiar complexity of modernist primitivism in settler societies arises primarily from intersecting and coincident movements of indigenous resistance to colonial domination and national identity formation." Anglo-American artists began incorporating images from Native America in a move toward distancing themselves from European influences, just as the "Indian room" signaled an annexation of Indigenous material culture to be displayed as an assertion of an original American aesthetic.[36] Jacobson tried on this expression as one of his many self-presentations, but he also carried with him the impressions from the art in the Swedish Pavilion at St. Louis, and its call for a return to specifically Swedish origins.

All was not play, however, and Jacobson appears to have worked diligently. In 1906, he was awarded the Henry F. English prize, receiving it from the hand of the university president. It was duly reported in the *Lindsborg Record*, proudly announcing that, "Bethany boys are coming to the front in all lines."[37] In 1908, Jacobson received a Bachelor of Painting from Bethany College and left art school to take up a position as art teacher at Minnesota College. He stayed there until 1911 when he assumed an assignment at the State College of Washington, located in Pullman.

JACOBSON AND SWEDISH AMERICAN NETWORKS

As a young and emerging artist, Jacobson became part of a network of Swedish American patrons of the arts. In her study of Swedish immigrant artists' patronage systems between 1880 and 1940, Mary Towley Swanson described this network as "uniquely vigorous and, although diffuse," frequently "interconnected." A collaboration between artists, journalists, exhibitors, collectors, businessmen, all of them with ties to Sweden and Swedish America, spread information about Swedish American artists and their work and encouraged readers and countrymen to purchase from the artists. Birger Sandzén, Jacobson's first art teacher at Bethany College, belonged to this network and arduously labored to describe the work of Swedish American artists in his contributions to the widespread publication *Prärieblomman* (The prairie flower). Sandzén brought Jacobson into the orbit of this association. Swanson stressed that, without such publications, "which provided free publicity for the artists, knowledge about the artists and the Swedish American art exhibitions would not have traveled beyond the small ethnic enclaves in Midwestern and East coast cities." These publications became efficient vehicles for spreading information regarding immigrant art and created a network of support for several generations of Swedish American artists.[38]

In 1908 *Svenska Tribunen* (Swedish tribune), the influential Chicago-based Swedish language newspaper, introduced Jacobson to their readers, and in 1910, his friend Victor O. Freeburg wrote an article for *Ungdomsvännen* (The friend of youth) entitled "An eminent Swedish American artist," which stressed Jacobson's talents as a portrait painter. The article also described how, through Jacobson's efforts, a group of Swedish Americans in the Twin Cities formed the Minnesota Society for the Fine Arts with the purpose of encouraging appreciation of the arts among Swedish Americans in the state.[39] The name "Society for the Fine Arts" carried a distinct class inflection and suggested that Jacobson embraced the ideals of the Swedish American ethnic elite.

If Jacobson chose to present himself foremost as a westerner at Yale, in Minnesota he fully embraced the role of Swedish American artist. A clipping in Swedish from the Minneapolis-based periodical *Nya Idun* (The new Idun), cut out without the author's name, reveals something of the nature of Jacobson's relationship to Sweden in this first decade of the new century. On a visit to Minnesota College, the writer met Jacobson and his students as they were in full swing painting and sculpting. The description of Jacobson read: "He is supposed to be ultra-Swedish in heart and soul, but that did not prevent that I almost got into battle with him regarding 'the preservation of Swedishness' or rather the possibilities thereof, which he pretended not to believe in. Pretended?! Yes, that he did not mean what he said but only fenced with wooden blades in order to get a discussion going was not so difficult to comprehend, since he in the same breath spoke fervently in favor of Captain McHold's lecture on 'Scandinavian contributions to American culture,' which would be held a few days later."[40]

Jacobson not only drummed up support for public lectures on the importance of Scandinavians, he also wrote and lectured on the characteristics of art in Sweden. He did so in terms that predate his methods in relation to the American Indian artists he would later mentor, when he advocated breaking away from foreign influences in order to develop an authentic national character. In a 1910 lecture at Minnesota College later printed in *Nya Idun,* in English, he spoke about contemporary art in Sweden. Jacobson ranked Sweden as one of the top art nations in the world, because of its "young men, vigorous and enthusiastic, who, after they have acquired an academic training, have thrown all conventionality to the winds and paint nature according to their own tastes and ideas." He asserted that after the Paris world exposition in 1900, Sweden was ranked as number two after France "as the most brilliant school of painting" and continued to hold that position at the 1904 St. Louis Exposition. He went on to identify the roots of this development in the late seventeenth century when the royal court imported art teachers from continental Europe. The positive effect of this was that Swedish artists became trained at a high standard of technical excellence, but it also led to an excessive imitation of foreign customs, particularly those of France. In the late nineteenth century, young artists began speaking of "the artistic possibilities of their own land with its freedom, poetry and beauty. They talked of its rugged mountain sides, its plunging cataracts, its peaceful ravines and nestling lakes. They saw the possibilities in the sturdy peasant behind the plow, of the Lapp gliding over vast stretches of snow under the starry heaven of a northern night." The consequence of this new movement, known as *Konstnärsförbundet* (League of artists) or simply the Opponents, was, in

Jacobson's estimation "that in no other country of the world is art more national, more animated or more true than in Sweden today."[41]

In an extensive article in *Nya Idun* entitled "The Modern Art in Sweden," Jacobson elaborated on this theme. "The Swedes are the broadest, boldest and most ingenious of realists. They are the men of all Europeans who draw and paint the thing as they see it. . . . And if they do not actually sit in polished chairs and paint immense, minutely finished, canvasses, it is because they prefer to stand upon their sturdy feet and keep ready to move forward in search of new truths." This quality of sturdiness and manliness adhered also to female artists, he asserted, "Their work is racy and bold. It has the rugged accent of masculinity even that of the women." He concluded, "The Swedes have just the qualities that one might logically expect to find in American art. This is a country of big things, and everywhere we find the spirit of initiative, exploration and unconventiality [*sic*],—I was even about to add adventure. But it is the Swedes, not the Americans who show this trait in their art. Our art does not seem like the art of a young and independent race."[42] Jacobson's admiration for Swedish art is apparent, but he was ambivalent in his own identification and wrote primarily as the initiated conveyor of the nation's qualities to an American audience. "Our" art refers to his critique of the art produced in the United States, and the pronoun "their" in the previous sentence underscores that he made a difference between Swedes in Sweden and in America.

Jacobson's lecture and article supplied ammunition in a debate that engulfed Swedish American elite society during the opening decades of the twentieth century. The discussion concerned Swedish contributions to the construction and character of America, and it struggled to dispel deep-seated notions that Sweden lacked an advanced culture with which to make a contribution.[43] "Don't forget to read Prof. Jakobson's article about 'Modern Art in Sweden,'" the editors of *Nya Idun* admonished their readers. The article was published in English, "the language in which it was held," specifically "so that it can prove useful and enlightening not only to genuine Swedes, but also to Americans and the younger version of Swedish Americans, who to a very small degree have an idea of what Sweden really is and has to offer in terms of 'fine arts.'" Such ambitions to combine the best of Sweden and America were common. Literary scholar Anna Williams describes a dual and nonexclusive identity as both Swedish and American in which "loyalty to America was entirely compatible with an active ethnic consciousness." This placed Swedish American writers in the Swedish tradition and referred to a long line of prominent Swedish authors to place Sweden on the literary map of the world.[44] It was a conscious rejection of the melting pot vision for American society, and one that Jacobson obviously shared.

Jacobson's tenure at Minnesota College coincided with the appointment of George M. Stephenson, who went on to become a prominent historian at the University of Minnesota and one of the pioneers of immigration history in the United States. Jacobson appears solidly ensconced in a web of Swedish Americans, and his social circle in Minneapolis included notable Swedish Americans as well as Swedish visitors, such as the astronomer and Nobel laureate Svante Arrhenius. However, a brief note in the Minneapolis *Picayune* reveals that he had not entirely shed his western persona when he invited colleagues to a "coffee carnival" in his "wild west abode."[45]

Historic connections took on a particular meaning for immigrant claims to belonging in America, and for Swedish Americans two events were especially salient. The supposed settlements of Vikings in North America in the eleventh century constituted the first of these, and the short-lived Swedish colony on the Delaware River in the seventeenth century the other. The Vikings united Norwegians, Danes, and Swedes in celebrating a special place in the settlement of America and ethnic leaders avidly sought to prove that the Vikings had been the first Europeans on the continent. While the presence of Vikings on American soil was largely speculative, New Sweden provided a tangible instance of Swedish settlement, and in 1888 the 250th anniversary of the founding of the colony turned into a major celebration of Swedish American history. "It is telling," argues Dag Blanck, "that the celebrations took place in Minneapolis, a rapidly growing center for nineteenth-century Swedish Americans, and not at the original site in Delaware." Then, at the peak of Swedish immigration to America, a link was metaphorically forged between that early and soon dispersed settlement and the waves of migrants arriving more than a century later.[46] Jacobson would participate in and draw strength from the commemoration of both these events.

In 1911, while still at Minnesota College, Jacobson participated in the staging of *Minnesota History*, a pageant set up to benefit the art school in

St. Paul. This production took shape as a collaboration between different immigrant groups in the Twin Cities, and it included nine different acts. Jacobson was in charge of staging the "Norsemen's scene," and he himself dressed up as a Viking. Act 2 of the pageant depicted the "Coming of the Vikings" and consisted of three scenes, beginning with the arrival of a Viking ship and ending with the erection of the Kensington Rune Stone, a slab with runic inscriptions presumed to have originated with fourteenth-century Scandinavian explorers, "by Survivors." The middle scene showed an Indian attack in which most of the Norsemen were killed.[47]

One of the opening scenes was to show "the Indians in their full domination over this state." The inclusion of Indians in the pageant obviously mattered to Jacobson. He included in his scrapbook an article from the *Pioneer Press* in St. Paul entitled "Indians Play Big Parts in Pageant." Members of the Minnesota Boat club dressed up as "Indians"—with one addition: the role of Hiawatha was played by Dakota author Charles Eastman (Ohiyesa). The article introduced him as "Dr. Eastman, one of the most prominent Indians of the country, and a man who has made a study of the tribal relations and conditions of his race, both past and present, has been cast for the role of Hiawatha." Notably, the pageant makes no mention of the Dakota Conflict in 1862, in which Dakota warriors took to arms in a desperate measure to try to stem the influx of settlers in their territories, following a long season of starvation and abuse. Instead, the penultimate act described the "passing of the Indian from Minnesota," thus completely erasing any hint at violent conflict. "A lone Indian is discovered asleep and his canoe is seen on the river bank. A dance of the Indian spirits provides an effective scene, but then the Indian awakes, gets into his canoe and slowly paddles away." The final act of the play then, predictably, portrayed "modern Minnesota" and "patriotic songs and choruses will bring the spectacle to a close." The pageant participated in a long tradition of what historian Jean O'Brien has called "firsting and lasting" of American Indians, a process in which she argues "non-Indians actively produced their own modernity by denying modernity to Indians."[48]

A small item in the newspaper demonstrates how perceptions of "Indians" firmly placed them in a fictional and exotic realm. The headline ran: "No Pajamas for Indians; Pageant Costumes a Mystery." The brief column described a problem regarding the clothing that participants in the Minnesota history pageant would wear as they portrayed Indians. The men who had consented to play Indians were concerned that they would be cold on the stage if they only wore scant coverings, and that it would also prove embarrassing. "They proposed wearing their pajamas, but Mr. Ziegler, anxious for the artistic integrity of the scene, would not listen to pajamas. It must be walnut oil or nothing." The piece concluded tantalizingly that "a compromise had been reached, and the brown braves are to wear—but that would be telling."[49] Again, as when Jacobson portrayed the Pawnee chief at Yale, authenticity required Indians to be portrayed as nude, a nudity that scandalized and titillated spectators and drew the line firmly between civilization and savagery. There is no mention of how Charles Eastman reacted to this binary. Indians, too, were expected to play along.

In 1913 Jacobson continued to develop the topic of Scandinavian contributions to American culture, and this time turned his interest to New Sweden. In an article entitled "How the Scandinavians Have Made Good in America," he began with the arrival of *The Key of Calmar*, the first ship sponsored by Swedish interests sent out to establish a colony along the Delaware River in 1638. He meandered through colonial history, finding Swedish connections in John Hanson, one of the signers of the Declaration of Independence and officially named "the president of the United States in congress assembled" and revealing the surprising claim that George Washington had remote ancestry from Skåne in southern Sweden. Then he went on to describe the mass migration of the previous century:

> Nearly all of the Swedish (and for that matter, Scandinavian) immigrants came from the sturdy, healthy (morally and physically) middle class—the small farmers, trades people, fishermen, and sailors. Generally it was the progressive and adventurous young men who found the severe military service and the overbearing attitude of the upper or aristocratic class irksome. . . .
>
> Racially, the Swede is a home-loving man. To have a plot of ground and a house that he could call his own has always been the ambition of the northerner in spite of the fact that he has always been at the same time of a restless and adventurous nature, always seeking new fields of conquest. Likewise he has always been a free man, somewhat proud and stern of temperament.

He rebuffed the notion that Scandinavians were only fit for manual labor and service and set forth that Swedish communities in America "stand for the highest type of rural civilization." Some of them had even achieved national recognition and among them Jacobson found his own hometown, Lindsborg, which he asserted was known around the world for its music and art. "Honesty and sturdy manhood" typical of the "ancient Viking sea kings" still characterized Scandinavians. But in all Scandinavian honesty, it must be admitted that they also had faults. One was their tendency to lose their identity in amalgamation with other nationalities. Another, which perhaps was not so much a fault as a marker, "is a rather heavy, but tender, melancholy temperament, due undoubtedly to thousands of years of living in the far dark north."[50] As a description of Scandinavians in America, the piece was rather trite and unoriginal. But was he really describing the over two million Scandinavian descendants in the United States and Canada? Was it not, rather, his own experience, and his own sense of in-betweenness? The young man avoiding grueling military service could have been his older brother Emil. His hometown of Lindsborg exemplified the lofty achievements and cultural advancement of Swedes on the plains, and he himself was an example of the amalgamation of identities—a westerner at Yale, an easterner in Pullman, and always poised to defend Swedes.

COLOR, LIGHT, AND FORM

Not surprisingly, Oscar was fascinated early in his life by the art of Frederick Remington and Charles Russell. He looked to the landscapes of the West when he painted. But unlike those artists he rarely depicted human beings in his sceneries. It is clear from his own early writings that his influence also came from the Swedish landscape painters, such as Liljefors and Schultzberg. Little is known of what Jacobson did in his art classes at Yale, but a description he wrote about Remington may well pertain to himself as well. "His strong personality rebelled at the rigidity of academic teaching, so . . . he left Yale and went west," searching for "more freedom of expression than is customary at Yale."[51]

Newspaper clippings indicate that Oscar was best known for portraits during his early years of teaching at Minnesota College and Washington State College. *Svenska Tribunen* described him in 1908 as a promising young Swedish American artist. "His specialty is portraiture and his early life and environment in the . . . so highly beloved wide west is often noticeable in his work, because he is happiest, when he can represent on the canvas some character from the domain of 'the cowboys.'" His portraits included US Forest Service research scientist T. T. Munger, Minnesota governor John A. Johnson, and young prince Chu of China. The portrait of Johnson, painted after his death and bought by Gustavus Adolphus College, attracted considerable attention and was shown at the Alaska-Yukon-Pacific Exposition in 1909.[52]

But it was nature, not studio portraits, that came to dominate his production. "Nature for Jacobson was more than a backdrop for his canvases." Instead, his art grew out of his passion for the rugged strength and transcendental reach of the natural world unadulterated by human presence. According to one of his earliest students, William Cunningham, Jacobson always "considered life more important than art," but the two intertwined to produce unique paintings suffused by poetry.[53] Jacobson, according to art historian Mark White, "hoped to convey the sensations and moods of the wilderness through form and color," and his "lofty beliefs in the spiritual and emotional import of painting were anchored in a tangible experience of nature, specifically the pristine wilds of western North America." However, he did not define himself as a romantic, instead seeing his work "as inherently modernist." Mayrene Bentley notes that his "most characteristic work was marked by bold depictions of sky, terrain, water, and horizon in flat, definable strokes of paint with strong delineations of color."[54] His form and technique altered over his life and a fascination with the desert landscape shaped his content, but he maintained the inspiration he received from Schultzberg's and Liljefors' paintings of nature "undisturbed by man."[55]

Jacobson's connection to Birger Sandzén, which lasted until the end of the latter's life, had a profound impact on his development as an artist. Together with Sandzén Jacobson explored the light, colors, and forms of the desert landscape. White explains that an "empathetic interpretation of light and color seem[s] to have been Jacobson's primary interest, and vigorous, linear strokes in the secondary colors acknowledge not only Sandzén's impact, but also that of Vincent van Gogh." Sandzén continued to encourage Jacobson, critique his artwork, request that he contribute pieces for exhibitions Sandzén organized or heard about, and the two discussed art and the conditions for artists and teachers in their correspondence. "Yes, you are right about the world we are living in. It certainly does *not* pay to be an idealist, an artist, teacher or writer, unless you Commercialize your talent and write or paint easily distinguishable stuff," wrote Sandzén in 1920. Sandzén's great project was a colloquium of southwestern painters independent of the establishments on the East Coast, and he constantly sought Jacobson's support and participation. In the 1930s, he formed the "Prairie Water Color Painters" club, which held its first exhibition in 1934 at Kansas State College. Jacobson was a member and exhibitor from the start. Sandzén continued as mentor and constructive critic. In 1942 he told Jacobson that, "I am proud of your paintings, because you bring out essentials in a very convincing way. Form and design are always there." Two years later Sandzén sought to bolster Jacobson's confidence, writing to him that, "I am glad that you are painting. I have told you repeatedly that you are too modest about your own work, which is very fine." He lived to see his young disciple achieve recognition in both his hometown of Lindsborg and his adopted state of Oklahoma and commended him in 1947: "You combine good, decorative design and fine understanding of nature's varied suggestions. In other words you are doing high quality painting."[56]

WEST OF THE WEST

In September 1911, Oscar Jacobson arrived in Pullman, Washington, to assume his new post as professor of art at Washington State College. His nimble dance between identities was about to acquire another step as he traveled farther west than he had ever been before. He continued to write for his community of Lindsborg. In October 1911, after a month in Pullman, he composed a letter to his friends, which was published in the *Lindsborg Record.* He now found himself in the curious position of having switched sides: "I have now lived here a short and very busy month and have as it were become acclimated and had time to observe the many peculiarities new to an easterner." The self-styled westerner in New Haven had now become the easterner discovering the majesty of the Pacific Northwest. "The northern Rockies are opalling [*sic*] in their grandeur and the pine and spruce forests and the lakes of the northern Idaho country the most glorious and infatuating I have ever beheld—even rivaling the splendors of Hudson river scenery." He concluded, a little cautiously: "I like the westerner and I hope he will like me."[57]

Presumably, Jacobson had explored the "splendors" of the Hudson River valley while at Yale, although there is no record of it. However, doing so would have been required fare for a landscape painter. But it is also possible that this is a dig at the self-assumed superiority of the East, evident in the canon of American landscape painting, which Jacobson and Sandzén often criticized. In d'Ucel's memoir, written half a century later, Oscar's momentary identity crisis had already been resolved. She remembered a meeting on a train as they were returning from their honeymoon trip: "We were amused by an Easterner who, seeing that Oscar sketched, began to tell us about the Hudson. He was surprised that we knew it; eventually, he had to admit that the Columbia compared not unfavorably with his home river."[58]

At Christmastime 1911, he found himself in Idaho, on a trip into the high country. With a mixed group of colleagues, Jacobson was to spend this Christmas "on an old Indian Reservation." He wrote an account for his community back in Lindsborg. His descriptions of the Nez Perce people he encountered on the train are full of racial stereotypes and particularly offensive in describing women, as he pandered to the imagination of an eastern audience:

> Red men are filling up the vacant seat [*sic*] in the coaches. Bright colored neckerchiefs and hat bands are to be seen all about and long coarse bluish-black hair is concealing the neck and shoulders of three-fourths of the travelers. Often a long feather or skunk tail adorn the immence [*sic*] black felt hat men with handsome, stern, immovable, hatchet faces silently slip in and out at every stopping place. Less handsome squaws, fat and squatty, hiding in shawls and blankets of all possible and impossible color combinations follow as silently and unostentatiously their masters. Often the rear view exposes a pair of bright beady eyes of a little papoose fastened by some ingenious contrivance to its mother's back. Tepees and camps litter the valley all along the way, before we realize what has happened we are in the Nez Perse Indian country.[59]

After a long train journey, the trip ended on a stagecoach that would "take us still further up into the unknown." A difficult climb up the canyon followed, which was "fatiguing both for the party and the double span of ponies. The grade was very steep and the trail narrow and rough, hugging the mountain side in wonderful curves, some lines overlooking abysses thousands of feet below." But the effort was well worth it. On arrival, they found a country of wonders. "The frontier of civilization,—in a virgin forest of evergreen as far as the eye could reach—and in a blinding snow storm." Two men and a little girl on horseback met them, and Jacobson exclaimed that, "never have I received such a wonderful impression as this group awaiting for us on the high mountain side in the snow storm gave me. It was wild and grim and awe inspiring. It was a picture of real men in a natural setting of a great country."[60] Jacobson felt that he was sent back into the past, and he imagined what it would have been like in Lindsborg when it was settled by hardy Swedes.

> Here were the people, the frontiers man and the pioneer, such as we used to read about in our school books, rough, uncouth and uncultured? Yes, Humanity with the bark on yet no less good timber and sound to the core. The leaves of history were turned back for me, and I saw and lived with the people that settled the Smoky Valley 50 years ago.
>
> These unshorn and unshaven people would be pointed at and sneered at if seen on the streets of our cities, but we must not forget that these are the sturdy advance guard of a finer and nobler civilization. These hewers of the wild forest. These homemakers, these empire builders—if you please,—are the real back bone of the nation.[61]

Here then, Jacobson found a historical laboratory where the history of the winning of the West was still performed, and in his 1911 rendering, the Indians were nothing but picturesque backdrop, with every conceivable stereotype intact. This was also a country where men took center stage, despite lip service to the presence of women, even though in his very first description a little girl came careening on horseback through the snowstorm to bring the party deer meat to eat. Here, as in much of his early writings, he glories in a rendering of masculinity that appears quintessentially western yet also with clear parallels to how he describes Swedish manhood. Roughly hewn, tough, and honest, and untouched by the deleterious effects of too much refinement—that is how he viewed the ideal man. Just as he had referred to Swedish women painters as favorably touched by the masculine virtues of their culture, so he included women in his perception of the honorable westerner.[62]

Gone is the ambiguity of *Sunset* and its critique of the white man's expansive greed. Instead Jacobson expresses a Turnerian view of American

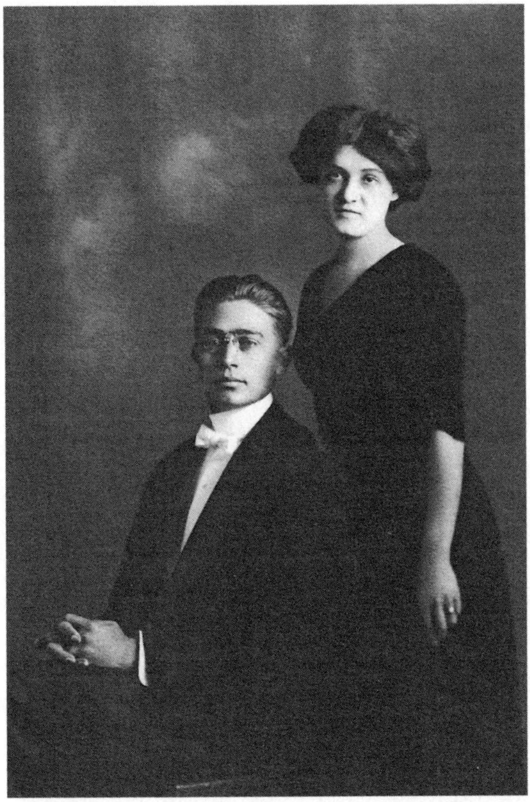

FIGURE 5. Wedding photo of Oscar Jacobson and Sophie Brousse, 1912. At the time of their wedding Oscar, unusual for his time, added Sophie's last name, Brousse, as his middle name. Courtesy of Sophie Sheppard.

(white) expansion, and the western experience as the origin of American democracy and values. By attaching these to the settlement work of immigrants, however, he linked his description to a well-established Scandinavian American rhetoric of emphasizing the importance of Scandinavians in building the American nation.[63]

Part of the allure of the midwinter wilderness experience may have been the presence of Mlle. Sophie Brousse, who had arrived in Pullman at about the same time as he had, to teach French. Sophie Brousse had a teaching degree, with English as her major, from Grenoble Academy. Their courtship was brief, and by August 1912 they were married. She became "Mrs. Oscar Jacobson," and he added "Brousse" as his middle name, ever onward identifying as the amalgamation I suspect he felt like—Swedish, European, and Western. His nephew remembers him describing his relationship to Sophie: "He said she gave up a beautiful, brilliant future as a writer and literary critic to become the ideal wife of a high strung, Swedish farm boy who never learned how to spell or shut doors." Instead she became his colleague and muse.[64]

At Pullman Oscar and Sophie lived their first year as newlyweds at a place named Cliff House, which they shared with several other professors and a minister. Around Halloween the inhabitants staged a housewarming party that caught the imagination. D'Ucel describes how they converted their apartment to the Cave of Endor (from the Old Testament book of Joshua). Jeanne dressed up as a witch, offering prophecies to their guests, while Oscar appeared as a ghost. James Robinson, the reverend, presided as Satan over his own quarters, arranged as Inferno. Arriving guests, guided by ghosts, assembled in the joint dining room "transformed into a Wild West saloon." This was during Prohibition, but "fierce looking professorial bar tenders" dispensed soft drinks "as if they were the real thing." The college president attended, and he complimented them "on the wonderful mise-en-scene."[65]

Together the two explored the western landscape, frequently going camping on horseback. But they also longed to go abroad. They spent their honeymoon traveling up through Washington and Idaho to British Columbia and on to Banff and Lake Louise. "Mobs of tourists had not yet found this region; so it was still largely unspoiled." In the spring of 1914, they had saved up enough to afford a long-awaited trip to Europe, to visit both Sweden and France, a Grand Tour that included visits to major art museums and inspired Jacobson to paint (see plate 1). While they obviously longed to see the places where they had grown up, Västra Eknö in Sweden and Aubernas in France, the abiding impression of the trip was of the ominous rumblings that would erupt that summer into world war. They were caught in the first skirmishes of the war while in Grenoble, and upon their return in September 1914 Jacobson wrote for the *Pullman Herald.* "Not until the train loads of wounded began pouring in did we fully become conscious of what was happening. When we saw the men who had left but a few hours before, return, their uniforms in rags and full of clotted blood and dirt, their heads, arms, and chests in bandages—then we were brought face to face with the sickening reality of war." He noted that "the cruelty and savage acts of the Germans can not be a question of doubt," but while his sympathies were clearly with the French and Belgians, he deplored the war and its instigators as such. "It is a glorious time for those who believe in war for war's sake, and an especially glorious time for the divine right of kings, for without this doctrine there would not now be the wholesale slaughtering of mankind. Perhaps, when the smoke of the guns has cleared away, it will not seem so glorious to the rulers upon whose heads rests the blood guilt of the most devastating war known in the history of the human race."[66]

THE LAST OF THE WEST— THE INCONGRUITY OF OKLAHOMA

Upon returning from Europe, Oscar Jacobson had been offered a new post as director of the School of Fine Arts at University of Oklahoma in Norman. In contrast to the majesty of the northwestern landscape, Oklahoma in 1915 must have appeared bleak. Jeanne d'Ucel remembered their arrival in Norman:

> When we arrived our hearts sank abit [*sic*] for the town was more primitive than we had expected. Emerging from the train at 1.30 A.M. we asked the coachman of the one and only, very dilapidated hack, to take us to the best hotel. The Grand Central looked anything but that and Oscar repeated his order. "Yessir" replied the man "thiss iss it." . . . We paid him and went in. No, there was no private bath, said the clerk, looking at us as if we had asked for the moon. It was hot, so we didn't need the unsavory looking blanket; the sheets at least seemed reasonably clean; we went to bed. But, before long, we arose; bugs were converging on us. We left them in possession and sat up the rest of the night.[67]

Norman compared unfavorably with both Lindsborg and Pullman, and its frontier crudeness seemed to lack the qualities inherent in the pioneer advance troops of civilization, which Jacobson had so admired in the Idaho mountains. Yet according to d'Ucel, Oscar had been ready to move again but wished to stay in the West, and so he was happy to accept the appointment "although the pay was low and it would entail much work." The dean of the Fine Arts College was another Bethanyte, Fred Holmberg, whose brother Sam had previously headed the fine arts department but died tragically at a young age. Sam and Oscar had known each other in Lindsborg, and Holmberg activated his Lindsborg network to find a replacement. Birger Sandzén had previously encouraged Sam Holmberg to apply for the position at Oklahoma, and now he seized on the opportunity and recommended Jacobson for the post. Dean Holmberg made it clear that the university was new and small and in need of development. Both he and the university's president, Stratton D. Brooks, "wanted to develop an art school of distinction and would stand right behind a willing worker."[68]

Letters from Sandzén during Jacobson's first five years in Oklahoma testify to the hard work involved and how the network of Swedish American western artists operated. Sandzén continued to support, encourage, and advise his former student both regarding his struggles to develop the art department and as an artist himself. During 1915 and 1916, Sandzén was particularly keen to bring Jacobson into his network of southwestern artists, and to advise him on how to best develop an art collection for the university. In January 1916, he wrote to Jacobson, "I feel more and more that we Western Artists have to work out our own artistic salvation quite independently of the East. We can not expect any support. . . . It gives me a very genuine pleasure to know that you are back to this part of the country *for good*." This disenchantment with the East informed his strategies for how to build an art department as well. "As a rule," he wrote in a previous letter, "there is very little satisfaction in getting an expensive loan exhibition. It is far better to invite a few artists and to save the money to buy something for a permanent collection." The Eastern loan Exhibitions, he continued in a letter four years later, "are expensive and . . . as a rule . . . very poor."[69]

Sandzén put Jacobson in contact with other western painters and art galleries in the Southwest. In November 1915 Jacobson sent two canvases to an exhibition in McPherson, Kansas, organized by Sandzén's friend Carl Smalley. Smalley owned a gallery in McPherson and for a while operated one in Kansas City and frequently organized art exhibitions that traveled across the region. Coming into Smalley's orbit brought Jacobson into a large network of southwestern artists. In 1920 Sandzén informed Jacobson that Charles S. Peterson, a Chicago businessman and publisher who was one of the wealthy patrons of Swedish American artists, "is going to take 100 pictures over to Sweden this summer. He wants me to go along and insists that I must go." Sandzén's letters suggest that he and Jacobson had an ongoing dialogue about their work as teachers and their endeavors as artists, and both of them apparently experienced exhaustion. "We teachers, and especially teacher-artists . . . are too awfully busy all the time. What is a person to do about it?" He expresses frustration with the Swedish American network of art patrons: "If those rich Swedish Am. fellows would understand that artists whom they want to help and encourage need checks and big checks rather than nice words."[70]

Jacobson's scrapbook testifies to a very busy life indeed. Already in January 1916, less than half a year after he had arrived in the art department at the University of Oklahoma, he organized an exhibition of eighty paintings by western artists, fifty etchings, and Chinese embroidered tapestries. Sandzén sent a canvas and was described by the *Oklahoma Daily* as "the greatest colorist in America." Several of the artists represented belonged to the Swedish American network, including Gustav Natanael Malm, Charles Hallberg, Samuel Holmberg, and Jacobson himself. His canvases were praised in the paper with the painting *The Mesa* demonstrating "the artist's enthusiasm for the past history of the interesting race which inhabited the great Southwest." Dean Fred Holmberg was cited in the paper: "The University of Oklahoma should be pleased . . . to have an artist at the head of the department of painting whose life's ambition it is to glorify in art the wonders and beauties of the great Southwest." Jacobson not only exhibited his own paintings from Indian country but also brought in several exhibitions and gave numerous talks on the topic of "Indian art."[71]

In 1917, ten years after statehood, it was time to reflect on Oklahoma's history in a pageant. Jacobson wrote the script and directed the play together with Holmberg. The third scene in the seventh act bore the title "The Passing of the Indian" and consisted of a procession slowly crossing the stage, "the savage, the Indian chief, the squaw, the modern Indian, the half-breed, the college man and girl." This suggested a seamless and inevitable change, which, just as the pageant commemorating Minnesota's history had done, eschewed any reflection on interracial violence and conflict in the creation of the state.[72]

Jacobson's fierce pride in the part of the West that he had made his own shone through in a speech he made in 1919 to the American

Federation of Art in New York City. In several stages he depicted the development of the region. He cast the westerner as possessing a "law unto himself" but also "a fine code of honor." He was independent, "but his hospitality knows no bounds. His word is good." The rough and untamed westerner may scoff "at anything intellectual but the songs and stories from the camp fire nights bear ample evidence of a longing for expression in art." Jacobson had developed a conviction that indigenous America was an indelible part of the state and of the nation and hinted at its special features. "If time allowed, I could guide you to a strange and pagan civilization still existing in this country, that has remained unchanged since long before Coronado—but that is another story." In a few years that very story would take center stage in his life, and Oklahoma was the ideal setting for it. "It is said that one-seventh of the white population of Oklahoma has Indian blood—could anything be more thoroughly American."[73]

In 1925 Jacobson received a sabbatical and he and Jeanne embarked on a life-changing trip to Europe and North Africa. By then the family had grown by three children: Yvonne, born in 1917, Oscar in 1919, and Yolande in 1921. When they returned in 1926, Jacobson had fallen seriously ill from typhoid, and his art style had changed dramatically. Jeanne wrote a book on Berber art, which was published by the University of Oklahoma Press, and Jacobson became known as an expert on primitive art.

The family first traveled to France, and after visiting exhibitions in Paris drove south and stopped at Jeanne's home in Grenoble, where Oscar sketched her ancestral castle, Château des Comtes d'Ucel. The greater part of the year away, they stayed in Algeria but also visited Morocco and Tunisia. They began assembling a collection of Berber pottery, jewelry, and textiles, which they subsequently sold to the University of Oklahoma. This material formed the foundation for the museum collection that the Jacobsons were hoping to build. The North African desert fascinated Jacobson and he wished to compare it with the American Southwest.[74] There is scant mention of why the couple chose to travel to North Africa, but as this region primarily consisted of French colonies at this time, it is likely that d'Ucel's origins in France contributed and that the trip was facilitated by French imperialism. Jacobson wished to paint the desert and he was fascinated with the dry Atlas Mountains, which reminded him of the Southwest. The same interest in the intersection between art and crafts, which he had developed in his Indian corner at Yale, brought him to "paint pictures and to trail to its lair the strange and beautiful peasant crafts that I suspect still exist among these primitive mountain folk."[75]

The sojourn in North Africa proved pivotal. Jacobson began to alter his form of representation, heavily influenced by the school of Art Deco and Paul Cézanne. These influences resulted in "a break with Jacobson's expressionistic tendencies of the 1910s in favor of a planar, angular style suitable to the representation of the severe landscapes of both North Africa and the American West." His paintings began to show a plainer brushwork and flattened planes, revealing the nuances of light and place. He became interested in the anatomy of nature, in the slow yet inescapable process of erosion, in the sculpting made by water and ice, the bending and scouring of the wind. After returning home he painted *Djedjelli, Algeria* (see plate 2) which clearly shows the change in his style. Mark White argues that it must have been one of his own favorite paintings since he exhibited it more than any other of his early paintings. Simple shapes and repetitious rhythms suggest the influence from the Art Deco style, and rocks, hills, waves, and clouds are reduced to elemental relationships.[76] Jacobson lectured extensively upon returning from the African trip, on topics ranging from "Islam in Africa" to "Arabian music" and "Djinns and Marabouts." Demonstrating his delight in costume play, he would often appear in Bedouin robes.[77] In some ways the sabbatical trip focused the various personas he had tried out during his years at Yale, in Minnesota, and in Washington. His active immersion in Swedish American networks and his exposure to Swedish nature painting combined with his identification with the American West to sharpen an interest in the visual representation of the natural world. His interest in "the primitive," most likely augmented through contacts with the art world of Paris, emanated from a search for cultural authenticity, and as Phillips argues, "as an immigrant Jacobson's primitivism was also something more, for through his painterly recreations of a raw and unsettled land he seems also to have been clearing a space in which he could root himself in America."[78] He honed his interest in "the primitive" and found a role as an authority on "primitive art." The trip to North Africa established the Jacobsons—in their own minds

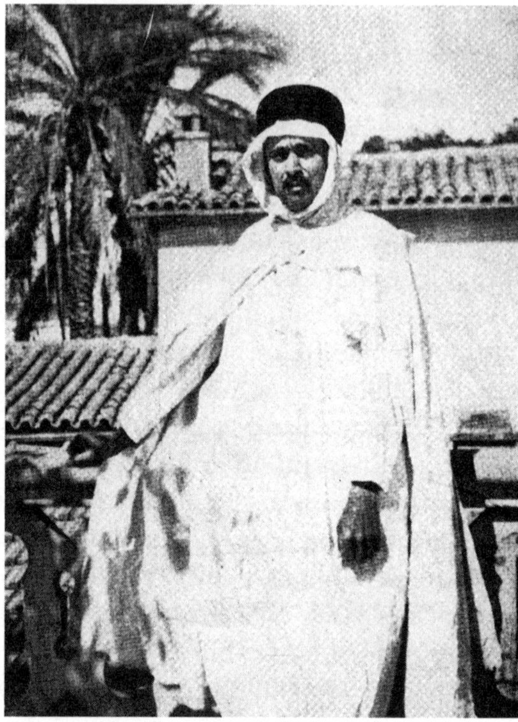

FIGURE 6. Oscar Jacobson dressed up as a Bedouin. The photo was used to promote lectures and presentations following the sabbatical he and his wife spent in North Africa in 1925. Box 4, Scrapbooks, OJC. Courtesy of the Oklahoma Historical Society.

and in the academic circles of the university—as not just immigrants or westerners but cosmopolitans. Oscar and Jeanne had traveled the world. With their art, lectures, and labor to build an art museum they sought to bring the world to Oklahoma. Now they were ready to bring Oklahoma to the world.

CHAPTER 3

Dancing in Place, 1900–1920s

INTENSELY BROWNISH-RED ROCKS LINE the Redstone valley in central-western Oklahoma. The sandstone protrudes in places where erosion from the ceaseless wind has swept away the soil, forming gullies and ridges in the otherwise rolling prairie landscape that enfolds the large granite outcrop of the Wichita Mountains (see plate 15). The Redstone valley lies north and east in between the towns of Carnegie, which now hosts the Kiowa Tribal Headquarters, and Anadarko. Stephen Mopope was born there in 1898 and is noted in the census record of 1901 as the three-year-old son of #316 George Mo-pope, thirty-five, and Hattie Pau-kee-gope, twenty-one. He had two elder half siblings alive at that time, Clara, age twelve, and Donald, age nine. A younger brother, Robert, was born in 1901, and later on, Clyde, Gilbert, and Roland followed. Stephen was Pau-kee-gope's first child, and Clara and Donald most likely were George's children from an earlier marriage. Stephen remembered several children who died in infancy from common diseases like flu and pneumonia, and who were buried on the allotment.[1]

Stephen Mopope grew up in an era of transition and turbulence. The Kiowa diaspora had led to a circumscribed existence on land to which they recognized a connection but over which they had little influence. Kiowas and their neighbors endured conditions of excruciating poverty as they were forced to adapt to life on restricted allotments, while white settlers continued to encroach on the reservation. Increasingly, Kiowas became a managed population, constrained in their movements and choices, controlled by Indian agents, missionaries, teachers, and field matrons. Mopope's upbringing placed him in this net of white officials, but it also rooted him firmly in the Kiowa struggle for cultural, spiritual, and social survivance.[2]

In the early part of the twentieth century, many white reformers and promoters of Indian art and culture viewed many Oklahoma Indians as being too assimilated, too acculturated, to count as real Indians. Oklahoma remained a highly diverse place after statehood. The multitude of tribes forced together in the Territory prepared the ground for intertribal exchanges and meant that Indian people were visible, even impossible to ignore, in almost every corner of the state. Specific practices and ceremonies were shared among tribes, contributing to the white notion that these practices would become diluted, but in many cases sharing them led to their maintenance and survival. Yet, in the eyes of authorities, visitors, and eastern tribes, the western part of the state stayed wild and savage. Kiowas, Comanches, and Apaches held a special place among the class of "wild Indian tribes," being considered "as yet close to untouched by culture or civilization." Around the time of Oklahoma's formation as a state, it was commonplace to describe the Kiowas as a "savage" people with "less honor, gratitude and general reliability than perhaps any other tribe on the plains," as anthropologist James Mooney did in 1898.[3]

The tension between perceived savagery and civilization did not just cut through the new state but infected relations within the reservation as well. The Kiowas and their neighbors divided over the issue of how to maintain Indian life in the midst of an aggressive white majority population. For some, embracing a way of living that resembled that of their educated white neighbors seemed the best way forward, and this often included adherence to Christian tenets and customs. For others, and the Mopopes and their neighbors in the Redstone valley were among them, preserving, protecting, and reshaping specifically Kiowa religious practices and cultural mores seemed paramount. Nursing and maintaining a connection to the land through dance, ceremonies, and art became essential tools as they strove to endure as a people. Yet, there was no definite binary between one belief and the other. Rather, most Kiowas of all generations combined aspects of religious expression and participated in different practices. Few exchanged tribal beliefs for Christian ones in a linear and permanent fashion.[4]

Oscar Jacobson's experiences before arriving at his encounter with Kiowa artists mainly derive from sources directly relating to his life, and in many cases his own words. By contrast, material concerning Stephen Mopope's life and those of his Kiowa friends and contemporaries is much more circumstantial. Writing Indigenous history poses different challenges for the historian. The Kiowas rarely wrote anything themselves that has been preserved in archives or in print, and contemporary information about them emanates overwhelmingly from persons who were placed in charge of them and who reported on them with a very specific purpose in mind—assimilation. Even when these people were sympathetic to Kiowa needs and desires, this ultimate goal colors the choice of information included in these sources and their interpretation of actions and events. I have consulted reports from field matrons stationed in the Redstone valley, Indian agents, missionaries, and schools, and I have related these to reminiscences that Mopope passed down to his granddaughter Vanessa Jennings.

GROWING UP ON THE RESERVATION

The Indian agent's report from 1907 described the Kiowa Agency's location "on the Washita River, north of and adjoining the city of Anadarko, Oklahoma, on the Chicago, Rock Island and Pacific Railway." The report counted 580 Kiowa males and 655 Kiowa females. Of these slightly more than 1,200 people, 363 were schoolchildren between the ages of six and eighteen. Generally, the prospects were good, the report asserted, which meant that the Indians were well on their way to assimilation. "The male Indians, with but a few exceptions, have adopted civilized dress." The females, however, "in a great part cling to their slip dresses." That year, as in so many others, the crops had failed, this time because of the "green bug." But the agent had good hopes that a later crop would grow to fruition "if late rains are had reasonably." The agent could report a most encouraging development among the Kiowas in particular: "Many have fields of good acreage, and their crops evidence good attention. Many have good homes that are well kept, and barns have been provided by them for their livestock. It is gratifying to see that a large number of Indians have bought good farm implements and machinery, and their fields show these implements to have been used to good purpose. Improvement is also noted in the home making and housekeeping by Indian women." The field matron at Redstone, Lauretta Ballew, described a most satisfactory year. The Redstone Women's Society had met diligently and made sixty quilts in addition to other household items, "earning this year with their own hands, $162.42. They spent for material to work with, $24. They gave $10. to help the Mexicans in Mexico, and they have in the treasury

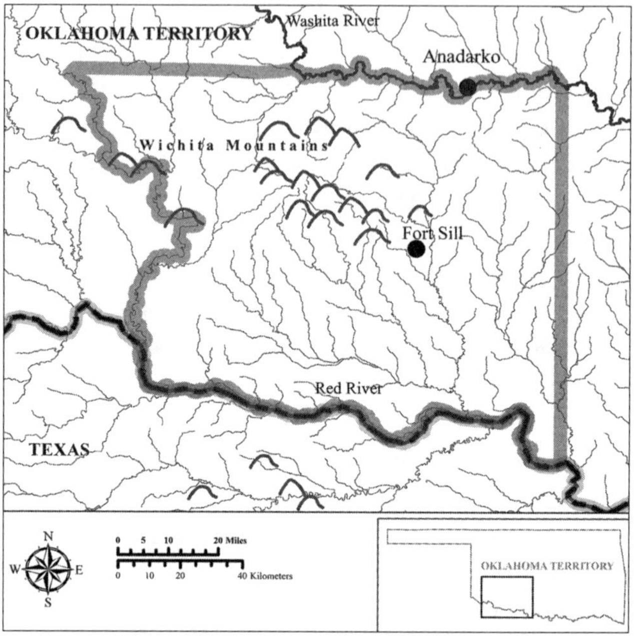

MAP 3. KCA Reservation around 1900. The Redstone valley extends just west of Anadarko and northeast of the Wichita Mountains.

now, $128.52." Such success notwithstanding, however, her account attests to the tensions at play on the reservation. "An old man began to tell stories to discourage the people, but was asked by another man, not to bring any more stinking meat to the people they had enough of it and cut it off today. It was a peculiar way of telling the man his words were no good but was very expressive."[5]

Despite the hopeful note in the report from 1907, poverty accompanied the Kiowas' existence on the reservation. The land was arid and not well suited for farming. In her June report of 1911, the matron at Redstone, Katherine Ellis Treat, remarked that most of "our Indians have been trying pretty hard to raise a good crop. Many have planted two or three kinds of seeds such as corn kaffer [kaffir] corn, cotton, oats etc. But the dry weather, the hot winds and grasshoppers have ruined everything. So there will be hard times all over this section of the state." Disease and infections constituted a constant scourge; trachoma, measles and dysentery, tuberculosis—and then there were the attacks of scabies. In September 1908, a letter from the field matron, Ida M. Schofield, to Agent

Stecker reported sickness among many of the Redstone inhabitants, including Keintaddle and also George Mopope and Paukeigope's young son. In late 1912, the parents applied to the agent to allow them to use available funds that were kept for their children in order to erect a new home and barn. Superintendent Stecker authorized the use of $102.01 from Stephen Mopope's balance as part payment on a seven-room house for the large family, and a new barn. Paukeigope had land funds, but these were not enough, and "they desire[d] to use their children's funds for completion of improvements." Despite the new house, the winter was hard, and in the spring of 1913, the parents again applied to the agent to use resources belonging to their children. The first petition reads: "The parents of this minor have no funds. On account of the severe cold and wet weather the children were without the necessary clothing, shoes and food." The following spring the family again were forced to dip into the children's assets as the parents "needed money very badly and that they had none of their own."[6]

These brief notations offer evidence that the Mopope family lived on the edge, as did almost all of their neighbors. A list of what goods the family had purchased from the trader Hugh Graham between 1905 and 1909 may illustrate the needs and necessities of an Indian family on the reservation at the turn of the century. Most of the items purchased were materials and clothing. By far the most common items were shoes, stockings, and ribbons. Among the purchases there were also a few more expensive items that would have been considered for extra adornment, such as a fascinator (a kind of hair decoration) for 75 cents, velvet material for $1.50, earrings for $1.50, and six curtains for $2.50. One item stands out. On December 24, 1906, someone in the household bought a musical album for $4.25.[7]

The list demonstrates that the Mopope household belonged to the group of Indians that had adopted "citizen dress" that the agent found so hopeful in his 1907 report. Suits, shirts, overalls, muslins, dresses, gloves, hats, and suspenders are listed among the purchases. One might suggest that the Mopopes were engaged in their own version of pageantry, but one that was considerably less voluntary than the role-play with which Oscar Jacobson entertained audiences at Yale. Appearing in citizen clothing meant more than functional wear for farming, it could mean the difference between food on the table and starvation, as authorities threatened

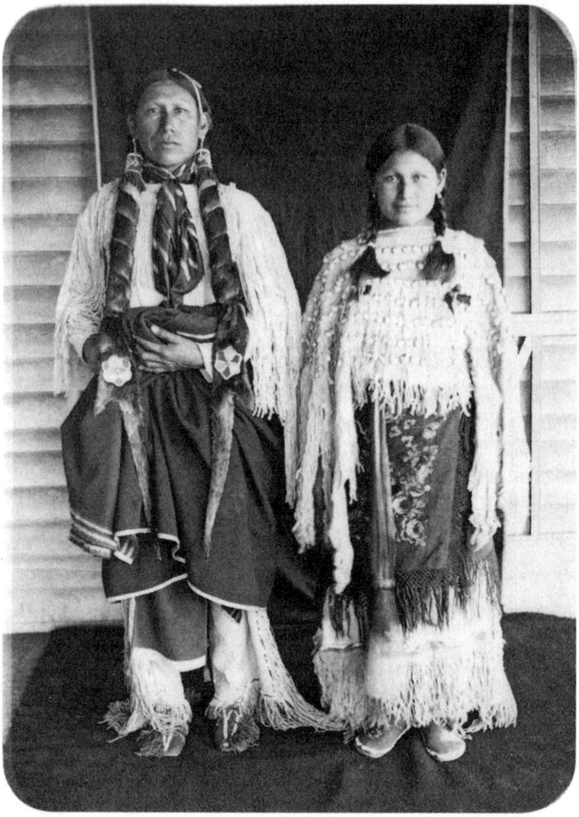

FIGURE 7. Stephen's parents—George Mopope and his wife, Paukeigope—in Kiowa regalia. Photograph taken in 1901. Kiowa interest in family photographs flourished in the early decades of the twentieth century. In their choice to be photographed in regalia, they conveyed a message of Indigenous survival and endurance. Photograph by Annette Ross Hume. Virgil Robbins Collection #16436. Courtesy of the Oklahoma Historical Society.

to withhold rations to those who kept to the old ways. Two photographs of George and Etta (Paukeigope)—one taken in 1901 or 1902 and the other sometime between 1910 and 1920—suggest a balancing act. The first shows both of them in Kiowa regalia. Paukeigope wears a heavily fringed dress, lavishly decorated with elk teeth, a store-bought shawl around her waist, a beaded bag, and fully beaded moccasins. George is in a similarly fringed shirt and leggings, wears a blanket around his waist, beaded moccasins, and medallions on his sleeves. His braids are wrapped in fur,

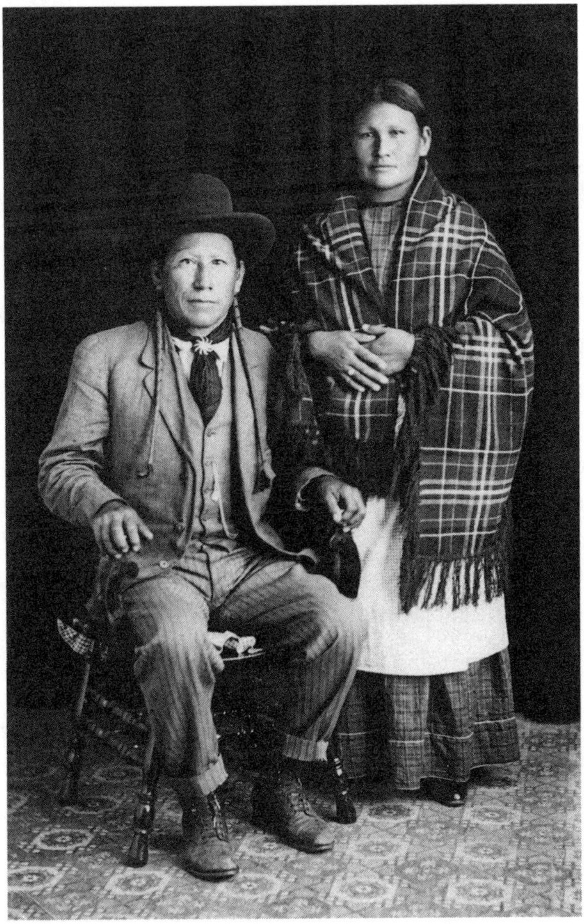

FIGURE 8. George Mopope and Paukeigope in citizen dress. Photograph taken some time between 1910 and 1918. In George W. Hicks, Rev. Collection # 22117.31. Courtesy of the Oklahoma Historical Society.

signaling standing and prestige. He, too, sports an imported item in the silk handkerchief that hangs around his neck. In the later photograph they are dressed in citizens' clothing. It is a studio portrait of a seated husband in a three-piece suit, felt hat, laced boots, and watch chain. However, he is still wearing his hair long and tightly braided. The wife stands beside her husband in a long muslin dress, white apron, and a woven checkered shawl. Her right hand covers her left and shows off a wedding ring. Laura E. Smith, in her book about the Kiowa photographer Horace Poolaw, notes an impressive rise in Kiowa interest in owning and commissioning family photographs in the late reservation period. "More than in the average white middle-class portrait of this period," she writes, "the poses, facial expressions, and clothing in Indian portraits convey the impact of colonial oppression, as well as subversive messages of Native perseverance and self-determination." Decorated clothing items testified to the women's skills and standing in the community, but it was also, according to Jacki Rand, a political act. As federal policy sought to alter both practices of labor and outward appearances, "the persistence of women's beadwork and other labor patterns defied the U.S. attack on tribalism." Thus, both prestige and perseverance could be communicated within and between families via these representations.[8]

But how did Stephen's parents afford these items of clothing and the photographs when they were in such dire circumstances as indicated by the request to use their children's funds? Smith suggests that photographs by this time had become relatively affordable and that leasing allotted land to ranchers and farmers meant that Kiowas "had sporadic periods of cash wealth." Initially, the Dawes Act had prohibited the leasing of Indian allotments, but subsequent modifications by both Congress and Indian commissioners allowed non-Indians to lease Indian land. Fred Hoxie describes the process as one in which the United States took over complete control of American Indian resources. By 1920, "the Indians' land had devolved from protected property to areas resembling the United States' overseas colonies." Allotted lands contained some of the most desirable grazing land in the region, and white farmers and ranchers were eager to lease allotments. This included not least land owned by minors such as Stephen Mopope and his siblings. A list of land apportioned to Kiowas from 1900 shows Keintaddle, Stephen's grandmother, and her brother, Oheltoint; Mopope (George) and Paukeigope (Etta), and their children Ghoulehe (Donald) and Woodcoy (Stephen) with their allotments of 160 acres each (80 acres for the young boy Woodcoy). Every year the Indians on the reservation leased out land to white farmers. In 1913 a small note on a lease application testifies to disagreements regarding the rent. A local farmer, Lemuel P. Clark, applied to lease land from Woodcoy for $50, but a handwritten notation on the form states that "Mopope agrees to rent for $85." Clark wished to lease 65 acres for planting cotton, corn, and feed and had previously rented this land for five or six years. George

Mopope negotiated the lease for his son. Clark was the only bidder, and yet Mopope demanded $85 and would not change his mind. Clark eventually agreed to the amount but later withdrew his bid as the drawn-out decision made it too late to put in a crop for the year. The sources do not reveal why Mopope suddenly increased his demands for rent, but it is possible that the dire situation of the family in 1913 left him little choice.[9]

In late December 1912, field matron Katherine Ellis Treat reported from Redstone that it had been a good year, and the Kiowas had received a good income from their crops. "Nearly every family has received lease money, and they have lived lavishly." The women had been busy taking care of their homes, making clothes, and "a good many do bead work on buckskin." Some had picked cotton for white farmers.[10] Such a report appears contradictory when placed alongside the Mopopes' petition to use their children's trust funds to survive the spring. This demonstrates how precarious and unpredictable conditions were on the reservation and qualifies the positive progress reports of matrons and agents.

THE EDUCATION OF A KIOWA YOUTH

Three government-run boarding schools operated on the reservation—Riverside, Rainy Mountain, and Fort Sill—and together they taught some five hundred students. In addition, the 1907 agency report included four mission schools that served the children of the agency. St. Patrick's Mission (Catholic), the Methvin Institute (South Methodists), the Mary Gregory Memorial School (Presbyterian), and the Cache Creek Mission (Reformed Presbyterian) together had some two hundred children. In general, institutions reported enrollment success, and a satisfactory pride of Indian parents in what their offspring produced in school. However, there were some more sinister developments. At Fort Sill, several fires in the girl's dormitory led to suspicion of arson, but no sufficient evidence emerged to support charges. From Rainy Mountain, the school principal found great reason to rejoice as the boys who came through the school generally stayed sober and refrained from excessive gambling "though gambling is a tribal vice that would come by inheritance." He found, however, that like "all Indians they are improvident with their earnings. . . . Taking into consideration the fact that the development of the Kiowas is hampered by the semi-annual receipt of large sums of money which in a measure, removes from them the necessity for work, I do not see how they can be expected to do better than they are doing." The girls, too, are "a vast improvement on their mothers as housekeepers and caretakers of their children."[11] Such reports expressed adherence to an ideology of assimilation, which did not reflect realities on the reservation or Kiowa perceptions of proper behavior. Kiowas considered generosity to be a central virtue, as well as a necessity in such stark circumstances, and what the schoolmaster may have viewed as squandering, Kiowas thought of as a moral obligation to share.[12]

While poverty and hardship accompanied Stephen's first years, his grandmother Keintaddle was adamant that he should get an education. She took care of and nurtured her grandchildren, as George Mopope struggled with tuberculosis, which eventually took his life in 1927, and Paukeigope worked in the fields and with her beadwork in order to feed her family. When Stephen was about ten years old, Keintaddle loaded up her camp and took her grandson to St. Patrick's Indian Mission in Anadarko. She told him they would teach him and feed him. He did not want to leave, but she calmed him saying that many of the other children in the school were his relatives and she wanted him and his brother Gilbert to be in a "safe place with food" in case something would happen to her and she could not look out for them. Vanessa Jennings wrote down the story of the trip to St. Patrick's:

> It was Stephen Mopope's first step into the wide world. Finally, they arrived at St. Patrick's and Keintaddle pitched her camp not far from the school. Inside her lodge, she placed her bed on the west side. My grandfather was her aw-day-tah-lee (the special one)! His special sleeping spot was in his grandma's bed!
>
> Keintaddle had devised a plan that was acceptable to my grandfather for her leaving. He was allowed to sleep in their bed for four nights. After that, a pallet was made on the ground. It touched her bed. Each night his pallet was moved further away from Keintaddle. Step by step, she was breaking the physical tie that holds most Kiowa children to their grandparents. The second week of camp finally found my grandfather's pallet near the opening of the lodge. He had found his cousins playing in the school yard and become comfortable with his new surroundings. The next night my grandfather slept for the first time in the dormitory. It was now time for Keintaddle to break camp and return to Redstone.[13]

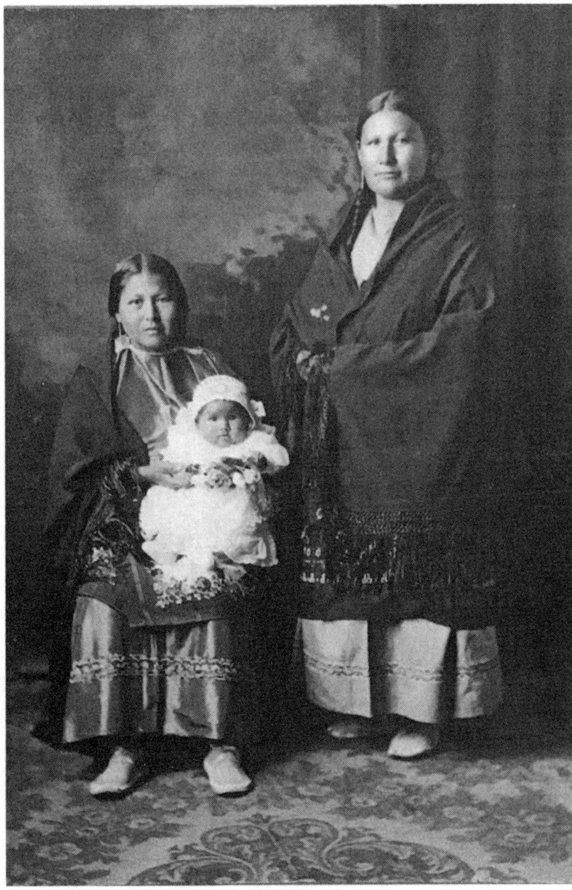

FIGURE 9. Keintaddle, Paukeigope, and Stephen Mopope, ca. 1898. The women are wearing their best cloth dresses. They wore cloth dresses for everyday wear. Ceremonies required buckskin dresses or best cloth dresses. Courtesy Vanessa Paukeigope Jennings.

Stephen was soon accustomed to living in the boarding school. He grew in confidence and soon led a small group of boys in diverse antics. The group of friends included Jack Hokeah and Spencer Asah, who both were several years younger. In secret, they sang war dance songs and spoke Kiowa. One moonlit night Mopope woke up his friends and they quietly slipped out of the dormitory. The small band of boys listened as Stephen told them that "the grapes were sweet and ready to pick. We're going on a raid!" They proceeded to the school vineyard, found a secret entrance through the fence and began harvesting the luscious fruit. What they could not eat they put inside their shirts for later. Stephen led the return "holding his precious grapes at his tummy inside his white shirt. He was telling Jack how good the grapes tasted as he exited the hole in the vineyard fencing. As he cleared the exit, Sister Olivia, was there to swat his behind. A second nun pulled him out of the way as the next grape bandit got the same treatment until all the guilty were rounded up and led back to the dormitory."[14] Jeanette Berry and her younger sister Cynthia also attended St. Patrick's at this time and they worked in the laundry room. Several years later, Jeanette would marry Stephen, and she would tell her granddaughter about this incident. The grapes had smashed across the boy's shirtfront and no amount of boiling would get rid of the stain.[15]

It is difficult from the extant records to ascertain exactly when and where Stephen Mopope went to school in addition to St. Patrick's. A handwritten note from 1912 places him in Bunker Hill school, a small two-teacher off-reservation school located near the town of Ardmore, Oklahoma. He had been present for 71 days, while his younger brother Roland ("Rollin") had attended for 38.5 days. The following year, however, the annual school reports from the agency listed Stephen, Roland, and Gilbert Mopope among the pupils at Redstone Mission school. Stephen attended fourth grade, Roland second, and Gilbert first.[16]

Field matrons frequently complained about attendance as well as content in the Indian schools. Katherine Ellis Treat blamed absences on camp life. In 1911 she counted only 49 families living in houses, while 125 still lived in tipis in the Redstone district. She felt she fought an uphill battle. "What report can you make with reference to returned students? Often we can do very little for them. We try to furnish them with good literature, and to encourage them to not go back to the old ways. But many of them are *failures.*" A field matrons' conference in 1912 connected the need to improve the morals of the young Kiowa women with the school curriculum. They resolved that one of the greatest requirements of the Indian School was that it needed to "teach the girls home making on the family scale" as well as "practical living" in houses.[17]

Reservation period education for Indian children was segregated not only in location but also in content. It was initially set up to train children to become American citizens and it was primarily vocational. A manual for Kiowa schools instructed teachers of history to focus on national heroes and holidays. A pedagogical approach that entirely eschewed dates and time lines was combined with conventional topics such as Columbus Day, Statehood Day, and Washington's and Lincoln's Birthdays. Third graders should be told about the Mayflower, Kit Carson, and General William Tecumseh Sherman. Pictures were central to the focus on narration and included "Washington crossing the Delaware," "the battle of Bunker Hill," and "Indian Pictures and the First Thanksgiving." In fourth grade, students were to hear about "L[eif] the Lucky. Marco Polo and Columbus. How and why America was named. The Spanish, French, and English explorations and settlements. Troubles of the Colonists: With the Indians; with England."[18] The manual made no note of the irony of teaching Indian children to honor as heroes those who fought against their own ancestors. "Perhaps no discipline was more trying for Indian students than American history," write Clifford E. Trafzer, Jean A. Keller, and Lorene Sisquoc in discussing the curriculum in American Indian schools. Educators on reservations around the country expressed distress at having to teach in this manner, but the Indian Office encouraged them to see that the future of Native people depended on their acknowledgment of the manner in which indigenous cultures fit into the grand historical progression from barbarism to civilization.[19]

These elements of training, including the stress on vocational training and a simplified focus on stories and pictures to encourage the right kind of patriotism, was in line with the Indian Office strategies for education during the first decades of the century. Indian educators no longer believed that through schooling Indians could be brought into society as full-fledged members but championed a "realism" based on a firm separation of races. Estelle Reel, who became superintendent of Indian education in 1898, emphasized manual training and a curriculum designed to apply concretely to the experience of the students in order to lead to practical self-sufficiency. She disapproved of spending time and resources on unproductive pursuits, such as when she criticized the superintendent at the boarding school at Chemawa, Washington, for letting girls learn to play the piano. Indian girls should "become proficient in cooking, sewing and laundry work," not spend time "in useless practice upon an expensive instrument which in all probability they will never own." Reel's successor, Francis Leupp, insisted on lowering expectations on Indian development. An Indian stayed childlike with "the physical attributes of the adult with the mentality of about our fourteen-year old boy," he told the National

Educational Association. He later reported that the new Indian education had success because it recognized the existence of "racial traits of the Indian, such as his lack of initiative, his hereditary lack of competition, etc." Such policies had direct consequences in favoring reservation day schools rather than off-reservation boarding schools, in hampering the integration of Indian students in non-Indian local schools, and in the format of subjects and courses. Textbooks were kept to a minimum in favor of visual and oral instruction, and simple vocational training dominated. "They were meant to be servants," says Jennings. "They didn't think they had the capability of being more. . . . [T]hey're teaching them how to farm, they're teaching them house chores so they can be like a butler, they're teaching the girls how to sew so that they can mend clothes for the white women."[20]

REGULATING THE INTIMATE

Stephen Mopope grew up with his grandmother's stories, immersed in a web of kin relations that stretched across the reservation from its center in the Redstone area. Life there pivoted around Keintaddle, who was at the heart of both the traditional ceremonial life and in adjusting to new requirements. She donated the land on which the Redstone Baptist parsonage was built, and several of her direct descendants became pastors in the church. In 1908 she was elected vice president of the Women's Society at Redstone, with one of her daughters serving as president and another one as treasurer. Yet she and her family were also deeply involved in reviving and maintaining the ceremonial societies of Black Legs and Ohoma. As a child she had been an *auday mata'un*, translated as very special girl in the Black Legs Warrior society, and she later held leading positions in several other Kiowa societies. Her grandson Stephen professed his lifelong loyalty to the Ohoma society. But upholding a balance between adherence to Kiowa values and the expectations, demands, and opportunities coming from agency officials and missionaries proved both complicated and divisive.[21]

Like people on all reservations, Kiowas were under constant surveillance. Restructuring family relations was central to the assimilation project carried out on the reservation. Indian commissioners, agency officials, missionaries, schoolteachers, and matrons all participated in seeking to "civilize the Indians," and all of them, despite differences in emphasis, agreed on the necessity to restructure intimate relationships. Proper marriages, stable nuclear heterosexual households, permanent houses, and patriarchal family structures all formed part of the goal, while dances, camps, giveaways, multigenerational families, and their different way of regulating sexual behavior, as well as proper behavior between men and women, appeared to be the obstacles.[22]

Already in March 1890, Commissioner Morgan emphasized the importance of inducing Indians to adopt patronyms, so as to avoid confusion regarding inheritance and property when Indians fell under state laws. It was through the reshaping of domestic relations that Indians were expected to recognize the value of individual property. Thus, agents and school superintendents were encouraged to "systematically endeavor, so far as practicable, to have children and wives known by the names of the fathers and husbands." J. W. Powell, director of the US Geological Survey, noted in his support of the commissioner's strategy regarding the adoption of patronyms that an added benefit would be to work "toward the breaking up of the Indian tribal system which is perpetuated and ever kept in mind by the Indian's own system of names." In addition to name changes, this required detailed attention to marriage customs and housing practices. In a letter to all Indian agents dated August 1890, the commissioner asked them to collect as full and explicit information as possible "on the subject of marriage among Indian, the customs observed, and the rites and ceremonies practiced; the sacredness or looseness with which marital relations are held; the terms on which marriages are made, &c., every detail which will give a clear idea of the manners and habits of the different tribes in regard to betrothal and marriage." The reason for this inquiry, the commissioner stated, was to "preserve knowledge in regard to Indian peculiarities which are being displaced by civilization and about which, in a few years, it will be difficult to acquire reliable information."[23]

The commissioner was overly optimistic. It took more than a few years to eradicate Indian marriage practices. In an exchange in 1908 between the commissioner and the agent at the Kiowa Agency, the latter confessed to scant success in persuading Indians to "become legally married and lay aside their custom of throwing away their wives." He asked that the agent should be authorized to withhold payments to Indians "until they furnish him with positive proof that they are legally married." However, the commissioner pointed out that according to the Statutes of Oklahoma, section

3499, all Indians with allotments in severalty and "married according to the Indian custom and were living together as husband and wife" were regarded as married, so punishing them through withholding rations would be illegal.[24] There were already other measures in place. After 1897 allotted Indians who did not procure a license and marry according to the law were subject to heavy fines. Still, the marriage issue continued to trouble officials on the reservation. Katherine Ellis Treat commented in her report in April 1911 on her efforts to convince couples to "marry legally. This is a hard thing to do, to make them see that it is necessary to marry by law."[25]

Variants of names noted in the official sources demonstrate how these policies impacted each individual. Stephen Mopope's mother was variously referred to as "Hattie," "Etta," and Pau-kei-gope. Allotment records from 1900 listed "Ma-pape," "Pau-kei-gope," "Gho-le-he," and "Wood-coy," but on a later list "Pau-kei-gope" had become a surname held by "Hattie," recognized as the wife of "George" who was designated "Father," and "Mo-pope" was now a patronym for their children. A nuclear family had been created that revealed very little about the significant relationships and kin bonds that situated these people in the Kiowa tribe.[26]

The next step in the reshaping of the intimate geography of Kiowa life concerned the structure of households. Here field matrons became the spearheads. At a field matrons' conference held in Anadarko in 1912, matrons discussed their various districts and resolved that "one of the needs of the Indian Schools is to teach the girls home making on the family scale instead of the large one that generally prevails." Agent C. V. Stinchecum concurred. In his experience, he wrote in 1916, "too many houses are inhabited by more than one family. For instance the younger member of the family marries and the husband or wife is brought home to live with the old people." To combat multigenerational households, he enlisted the matrons. "This is so productive of harmful results that I wish you field matrons and farmers to discourage this practice and encourage the young people, when they marry, to go and live by themselves and try to make a living for themselves." In 1919, Susie Peters deplored the habit of camping around the different churches at Christmastime: "I think this very bad for the Indian from a health standpoint, as large families and a great many visitors cook eat and sleep in one tent or tepe. All camps are crowded causing the spread of infectious diseases." To accomplish their aim, the matrons awarded prizes for the best-kept homes and the most sanitary conditions. In 1916 Stephen Mopope's future mother-in-law, Anna Berry, received commendation for keeping a clean house and her children ready for school, and in 1922 Susie Peters found George Mopope's family in a clean home ready for inspection. "These family homes," she reported, "were in excellent condition, their yards clean. Nice gardens, and all at home waiting for inspection."[27]

Sanitary conditions may have been the ostensible goal of these policies, but promoting living in houses was as much ideology as practicality. Karen V. Hansen, who discusses similar interventions at the Spirit Lake Dakota Reservation in North Dakota, notes that living in tipis was in fact often more sanitary than houses. "When Dakotas lived in tipis with smoke holes at the top, ventilation was not an issue, and seasonal relocation allowed them to refresh their campsites." In 1913, some families "still lived year round in tipis or tents on their property, which they viewed as more hygienic, warmer, and less smoky than log houses."[28]

For authorities, sanitation issues combined with moral concerns. Multigenerational camps were seen as breeding grounds for immoral relations. Indian dancing came under attack, and in 1913 Superintendent Stecker wrote to the commissioner about leaders of "Give-away dances." Stecker proposed that anyone who participated in "'Give-away dance' or any other detrimental dance, will be punished by forfeiting their right to share in the annuity payment following such dance." Furthermore, Stecker expressed concern regarding the revived Ghost Dance, which he described as "semi-religious." It has been the practice, he wrote, to permit the Indians to perform this dance around the Fourth of July, "with a view to controlling the dance and also on account of its semi-religious nature." But he deemed it unwise to continue doing so "as it has a tendency to awake in the Indian nature 'The Calling of the Wild,' which results in other dancing when they should be at work in their fields."[29] Stecker strongly urged the commissioner to extend regulations against these dances to apply to the Kiowa, Comanche, and Apache (KCA) Reservation, as it now did at the Sioux Agency. The matrons may have been the first to report illicit dancing to the agent, and their reports constantly worried about the deleterious effects of dancing and camping on Kiowa people. They did not always know who to blame, as in Katherine Ellis Treat's report in June 1913, when she wrote that "with the coming of the Fourth of July and the many attractions which the White people offer in the towns, and the encouragement from the white people to go into the old time dances they are getting unsettled and are planning for the dances for the summer." She and her successors as field matrons worked hard to keep the Kiowas in their houses and away from the camp life.

> If we could hold them at home from these old dances we could save many more of the boys and girls from going wrong. The old camp and the old dance brings the temptation which so often catches them. My most serious problem is to find a way to meet the needs of the young people so that they may overcome temptations. There are several young widows and grass widows who are exerting a bad influence upon some of the young people. I am trying to overcome this influence, and also save all parties. Yet these dances as planned by some of the older Indians offer good chance to the temptations so that I may not overcome them.[30]

Matrons connected the dances with two troublesome features in particular: the dances provided opportunities for immoral sexual relations and they contributed to spreading disease. In the summer of 1913, the matron reported on six deaths in the area of Redstone, three of them from tuberculosis, and she blamed them on the dances. "In fact all our serious sickness has been among the families that have chased around to the dances. These dances have been held almost every week in some place or other during all the quarter. One infant a few months old, and two children between two and three years died from dysentery. Each of these were contracted at these old camp dances, brought home too late for us to give them much help. These dances are a menace to the health condition as well as the moral nature." The matron expressed her conviction that specific Indian practices threatened their moral and physical health, but it is more likely that it was the imposed reservation conditions that caused illness and death. Poverty was a major contributor to the spread and disastrous effects of diseases such as tuberculosis, dysentery, and measles, and so were the cramped conditions in the residential schools and the inability of government employees to handle epidemic outbreaks among schoolchildren.[31]

In the minds of matrons and agents, the immorality of the dances was every bit as threatening as the spread of diseases. Complaints surfaced frequently throughout the 1910s and early 1920s: dances made people move around, offered opportunities for young people to meet and engage in illicit sexual relations, provided occasion for gambling, and made people neglect their farms. While attention to what missionaries and government officials viewed as "adultery," "immorality," or "leading a life of shame," had a strong moralizing component, it also expressed unease with the challenge that Indian family practices posed to issues of property and inheritance. To Kiowas, children could not be "illegitimate," as they all belonged to a network of kinship relations responsible for them and toward whom they had obligations. "Each child," described Katherine Ellis Treat, "legitimate or illegitimate gets its share in the payment" from annuities or land.[32]

As late as in the 1920s, another dispute regarding dances brewed over into letter exchanges between agency superintendents and the Office of Indian Affairs. This time the controversy concerned the supposedly deleterious effects of the "49'er dance." Superintendent Stinchecum again invoked the threat of withholding accounts. His letter attests to the concern with the evils of camp life. "A dance of any description, irrespective of its significance, forms an opportunity for the mingling of the sexes. In the excitement of the dances the restraints of home are cast aside and practices are indulged in which would not have occurred had the camp not been in existence. I have made it a constant policy for the last seven years to discourage camps of every description for the very definitive reasons just enumerated."[33]

This clearly expressed a misrepresentation of Kiowa morality, as well as the appropriate demeanor during ceremonies. Kiowa protocol was very strict in terms of how men and women related to one another. Jennings recalls a memory that her grandfather passed on to her regarding an altercation during a secret gathering of one of the warrior societies: "Children played, young people milled about. One old man had his son and wife along. [The young man] was a jealous husband and began to argue with the beautiful young woman. It seems some other young man in the crowd had given too much attention to his pretty wife. The old warriors jumped up without hesitation, ready to resume their old role as camp police, enforcers of social order, to put an immediate stop to the squabble. Such unseemly conduct was certainly *NOT* appropriate at such an important event."[34]

The struggle against dances and immorality concerned a lengthy effort to restructure Kiowa social organization at the most intimate level, and policing dances was not primarily an issue of religious freedom but one of social revolution. The Kiowa artists Stephen Mopope, Spencer Asah, Lois Smoky, Jack Hokeah, James Auchiah, and Monroe Tsatoke—grew up in a time when all aspects of Kiowa identity were under pressure from the people directly in charge of their daily practices and resources. Vanessa Jennings explains: "The Indian Agent with the backing of a heavily-armed military fought relentlessly to erase all Kiowa warrior societies. The missionaries fought with their Bibles to erase our songs and dances. The Field Service Matrons fought by canning peaches and teaching housekeeping to erase our clothing and traditional home life."[35]

The Mopopes and their neighbors did not silently accept these attacks, but they did not reject everything white society had to offer. The move between citizen's dress and regalia evident in photographs could be paralleled with the intermittent use of houses and tipis. People found them useful for different things and continued to practice a migration between the two kinds of homes. Women often appreciated the women's clubs that matrons organized and learned new ways of cooking and preserving while also developing beadwork for both sale and personal use. Lauretta Ballew reported some of them telling her: "dont hurry us too fast, we are coming into the white man's road just as fast as we can understand." Deeply concerned with the well-being of their children, many refused to give up dancing precisely because it represented a proper education and a measure to maintain health and healing.[36]

THE DANCE BANS

Nowhere was the tension between Indians and agency officials greater than in the conflicts over dancing. Deeply imbued with Kiowa values, dancing to some people expressed the heart of what it meant to be Kiowa, while for others it was precisely that heart that needed to change if they were to stand a chance in their new world. It was around dancing that Kiowas rebuilt their community after the disasters of war and destitution on the reservation. Dancing caused tension within the community and divided white people in their perceptions of its practice.

Indian dancing represented a rejection of what white society viewed as civilized behavior and created community values around a fundamentally different way of life. Beginning in the 1890s and until 1916, during Stephen Mopope's childhood and youth, the Ghost Dance—or Feather Dance, as the Kiowas called it—caused the most anxiety among authorities and missionaries on the reservation. It began as symbolic resistance to allotment in severalty, conversion to Christianity, and coercive attempts to force them to abandon their camps to live in individual houses. Kiowas also believed that the ritual could bring back the buffalo and thus make possible a return to traditional life. The Kiowa ritual combined Kiowa and Christian beliefs with Peyotism. Many who participated in the Feather Dance also belonged to the Native American Church and practiced the Peyote Ceremony, which had come to the Kiowas in the 1880s.[37]

In the late 1880s, Indian commissioners launched a veritable campaign to end the central Kiowa Sun Dance ceremony for good. In 1889 Commissioner Morgan made his position abundantly clear in a letter to Agent Myers regarding the Kiowa "medicine dance": "It is my wish that the dance shall be prevented, and that you will call upon the military to assist you if necessary. Should the dance be held contrary to orders, you will cause the arrest of all engaged in it." Apparently, the agent did not hold a similarly sinister view of the Kiowa dance, and a year later the commissioner again wrote sternly to the new agent, C. A. Adams, that he had learned that "the Kiowas have just held their medicine dance which continued during an entire week; also that the white people at the agency visited the dance and thus lent encouragement to this heathenish practice." He continued to stress the demoralizing influence of dances on both participants and spectators and chastised the agent for not preventing it. The efforts to educate Indian children, he argued, were "largely neutralized by such exhibitions as these, and when white people of an agency, by their presence, lend their countenance to such things, it throws the weight of white civilization into the scale of barbarism." Instead of Indian dances of various kinds, the commissioner suggested that Indian schools should be responsible for "the inculcation of patriotism" through the observance of national holidays such as "'Franchise Day,' 'Washington's Birthday,' 'Arbor Day,'" and—of course—Independence Day. The commissioner and agent backed their opposition with military threats forcing Kiowas to abandon the Sun Dance in the late summer of 1890.[38]

It was the same year that the US Army's Seventh Cavalry massacred over one hundred Minniconjou Sioux Ghost Dance believers at Wounded

Knee, South Dakota. The Ghost Dance had originated with a Paiute prophet named Wovoka. Kiowas received news of the dance during that summer of their last Sun Dance attempt. A large dance was held in the fall and persuaded one of the most prominent of the Kiowa leaders, Ahpeahtone, to travel to the Pyramid Lake Reservation in Nevada to meet with Wovoka, and in 1891 he publicly declared that the dance held no power. The government awarded him with a house and a medal for denouncing the Ghost Dance, but on the day of his report there was no rejoicing even among those who opposed the ceremony. Several "remarked that it was one of the saddest days in their memory." Agents and missionaries preferred to think that this problem had been conquered with the demise of the Sun Dance practice and the efforts of Ahpeahtone to expose Wovoka. Other prominent Kiowa chiefs, such as Big Tree, Lucius Aitson, and Delos Lonewolf, joined the anti-dance faction and reported to the agent about those who led dances. But the troublesome dancing continued. Three years later Ghost Dances were held again in different locations on the reservation, and in 1907 a letter informed the agent of a large encampment at the camp of Sitahpate, where "nearly all of the Kiowas from every district" were present for a Feather Dance held on July 8. The Kiowas continued with the Feather Dance until 1916. Among those who danced could be found some of the men who had returned from imprisonment at Fort Marion.[39]

Field matron Maryetta Reeside gave an illustration of how the Kiowas sought to keep their ceremonies shielded from the censure of the agency authorities. The dance, she reported, was led by Sit-ah-pay-to (Afraid of a Bear), who claimed that "Jesus tells him Christianity and the Bible are for the white people, but he wishes the Indians to keep to their old ways, and worship him this way." Furthermore, he told them that that there is a "good home above where there is plenty of land and buffaloes and no white people." They must dance, and if "their rations are cut off they must still dance, if they die of hunger, it is good for they will the sooner be in that good land." Reeside also observed the discipline and secrecy of the Kiowa dancers, who made sure not to exhibit any offensive behavior when white people were present to inspect their dancing, "but at other times they dance and sing in a wild manner, throw themselves in the dust and grovel, go into trances, become prostrated and so on." This behavior, Reeside argued, contributed to debauching the Indians. "We see the pitiable effects of this savagery and wickedness. The young demoralized and drawn back to the old ways and clothing. All efforts at work and progress are paralized by these dances."[40]

Relations on the reservation—whether alliances, dependencies, friendships, or animosities—were far more complex than can be conveyed through simple categorizations of whites and Indians, or tribes. Indian agents and matrons faced a very different reality than did officials in Washington, and missionaries from several denominations chose varying approaches and forged a myriad of ties with converts. While all of the Kiowa artists who became known outside the reservation belonged to what was known as "the dance crowd," all of them had familial ties and personal bonds to other Kiowas who chose to take a stand against dancing and traditional ceremonies, as well as ties to individual agents, matrons, and teachers.[41]

After 1910, Kiowas again attempted to make space for their dances on the reservation and the conflict with authorities resurfaced. Some of them made efforts to clarify their legal position and, according to Agent Stecker, sought advice from "a class of cheap lawyers" who told them that "they are citizens, and that there is no law to prevent them dancing as long as the[y] violate no state law." Indeed, in 1916 James Ahtone asked permission to hold "a picnic and old time dance," but the assistant commisioner responded cautioning him that Ghost Dances were unacceptable.[42]

CLANDESTINE DANCING IN THE REDSTONE COMMUNITY

The diaspora experience divided Indians on the reservation regarding whether history and traditions could play a role in their future, and if so, what that role could be. Kiowas and their neighbors actively engaged in responding to government restrictions and surveillance. Reviving, staging, and questioning the role of the past and of ceremonies were issues of pressing concern for the community. That George Mopope's family maintained what field matrons viewed as a respectable family home did not mean they abstained from camp life. Stephen grew up immersed in a culture of dancing, and to gather for dances and ceremonies required living in tipis. The protracted controversies with reservation authorities over the practice of Indian dancing would have a significant impact on his life. Most of the Kiowas who would become known as artists had close ties to this community of dancing at Redstone, and they came from high-ranking families in Kiowa society. Vanessa Jennings describes them: "He came from, he and Spencer Asah, ah, those young men, including Miss Smoky, they came from that upper level of people. . . . They had actual, the men who had the buffalo doctors, you know they were the ones who repaired those horrible wounds from the wars—they were still here. They were active. They were walking around here. And, you know, bundle keepers. They were important people. And this is who my grandpa came from."[43]

The Mopopes and their neighbors and relatives participated in the Ghost Dance early in the century and were closely involved in the Ohoma society, the one Kiowa society that did not cease its activities in the reservation period and continued its practices unabated during the years of bans against ceremonial dancing. The Ohoma (Omaha) society came to the Kiowas as a gift from the Cheyennes in early 1880s. It originated as a war dance and was shared among many of the prairie nations, like the Kiowas, Arapahoes, Cheyennes, Poncas, Osages, and Pawnees who had come to live closely together in Oklahoma as a consequence of American colonial resettlement policies. Gift giving was a central element of the dance, and among the Kiowas, similar stories about the giving of a feather connect the Ohoma and the Ghost Dance (called the Feather Dance among the Kiowas).[44]

Many also participated in peyote ceremonies, and the Native American Church became a significant influence in the lives of the young artists. Comanches, Kiowas, and Cheyennes had come in possession of the knowledge and experience of peyotism via their raids into Texas and Mexico during the nineteenth century. Ceremonies involving the tops (or buttons) of the peyote plant had long been part of indigenous religious practices in northern Mexico and southern Texas. As these practices arrived in Kiowa and Comanche country they were reshaped and evolved into the present-day Native American Church. All-night meetings, usually held on Saturday nights, involved eating peyote buttons as a sacrament, in a unique religious ceremony. Ingesting the peyote button produces, writes Omer S. Stewart, "a warm and pleasant euphoria, an agreeable point of view, relaxation, colorful visual distortions, and a sense of timelessness." It is not addictive, although US authorities consistently fought against its use and argued that it was a dangerous drug. In the beliefs of the church, peyote is the sacred medicine, it teaches, protects, and allows participants to see into the future, it helps find lost objects and offers power to the users. Peyote beliefs can be combined with Christian ideas.[45]

From the 1880s, aided by the establishment of railroads criss-crossing the territory, Oklahoma emerged as the "cradle of Peyotism" in the United States. Tennyson Berry (a prominent Apache leader and Stephen Mopope's future father-in-law) and Jim Waldo (Mopope's uncle) were both peyote men, and they exemplify the generation of American Indians who had gone to boarding school, learned to speak English, and upon their return to the reservation continued traditional practices centered around the peyote ceremonies. Both of them traveled to spread the beliefs and simultaneously worked to counter efforts to suppress the practice in the early 1900s. As a young man Berry traveled to Washington, to translate for the three chiefs Ahpeahtone, Quanah Parker, and Apache John, who all embraced the peyote beliefs. In 1907 Berry took part in a delegation of peyotists to argue its case before the Oklahoma Constitutional Convention. Jim Waldo became a peyotist before 1902 and was also one of the men who argued before the territorial senate. He told them in 1908 that it was the "worship of the Lord," and to him peyote resembled "Lord Jesus." At the same time, Waldo belonged to the "dance crowd" that perpetuated the Ghost Dance and the Ohoma Dance.[46]

The year 1917 was a hard year, and Kiowas suffered from a spell of drought that made farming nearly impossible. The wheat died on the stalk and many worried about how to get through the winter. In July 1917, Kiowa Jim Tongkeamha requested to hold a give away dance at his home south of Carnegie, but Superintendent Stecker informed him that "give away or the ghost dances are prohibited" and cautioned him that "participation in either one of these dances will make it necessary for me to withhold from payment at the next annuity payment the shares of those who participate therein, or who were in attendance." Government officials equally opposed give away dances associated with the Ohoma society and the Ghost Dance.[47]

Despite such threats the Ohoma society members continued dancing. Benjamin Kracht notes that in central and western Oklahoma, dances did not cease following government bans, but they went underground. "Hence Indian dances became surreptitious activities or assumed different forms in order to bypass prohibitive Indian Office policy." Kiowas following the "dance road" held many such dances "under the auspices of church picnics or national holidays like the Fourth of July."[48] The people in the Redstone area danced for their lives in the ravine below the Whitehorse allotment. Dorothy Whitehorse describes how they "practiced war dancing, they practiced ghost dancing and went to peyote meetings," despite being threatened with jail sentences. They would "erect a tipi down there at the creek and get it up after dark go in and worship the lord all night and then come out and tear it down before the government could find them. They shortened their rations and I don't think they gave them much." She emphasizes that they "never quit dancing." They composed a song, known as the "Resistance Song," in which the leader told the dancers "don't give this up, don't quit dancing, even if we have to go to jail." Today, Ohoma society members remember with pride that theirs was the only Kiowa society that never stopped dancing despite persecution.[49]

George Mopope was among sixty-seven people who did not receive any funds in January 1917. By May, a large number had relented and "signified their intention not to indulge again in such dances," but Mopope was not among them. Those who changed their minds, hunger no doubt influencing their decision, received their withheld checks, but the shares belonging to the thirty-five who refused to sign the affidavit were returned to the treasury.[50]

As late as 1927 Edgar Keahbone, who was married to George Mopope's sister Sendehmah (Sindy), requested from the commissioner permission to hold one last Sun Dance. The request was passed through Major General Hugh Scott at Fort Sill, and Keahbone signed his letter "Ex. Service and Comrade." Keahbone had been a member of Troop L, Seventh US Cavalry, which Scott had commanded at Fort Sill between 1891 and 1897. Keahbone wished the occasion to demonstrate Kiowa traditions to the younger generation. He proposed that this Sun Dance would be the last, and he desired a photographer to be present to document every detail of the ceremony. He ended the letter: "We older people do not wish to have our young generation to follow our customs, but this is one thing we want as a tribal history to be preserved and kept."[51]

The request demonstrates how thorny these issues were for the officials in charge of Indian policy. Scott passed the letter along to the commissioner commenting that he thought the Kiowas would be willing to give up the Sun Dance entirely if given this final opportunity. The commissioner apparently gave permission for a dance to be held in 1928 and the superintendent at the agency, J. A. Buntin, reluctantly lent his support as long as the Kiowas agreed to remove self-torture from the ceremony. However, organizing a Sun Dance was costly and demanding, and other matters arose that made Keahbone decide to postpone the event. In 1930, he tried again and together with Lewis Ware, a Kiowa lawyer, wrote a letter to the commissioner. They assured him that they would "not perform any of the undesirable part of the ceremonies." Buntin, this time, expressed concern. "From a legal standpoint, since these Indians are citizens, there would be no law by which such a dance could be prevented, however, to give such a dance moral support would most likely result in more or less criticism by various Church organizations and the Indians who oppose the Sun Dance." The commissioner responded to Lewis Ware that his office had never issued a permission to hold the dance in 1927, and since then "a letter was received from one of the older members of the tribe objecting to renewal of the dance owing to the present advanced status of the tribe." He then continued in a most derogatory manner: "We have no objection, of course, to innocent recreation; but the Sun Dance exercises a harmful influence and does not conform to the present-day standards among the majority of the Indians. The older members of the tribe can amuse themselves in a much better way that will not have any harmful tendencies. The old conditions will never return and the Indians should adapt themselves to the circumstances of modern life so far as practicable."[52]

For Keahbone and the Kiowas around Redstone, organizing a Sun Dance was certainly not a question of providing amusement but, rather, part of a fundamental struggle for what Vizenor termed survivance through resistance and remembering. The letters indicate how intimately connected ceremonies and dancing were to political developments in relation to the reservation, but they also reveal a conflict with other Kiowas who had chosen the different strategy of adapting to American society and embracing Christian beliefs. The controversy over dances continued to drive wedges into and through Kiowa society. People had to make difficult choices regarding what strategies to pursue so as to ensure cultural and physical survival as Kiowas within the larger American nation. For some, the dances and traditional societies prescribed ways they believed would enable health, well-being, and propriety. For others, the different Christian roads appeared to offer a better alternative.[53]

Sometimes contention pitted relatives against one another. An early marriage between Stephen Mopope and Kiowa Bill Montkee's daughter ended when their first child died. For some, this was perceived as punishment for their involvement in dances and other traditional practices. Like George Mopope, Kiowa Bill was on the list of people who refused to give up dancing. For the Kiowas who opposed the dances, persisting had a price, and the young couple encountered their opposition: "and all of their Christian relatives told them 'God will punish you' . . . 'God's going to punish you, you're doing all this nasty, evil stuff, you're dancing, you even have the audacity to be recording them and painting them on the walls. God's going to punish you.' So when their baby was born, the baby died shortly after birth."[54] The marriage did not survive this tragedy.

Missionary records from Redstone Baptist Mission offer indications of the vacillations within the Redstone community itself. In February of 1925, Jim Waldo, Stephen Mopope's uncle who served on the Tribal Business Committee, was excluded from the Baptist congregation because he had assumed an official role in the Native American Church. The records noted: "Pastor has been laboring with him for three or four years—and . . . he confessed he was in the peyote church as treasurer. It was *voted* to exclude Him." At Christmastime 1926, Etta Mopope, among several others, came forward "earnestly seeking to consecrate their lives to the Master and His work." She and George "both solemnly promised to deliver themselves and sons to God. No more running around to dances or social gatherings." The decision was not an easy one for George. He later confessed that "he was still clinging to some old roads" but promised "to consecrate himself fully to God."[55]

In 1923 Stephen Mopope married Jeanette Berry. Jeanette was a resourceful Kiowa Apache woman whose father, Tennyson Berry, had been educated at Carlisle Indian School in Pennsylvania and sat on the Reservation Business Committee. Jeanette and Stephen had met as students at St. Patrick's. She had not been married before, she owned property, and according to her granddaughter, had her eye on someone else. But Stephen was persistent. When he first walked up to her father and said that he wanted to marry Jeanette, her father flatly refused. The next time he brought gifts but the answer was still no. He then enlisted the help of his uncle, Jim Waldo, and finally succeeded in securing permission. The couple first lived with her parents, but tensions mounted and

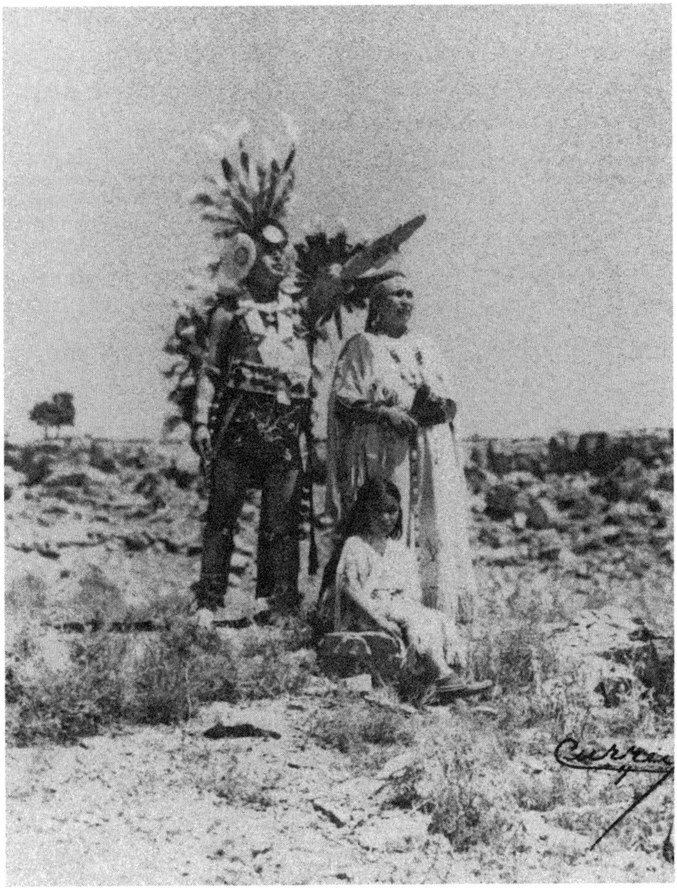

FIGURE 10. Stephen, Jeanette, and daughter, LaQuinta, early 1930s. The photograph was taken at Medicine Lodge, Kansas, and was used as a promotional photo for tourists. Courtesy Vanessa Paukeigope Jennings.

they moved to Redstone. Jeanette sold her own allotment and bought one from Pa-quoot, Jack Hokeah's grandmother, and through that purchase acquired land in the Redstone valley adjacent to that of George and Etta Mopope. From then on, the family lived on Jeanette's allotment, while Stephen steadily acquired land stretching from the Washita River in the north to the Red River in the south of the reservation. They farmed some of their land and leased some to white farmers in the area. While apparently creating a successful partnership between Jeanette and Stephen, their marriage caused disapproval, not least from Jeanette's own mother,

Anna Berry, who did not appreciate that her daughter married an artist, and a man who held on to what she perceived as pagan practices. They began a family, but even though they had ten children together, only two daughters survived to adulthood.[56]

CHAMPIONSHIP DANCER

Stephen's cousin Hannah was something of a flapper. She wore her hair bobbed and flouted temperance laws on the reservation. Her mother was Sindy Keahbone, who was George Mopope's sister. She held on to Kiowa traditions, maintained a large tipi, and "treasured . . . the things pertaining to the old life." Her eldest daughter, Katie, longed to buy herself a fur coat and no longer wished to wear her beaded buckskin dress. Young people on the reservation clearly faced a crossroad as they shaped their lives in relation to external cultural influences and traditional expectations. This caused strain between the generations, but Laura E. Smith cautions against exaggerating the distance between parents and children. In analyzing a photograph Horace Poolaw took of Hannah and Sindy Keahbone, she argues that despite Hannah's Clara Bow–like look and Sindy's reverence for her Kiowa traditions, the two "are connected by intergenerational signs of Kiowa female authority and self-determination. They are uniquely engaged with their present and their heritage. The complexity of women in Poolaw's imagery reflects the reality of conflicted identities, as well as the individualistic responses to Kiowa cultural transformation." For young people such as Stephen Mopope, being a traditionalist Kiowa did not preclude going to the picture shows in Anadarko and dreaming about movie stars in Hollywood, or filling up a car with cousins and driving to "picnics" where they could dance away from the eyes of the reservation authorities. Mopope "loved all that the modern world had to offer," Jennings writes, but "he was too culturally entrenched to ever leave our Redstone community."[57]

Stephen Mopope wanted to be a warrior and a buffalo hunter, but he was born too late for that. Instead he excelled in the dances that had developed in combination with these pursuits, and by the 1920s he was well known in the Southwest as an outstanding dancer. Mopope, Jack Hokeah, and Spencer Asah all grew up dancing in the Ohoma. "I'm Ohoma, I could belong to anything I wanted to . . . but I'm Ohoma," Mopope told his granddaughter. "And I'll be Ohoma until the day I die."[58] The Ohoma

Society had become the foremost of the Kiowa men's societies for war dancing, and it contributed elements that emerged in powwow culture as Straight and Fancy Dance styles.

Powwow dancing was at once uniquely modern and deeply traditional. Clyde Ellis has portrayed the growth of a Southern Plains powwow culture paradoxically emerging out of this period of severe repression against all forms of Indian dancing. Despite misgivings among Indian commissioners, agents, fieldworkers, and missionaries, the public appetite for viewing Indian dancing could not be curbed. "Reformers and bureaucrats soon learned that influences largely beyond their control were reshaping dance culture so that by the 1930s a new form of dance that was public, performative, and intertribal appeared all across Indian country," writes Ellis. Official dance bans and attempts to curtail dancing by withholding rations served to render some dances more secret while others transformed into shapes less offensive to white authorities. The powwow and exhibition dancing that emerged on the Southern Plains during the early and mid-twentieth century was truly an Indian invention that had a profound impact on the surrounding white community, as well as on the strengthening of Indian identities. Kiowas and their Indigenous neighbors danced in all kinds of contexts, from the clandestine ceremonies after nightfall in remote river valleys to open and vigorous exhibitions, and private shows, or in expressions of mutual belonging and support. Dancing expressed culture, faith, hope, and connections to place; but it also meant an opportunity to publicly demonstrate valor, agility, and prowess. Not to be neglected, it also provided a way to augment one's income, to meet people beyond one's own circle, and form new friendships and families. White people were touched and intrigued by it, and some sought to capitalize on it, turning ceremonies and regalia into dances and costumes for consumption in a capitalist market. For all this, it remained dependent upon Indians themselves—Indians such as Stephen Mopope.[59]

Scholarship on the development of powwow dancing debate whether it created a pan-Indian sentiment or evolved in tribally specific ways. Another issue of contention is whether powwows served to take the edge off hierarchies and competition, or if, instead, they strengthened them in new forms. The sources approached for this book confirm that for Mopope and his friends and colleagues, powwow dancing was deeply competitive and sometimes divisive, yet simultaneously it offered adventure and camaraderie. They danced at all kinds of powwows, fairs, and expositions. They represented the Kiowas, but often they danced together with champion dancers from other tribes.[60]

Mopope, Hokeah, Asah, and other young men were traditional in their loyalty to their societies, but they contributed to revolutionizing the dance style, clothing, and ornamentation. Ellis notes how "Kiowas and Comanches were introducing elaborate new dance clothes and styles with bustles worn not only on the back but also on the arms and neck. Color-coordinated beadwork harnesses, dyed long johns, long strips of bells, and large feather-crest headdresses completed the ensemble that shortly came to be called 'Fancy Dance.'" Mopope's considerable skills made him attractive to audiences. Anthropologist Bill Meadows who interviewed Kiowa elders, learned from them that Mopope and his close friend Chester Lefthand (an Arapahoe married to a Kiowa), who always danced together, introduced the new fancy steps. In 1926, at Haskell Indian School in Kansas, Mopope and Lefthand faced off against the Ponca star dancer Gus McDonald in a competition to determine the world champion war dancer, a contest that McDonald narrowly carried. For years to come, crowds would gather to watch these men dance and perform, and their names topped the bills on powwows, exhibitions, and fairs all across the Southern Plains and the Southwest, mingling red and white audiences in awe of their athletic and artistic accomplishments. World champion fancy dancer Elmer Sugar Brown (Oto-Missoura) told Clyde Ellis that he learned many of his steps and moves from watching dancers such as McDonald, Lefthand, Mopope, and Reuben Snake, "I watched them. That's how I got to be world champion."[61]

Modern American warfare provided young Indigenous men with opportunities to create a new warrior ethic, based on traditional notions of valor, honor, and prestige. The two world wars formed links between pre-reservation customs and rituals and the revival of dances. Many American Indians viewed participation in the nation's armed forces as an obligation required of citizens and an affirmation of specific tribal warrior traditions. They connected service in the US military with traditions previously practiced to support and honor departing and returning warriors. Powwows and ceremonies honoring soldiers abounded as the return of First World War veterans inspired victory and scalp dances, bestowing new names on warriors. Sindy Keahbone organized such a dance when Mopope's cousin Mark was leaving for France, naming him after a distinguished warrior. Jennings stresses that her grandfather enlisted at Fort Sill and was prepared to fight for the United States in Europe. However, his name does not appear on lists of enlisted soldiers. Instead, an inventory of Kiowas between eighteen and forty-five years of age who had not yet registered for the draft contains both Stephen Mopope's name, and that of his future father-in-law, Tennyson Berry. By September 1918, the local draft board possessed a registration card for "Stephen Mopope, color: Indian." He became a recruit at Fort Sill, but he never saw any action overseas. Like so many others, he caught the dreaded Spanish Influenza, which cut a swath across the world in 1918–19 quite as wide as the devastation of fighting itself. He did not improve while in the camp and was sent home to die. In the end, what saved him was Indian medicine, and this would have a profound impact on his life and art. Like many other Kiowas, he knew from firsthand experience that Kiowa medicine had power and thereafter did not doubt its efficacy.[62]

ART EDUCATION

Instead of becoming a warrior, Mopope found another arena in which to express his respect for Kiowa traditions and his masculine pride. He grew up immersed in a Kiowa artistic heritage. Keintaddle was a highly respected beadworker, and she passed on her knowledge to her daughter Paukeigope. She tanned hides, staking them to the ground on top of canvas, then made buckskin dresses and leggings. She was known for her cradleboards both for her own family and for other people who came to her when they had newborn babies. One account says that she obtained her beads from northern tribes, probably the Cheyennes and Arapahoes, illustrating the intercultural exchanges occurring on the reservation. Her grandchildren remember her diligence. She worked indoors all day at her beading, while the children played outside. She also fulfilled the obligations of a Kiowa grandmother in passing on the history of their family on to the grandchildren through frequent storytelling. Keintaddle's brothers Oheltoint and Silver Horn were both accomplished artists, and Silver Horn in particular was regarded as a "master illustrator" who painted on muslin covers and shields. He was a calendar keeper. He made the transition to painting on paper and became prolific in that medium.[63]

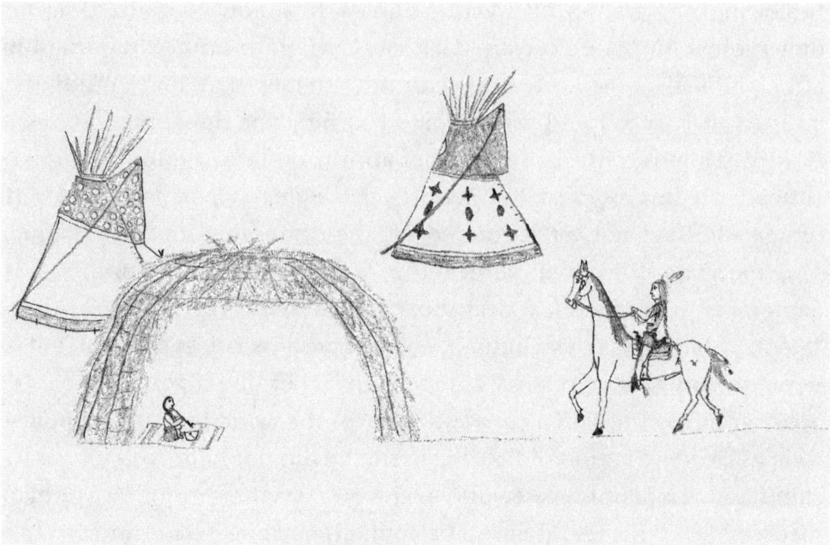

FIGURE 11. Stephen Mopope's sketches for illustrations on Dohausen's battle tipi, ca. 1916. He later drew a series of soldiers on horseback pursuing a Kiowa warrior. Courtesy Vanessa Paukeigope Jennings.

In the hot dry summer of 1913 the brothers gathered together with other senior men, and Silver Horn conveyed a message to his sister Keintaddle: "Send my nephew, Stephen Mopope." The object of the gathering was to renew the famed chief Dohausan's battle tipi with representations of war deeds. Fifteen-year-old Stephen was given the task to record narrated war deeds in pictures that would be painted onto the tipi.

> The stories recalled the battles of the Free Days. Each warrior was given an opportunity to recount an important war deed. The stories poured out in a seemingly endless and seamless flow. With each nod, Mopope drew quickly and easily. He was struck by the stories of Big Bow and his wife fighting the enemy from behind an earthen berm. That story was placed on the north ear of the lodge. The other story that impressed him was of Heart Eater's war honors. His penchant for a bit of each his victim's heart. Each were honored by placement of a tomahawk, his favorite weapon, on the spine of the tipi cover. The tomahawks ran in a commanding upward motion as the last pole lifted the cover into place on the pole frame.[64]

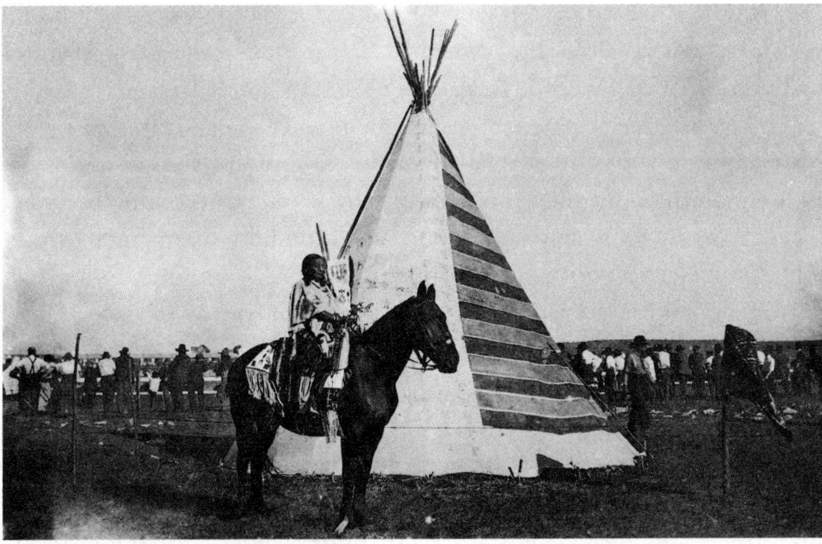

FIGURE 12. Mary Buffalo and the "Tipi with Battle Pictures" from a scene in the 1920 silent film *Daughter of Dawn.* Mary Buffalo was married to Keintaddle's brother Oheltoint (Charley Buffalo). In Mary Buffalo Collection. Courtesy of the Oklahoma Historical Society.

Mopope credited his uncles as his first and most significant art teachers. Silver Horn had learned painting techniques passed on from the pre-reservation era, but he transformed them as he became a professional artist who also produced artwork for a commercial market. His images connected to forms and topics of importance to Kiowa male identity, extending into his present the link between masculine exploits and figurative art from the previous century. He worked in many mediums and with different techniques, from painting on hides in the tradition of the calendar count, to ledger book drawings, and paintings on muslin and paper. He also made shields and rattles and created objects in silver. During his long career he was extremely creative, producing works of art for ceremonial use and for sale, as well as at the request of museums. He stood in close contact with anthropologist James Mooney and Major General Hugh Scott, who was his commanding officer in 1891–94 when Silver Horn was enlisted in Troop L of the Seventh Cavalry and stationed at Fort Sill. Both Mooney and Scott bought his work and commissioned him for pieces. He also met the Chicago-based portrait painter Edward Ayer Burbank, who noted that Silver Horn "is in love with his work, and is always at it." Burbank visited Fort Sill in 1897 and was impressed with Silver Horn's talent. Silver Horn watched him work and was much inspired by Burbank's novel methods and concepts.[65]

In several ways Silver Horn stood as a model for his great-nephew. His connection to a past of martial valor, his love of art, his connection to influential white patrons, and his willingness to learn new methods and to experiment while staying close to a traditional visual content are all aspects that characterize Mopope's own career. His great-uncle's support, patronage, and endorsement—in deeming him worthy of decorating a battle tipi—meant more to him than all the awards and certificates he would later earn. In addition to learning Kiowa forms of artistic expression from his uncles, Mopope also learned an important lesson about the connection between art, cultural preservation, and social relations, and this would have enormous significance for his own later work. Painting the tipi became an occasion for reaffirming history and Kiowa society. Many people attended this gathering to hear recitation of war deeds and to feast in memory of their history. "The elders participating in this storytelling had their families with them. They wanted the children to remember this important occasion."[66]

Another form of art education took place at school. At St. Patrick's, Stephen and the other young Kiowas met Sister Olivia who would become one of their most influential teachers. Music may have been viewed as frivolous in the Indian schools, but arts and crafts were deemed suitable. Sister Olivia, who was herself Choctaw and Chickasaw, introduced the young students to oils and took an interest in their education and noted their passion for artistic expressions. Lois Smoky recalled her experiences in an interview with Arthur Silberman: With colored chalks the students "would draw paintings on the blackboard." Each student would draw on the board and transfer it onto paper. "Sister Olivia taught the fourth, fifth and sixth grades," and seeing the skills of her students she picked them out when matron Susie Peters came over to "talk to Sister Olivia about her drawings and things." Peters then "got in touch with this art teacher from Chickasha, Willie Baze Lane."[67]

The WPA records from Oklahoma in the 1940s include a story about Susie Peters that appears to be based on an interview with her. She first came to the Kiowa Agency as field matron in 1918 and immediately became deeply interested in Kiowa culture and history. She "loved their dances, which at that time were against the ethics of government employees to encourage by their presence." Her posting at Redstone Mission put her in contact with the young aspiring artists. "In 1918 these Kiowa artists were small boys, who loved to play at their tribal dance, where their people were camped around their mission church at Christmas time; they would beat a drum, or tin pan, or tub upside down, and dance and sing wildly, until late at night." She remembered them as "little boys" who "were full of fun." They would bring her drawings, and she would tack them on her office wall for visitors to see. Peters started a "Fine Arts Club" and furnished paper and canvases, as well as art supplies for the participants, starting with colored pencils and going on to watercolors and oils. Apart from the young men who would go on to become famous, the first group consisted of Teddy Ware, who would later become a Methodist minister, "and two girls, who were outstanding, Lois Smoky and Emma Ware":

> Twice a week these boys came to Mrs. Peters' home and drew pictures and painted. Steven Mopope undertook the first large oil painting; he sat on a tin lard bucket with his huge canvas on a chair, the picture of Big Tree, one of the famous chiefs of his tribe in his left hand while they all looked and laughed—Spencer Asah had his dance picture tacked on the wall and painted from memory. He would paint awhile and Monroe Tsa-Toke or James Auchia would begin to sing a war song and beat on an imaginary drum, Asah would dance, and sometimes Mopope would bubble over and join the dance.[68]

Stephen Mopope was already in his early twenties at this time, and the other "little boys" in their mid-teens, but Peters's story captures well the sense of excitement at expressing themselves visually, which also comes across in Smoky's and Auchiah's reminiscences from interviews in the 1970s.

In addition to the six who would later attend the University of Oklahoma, the group included Emma Keahbone, Ruby Pedrick, and Emma Ware, all of whom came from Redstone. Older Kiowas, like Laura Pedrick, also participated. Apparently, it was Lois Smoky's father who paid for classes for all of them. James Auchiah, like Peters, regarded Lois Smoky and Emma Ware as the outstanding students of the group, and Ruby Pedrick advanced the most under the tutelage of Willie Baze Lane.[69]

Lane would come to Anadarko on Saturdays; she brought materials and set up a studio in a vacant room behind the jail in the old city hall. She taught her students color mixing, how to keep their colors clean, perspective, and economy. They painted mainly landscapes in oil, but Smoky remembers that sometimes Lane would take her students out to a park and "we would use that charcoal and we'd sketch." Lane wrote later that her class consisted not only of young Kiowas but also children of Indian Office employees, of the town editor, and some local high school students. In time, the older students began to do research, "talking with the older Indians—attending ceremonials at Washita and Saddle Mt. with a new field to conquer—to get all Possible tradition before some passed on." Among this group were all the students who would later go on to Norman. At the time of Lane's teaching, however, Stephen Mopope already had a family of his own and could not always come to classes, as he had to tend to his crops.[70]

As the 1920s drew to a close, Stephen Mopope knew that he had a passion for painting, and he was making a name for himself as a fancy dancer. He had a family and was deeply enmeshed in responsibilities to the Ohoma Society and the Native American Church. Unlike Jacobson, who was undoubtedly exposed to Indian stories in Sweden, there is no reason to believe that anything in Stephen Mopope's and his friends' upbringing or education prepared them for encountering a Swedish immigrant. No cultural stereotypes circulated widely regarding Swedish traits or customs, and the ones that did were very unlikely to make their way to the KCA Reservation, unless they heard stories from their Delaware neighbors about a people from the Far North who had come to the shores of their original homeland in the Delaware Valley.[71] But this did not mean that Mopope and others would not have recognized the complicated navigation between and performance of identities that characterized the lives of Jacobson and his friends from Lindsborg. The Kiowas lived in a multicultural world, albeit a severely restricted one, and they too struggled with the divide between East and West, and between a call to conform to a certain form of modernity and the tug of traditions. Norman, Oklahoma, would become the site where the concurrent lives of American Indians and immigrants joined and became inextricably entangled.

PART II

ENTANGLEMENTS

CHAPTER 4
Encounters in Norman, 1926–1930s

"STEVE MOPOPE IS A NEW FIGURE in the world of Oklahoma art. It is less than six months since Mopope first appeared on the campus at Norman as a special art student under Oscar Brousse Jacobson, director of the school of painting and design at the university. But in every sense of the word Mopope has 'arrived.'" The arrival in 1927 of four—later six—young Kiowas in Norman, enrolling at the University of Oklahoma as special art students, caused a stir. Tsatoke, Asah, Hokeah, and Mopope—"their very names speak of an ancestry that whirled savagely and mightily over the western plains," reported *Oklahoma News* in June 1927. The four began taking lessons in January 1927. A year later, Lois Smoky (Bougetah) joined them and constituted the fifth member of the group. James Auchiah eventually replaced Bougetah, who returned to the reservation after only one semester in Norman.[1]

What was it that had happened in 1926 to set in motion the collaboration of the young Kiowas and Oscar Jacobson? Each had, in their manner, been preparing for this encounter. The Kiowas had begun to paint while in school at St. Patrick's in Anadarko. Later, through the initiative of Susie Peters and Willie Baze Lane, they participated in art classes held in various locations and studios in Anadarko, paid for by Lois Smoky's father, Enoch Smoky. Under Willie Baze Lane's tutelage they learned to paint with oils and practiced making landscapes and camp scenes. Susie Peters's efforts included forming the Mau-Tame Club for women to encourage the arts and crafts, which became a powerful node for the development and transmission of beadwork among women of all ages. This also involved the male artists, who contributed designs for the beadwork. The growing interest in Indian dancing embroiled Mopope and Hokeah, and during the 1920s they and others traveled regularly to

Indian dances and ceremonials held across Oklahoma and the Southwest. While suspicious of Indian ceremonials and an outright critic of the social dances such as the 49'er dance, Peters keenly sought out opportunities to act as agent for various groups of Kiowas who received invitations to perform dances. The opportunity to take art classes at Oklahoma University (OU) was a chance that Stephen would strive to make the most of. He was already close to thirty and there were unlikely to be other chances. The other prospective students were in their early twenties and not yet married, with the exception of Monroe Tsatoke who brought his wife and two daughters to Norman.[2]

Oscar Jacobson had nursed a fascination with Indian culture for a long time before he met the Kiowa students. He and his wife traveled extensively in the Southwest and admired the Pueblo peoples, because they remained "in their primitive state," and "their manner of living is the same as it was hundreds of years ago." He lectured on "Indian art," and in the 1920s he involved himself in Pueblo and Navajo concerns with abrogation of their water rights. Jeanne d'Ucel describes in her memoirs how in 1922 Jacobson had traveled with a friend to the Southwest for a vacation but returned "heartbroken and indignant" because of the oppressive conditions on the reservations. She suggested that he expressed his indignation in a painting, called *White Shadows* (see plate 3) depicting the ominous clouds of oncoming settler invasion on Indian land. Mexican squatters tapped the water supply for irrigation, leaving Pueblo fields dry and parched. The political leadership of New Mexico protected the squatters, who had citizenship in the state. In Washington, Albert Fall, secretary of the interior, lobbied to tear up the communal ownership system of the Pueblos, which would enable further appropriation of Indian land and water. He asked the New Mexico senator Holm Olaf Bursum to draft a bill that would ensure the rights of non-Indian squatters on Pueblo land. The bill also introduced a provision that, in the future, state courts would be permitted to review all conflicts over Pueblo land titles. Pueblo people enlisted their white allies to oppose the bill, and according to d'Ucel, desperate Pueblos and Navajos "spoke frankly to Dad whom they knew as a friend. Some of the young men felt they must take matters in their own hands; they threatened to go on the warpath. Dad dissuaded them as he explained that such a move would only be disastrous." Jacobson began writing letters to colleagues in the arts and universities, including his contacts in Santa Fe, and they "immediately joined in his endeavor." He had frequently lectured at women's clubs and now he contacted them about the situation in New Mexico and asked them to involve their members in writing to their representatives to protest the measures against the southwestern tribes. He explained the situation to the president of OU, Brooks, who in his turn wrote to presidents of a large number of colleges and universities. D'Ucel argues that this "avalanche of protest caused Congress to take a second look at" the Bursum Bill and "it was soundly defeated." An investigation into Secretary Fall's questionable business activities followed on the defeat of the bill, and d'Ucel concludes that it, "is possible that the Teapot Dome scandal would have been uncovered anyway; but the rumpus concerning the Indian lands of New Mexico probably hastened this."[3]

The controversy surrounding the Bursum Bill had energized a substantive part of the New Mexico art community and protestant reformers in the Indian Rights Association. John Collier, the future commissioner of Indian affairs, employed direct action methods in the struggle to defeat the bill and helped organize the Pueblo villages' own protest. The Jacobsons maintained close contacts with several of the Santa Fe–connected artists and activists, such as the sisters Amelia and Martha White. The involvement of women's groups, as well as individual women who had relocated to southwestern artistic communities, is well documented in previous scholarship, while Jacobson's role in these protests has received far less attention.[4] With hindsight, however, the situation in New Mexico mirrors that of the Midwest in the previous century, when immigrant groups, Swedes prominently among them, were deployed as spearheads of US colonialist strategies to take over land from Dakotas, Ojibways, Ho-Chunks, Kaws, Pawnees, and others who had as yet not surrendered their territories. Holm Olaf Bursum, son of Norwegian immigrants in Iowa, and Oscar Jacobson were both beneficiaries of such policies of settler colonialism. Nothing in Jacobson's own or d'Ucel's writings suggests that they themselves made such a connection.

It is unlikely that Jacobson's influence was as great as d'Ucel suggests in defeating Secretary Fall's proposal. In her manuscripts, she frequently emphasizes her husband's role in events. There is no indication that she intended the memoirs to be published, rather her manner of referring to Jacobson as "Dad" suggests that she wrote for the benefit of their children and certainly so with the ambition to demonstrate his greatness. Nevertheless, her manuscripts are among the very few sources to the personal and private sides of the relationship between the Jacobsons and the Kiowa artists and therefore useful. While they must be used with caution, and while she sometimes exaggerates the qualities of Jacobson's deportment in relation to American Indians, I have found that in instances when it has been possible to corroborate her accounts with others, some unique features emerge.[5]

By the mid-1920s, then, Jacobson had experience from involvement in campaigns on behalf of Indian claims, and he had begun to establish himself as an expert on "primitive art," not least in the aftermath of their trip to North Africa and the many lectures that followed. At the University of Oklahoma, a trickle of American Indian students had begun to appear. Jacobson offered a course in American Indian art history, a course that, according to d'Ucel, was the first in the nation to consider "Indian art as a living force and from the esthetic point of view, not merely as an anthropological and archeological study."[6] A portrait in *Oklahoma Magazine* in 1927 described his energetic pace, his modern use of technology, his dual occupation as artist and teacher, and his mixed identifications:

> Jacobson, for the past two years, has been lecturing over the entire United States, carrying with him canvasses of his own work, with which to illustrate the lectures which deal with many phases of art from that of the artist and the public, through the art of the American Indian and on into lectures on religious architecture and the evolution of the dwelling house . . . Jacobson is a Scandinavian. . . . Two years ago . . . he penetrated the heart of Africa emerging with sixty new oil paintings, a thousand photographs and a collection of African artisanship which is exceptional in the United States.[7]

A St. Louis art critic had lyrically lauded his paintings, stating that, "Jacobson can fling the tradition of the schools to the four winds—thereby proving that this young Scandinavian is as truly American in his spirit of pioneering as were the forefathers of you and me when they settled up the wilderness."[8] Beneath the laudatory tenor ran a note of suspicion against immigrants; this one had proved he was as good an American as those who crossed the plains in oxcarts, but he was not automatically enclosed in the community of "you and me." Perhaps such pointed comments contributed to his and his wife's desire to side with other people who were not included in the nation's "you and me."

He had already established many contacts among the Pueblos and Navajos on his trips to the Southwest, and he appreciated the mixed ethnicities and heritages present in Oklahoma, although he never expressed awareness of racist and colonialist inequalities such as those he identified in the Southwest.[9] In what appears prophetic in light of later developments, d'Ucel describes a visit to Santa Fe in the summer of 1915, just prior to the couple's arrival in Norman. Oscar was visibly upset as he viewed the trinkets Indians sold on the market, and one incident in particular angered him. The couple attended an exhibit designed to demonstrate how far New Mexico's Indigenous peoples had come "in the white man's way." The Jacobsons noted only what they viewed as "a total absence of Indian inventions and methods." Chancing upon a representative of the Indian Bureau, Jacobson lashed out and expressed his deep displeasure: "It's a crime to destroy the sure and inborn sense of beauty of Indians and to debauch them to the worst and poorest in white art," he raged. "Why! We're civilizing them," responded the bureaucrat. "Civilizing them! And to think you don't even realize there's much you could learn from them," Jacobson retorted. The Jacobsons left the building and d'Ucel remarked that it would be a fine thing if her husband would help some young Indians to develop their own artwork. But Jacobson "shrugged his shoulders as he replied 'But what would one do with them afterwards? And what good would it do them in a world unfit to appreciate them?'"[10]

The story sets up a pattern that occurs several times in d'Ucel's memoirs, of Jacobson as an interpreter of Indigenous art, exhibiting greater understanding of Indian culture than other white people. In this account, d'Ucel inserts herself as a cocreator of his important future work, a role he later also credited her with. Whether they already at this time saw themselves as patrons for the Indians or not, a decade later he was poised and ready when the Indian agent J. A. Buntin approached him on the recommendations from Susie Peters, regarding the group of talented Kiowa art students.

AN IMMEDIATE SENSATION

Whether by Jacobson's savvy or by the growing exoticization of American Indians of the day, the arrival of Kiowa special students on the Norman campus caused immediate excitement. "In no time the four boys were one of the sensations of the campus," *My Oklahoma* exclaimed in August 1927. The magazine ran two feature articles about the artists in May and August 1927, and *Oklahoma News* described them at length in June of the same year. The purpose of their studies, this article noted, "is to preserve the heritage of this ancestry." Realizing that "their Indian ceremonies and costumes are in danger of being lost they are making an attempt to preserve them." Thus, it was heritage preservation that motivated their presence at the university, rather than skills in "art as it is generally understood." Nonetheless, "it is primitive, genuine art, expressing the Indian as the Indian sees and feels," an ethnic art of some interest, their "colors are flat and bright; there is swing and verve to their figures."[11]

The urgency of preservation resonates in the account in the May issue of *My Oklahoma* as well: "Jacobson visions a place in art history for the contribution of the red man. He seeks, too, to establish in Oklahoma a museum to house the relics of this passing race. He would retain samples of Indian culture in this state, the last home of so many of the great tribes of plain and forest, before it is too late. That is one reason why he is so interested in these Kiowa boys. Another is, that being a true artist himself, he sees in their work an art that is of itself of value and a thing of beauty." Since Jacobson was likely the source of information for both articles, it seems reasonable that it was his views on the urgency of preservation that came across, with the value of the artwork almost as an afterthought. There is no doubt that Jacobson appreciated the aesthetic qualities of Indigenous art forms, but it may be that this was overshadowed by his concern that Indian culture risked obliteration, a worry he shared with other "Indian reformers" of his time.[12] His concern set the tone for the endeavor—it was a project to salvage a timeless and original Kiowa aesthetic expression before it was too late. There was little room in this representation for the enormous creative outpouring of cultural assertion on the reservation, evident in the revitalization of dances, the spread of peyotism, the twin developments of beadwork and adaptations of visual expressions to new media and markets such as painting and photography.

Few documents exist that clarify the decision to create a special program for the Kiowas at OU. Later on, several of the participants would write letters, articles, and memoirs and hurl accusations at one another for not recognizing their own significant contribution, but at the time it appears not to have been a decision anyone felt inclined or obligated to put down on paper. The earliest references from Oscar Jacobson's own pen regarding the Kiowa special students are found in brief descriptions of the artists, made in preparation of a manuscript on Indian painters of Oklahoma. Jacobson included in his account information that could only have come from Mopope himself: "Steve Mopope's childhood was spent near Redstone Mission with his grandmother, in the purest Indian tradition." His interest in painting and drawing appeared early as he drew designs in the sand and on hides. Jacobson wrote: "It was therefore natural that Steve should be one of the original group of Kiowas whom Miss Mahier and I launched on their career. His Indian name, Painted Robe, had been prophetic. He found his greatest joy in painting, and like his colleagues, his main source of inspiration and subject matter came from the Indian rituals and Indian traditions."[13]

An account Jeanne d'Ucel wrote only three years after the arrival of the students at University of Oklahoma, established a perspective that has often been cited:

> About three years ago the attention of Professor O. B. Jacobson of the University of Oklahoma was attracted to these boys. Mr. Jacobson is an authority on primitive art and primitive art is his joy. He at once took these young fellows under his protection. With the assistance of Miss Edith Mahier of the Art Department, he directed them, helping them to develop and especially keeping them from being spoiled by contact with white art.
>
> At first timid and hesitant, these young men soon took heart; finding someone who did not look on Indian things as inferior things, their racial pride reasserted itself; they felt no need to apologize for what they did but threw themselves into their work with joy and enthusiasm.
>
> Under their brush dancing figures spring magically and, like a living frieze, evoke all the sacred ritual of Indian life and lore. Eagle dancers resplendent in their fantastic wings, the flute man at his wooing, the medicine chief making incantations, the smoking of the peace pipe, the beat of the war dance, all that which means most to the Indians is there idealized in rhythm and harmony.[14]

In her text d'Ucel established Jacobson as an authority on "primitive" art.

It was through his expertise that his efforts to ensure the Kiowas escaped white contamination achieved credence. Primitive art existed in a premodern state, and as such it was timeless and unspoiled by change and fashions.[15] Jacobson's authority in this area also enabled him to communicate respect and trust to the Indians.

In the early 1970s Arthur Silberman conducted extensive interviews with James Auchiah, and these shed more light on the events and are particularly valuable for their rich detail. According to Auchiah, Jacobson had been aware of the Kiowa painters from submissions the superintendent sent to him early in the 1920s. From then on, Jacobson encouraged Susie Peters and Willie Baze Lane to continue to train the students, in the hope that the university would one day establish a scholarship fund to bring the artists to Norman for further education. Jacobson also visited St. Patrick's in Anadarko, met the students, and shook hands with them. He talked to Lane, Peters, and the superintendent and said that the "paintings were great, unusual, very primitive." However, he did not approve of Willie Baze Lane's teaching, as she encouraged the students to paint in oils. He considered this too European and wanted them under his own control so that they would stay in an Indian style. After the initial meeting, Jacobson visited the reservation regularly—as often as once a week by Auchiah's recollection.[16]

The interview with James Auchiah clearly emphasizes the importance of the Kiowa students' own agency and desire to learn further. Their ambition should not be downplayed when accounting for these unusual events. They all longed to paint and were willing to accept sacrifices to make that possible. "Anyone could have helped these boys because they were just craving to go to school. They wanted to go to school so bad and they sold everything they had. Mopope sold some livestock. So did I and anyway that we could raise money, to go to OU."[17]

In no one did ambition burn as hotly as in Mopope, and he was willing to adapt his story to fit with Jacobson's expectations. The information about his background that Jacobson included in his early biography must have come from Mopope, but it is just as clear that it was only partial. He was, indeed, fascinated with Indian traditions, but he had also learned to paint in oils and had created several canvases of motifs that had nothing to do with Kiowa rituals. His decision to come to OU as a grown man with a family to support caused a rift among his own relatives. Vanessa Jennings recounts the reactions of Mopope's family to his choice of accepting art education at the university. Her story, like d'Ucel's, focuses on a conflict or dichotomy. On the one hand, there is the art of the Kiowa students, connected to traditional motifs and customs, but while d'Ucel and Jacobson viewed it in opposition to white art, Jennings identifies a conflict with certain Christian values, which some Kiowa people themselves had adopted. Jennings points out how difficult it was for the Kiowa students to leave the families who needed their labor during the harsh years of the Depression. Mopope depended on the support and encouragement of his wife, Jeanette Berry, to be able to carry on with his studies in Norman. He also ran into opposition from Baptists and Methodists who wielded considerable power in the rural reservation communities. "They thumped their Bibles and screamed *'SINNER,'* loudly and without shame," writes Jennings. "Their power was so strong that it was not unusual to be denied a funeral based on your association with 'sinful heathen traditions' with the O-Ho-Mah Society Ceremonies or the Peyote rituals. My grandfather was guilty of keeping his Indian traditions." At one time Christian relatives summoned Paukeigope to a meeting in Anadarko and asked that Stephen join them there:

> My grandfather arrived at the appointed hour. When he entered the living room he knew exactly what was going to happen. His mother-in-law launched into an explosive verbal attack on him. She was angry that he would abandon the small income he made at farming to support his family and go to study art, especially to record the very sinful traditions that the Christians objected to so much. The attack escalated as each person in the attendance used the visit as a chance to beat the "wanton heathen" verbally and then pray for him with Christian charity to save his soul. It ended mercifully when Paukeigope stood up, took him by the arm and led him outside away from the frothing zealots! She kissed him on the cheek and asked him to return to the University right away.[18]

That night, Mopope wrote a letter to his mother:

> Dearest Mother,
>
> I apologize for any heartache that I have caused you. However, by asking me to stop painting—it is like asking me to stop breathing. I

can not stop painting. I can not explain why my art is so important to me. Jeanette understands. She encourages me to continue my artwork. I could not do this without her support. Someday I will become famous with my art. At that time, you will be proud of me.

Lovingly,
Stephen Mopope[19]

He again expressed his deep commitment to a life of art in a letter to his mother written in 1934 when he was away from his family painting murals in Tahlequah: "Dear Mother:—Just a short note letter to remind you that you have a son doing Art Work—and a real good *Artist* for you to talk about in the future.—I know you feel hurt for what had happen in the past time. But Mother—you must think about me and my little one's And brace up—be happy—So that will start a life better + happier to all of us in the family while we're living."[20]

A sensation they were, these young Kiowas who entered college as special students with an irrepressible desire to paint. But they paid a high price for their commitment, as Mopope's letter to his mother reveals. While a number of issues influenced the growth of a special program for Indigenous students in art at the University of Oklahoma, it may well be that the glue truly holding it together was this passion for art, this equation of art with the very breath of life, surpassing the obligations to family and community, that characterized both Oscar Jacobson's life and that of Stephen Mopope.

EVERYDAY LIFE IN NORMAN

Norman, situated in the center of the state, became the location of the University of Oklahoma in 1890. Campus buildings were modeled on the red brick of the prestigious institutions on the East Coast and its streets landscaped to create a lush green oasis on the flat Oklahoma plains. As all Oklahoma state institutions in the 1920s it was strictly segregated, and open only to white students, although students of mixed American Indian and white descent had been admitted earlier in the century. Two major issues confronted Jacobson as the Kiowas arrived in town—where should they stay and where could they paint? A provisional solution to the first problem was to place the Kiowa men in Jacobson's own basement on Chautauqua Street. However, the presence of a woman, Lois Bougetah

Smoky, required other measures. Smoky recalls how Susie Peters came over to her parents and made arrangements about accommodation in a two-storied house in Norman. Smoky and her mother stayed in the backroom, and Monroe Tsatoke and his wife and children had one apartment, and Stephen Mopope and Jeanette Berry occupied the apartment upstairs. Spencer Asah and Jack Hokeah stayed in a place that operated like a boardinghouse, according to Smoky.[21]

Painting took place in a makeshift studio, set up in a long narrow room next to art teacher Edith Mahier's office in the OU art building. An everyday pattern developed, and the Kiowas went to the art department at eight o'clock in the morning and began painting. By noon they had a lunch break and then after that continued to paint all afternoon. Edith Mahier supervised them all day, and sometimes in the mornings and sometimes after lunch Jacobson would come in and look at their work and offer comments. Or simply just shake his head slightly and they knew it was something he didn't like: "anything modern why he would kind of shake his head and just go like that you know he want us to stay in that real Indian flat work," Lois Smoky recalled. At regular intervals Jacobson would call in the students and evaluate them. Auchiah remembers being "called down" for being too hasty, for lack of improvement, and for a lack of balance in his paintings. At the end of semesters Jacobson assigned their work a grade. Stephen Mopope kept his credit book, which revealed that in 1927–28 he took three credits of Art and earned a B.[22]

The Kiowa students studied according to a specially devised plan, "extracurricular" as Auchiah expressed it. It contained an introduction to a variety of topics, such as oil painting, technique training, some sculpting. Mopope recalled doing some soap carving and batik dying. They attended lectures together with other art students. Auchiah remembered one evening class on Egyptian art. Sketching was done in the classroom and brought home to work on during the evenings. Jacobson would come in and offer concrete suggestions, such as pointing out that "hands should be the size of face," or that big feet and small hands were out of proportion. On one occasion, Mopope had drawn a buffalo hunt depicting two Indians with two horses and buffalos. It turned out that one of the horses had five legs. All ran together and it took all of them counting legs to discover that there were too many of them. Auchiah told Arthur Silberman that Jacobson would give each of them individual attention. One evening he would single out Mopope and spend the whole evening talking about just one of his pictures. Next time it would be Auchiah's turn, and so on. He recognized each artist's personal style and encouraged them to stay with it. "He was very good at it. Was responsible for keeping everybody with a distinct style." Such personal preferences included colors, detail, and topics. Mopope liked orange, while Hokeah often used white; Hokeah emphasized detail, but Asah did not; Mopope often painted the buffalo dance (see plate 4).[23]

Jacobson also provided a fixed framework for their painting styles. He chastised them for using colored paper and preferred them to use brown paper. "He always wanted to keep everything Indian. Like brown represents skin you know." It was too modern to paint on a green or blue-green board. He also did not like metallic paint. Once Auchiah used some bronze paint in his work and Jacobson told him he did not like it. When Arthur Silberman asked Auchiah what happened when Jacobson disapproved of something, the response was that the Kiowas stopped using it, although extant paintings demonstrate that they continued using metallic paint and colored paper. Watercolor was the preferred medium at OU. In Jacobson's view it was the best technique for showcasing the particular Indian style, perhaps because it most readily resembled the painting done on buffalo hides and tipis. Auchiah stated that they did not do any oil painting at OU, yet on the side they did occasionally. "People came and wanted a landscape painting, with Indians camping. We did some of them. . . . Nothing to do with our class work."[24] Four oil paintings remain in the possession of Mopope's descendants, evidence of his experimentation with a form of landscape painting that was more similar to Jacobson's own than to the flat style "Indian" painting (see plate 5).

Detailed learning and practice at OU involved planning pictures by drawing lines on fine tracing paper and then transferring it onto drawing paper. Jacobson would look at sketches and suggest changes in dimension or balance. When he was satisfied, the artists would take the sketches home and finish the paintings. The tracing paper would be kept for future use, in case other customers requested a particular painting.[25] Mopope continued the practice all his life, leaving a large number of sketches on tracing paper, as well as on any other piece of paper available. Many years later, Scott Fulton would give an account of the technique with which Mopope constructed his paintings, a basic practice probably begun at

OU. Fulton, who worked at one of the art galleries in Oklahoma City in the late 1950s, once watched Mopope finishing a painting for sale in the gallery. Mopope worked with a set of basic cardboard designs from which he carefully outlined the motif and proceeded to add colors one at a time:

> If there was red in the bonnet he'd paint that red and then he'd go down to the loin cloth. . . . He'd go down to the moccasins perhaps and put it there. Then he'd clean that brush real carefully and he'd study the painting a little bit and then he'd choose another color and then he'd paint those colors in . . . instead of blending each color in a certain area as he went like I was used to seeing painters do. He didn't do that at all. He painted mostly all of the reds together then he'd paint all the blues together he'd paint all the yellows together and then all the whites together and just kind of moved in and around the painting and it finally became a whole rather than just working in one area at a time.[26]

D'Ucel commented on the Kiowas' use of color. "The Indian loves color," she wrote in 1930, "his taste in color is not anemic but it is much more subtle than civilized people usually give him credit for, his harmonies are often exquisite and when he produces a strong contrast there is good esthetic reason for it. The way he handles his colors, how surely he selects them and juxtaposes them is something to make a white artist despair." In a later article, she wrote that the Kiowas, in particular, handled paint cleverly. "They use it thick in spots, lines, etc. against the velvety texture obtained by washing it in, and as a result their paintings show a jewel-like brilliancy that is indescribable."[27]

She also made a reference to the use of molds in sketching the outline of paintings—and to an occasion when this was not used. In the spring of 1930 Monroe Tsatoke and Stephen Mopope had been given the task of decorating the University Auditorium in Holmberg Hall with one large panel each, flanking the presidential box:

> They were shown how to square their sketch and the large canvas in order to find themselves. However, for the sake of harmony and to balance better the work of Tsa-to-ke, who had already begun, Mopope decided to work without a previous sketch, as all the dancing figures which he had and which were suitable faced to the left, therefore away from the stage. Miss Mahier was a little

dubious concerning the results of this improvisation, but Mopope in his quiet, smiling way remained obdurate. And he succeeded in painting a canvas twenty times as large as any of his previous works, retaining his sense of proportion even tho he had to work at close range. "It was fun," he said.[28]

The students were expected to deliver five to six pictures per week. This requirement served both educational and financial purposes. Their work was not only evaluated quantitatively, for Jacobson also expected improvement in their production. Jacobson then bought the paintings and this served as income for the students who received no other allowances or salaries. The general price was ten dollars per painting. This meant that each student earned from fifty to sixty dollars per week, which helped them pay for accommodation and meals. Jacobson seems to have bought most of the paintings, and he continued to sell them for many years out of his office in the art department, but he also encouraged other buyers, and Auchiah remembered selling to other art dignitaries in Oklahoma, like Anita Howard, Martha Avey, and Nan Sheets. Oklahoma oilman Lew Wentz supported the students financially through buying their paintings and donated many of them to the Art Museum at the university.[29]

Undoubtedly, the Kiowas benefited greatly from the critique, guidance, and experience that Jacobson and Mahier offered them. It aided them in developing techniques and motifs that they had already encountered on the reservation. Mopope's way of painting may have been a procedure he learned from his great-uncle Silver Horn. Candace S. Greene describes changes and developments in Silver Horn's technique from the 1880s into the first decades of the twentieth century. Drawing books from the earliest period developed the ledger art, which in turn grew from an earlier form of warrior art. "Figures were drawn in hard outline then filled in with solid blocks of color." In the 1890s Silver Horn became acquainted with watercolors and continued to apply paint in solid blocks, but sometimes he varied brushstrokes and thickness to indicate different textures. Later still, he painted shield designs on buckskin. "On shields with pictoral images, finely detailed figures are drawn in pen and ink, using much the same style as in his works on paper. For geometric designs, the paint is applied in lines of various widths as well as in solid blocks of pigment, and the color is smooth and even throughout."[30]

Many accounts stress that Jacobson did not wish the Kiowas to be influenced by European art forms. D'Ucel commented in her manuscript that "Dad was determined not to let them be 'contaminated' by white studies" but that they were free to choose subjects, techniques, paints, colors, and so on. "If you are looking for a career in art," he told them, "don't attempt to work in the white manner where the white artists, 50 000 of them, will always have some advantage over you." In this there may have been some criticism of the style of painting that Willie Baze Lane had imparted to them in Anadarko. It is likely that his desire to isolate the Kiowas sprang from ideas that were current among whites who wished to reform Indian policy regarding the need to salvage Indian culture before it had been eradicated entirely. It was a notion that located Indianness in a particular racial sensitivity from which came their aesthetic expressions. Too much contact with whites would ruin this sense, as Jacobson had witnessed in Santa Fe in 1915. While in Norman, Jacobson remained in control of their aesthetic development and its impact. He appeared adamant that the Kiowas should not depart from the flat painting style. Jeanne d'Ucel described what seems to have been his rationale in an article published in 1938: "The artistic works of the Red Man show very plainly his Asiatic origins. Most young Indian painters tried at some time to imitate white artists, to put in their pictures *chiaroscuro*, modeling, perspective; discriminating white patrons have led them back to their racial tradition in which their instinct lies, that permits them to produce masterpieces with an absence of background and the use of flat surfaces, thus securing not merely realism but the decorative synthesized quality for which they unconsciously strive." Therefore, there was to be no background in the pictures, no shading, and no curve marks.[31]

There is an irony, which went without comment, that Jacobson needed to teach the Indian students how to paint according to "their racial tradition." The students may have accepted this because Jacobson was an authority figure, or they may simply have accepted it along with the very tangible opportunities he offered to expose their work to the larger art community. Jacobson actively worked to promote the acceptance of American Indian art in the established art world and by the general public. These two goals—of protecting the students from Euro-American corrosion and introducing them into galleries, museums, and collections—seemed incompatible but would have a dominant impact on how

Indian art was taught and promoted in Oklahoma and in the Southwest in the following thirty-five years.[32]

However, in practice, their time in Norman included exposure to many forms of aesthetic expression, some obviously encouraged by Jacobson and others beyond his control. Jacobson's insistence that the artists should attend classes with other students and become familiar with different techniques seems to belie his overarching purpose of segregating them from corrosive influences. Auchiah recalled that at times the Kiowas would join with other art students for lectures, demonstrations, and in watercolor painting at Jacobson's request. Mopope left behind a collection of art postcards and magazines, demonstrating a wide interest in art and form, which the years in Norman had introduced him to.[33]

The artists developed their distinct styles, and over the years their perspectives and motifs changed. "There is as much difference between a Tsa-to-ke and an Hokeah as between a Velasquez and a Rubens," wrote Jeanne d'Ucel in the early 1930s, and she described the unique character of each of the six first artists. A "musical quality permeated all his work," she wrote about Tsatoke, "and there is no ignorance in his subtle color harmonies and his rhythmic compositions." Mopope, while influenced deeply by his dancing, showed in "all his paintings in spite of their virile quality a something which can only be described, altho inadequately, by the name of rococo, a love of swirling lines, of delicate pose, of subtle balances." Asah, she said, depicted "principally the magic and mystery of Indian medicine," and Hokeah's "paintings seldom show motion like those of Tsa-to-ke, or elegance like those of Mopope; there is about all of them a quietness, a reserve that well reflect his temperament. He seems to prefer depicting the contemplative and purely spiritual side of Indian life, he might almost be said to paint prayer. . . . On the other hand, there is sometimes an element of the grotesque in his work, and his paintings are both more decorative and more barbaric than those of the others." Auchiah, the latest arrival in the group, she deemed to have the surest color sense, and "he has an uncanny instinct for métier in bringing out all the qualities of water colors and all their resources for texture and brilliancy. He is also endowed with a remarkable sense of balance, his compositions are well handled. . . . In all his works there is a sense of humor that often broadens into profound irony, altho his paintings are never caricatures." D'Ucel, however, had little to say about Bougetah. She was talented but had been educated among whites and "had difficulty at first finding herself. Little by little she reentered the old racial tradition and she produced some very creditable things; her subject were mostly Indian women and children."[34]

Much later, the art historian Maybelle Mann evaluated Mopope's paintings in an article where she discussed the early works of the Kiowa artists. She pointed out that "Mopope also painted rearview figures [see plate 6]. The portrait-style heads, small groups, and single figures that appear in his Kiowa paintings are distinct from other Plains paintings, such as those done in San Ildefonso, where the artists generally painted large groups of people. . . . He handled the brush with additional delicacy and his figures are distinct one from another. Even the faces he painted reflect expression missing in some of the other work. In the *Squaw Dance*, an outstanding piece, the faces of the men indicate pleasure while the brightly clad rearview figures execute their dance."[35]

By all accounts, the sojourn at OU meant hard work but also some play for the young Kiowas. Mopope tried his hand at boxing, with rather disastrous results. Jennings describes his first and only match:

> Jack Hokeah promised to be his "corner man." When the date arrived, Grandpa Steve was able to come up with the required equipment. He was excited and ready! The referee called him into the middle of the boxing arena. Grandpa Steve said he looked at Jack for courage and clearly saw him chewing gum as he reassured him that it would be an "ea-ea-eazy win!" Grandpa's friend stuttered slightly when he was excited.
>
> The referee gave his instructions for a "good clean fight." He remembered touching his opponent's glove. Then, he heard the bell ring. . . .
>
> When Grandpa woke up he was being carried down the hall by two large men with Jack frantically waving a towel at him. "St-St- Steve, wake up! Ar-ar-are you OK? Pah-bee, open your eyes! Jeanette's gonna k-k-k-k-Kill me if anything happens to you! Wa-wa-wake up! Pleasssse!!!"
>
> That was the end of my Grandfather's boxing career. He kept his boxing gloves as a souvenir and they passed to me when he died. He told me this story many times.[36]

They enjoyed the opportunity to participate in sports and became enamored with the prime spectator game in Oklahoma—football. Auchiah, in fact, credits them with coming up with the idea for "Little Red," the OU football mascot, which came under heavy fire in the 1980s for being a racist and derogatory symbol. The Kiowas were also engaged on various occasions to provide entertainment with Indian dances. They, and other Indian students calling themselves the Sequoyah Club, participated in setting up a "wig-wam right at football grounds and make medicine." A dance was held on the evening before games. On game day, however, no one wore Indian regalia in the stands. Lois Smoky recalled all of them belonging to the Indian club at the university and going to basketball games and baseball games together.[37]

Other students, contemporaries of the Kiowas, remembered bantering and play as well as concentrated labor. Olinka Hrdy, one of Oklahoma's first modernist painters, liked to "sneak in" to their room where the Kiowas were painting under the supervision of Edith (Ely) Mahier, because Mopope and Hokeah "loved to play tricks on each other and they laughed and throw darts and things." She recalled one occasion when Jack Hokeah took a brush and walked over to Mopope and painted him up and down his body. Hrdy told him "don't just use red how about a little blue and white and may as well be patriotic" so Hokeah painted Mopope's back full of stars, all to Mopope's amusement.[38] Hrdy was known to exaggerate her stories, but that Mopope and Hokeah, who were neighbors in Redstone, liked to banter and play is supported by Jennings's accounts as well.[39]

DANCING AT OU

As Auchiah pointed out, the Kiowas and other members of OU's Sequoyah Club organized intertribal dances. The club must have been important for the students far away from their families and home, but they were already accustomed to performing dances for entertainment and it is not surprising that dancing for white audiences became a feature of their tenure in Norman. Auchiah asserted that they were all dancers. "Mopope and I belong to the same dancing group. We were war dancers, costume dancers, feather dancers. Asah, Mopope, Hokeah and Auchiah all belonged to Ohoma Lodge. Tsatoke don't dance." The Jacobsons knew enough about Kiowa culture to understand that dancing and music held profound meaning for the young artists. These expressions of culture were interwoven with their works of art. "On first seeing these Indian paintings," wrote d'Ucel, "one is struck by the action, the rhythm with which they vibrate: the dancers dance, the deer leap, looking at them one seems to hear the tom-tom and the flute, for all the figures are remarkably, radiantly alive." She recalled first seeing Tsatoke at a dance, singing and drumming. His "soul is music" and ever since childhood he had listened to old men sing and learned songs that were all but forgotten. He knew not only Kiowa songs, but also songs from neighboring peoples, and he even knew a little French song that delighted her. Mopope, she knew, was "the champion dancer of all Oklahoma Indians" and she described watching him dance. "It is a joy to see Mopope in his Eagle dance. Wings made of eagle feathers give him the appearance of soaring, his powerfully muscled body sways and revolves portraying the flight, the loves of the king of birds; under his fantastic headdress his naturally haughty face becomes proud and daring." D'Ucel and Jacobson learned, no doubt through their connection to the Kiowas, of the significance attached to dancing to maintain courage and hope during the difficult reservation and allotment experience. D'Ucel understood that dancing "gave release to their crushing emotions, it proved a viatic for the beauty hungry, it brought to the earth-bound a little cosmic joy." For those reasons "the ritual of the dance is at the core of Indian life; it has been lovingly and tenaciously guarded and it is the foundation of the modern Indian art renaissance."[40]

Since several of the artists were already seasoned performers and had traveled with Susie Peters to Indian fairs around Oklahoma and neighboring states, dancing, singing, and selling their paintings, they were keenly aware of the usefulness of dancing and music as ways for the artists to enter the awareness of the general population of Norman and surrounding communities. Jacobson soon realized that it offered an avenue for financial support for their studies and work as well. Their skill was considerable, with Mopope and Hokeah being particularly outstanding dancers. Olinka Hrdy described an occasion when she, Mahier, and Jacobson watched the Kiowas dance in the auditorium of the art department. "Jack was the greatest dancer of all" and when he danced "I saw Jacobson cry tears running down his face." Hrdy alleges that she got all the Kiowas dancing and she, Jacobson, and Ely (Mahier) sat in their little studio and watched them with amazement. Jacobson asked them if they had any dance costumes to wear and they responded that they could go to Anadarko to get them. Jacobson said "well I'll talk to president Bizzell I'll go right now and talk to him and we'll get you lined up to dance on the stage at the University. So they did."[41]

Hrdy's claim to have discovered that they danced is hyperbole, but from early on, their presence in Norman became connected to dance performances. On Sunday, March 11, 1928, the *Oklahoma Daily* announced a "novel entertainment" to be offered in the university auditorium the following Friday by four "Indian artists of the Kiowa nation, who are University students." Asah, Hokeah, Mopope, and Tsatoke would dance, assisted by "an old Kiowa Indian," who was to play two flute solos. The following fall ten Oklahoma City women's clubs sponsored a program, aimed at raising funds for the Kiowa students at the Shrine auditorium in Norman. A crowd of two hundred attended, and artwork was for sale in the lobby, including an auction for a poster made by Olinka Hrdy, which sold for twenty-five dollars. Mopope performed a solo, which inspired the attending journalist to poeticize: "He dances with an utter abandon that suggests the Charleston. After a particularly high kick he grinned through his paint and gave his shoulders a twitch that set every muscle in them writing [*sic*]. 'Ki-yi!' he yelled, and the strange quavering notes of the chanters echoed the spirit of the dance."[42]

The combination of cultural performance and art exhibition and sale developed into a pattern. Jacobson arranged for the Kiowas to dance in many cities and towns in Oklahoma and beyond, and the Kiowas came to rely on him for advice relating to contracts and conditions. But, in contrast to the art education, Jacobson did not have aesthetic control over their dancing. The addition of other Kiowas in the dance performances, such as a flute player and women dancers, shows that the repertoire relied on the Kiowas' own contacts on the reservation and experience in organizing such programs. Initially, at least, Jacobson showed little understanding of the multilayered meanings of dance for his Kiowa students. He appreciated the dancing as "magnificent performances and an art expression of a high order," but appears to have believed that in the present they were "given but as an artistic spectacle only."[43] He seems to have learned as his connection with American Indian artists deepened over the years, but it was the Kiowa artists themselves who fashioned and developed the important link between painting and dancing.

EXPANDING THE MEANING OF FINE ART

Much of what occurred in Norman appears to have followed general trends in the 1920s and 1930s. The Indian Arts and Crafts Board encouraged the production of arts and crafts as a viable source of income for Indians on reservations, and since the 1890s Wild West shows and fairs had offered Indian dancing as entertainment for white audiences. What was innovative was Jacobson's effort to introduce the art of the Kiowa students into the mainstream of art galleries and exhibitions in the country and beyond. He and his wife both insisted that American Indian art contributed significantly and fundamentally to the aesthetic life of the nation. In this they built on the emerging wave of interest in Indigenous art, championed by prominent artists and patrons in the Southwest, such as Marsden Hartley and John Sloan who began exhibiting Pueblo painters and Amelia Elizabeth White who opened the first gallery devoted to Indian art in New York City in 1922.[44]

From the outset of Jacobson's tenure in Norman, he strove to build structures and networks that would allow Oklahomans access to quality artwork. He struggled with inadequate funding from the university and traveled tirelessly to promote the new department of art and to lay a foundation for an art museum. He based the curriculum of the new art program on that of Yale and emphasized art history. With the nearest public museum in St. Louis, five hundred miles from Norman, he argued for the necessity to collect art for the department so that students could come in direct contact with paintings and sculptures. He was engaged in various clubs devoted to the promotion of arts and culture and, in 1916, was instrumental in forming the Association of Oklahoma Artists. This association became an important venue for Oklahoma art students to display their work. In 1916 the art department at OU achieved recognition as fulfilling national standards. This coincided with a personal achievement for Jacobson as he received an honorary degree from the School of Fine Arts at Yale University. He gained confidence and recognition as both a teacher and an artist. In 1916 a journalist described his approach as "Jacobsonism," and in the following years he exhibited widely across the Southwest and Midwest together with a group of western artists associated with Birger Sandzén. In an impassioned plea for the opportunities in the American West, Jacobson managed to get the American Federation of Art to begin sending out traveling exhibits to the schools in the Southwest, and he organized a regular tour of exhibitions across Oklahoma, New Mexico, and Arizona. In the article "East and West," printed in the *American Magazine of Art* in 1924, he outlined a program for the improvement of conditions for art in the West and ended with his conviction concerning the value for the nation as a whole. The western artist, he wrote, may lack "the polish and refinement of the metropolitan painter," but instead "he shows a youthful and rugged strength that is wonderful. Lacking the companionship and association of art to be found in the large cities he finds his whole inspiration in that wonderland of America so little known or understood—those great silent plains and deserts of the southwest."[45]

Jacobson's description of the rugged strength and direct physical inspiration from the natural environment is reminiscent of his earlier characterization of the merits of Swedish nature painting. This points to the significance of his training and contacts in Lindsborg and through the networks of Swedish American artists in developing his program for art in Oklahoma. Immediately upon arrival in Norman, Jacobson began to build along the lines he had discussed with Sandzén, and already in January of 1916 he had organized what was to become an annual exhibition, at which Sandzén's painting *Mountains and Plains* won a medal. Letters from Birger Sandzén reveal how Jacobson's old teacher consistently advised him, and although Jacobson's replies do not remain, Sandzén's letters suggest a vigorous exchange between the two on how best to proceed in establishing the OU department as an art institution in its own right in the West. Building a collection of one's own rather than relying on loan exhibitions was an essential ingredient in this strategy. Sandzén wrote, "I believe your good president would be willing to let you purchase a couple of good paintings, at reduced prices of course, for your university. It would be for 'educational purposes,' of course. Many institutions do that now instead of spending the money on exhibitions." Jacobson began building a collection that would eventually form the basis for the Fred Jones Jr. Museum of Art, and he encouraged art students when they finished their degree to donate an artwork of which they were particularly proud to the university's art collection, which "proved to be a marvelous incentive as all strove to leave behind something they never would be ashamed of."[46]

In 1924 Oklahoma University very nearly lost Oscar Jacobson to the Broadmoor Art Academy in Colorado Springs. A unique art colony had been incorporated as an academy in 1919 and operated through the Second World War. Under the mentorship of illustrious American painters such as Grant Wood, John Steuart Curry, and Thomas Hart Benton, the academy's instructors strove to establish an essential American art. Several Swedish American artists were involved in the academy's work, and again, it was Birger Sandzén who lay behind the invitation to Jacobson to become the academy's new director that summer. Jacobson received an offer to continue as director and seriously considered staying on, but eventually he decided that he missed the contact with students and "the common search for esthetic and intellectual aims." There was also a concern that the directorship, although it paid much better than the university post, would make it difficult for him to continue his own painting. Before going back to Norman, he and Sandzén spent the summer together enjoying each other's company and showing their work in a joint exhibition at the Broadmoor Art Academy.[47]

From the very beginning of the Kiowas' sojourn in Norman, Jacobson strove to exhibit their work, often in conjunction with cultural performances. An article in the *Norman Transcript* from November 1928 carried an already impressive listing of the exhibitions where the Kiowas' work had been shown: San Francisco, Houston, Memphis, Kansas City, Missouri, Denver, the University of Kansas, the University of Missouri, Hartford, Connecticut, the University of Minnesota, New York City, Manhattan, Kansas, and Joplin, Missouri, and even European cities such as Paris and Prague. "Four Oklahoma Indians of the Kiowa Nation seem likely to outdo in the art of painting their white colleagues," proclaimed the *Kansas City Star* in April 1929. The article continued to prophesy international acclaim: "Wait until the modern Italians, the Russians, see their flat greens, their blues, reds, yellows, their use of the dancing, leaping figure in design. Why study, when an untaught American Indian can excel in the decorative field now most sedulously cultivated by modern artists?"[48]

Newspaper reviews record a vibrant debate about the nature and merit of the Kiowa artists' paintings. An exhibition at the Minneapolis Institute of Art in March 1929 caused an art critic to describe their work as a result of a peculiarly racial conditioning. "If this were the ordinary exhibition, the conscientious critic would begin by making comparisons between contributing artists. . . . But you will look long before you are able to distinguish a picture by Asah from one by Mopope, or a war dance by Tsa-Toke from a similar subject by Hokeah." But the Kansas City critic took exception to this and suggested that the refreshing directness, harmonious colors, and sinuous patterns of the Kiowa paintings offered "a new sensation, and, if we read the times aright, that is what most of the world is looking for."[49]

D'Ucel's description of the individual styles of the Kiowa artists certainly fed into this debate and demonstrates how the Jacobsons participated in reconfiguring American Indian aesthetic production as fine arts rather than primitive and exotic objects. Naming and identifying individual artists formed a central part of this endeavor. Jacobson began taking the Kiowas' paintings with him wherever he went for exhibitions. "Leaving for New York to attend an American Federation of Art Convention, he put a few Kiowa watercolors in his suitcase and said to me 'I'll see what they think of them.' I heard later, from other delegates that 'they' (the whole convention) found themselves spontaneously in his room to see the works he brought." He was subsequently encouraged to submit their work to the American art exhibit at the First International Education Association Convention, which was to be held in Prague in 1928. Jacobson selected paintings from his own collection, as it was summer and there was no time to contact the artists who were all back on the reservation. The showing of the paintings in Prague turned out to be hugely successful. Much later, D'Ucel encountered a woman who had visited the convention in Prague. "For three days, she told me, she could not get near the Kiowa room, so packed was it with onlookers." President Tomas Masaryk wrote to Jacobson to inquire whether it could indeed be true that American Indians "had painted these extraordinarily beautiful things."[50]

Less than two years after their arrival in Norman as special students, the Kiowa artists had international audiences thronging to view their work. It was indeed, as d'Ucel expressed it, "an international sensation." Building on this, the Jacobsons, who were fully aware of the contemporary trend of modern abstract painting and the attraction to the primitive, decided to seek to publish representations of the Kiowa paintings. A French publisher, C. Szwedzicki, contacted them and arranged for the publication of their work, and in 1929 a limited edition of *Kiowa Indian Art* appeared. The volume contained pochoir reproductions of thirty paintings. The pochoir print is an intricate and highly labor-intensive technique for reproducing images. The process involves stencils, one for each color in a painting, and it results in a remarkable print, which is quite similar to the original. "Scholars sometimes mistakenly think of the *Kiowa Indian Art* portfolio simply as the means for introducing the world to this artistic experiment," writes art scholar Janet Catherine Berlo. "But it was, in fact, the result of an intense interest worldwide in new American Indian paintings." The paintings of the Kiowa artists and their Pueblo counterparts tapped into the swell of attraction to what was so often described as "primitivism" in art, at the same time as it aligned with modernist Art Deco and its emphasis on flat, decorative patterns and strong color palettes.[51]

Jacobson's introduction to the volume combined a recitation of racially loaded anthropological terminology to describe the Indians, with an earnest insistence on their cultural survival and their rightful place in modern life. The Kiowas he described as one "of the fiercest and most independent of the western Indian tribes that harassed the ever closing frontier during the latter half of the nineteenth century," of "unusual virility" who despite "gradually adopting white ways" have "been able to retain their tribal characteristics and their identity." This tension shapes his text and produces the categories of traditional and modern as opposites. "They live in houses, they drive cars, they buy modern farm machinery," he wrote, "but the women still dress their hair in braids and wear the bright colored shawls of tradition," suggesting also that the binary had a gendered dimension. It is anachronistic to expect Jacobson to have freed himself from such stereotypic characterizations of Indians. But what is of interest is how he framed an eloquent argument for the value of Indians' aesthetic production as art—"the work of these pure blooded Kiowas will stand as a real contribution to art." This realization, I suggest, was as much a result of the Kiowa artists' insistence on painting culture with "a knowledge of the human body and how to draw it in action"—drawn from experience and from earlier Kiowa forms of depiction—as it was of his own effort to direct and influence their production.[52]

In the summer of 1930 the Jacobsons, on their way west, stopped in Santa Fe and were invited to dinner at the house of the White sisters, Amelia and Martha, who were both deeply interested in Pueblo art. They had heard of Oscar's work with the Kiowa artists and honored him with a dinner to which they also invited Jesse Nusbaum, Kenneth Chapman, and others with an interest in promoting Indian art. During the dinner, the party sketched out the idea for a National Exposition of Indian Arts and Crafts. The group asked Jacobson to chair the committee, but he had to refrain due to ill health. He involved himself in the committee as a member and worked to supply a sizable and impressive representation from Oklahoma, including not only paintings but also "first class examples of Bead work." The exposition took place in New York City in November 1931 with the aim of winning "the aesthetic appraisal of Indian art so long due," and "through awakened public appreciation and an enlarged market to encourage the Indians to continue to create and develop their art."[53] Jacobson had truly become acknowledged for his work with American Indian artists.

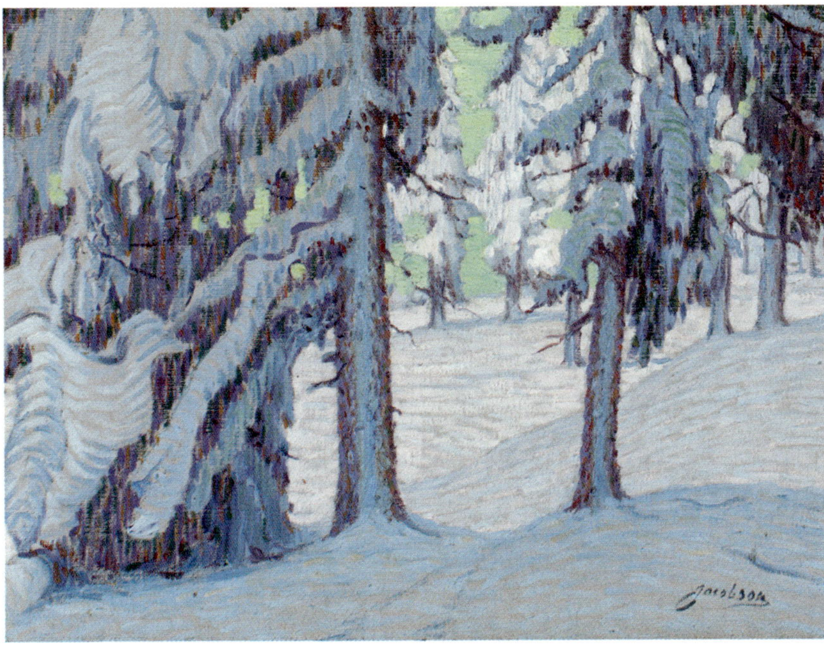

PLATE 1. Oscar B. Jacobson, *Winter Forest in Sweden*, ca. 1914. Oil on canvas 18 × 24 in. The light on the snow and the absence of human imprints on the landscape brings to mind the paintings of Bruno Liljefors (1860–1939) who is best known for painting nature and animals. Courtesy Fred Jones Jr. Museum of Art, Norman; Gift of Hal Johnson, 1983.

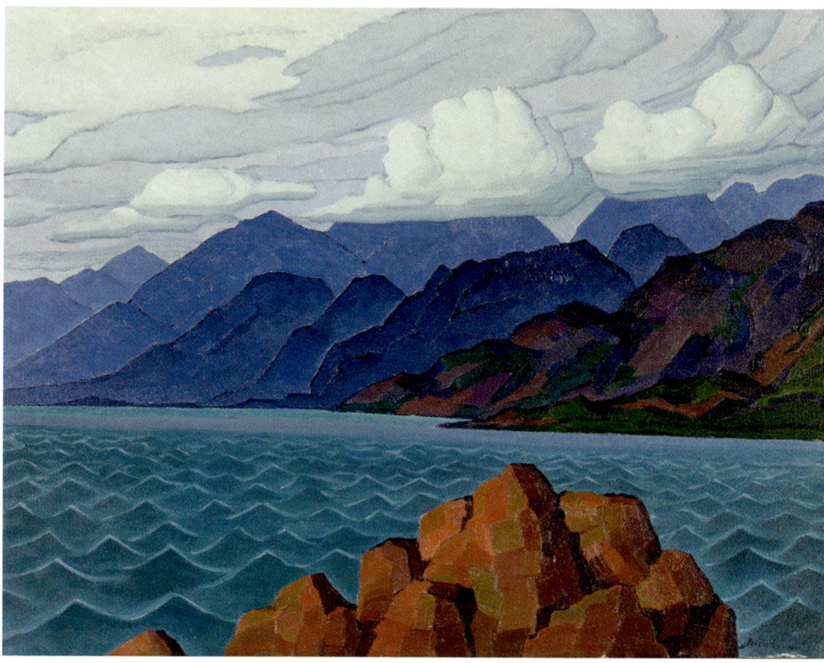

PLATE 2. Oscar B. Jacobson, *Djedjelli, Algeria,* 1926. Jacobson deemed this painting to be one of his best, and he exhibited it more than any other of his early paintings. Photo by Phil Shockley. Courtesy of Oklahoma State University Museum of Art, Stillwater, Oklahoma.

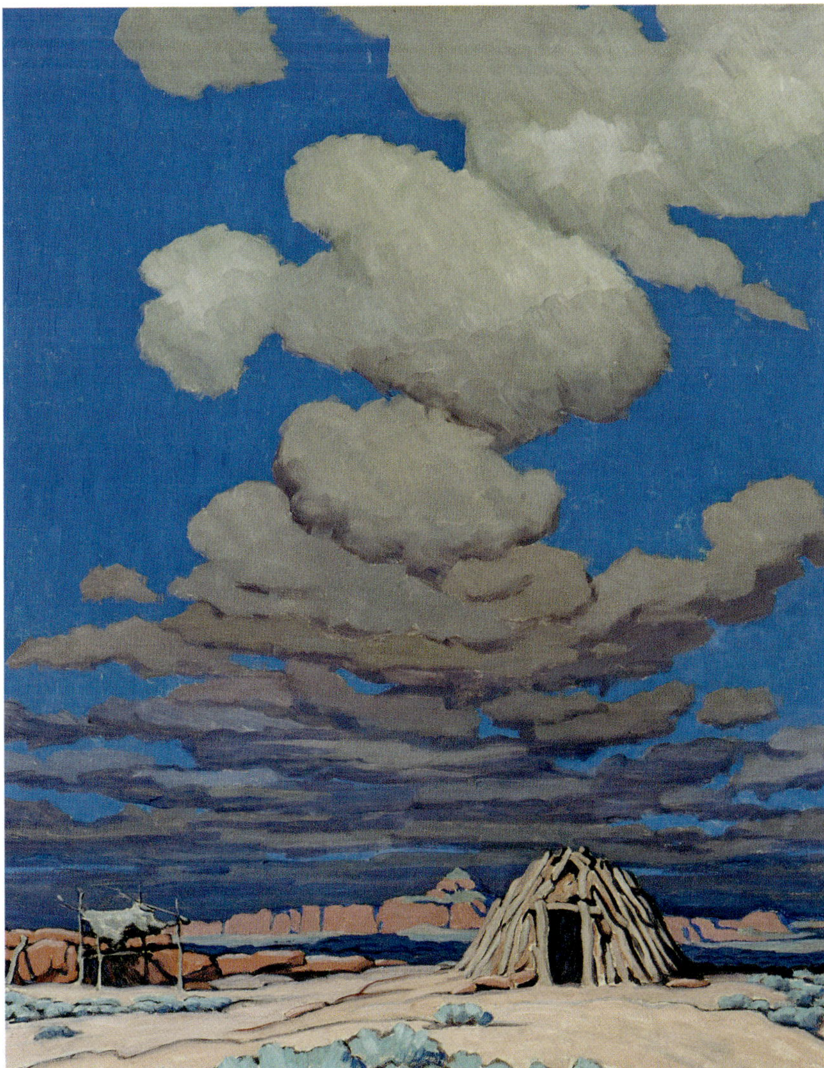

PLATE 3. Oscar B. Jacobson, *White Shadows—Among the Navajos,* 1922. Although the Navajos were not threatened by the 1922 Bursum Bill, Jeanne d'Ucel emphasized that Jacobson's meaning should be understood both figuratively and literally as the threat of "white knavery." From the Collection of Gilcrease Museum, Tulsa, Oklahoma.

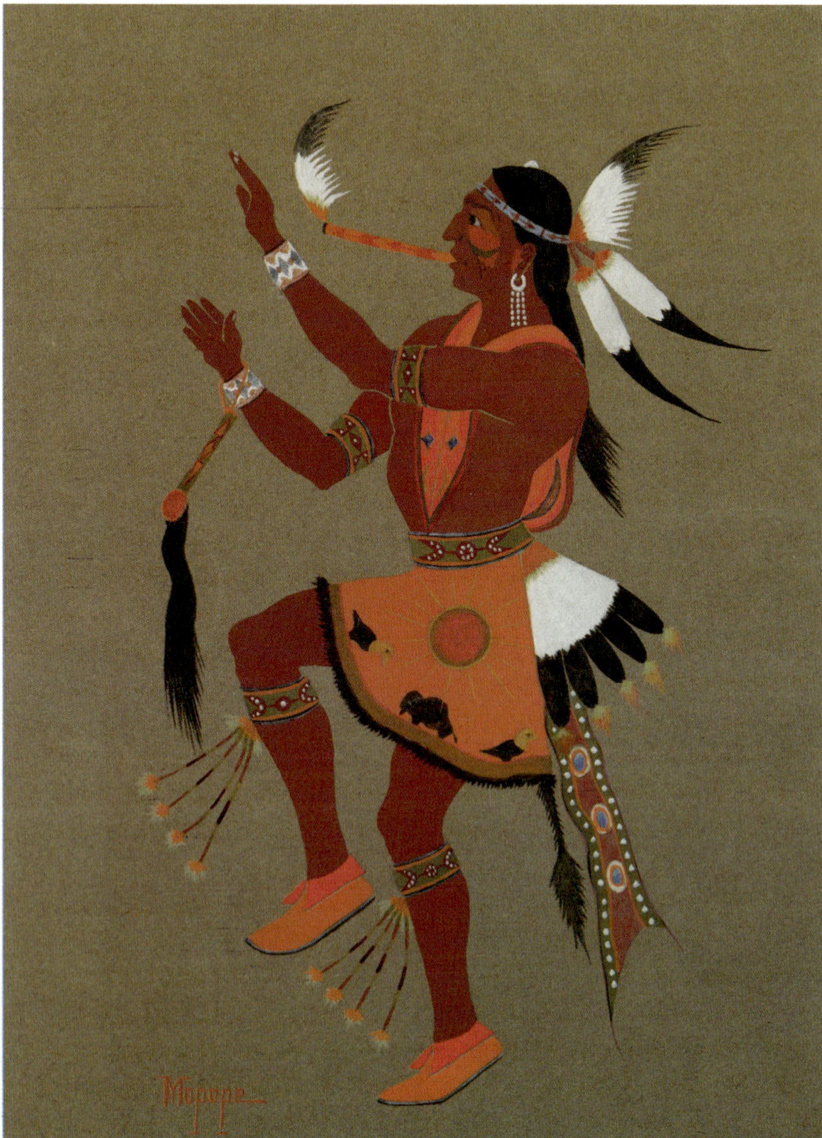

PLATE 4. Stephen Mopope, *Kiowa Sun Dance*, n.d. Tempera 11¾ × 9 in. Mopope liked to paint with the color orange. The painting is an outstanding example of the flat style of Indian painting that Jacobson encouraged. Courtesy Fred Jones Jr. Museum of Art, The University of Oklahoma, Norman; Museum Purchase, 1936.

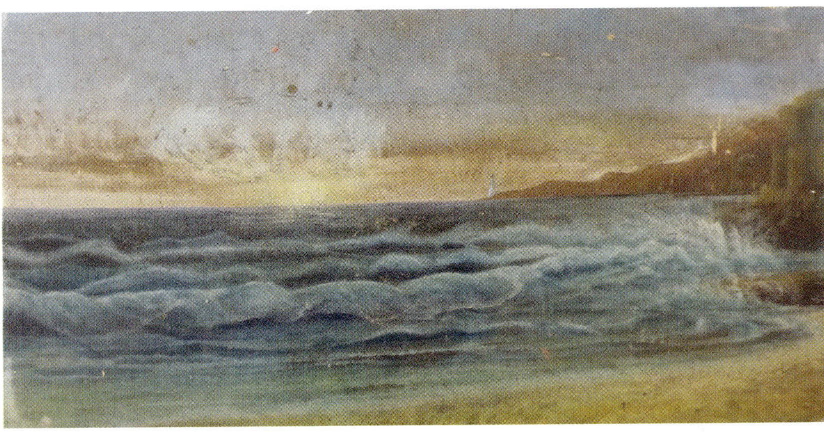

PLATE 5. One of four remaining oil paintings by Stephen Mopope. The date is unknown but may have been during the time he was painting with Willie Baze Lane. However, the shape and movement of the waves are suggestive of Jacobson's style of painting in Djedjelli (see plate 2). This ocean scene suggests that Mopope experimented with shapes and strokes to create an image of moving water. Two of the other scenes depict mountain and forest landscapes; the fourth shows one of the pueblos in New Mexico where Mopope had visited on several occasions as a dancer. Courtesy Vanessa Paukeigope Jennings. Photo by author.

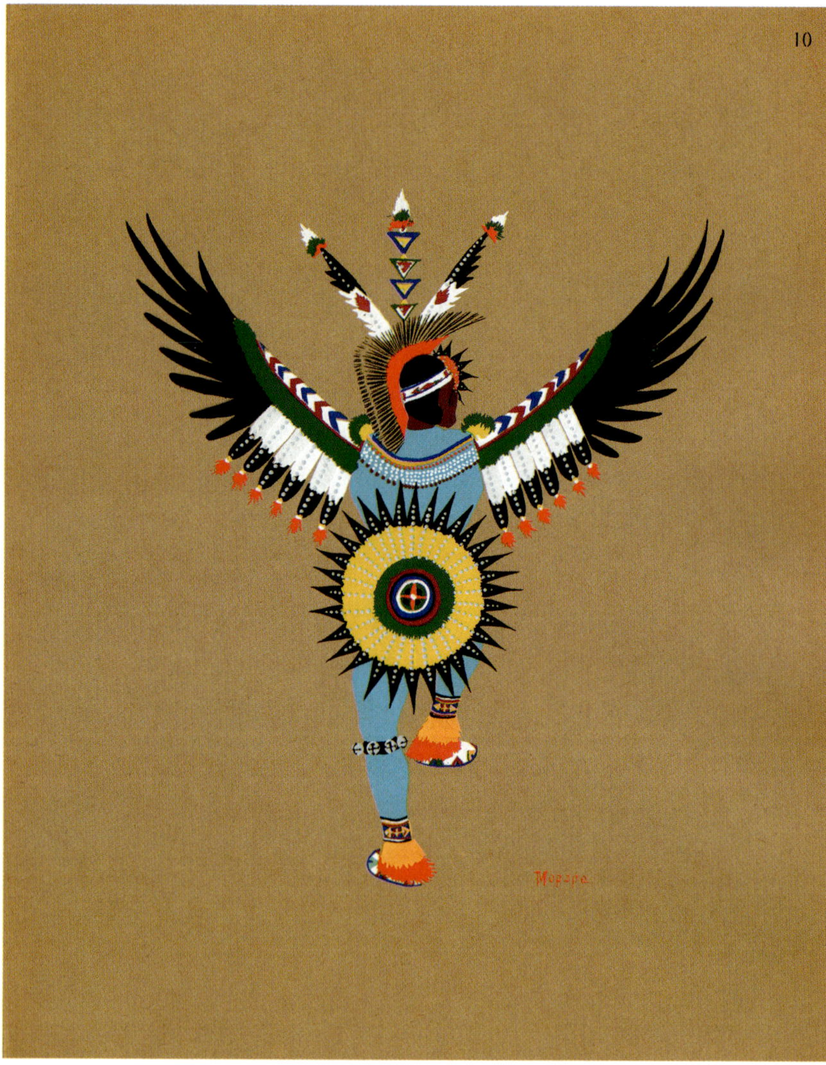

PLATE 6. Stephen Mopope, *Eagle Dance* (from the *Kiowa Indian Art Portfolio*), 1929. Pochoir (screenprint) 15 × 11½ in. According to James Auchiah, Mopope was influenced by northern tribes in how he performed the Eagle Dance. The painting shows a dancer with elements from Crow and Southern Cheyenne regalia. Courtesy Fred Jones Jr. Museum of Art, The University of Oklahoma, Norman; Gift of Elaine Bizzell Thompson, 1998.

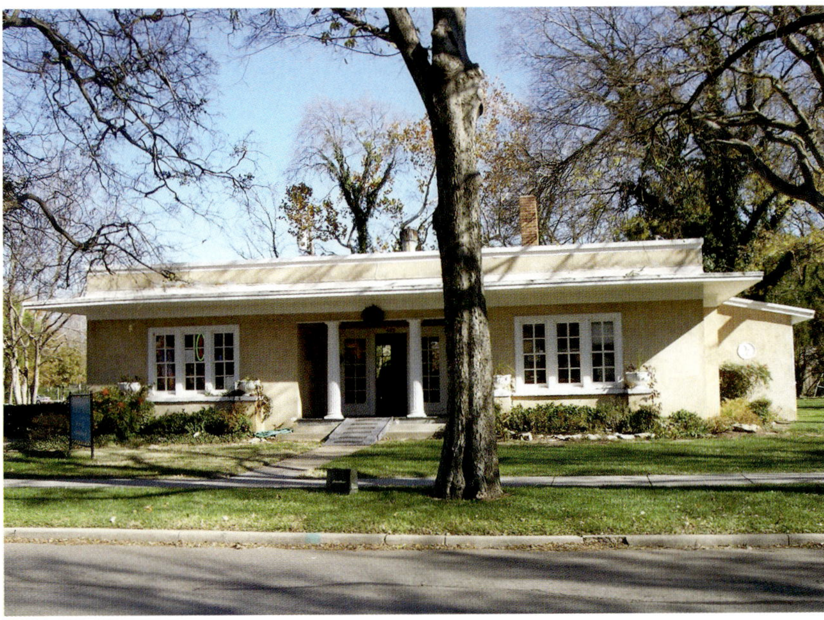

PLATE 7. The Jacobsons' house on 609 Chautauqua in Norman. The couple designed the house to represent Scandinavian and French architectural styles, and it stood ready in 1918. It is now the location of a cultural center, the Jacobson House Native Art Center. Photo by author.

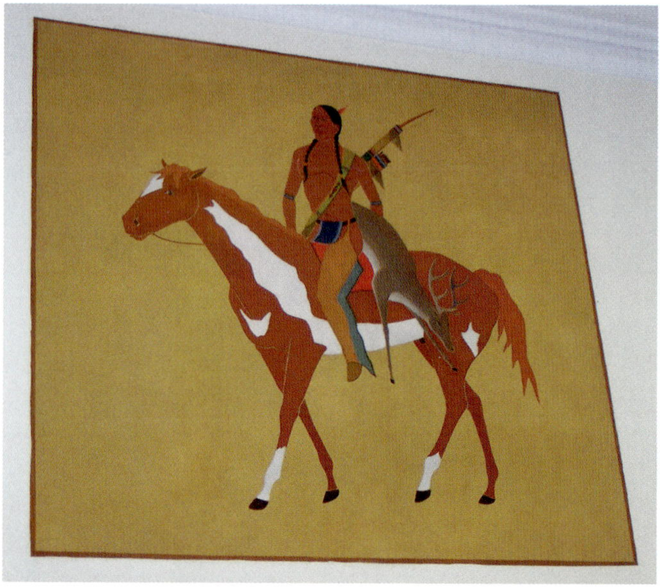

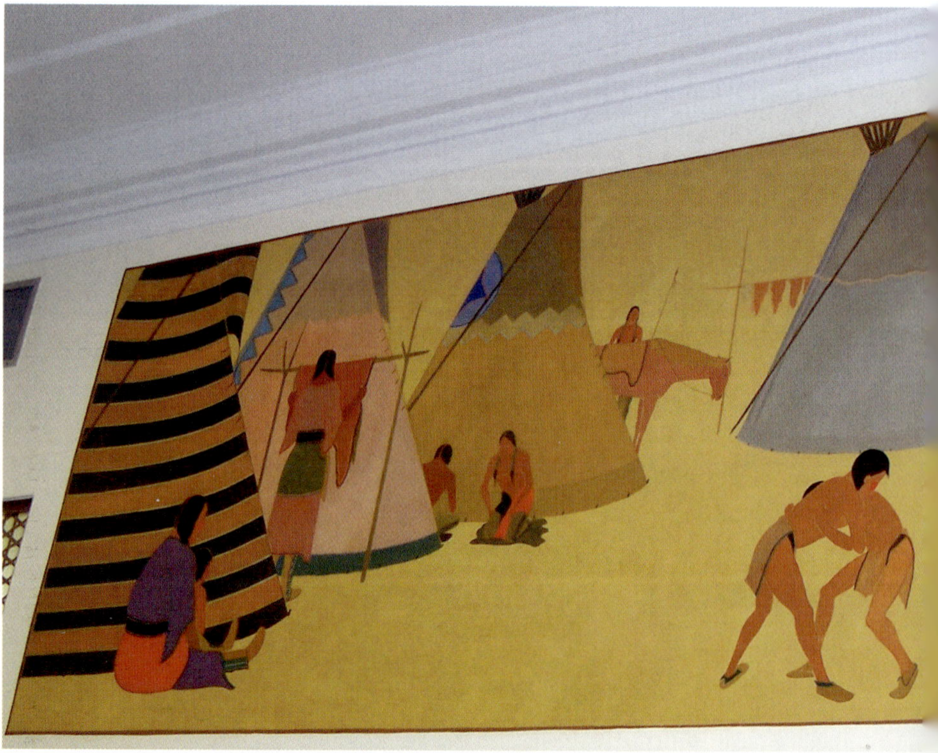

PLATE 8. Stephen Mopope, *Hunter on Horse with Slain Deer.* Figure 14 shows Mopope working on this image. Mural at the US Post Office in Anadarko, 1937. Used with the permission of the United States Postal Service®. All rights reserved. Photo by author.

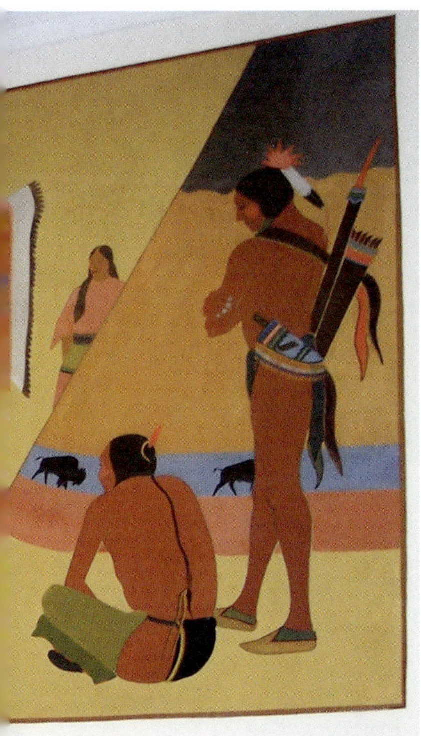

PLATE 9. Stephen Mopope, *Village Scene,* mural at the US Post Office in Anadarko, 1937. This is a village scene with women hanging meat to dry on racks. Kiowa women watching Mopope paint informed him that no one would have hung meat so close to the camp, but he argued for poetic license in his portrayal of the scene. Used with the permission of the United States Postal Service®. All rights reserved. Photo by author.

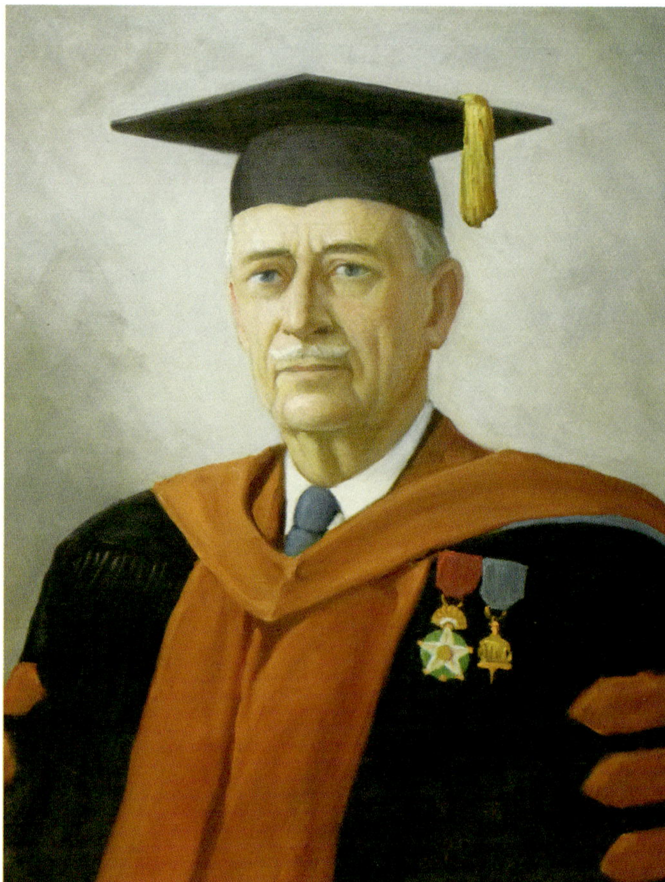

PLATE 10. Oscar Jacobson, *Self-Portrait,* 1954. Courtesy of the Sandzén Archives, Birger Sandzén Memorial Gallery.

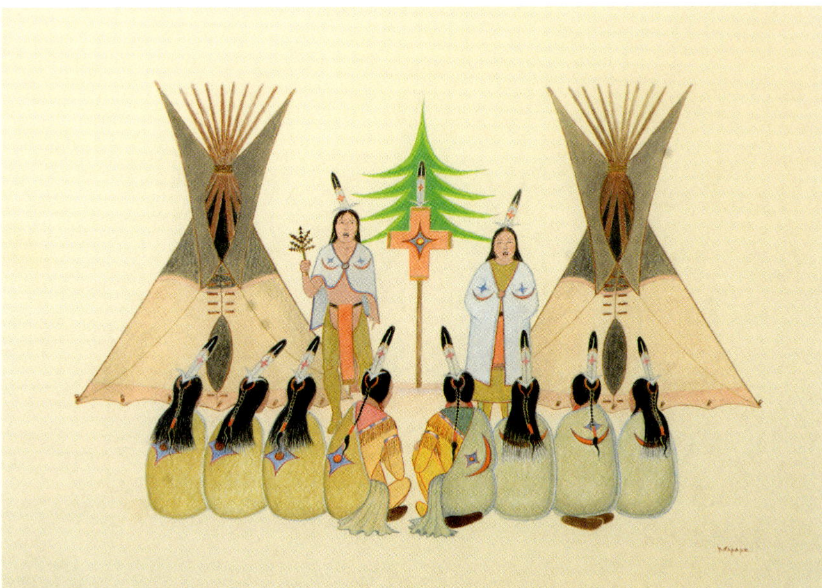

PLATE 11. Stephen Mopope, *Ghost Dance*, n.d. The Feather Dance held special meaning for the Kiowas, and Mopope often included the symbol of the morning star in his paintings. The painting shows Kiowas gathered for the ceremony with the sacred cedar tree in the middle of the dance ground. 68.28.191. Photo courtesy of the US Department of the Interior, Indian Arts and Crafts Board.

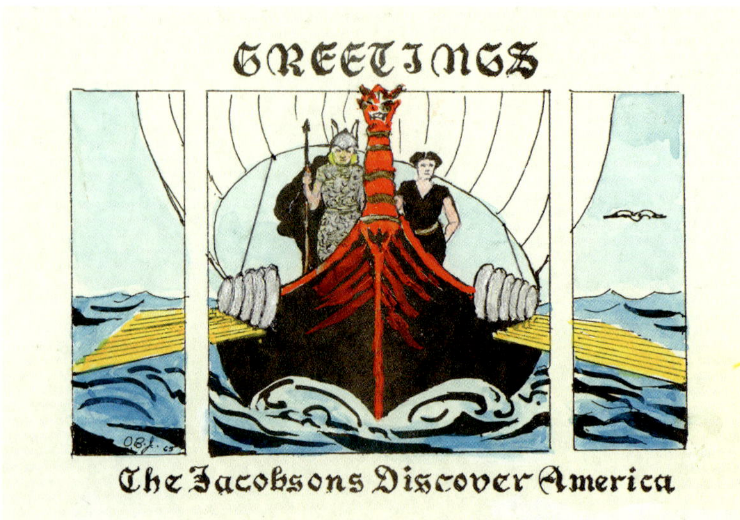

PLATE 12. *The Jacobsons Discover America.* Greeting card made by Jacobson featuring Oscar and Jeanne at the helm of a Viking ship sailing toward America. The couple used the image as their personal bookplate. Vol. 8, Box 7, Scrapbooks, OJC. Courtesy Oklahoma Historical Society.

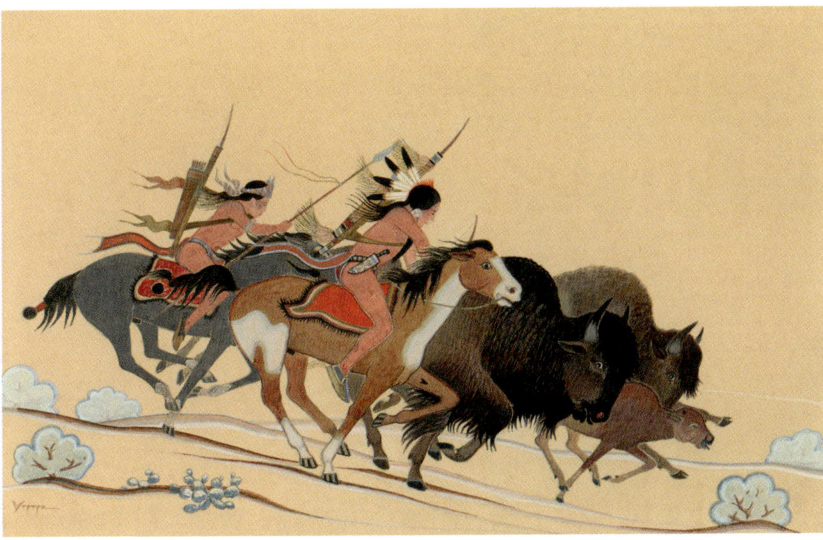

PLATE 13. Stephen Mopope, *Buffalo Hunt*, ca. 1930–40. Watercolor 15 × 22½ in. Mopope expressed a wish to have been born earlier so that he could have taken part in the buffalo chase. He often featured hunters and bison in his pictures. Courtesy Fred Jones Jr. Museum of Art, The University of Oklahoma, Norman; Purchase, Richard H. and Adeline J. Fleischaker Collection, 1996.

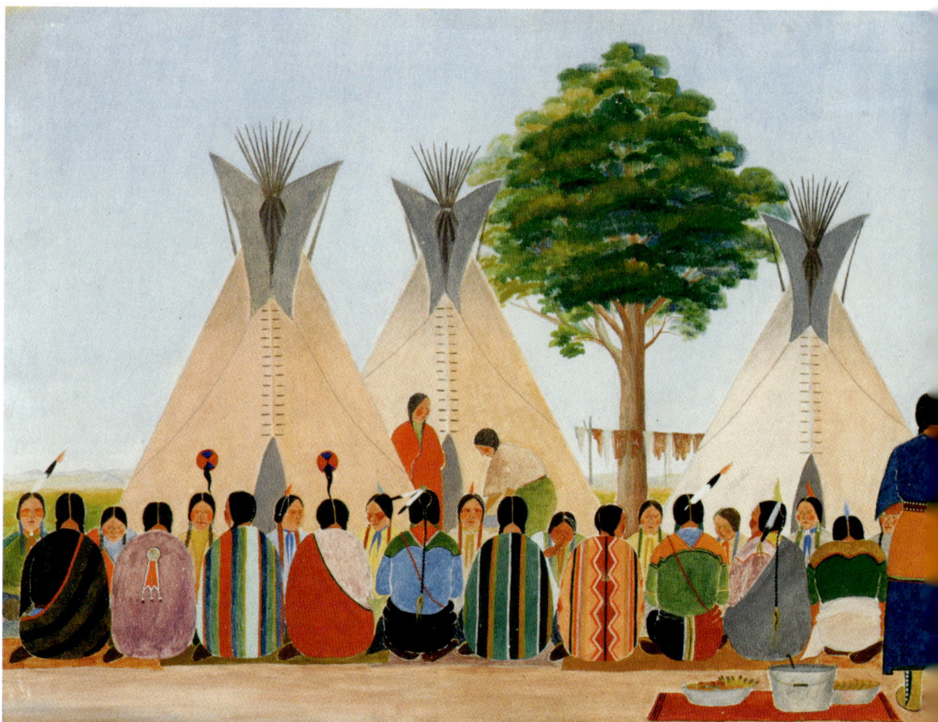

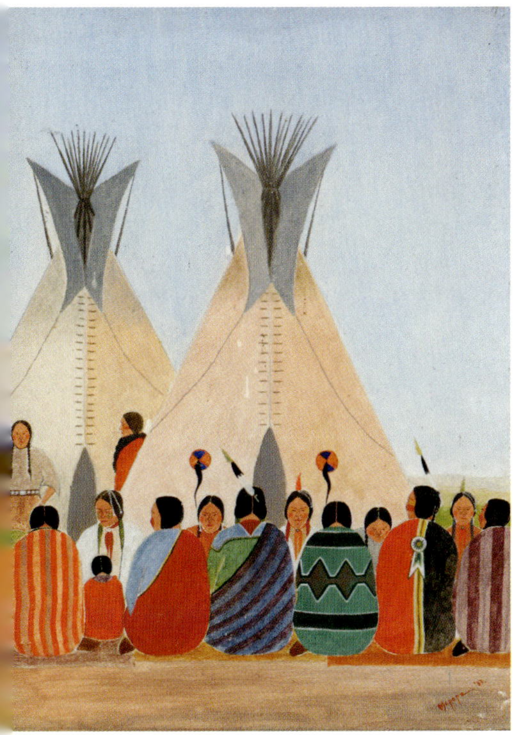

PLATE 14. Stephen Mopope, *Indian Gathering*, 1933. Mopope frequently painted people from the back. The painting differs from the usual flat style, and in this scene there is the outline of hills in the far back, and a cedar tree towering over the tipis. The woman in the foreground, wearing elaborately beaded moccasins, is waiting to serve food from tinned pots and a pail with soup. From the Collection of Gilcrease Museum, Tulsa, Oklahoma.

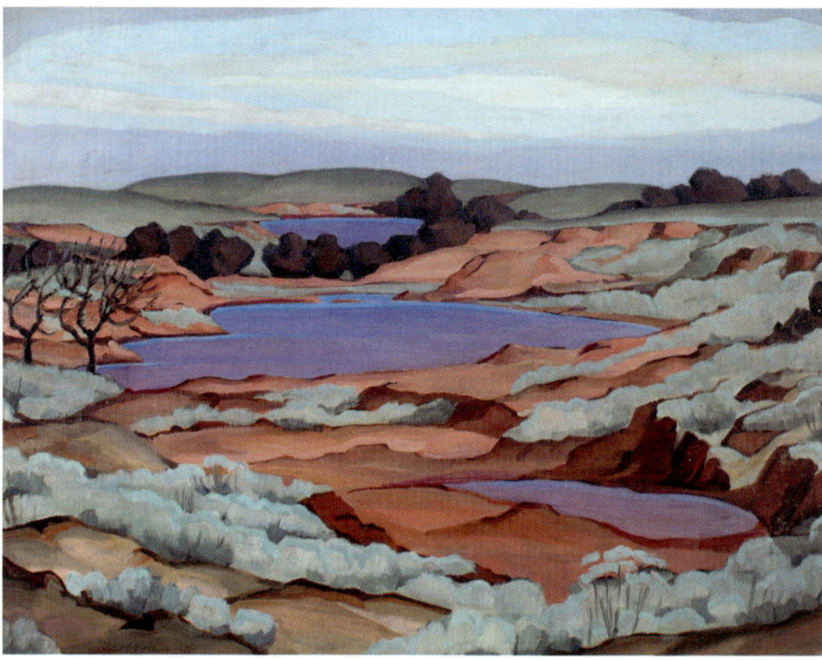

PLATE 15. Oscar B. Jacobson, *Oklahoma Mosaic*, 1936. Jacobson painted several pictures from the area around the resort town of Medicine Lodge near the Wichita Mountains. Donation, Leonard Good, September 1999. University of Oklahoma Libraries, University of Oklahoma.

CHAPTER 5

Negotiating Conflicting Cultures

THE ARGUMENT HAS BEEN MADE that reformulating Indigenous cultural objects from "artefacts" to be placed in museums to "art" to be appreciated for its aesthetic qualities formed part of a settler colonial project of political nationalism. This process, argues Ana Filipa Vrdoljak, "had a two-fold purpose: first, aiding the establishment of a unique national cultural identity; and second, enabling this national narrative to have its beginning in the 'timeless' past." In the United States this had a third consequence as it "elevated its commodity-value and suppressed historic-political implications of its possession by the dominant culture."[1] While such an analysis rightly exposes overall structures of domination and ideology, it fails to account for the ambiguities and complexity of the day-to-day negotiations surrounding these larger policies. Nor does it account for the struggles and oppositions emerging around this reevaluation of Indigenous American arts and crafts or for the investment American Indians made in it.

Jacobson's work with the Kiowa students was not done without opposition. Even on their own campus, d'Ucel writes, "there were people who thought he was foolishly wasting his time working with Indians." Jacobson may also have stretched the limits of what the university allowed when he accepted to oversee the tutelage of the Kiowa artists. In his introduction to *Kiowa Indian Art* Jacobson stated that since "none of the original Kiowas had the necessary entrance requirements for University study, they were given instruction rather informally, or, shall we say, 'illegally.'" He was adamant that at "no time did they attend the art classes." It may have appealed to Jacobson's rebellious nature to do something outside convention, but there is likely more to it than that. One interpretation of this is that he wished to racially segregate the students in order to preserve their "Indianness." However, as James Auchiah clearly asserted, the Kiowas participated in events together with other art students, such as lectures and even specific tutorials, and they painted together with other watercolor students because watercolor painting required a special kind of light. In addition, two art instructors circulated in the room and tutored the students. Stressing in print the informal nature of tutoring may have been a necessary strategy to circumvent regulations regarding both the eligibility of the Kiowas for university study and racial segregation.[2]

Joe Taylor, who joined the art department in 1932, remembered that Jacobson had encountered some complications with the university administration in "getting permission to simply enroll them and let them paint, without having them in highly structured classroom situation," which was the common procedure. Taylor also recalled Jacobson commenting on the success of *Kiowa Indian Art*: "That is typical, he said. These boys have won fame in France. Eventually they'll be recognized at home." This comment reflects, perhaps, the frustration that d'Ucel alluded to, that not all his colleagues at the university appreciated the Kiowa artists' presence. It is also not inconceivable that Jacobson encountered a fair amount of jealousy for the attention earned by his work with the Kiowas. In 1938 Edna Nyquist described Jacobson's work at University of Oklahoma: "A big man came to a little department, and because he stayed the department had to become big." Artworks decorated campus and murals adorned local hangouts, all in keeping with Jacobson's efforts to put "art in public places where the eyes of the people would become accustomed to it without their realizing what was happening." The work with Indian artists followed in the same direction, and it was "only incidental, that is, it is only part of his work that has developed naturally with the rest."[3]

Jacobson ran into considerable difficulties in the mundane tasks of organizing trips and collecting artworks for exhibitions. The Kiowas were not at liberty to move about freely. As the superintendent of the agency told him in January 1934, "you are advised that these men are restricted Indians and, therefore, wards of the Government." In this, the restricted movements of incarcerated Indigenous people contrast most starkly with the peregrinations available for a successful immigrant such as Jacobson. In order for the Kiowas to travel anywhere outside the reservation, they required a letter from the local magistrate proving their identity and asserting their good conduct. Oklahoma Indians had been citizens of the state since its inception in 1907, and under the Dawes Act they were promised US citizenship upon allotment. However, this turned out to be more complicated than envisaged in the late decades of the nineteenth century. Allottees on the large reservations in Oklahoma Territory, later the western half of the state of Oklahoma, were soon surrounded by aggressive settlers who refused to recognize Indian property rights and did not acknowledge them as fellow citizens. The problem, Fred Hoxie points out, "was to devise a means of providing greater federal protection without appearing to retreat from the government's commitment to Indian citizenship." Optimistic assessments of the speed with which Indians would assimilate into American society came to a halt as the new century dawned. Debates regarding the tension between citizenship and treaty obligations enveloped the political and judicial system. The Burke Act of 1906 strengthened federal supervision over all Indians, citizens or not, and came under heavy fire from both eastern reform groups such as the Indian Rights Association, who questioned the infringement of Indian citizenship rights, and westerners, who wished to do away with Indians' special protection. By 1916, the Supreme Court decision in *U.S. v. Nice* established that guardianship was not incompatible with citizenship and therefore the federal government's responsibility to protect Indians extended beyond franchise. This understanding, however, was no longer based on recognition of treaty obligations but on a perception of Indians' lack of "civilization" and their "backwardness." Indians were deemed racially inferior, and as such, in need of both guardianship and protection. This also meant that they fell under such restrictive state legislation as Oklahoma's notorious grandfather clause, which prohibited them from voting. Despite the congressional decision in 1924 to grant citizenship to all American Indians, their status as wards continued.[4]

Different systems of power thus structured the movements and constraints of white and Indigenous men. Jacobson took on the role as the Kiowas' guardian when they were away from the reservation. This came with obligations and unexpected duties. His thoughts about this are not known, but his wife's writings suggest that they were not immune to the prejudice of their time in relations with American Indians. One obligation arose from the financial setup of the Kiowas' studies in Norman. As mentioned above, Jacobson expected them to produce from five to six paintings a week (a rather exacting pensum), which were then sold to cover their expenses. This left the artist with an income of between fifty and sixty dollars per week from paintings bought by Jacobson and his friends. This equaled between six hundred and eight hundred dollars in 2014 value, measured as the "historic standard of living," and would have amounted to a sizable income. From this they had to pay for room and board and materials as well as contribute to the support of families back on the reservation. Jeanne D'Ucel describes the development of a special occupation of account-keeping emerging out of this financial arrangement, and she did so in language revealing the racial prejudice of her time. "This was absolutely necessary; they were as casual about money as true Indians are. They were always broke and they would borrow against future paintings. So the books dad kept were rather complicated. Often he had to gently persuade them against useless and unnecessary purchases, in which he knew or suspected they were egged on by interested parties. Sometimes, he had to prod them to produce the work for which they had already been paid, and had long since spent the money."[5] D'Ucel's evaluation of how American Indians related to money echoed what many of her contemporaries in the Indian Service believed, and in her concurrent world this amounted to difficulties. Kiowas likely viewed it differently as they had to abide by a Kiowa logic of honor in an economy of great austerity.[6]

Newspaper articles consistently exaggerated the youth of the Kiowas, presenting them as younger than they were. Furthermore, articles suggested that teachers and matrons had discovered their talents while teaching on the reservation and then made contact with the university, thus downplaying the agency and aspirations of the Kiowas themselves. The May issue of *My Oklahoma* wrote in 1927 that Mopope was twenty-two years old, and in August the magazine described him as "the Kiowa Indian boy who painted the design for the art cover."[7] By that time, he was already close to thirty years old. Asah, Tsatoke, and Hokeah were between twenty and twenty-two, but this means they had still been out of school for several years. They were experienced dancers (all but Tsatoke who instead focused on drumming and singing) and had performed before white audiences in many places beyond the reservation. The consistent use of "boys" to refer to these artists (and the almost ubiquitous ignoring of Lois Smoky's presence) signaled more than simple misconceptions concerning their ages. The loaded meaning of the term "boy" to describe men cannot be overstated in the American South in the 1920s, despite its frequent usage by both Kiowas and whites. Most commonly the term applied to black men, but in Oklahoma with a large population of Indigenous peoples, the term specifically marked them as racialized others. "Boy" also meant an infantilization of the Indians that defused any mature challenge they may have posed to American society. A 1937 article in the *Oklahoma News* described the artists as "depicting the life of the wandering Kiowas before the arrival of palefaces in prairie schooners. Half-forgotten legends, once whispered by aged chieftains around campfires and in tee-pees, are being preserved by the three youths for those who've never heard the weird throb of the tom-tom." Again and again the article refers to them as "youths," "schoolboys," and "shy." But in 1937, Mopope was nearing forty, and Auchiah, Asah, and Hokeah were all well into their thirties.[8]

While "the boys" mostly aroused curiosity in the academic community in Norman and entertained audiences across the state, they also regularly met with more sinister forms of the power inherent in racial categorization. By the 1920s American Indians appeared less of a threat to white America than in previous decades. "In the minds of many white Oklahomans, Native Americans had become picturesque reminders of a frontier past, not a real threat to white power," writes the historian David Chang. Nonetheless, class and race stratified and separated people in the local area around Anadarko, and white racist activity targeted Indigenous people well into the middle of the twentieth century, even though, as Chang finds, "Whites in Oklahoma shifted the unenviable role as foil to whiteness from Native people to African Americans." Jennings recalls the fear people had of the Ku Klux Klan. "And the KKK was here and they had it in their heads that these boys that were going and had been educated on their money, they saw the government as spending their money, they did not approve at these boys coming back and falling back into prayer meetings and things . . . there were actually signs that they would nail up 'We the Ku Klux Klan have our eye on you.'" Scholars have argued that by the 1930s the Klan had weakened considerably in Oklahoma, but in rural towns such as Apache and Anadarko, the fear of their threats still permeated American Indian communities.[9]

The Kiowas were wards of the government, and the reservation government officials handed out checks on a weekly basis, checks coming out of the Kiowas' own property. This did not end with citizenship, and Jennings describes the procedure from her own childhood in the 1960s: "I remember those long oak benches, I remember how long we sat on them, and you know we'd go there on Wednesday and then we'd go back on Friday, and then I remember it was fun . . . my Grandmother was scared of the elevator so we'd always use the stairs so you'd go down it seemed like a dark pit . . . then there's the last door on the left, it's kind of like a half-way open so you could never see in but you could hear their voices, and my Grandma standing there identifying herself, getting her, either her government check or her purchase order." When the artists came to Norman, Jacobson essentially took over the role as their guardian and as manager of their money.[10]

Both Mopope's daughter LaQuinta Mopope and granddaughter Vanessa Jennings recall being told about demeaning treatment and about acts of resistance. Mopope said there were places, mostly in the South, where the Kiowa artists could not go without Jacobson's company. LaQuinta recounted hearing her father relate how "they stopped at some restaurant and they told him to go around by the kitchen and he said I don't need to go back to the kitchen. He said I'll just go somewhere else. He said where is your biggest hotel. So that's where he went. . . . I just don't know why they did that to me. Because see when they were with Mr. Jacobson they went into the same place and they served them all, and then he said when I went to the same place myself and some of these other boys that was with me . . . they told us to go round by the kitchen."[11]

Paradoxically, Philip J. Deloria describes the opening of the twentieth century as a window of opportunity for American Indians. "In the early twentieth century's tête-à-tête with cultural primitivism, Indians could be objects, not simply of racial repulsion, but also—as they reflected nostalgia for community, spirituality, and nature—of racial desire."[12] The interest and engagement that the Kiowa artists' work engendered in the white community certainly opened doors for them and for subsequent generations of American Indian artists, but they remained restricted and supervised both on and off the reservation.

Kiowas also had their own internal opposition to contend with. Mopope's family and in-laws did not appreciate his leaving the reservation and his obligations there in order to pursue art. Bougetah Smoky returned to the reservation after only one semester in Norman to take up responsibilities in her family and concentrate on beadwork. Not only did the Kiowa artists need to learn to negotiate the novel world of the academic town and the expectations on them from tutors and buyers; they also had to take into account the reactions from the community back home on the reservation. James Auchiah's father told him not to paint any sacred emblems or designs. He remembered that the students often took pictures home to show to their parents and get opinions from the old people on accuracy. Paintings that were "too far off" were laid to the side. He experienced criticism in particular from peyote people who did not think it was proper to make drawings that incorporated peyote designs and sell them. However, at some point before 1930, a new group took over the leadership, and this new regime found the paintings acceptable. Auchiah and Mopope often conferred with one another regarding the propriety of their subject matter and the accuracy of emblems and symbols.[13]

One particular area of contention concerned expected gender roles. Tensions played out in the studio as well. Jacobson's comments caused competition among the Kiowas. Some evidence points to a rift between the male artists and the one female, Lois Smoky. She remembered in an interview how once Jacobson praised one of her paintings and Stephen Mopope got jealous. It may be that it was Mopope's burning ambition that caused his displeasure when another of the students received praise, rather than a dislike of Smoky's work. That is at least how Smoky interpreted his reaction: "then Oscar Jacobson come in and look at our paintings and [and] at one time he liked one of my paintings and then I remember Steven got jealous [laughs]. He didn't like me at all. He just wants to [be] the main one that do the fine work." It was also alleged that the men destroyed one of Smoky's paintings because they did not approve of her participation. D'Ucel wrote in her manuscript that the other four mistreated her, as "her taking up this masculine activity had been resented by the companions, causing her unhappiness. They went to the length of damaging her work sometimes, in fits of spite." Smoky herself was unwilling to acknowledge any such destruction, but she did tell Arthur Silberman she felt uncomfortable around the others, Mopope in particular. "He sure act funny you know. . . . That's why I didn't go around on their trips. Sometimes I didn't want to go."[14]

Defending her grandfather, Vanessa Jennings tried to reconstruct the thinking of many Kiowas at the time regarding a young woman doing artistic work in Norman. "You have to remember that there in the Kiowa world is very divided, you know, you go up to this line and this is all woman's territory then you go beyond that and all of that is male territory. You don't cross." She rejected d'Ucel's suggestion that the men demeaned Smoky out of spite. "But in the end you know there is kind of like a feminist view that came out that said that you know they were anti-women anti–Miss Smoky. And I don't know that. . . . I don't know, it's just me . . . it didn't look like she was really interested. So it was easier for her to come home. . . . She continued beading, but not painting." As mentioned above, Smoky did not wish to comment on this, but it is difficult to avoid the conclusion that the flat-style painting of the period was associated with male privilege and that Mopope was active in enforcing this understanding. In her dissertation, Jenny Tone-Pah-Hote clearly identifies gender as an issue in the relationship between the artists but argues that "it was not the only complication." It may well be, she writes, that the others took issue with Smoky participating in a form of painting that challenged what Candace Greene has described as "the rights of representation." Greene notes that Kiowas placed emphasis on family or personal experience as the foundation for the right to depict certain scenes and events. Tone-Pah-Hote suggests that the others "may not have felt that she had the knowledge or experience to depict the kind of warrior and visionary themes that were so prominent in their own pieces." Smoky's departure from Norman and from the group of "Kiowa Five," she argues, "reinforced that painting was men's artistic labor . . . and that men continued to present images of the Kiowa as a tribal nation."[15]

Although this may have been an unforeseen consequence of a strict gender separation, it did not mean that the artists only portrayed men and male activities. In fact, Mopope painted several camp scenes of women and children and ceremonies in which both men and women participated, and he pictured women's creative work. In James Auchiah's recollections, women figure prominently, and he mentions on several occasions that young girls and women were some of the most talented and ardent participants in art classes on the reservation. Emma Keahbone, Lois Smoky, Emma Ware, and Ruby Pedrick took classes from Willie Baze Lane, and Auchiah described Smoky and Ware as outstanding.

Yet it is telling that Emma Ware did not go on to OU. She wished to stay on with Lane and paint in oils, and she also had aged parents who needed her at home. Auchiah also describes the close collaboration between male artists and women performing beadwork in the Mau-Tame (Showing the Way) Club, which Susie Peters organized in 1921. The purpose of the club was to teach women on the reservation Euro-American homemaking skills, but Indian women also forged it into a central forum for beadworking.[16]

THE JACOBSON HOME

In 1918, after several years of planning and construction interrupted by America's entry into the First World War, the Jacobsons were able to move into their own home. The house on 609 Chautauqua in Norman formed the nexus for the encounter between the Jacobsons and their Kiowa protégés, not only because that is where many of their meetings took place but also because it stands for a powerful, multilayered production of ideas about home that changed over time yet also endured to carry meanings into new contexts. The Jacobsons had the house built according to their own specifications in 1918. In 1986, after years of disuse and neglect, it was inaugurated as the Jacobson Native American Arts Center, dedicated to both Scandinavian and Native American art and culture (see plate 7).

Home is central to experiences of diaspora, forming the opposite of the trauma of being forced into exile. The home left behind is strongly present and determines interpretations and feelings related to the new and foreign context. Neither Oscar nor Jeanne had left their previous homes because of violence or deprivation, but the house they built nonetheless meant much to them. "It seemed almost incredible," wrote Jeanne, "that, after all the drawbacks and disappointments, the dream we had planned so carefully could materialize. We always loved our little house and it is doubly home to me because it has some of the features of Provençal architecture."[17] Carol Whitney described the house following its restoration and dedication as a culture center: "Jacobson designed a home whose floor plan included the outside world as part of its living space." Verandas and porches served as outdoor family and sleeping rooms. The family frequently ate on the east veranda, while they mostly slept, even in winter, on the southeast screened porch. "Even in winter, we'd sleep on the sun porch. If the wind was blowing, Dad would lower the canvas window rolls to keep the snow off our blankets," remembered their daughter. The seamless connection between the outdoors and indoors dominated the layout of the floor plan and construction of the house with "large multiple paned windows that cover each exterior wall. . . . The open airiness of French doors and floor-to-ceiling side lights combine with three sets of Roman Doric columns on both verandas and within the living/dining areas to create the feeling of a covered pavilion—a passage way from one outdoor environment to another."[18]

Yolande Sheppard, Oscar and Jeanne's daughter, reminisced in 1981 about the Kiowa students: "They often came by individually or in groups particularly when they were disturbed about something would enter the house and then I remember clearly particularly Tsatoke. Dad would always leave them alone Mother would offer them coffee or something and he'd pick up always the Indian drum we had, drum it awhile. My father said not to hurry them."[19] In this way the Jacobson House seemed to serve as a home away from home for the Kiowas, a place where they could express themselves in their own way (such as play the drum) and their own time (not being hurried). They came when they were in distress, and the place and its inhabitants provided solace. There exist also some accounts that describe the house as more than a place of comfort in the confusing white world of the college town, it may also have been their abode. The men, at least during some periods, lived in the basement of the house.[20]

D'Ucel described how "living in town, away from the Reservation atmosphere, our protégés were often homesick. They would come then to see us, or rather our old drum. I'd say 'Let's have some songs.' Eagerly they would take the drum and warm it. They could sing for hours, and such songs! Not merely the more or less stereotyped ones of pow-wows etc. but little gems never heard by strangers." There is a familiarity to d'Ucel's account of "their" Kiowas, but she is also at pains to describe the learning process necessary for this cross-cultural connection. The whole household was enlisted in these activities. It took a little time for their children, Yvonne, Yolande, and Oscar (aged ten, eight, and six at the time when the first students came to Norman) to become accustomed to the presence of Indians in their living room. One of their new maids feared the worst when she opened the door to "a baker's dozen of Indians in braids and blankets," and she "slammed the door shut and fled with a scream to the kitchen." But when she saw that Jeanne "was not being scalped," she became curious and eventually consented to serve coffee to the visitors.[21]

Braids and blankets, scalping, singing, and drumming—common representations limiting and diminishing what Indians were like—infused d'Ucel's narratives. Did Jeanne and Oscar go beyond them in their contacts with the Kiowa artists and their families? Did they use such stereotypes for literary effect, or did they share the perceptions of so many of their fellow Americans? Extant sources do not suggest that d'Ucel questioned or critiqued these representations as part of an American colonial policy. But having American Indians as guests and friends in their house, visiting powwows, devoting their spare time and their extra money to support the Kiowas—all of that must have made the Jacobsons stand out in the Norman community. Perhaps it also made them objects of a mixture of jealousy and contempt?

In her writings, Jeanne d'Ucel offered glimpses from Kiowa visits in their home. They might come and ask Jacobson's advice on how to interpret a contract or on how to respond to pressures to assimilate. Invariably, he encouraged them to remain true to their Kiowa origins. Once Tsatoke, to whom the Jacobsons appear to have felt closest, brought a friend with him to their house. The new man "sat there with his braids over his shoulders" when their son Oscar came home from school, said "How do you do?" to the Kiowa guest, and went on. D'Ucel explained:

> Satisfied because he wasn't stared at like a beast in the zoo, the new Kiowa immediately asked Dad "Do you think I should cut off my hair?" "Why?" was the reply "if you like it long, I don't see any reason for you to cut it short." "Oh! but the preacher says I should, to be a good Christian." "What has the length of hair to do with that?" said Dad. "It seems to me that Christ himself was supposed to have rather long hair." The Indian thought this over a moment; then he chuckled, after which he became rather talkative. As they left, Tsa-to-ke said to me with a wink "Aren't Indians funny!"

LaQuinta, Stephen Mopope's daughter, also remembered vividly that Jacobson encouraged her father "to continue his expressing his traditional ways in paintings and everything and don't you know pick up things from the outside." D'Ucel recounts a small anecdote of Mopope from their first years of acquaintance. "He has a little daughter, a beautiful golden doll

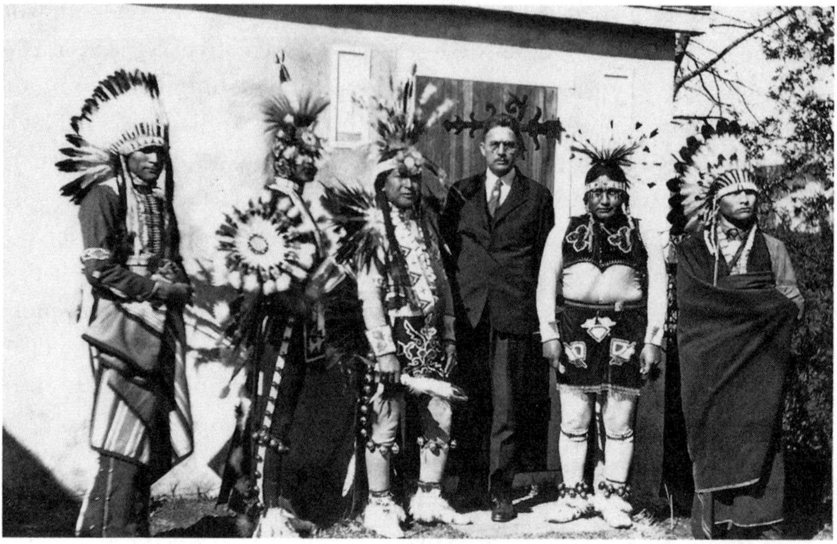

FIGURE 13. The most well-known photograph of the Kiowa artists and Oscar Jacobson, taken at the back of the Jacobson House in 1929. From left to right Monroe Tsatoke, Jack Hokeah, Stephen Mopope, Oscar Jacobson, Spencer Asah, and James Auchiah. Courtesy Sophie Sheppard.

whom I had not seen for some time. I asked how she was and 'stoicall, impassible Indian' that he may be, his eyes flashed and a beatific smile spread over his face as he eagerly, vehemently said, 'Do you know, Mrs. Jacobson, she is the nicest and best baby in the world.'"[22]

In her manuscripts Jeanne frequently emphasizes that she and Oscar knew more about American Indians than most white people did. Yet, at times she also misconstrued the meaning of certain exchanges. She related how she once asked the Kiowas to play the songs of the peyote ceremony, with the words "would you please sing one for me?" The Indians nodded and smiled, but soon quit their singing and left, and this was repeated on two more occasions. Jeanne felt confused but determined to find out the cause of their reticence. Finally, Stephen Mopope explained: "Well . . . you see . . . in peyote ceremony everyone sings four songs," and Jeanne understood that she needed to ask for the whole set. "Light dawned on me 'Sing four songs, please,' I said and at once had them. Knowing how sacred the number four is to Indians, I understood why they had not complied before, simply because they had taken literally my request for 'one' song."[23] Herein the joke appeared to be on Jeanne. It seems like a misunderstanding that can easily mar exchanges between strangers, especially as they cut across distances of class and culture. Jeanne learned and got to hear the songs. But her account also further established the distance between herself and the Indians, just as it set her aside from other white people. Knowing the significance of the number four "to Indians" affirmed that the Jacobsons had indeed come to know more about Indian culture than other white Americans, and yet there existed a distance between them, as suggested in her reference to the Kiowas'—possibly racially limited—literal interpretation of her request.

Important as the Jacobson home may have been to the Kiowas, they did not lose their links to their own homes. D'Ucel wrote: "The Indian artists stayed in Norman fairly content through the winter. But, with the first breath of spring nothing could hold them back. Shamefaced they would come to wish us a happy summer; always promising to paint while on the Reservation. On their return in the fall, they would be as shy as at first sight. It was amusing to see how we had to become reacquainted; yet we knew they truly liked us." There is no reason to doubt that they did, but this cannot hide the enormity of the decisions they had made. Leaving the reservation for Norman placed the artists apart from their own community every bit as much as the Jacobsons' decision to mentor them did in white society. It was an opportunity that must have stung others on the reservation, but it was also a frightening one. Lois Smoky related how they were asked to go to Europe to show their paintings, but "we all didn't want to go across you know. You know we were going to have a show of our paintings in Paris somewhere and we didn't go cause we're afraid to go on a ship." They were exposed to views held of them as both exotic and barbaric, and they had to step carefully in educating white Oklahomans about American Indians, and Kiowas in particular. The stakes were high, and they were all expected to contribute to the welfare of their extended families back home. Returning to the reservation was part of a necessary cycle for all the Kiowas. Several of them worked their allotments, and their prolonged stay on the Norman campus came at a cost to their families. A 1924 description of George Mopope's household reveals a sizable farm: "George Mopope is living on his own allotment eight miles west of Anadarko in a five room frame house. . . . He has a fair barn, six horses, four head of stock cattle, two milk cows, eight hogs and eight chickens. They raised corn to the value of $400.00 last year and garden to the value of $20.00. The family received in trust funds a total of $485.00. George Mopope is in poor health and his farm operations are principally carried on by a son. All considered the efforts of the family are making toward self-support are fairly good."[24]

Jennings describes her links to her Redstone allotment as a thread traversing her body and secured in the ground. Similarly, home tugged at the hearts of both the Kiowa artists and the Jacobsons; threads stretching across the distances between Norman and the reservation as well as across the Atlantic Ocean to France and Sweden. The Jacobsons created their house to reflect and perhaps defuse that tension. To be sure, the Kiowas had less choice, but association with the land from which they came was a key component in their assertion of cultural identity in the face of colonial erasure. They always sought to return to their allotments and the sacred places in the heart of Kiowa territory.[25]

MURALS—PAINTING THROUGH THE DEPRESSION

Soon after the arrival of the Kiowa artists at the University of Oklahoma, America was swept up in a devastating economic depression. On the reservation, where conditions had been depressed since its inception, the impact was noticed less keenly than in white society in general, but only because poverty, unemployment, and ill health had become a feature of normal life. In contrast, the opportunities that opened up for the artists must have appeared enormous. For Jacobson and his colleagues at the university, the Depression meant frozen or even lowered wages, and it directly affected the family's income. Oscar's brother Ernst found himself in difficult circumstances. He managed the family farm in Lindsborg and had sought to extend the property through buying land at inflated prices, with money he had borrowed from their mother. Now his entire holdings were reduced to debt, and with this disappeared any possibility for an inheritance for his siblings.[26]

Many of the artists and activists in the Southwest came to view Indian arts and crafts as a vehicle for alleviating some of the devastating poverty among Indian communities. In 1928 the secretary of the interior asked for a survey of the situation for Indians, and the ensuing report, the Meriam Report, observed that the government must enable American

Indians to manage their own affairs, while providing them with adequate levels of health care and education. According to the report, American Indians who wished "to merge into the social and economic life of the prevailing civilization of this country should be given all practicable aid and advice in making the necessary adjustments," while those who desired to "remain an Indian and live according to his old culture should be aided in doing so." Particularly, the Meriam Report recommended that arts and crafts instruction should be part of the curriculum in Indian schools, as the practice of it offered a potential source of income. The new administration under John Collier, who became Indian Commissioner in 1933, viewed artistic expressions and the continuation of traditional crafts as key components in a policy that would allow Indigenous peoples to maintain distinct cultures while participating in a market economy. The formation of the Committee on Indian Arts and Crafts in 1934 served to implement new policies for marketing Indigenous arts and crafts production, as suggested in the Meriam Report. Producing for markets would potentially lead toward greater self-sufficiency, but the report showed scant regard for self-directed production. Instead, it was assumed that American Indians needed the guidance of white patrons in order to know what and how to design saleable objects for these markets.[27]

Jacobson was in regular contact with the new commissioner and generally appears to have supported his new policies, but he also expressed doubts about overconfidence in a market for Indian art. He saw a "danger of oversaturating in a world ill prepared to absorb and appreciate their work, and to provide sufficient returns for them." He cautioned that the Indian artists found it hard to compete on a globalized market where undiscriminating buyers could purchase imitations of Indian craft "made in Japan and elsewhere," while the "genuine article could not be produced as cheaply." His analysis may well have derived from his own early experience as a collector of Indian and western objects, displayed in his rooms at Yale. Elizabeth Hutchinson has shown how the "Indian rooms" in many cases were furnished with objects purchased at department stores that had become part of a global circulation of ethnic material culture.[28]

Despite his wealth of experience and dedicated effort to augment the appreciation of American Indian art and crafts, Jacobson was not directly involved in shaping policy the way many of his contemporaries in the Southwest were. I can only speculate as to why. Art was his first and foremost passion, and he may have been unwilling to compromise with his exacting standards for the sake of commerce. His own ambition, d'Ucel writes, was to start an annual American Indian art exhibition, but he lacked the funds to do so. He may also have found it difficult to collaborate with other reformers and perhaps saw their work as competition. And possibly, his personal route as an immigrant growing up in Kansas, fostered in him a sense of separation from the predominantly Anglo artist community in Santa Fe, many of whom had strong connections to East Coast elites. Whatever the reason, both d'Ucel's memoirs and his own sparse comments place him somewhat apart from the political reform work in Washington and its advocates in the Southwest.[29]

He did, however, work with Washington to help his students. Two events appear especially meaningful and illustrate the continued involvement of the Jacobsons and the Kiowas: the projects to paint murals in federal buildings and the participation of the Kiowas in the First National Folk Festival. In 1934, Jacobson contacted Washington regarding the plight of the Indian artists, which he felt was as great as that of their white counterparts. As a result he was placed in charge of the Oklahoma branch of the short-lived Public Works of Art Projects, the first federal program to alleviate conditions for artists and writers and other culture workers during the Depression, which was subsequently followed by the Federal Art Project as part of the Works Progress Administration. In addition to his teaching and administrative load at the university this taxed him greatly. D'Ucel describes the demands of this work: "The P.W.A.P. consisted almost entirely of frescoes for public buildings, libraries, schools, court houses, etc. It required much traveling to inspect the various projects, see that they were up to standards. This meant that Dad had to contribute not only his time and effort; usually he made the trips in his own car, at his own expense." Jacobson also used all his available contacts—on the reservation, in Oklahoma, and in Washington—to procure commissions for the Kiowa artists.[30]

The Kiowas had already begun painting decorations for public places. In 1927–29, all five of the men were asked to paint murals in the chapel at St. Patrick's in Anadarko, the school they had all gone to and where they had begun their art training. Through his contacts in Washington,

Jacobson was able to secure contracts for several of the Kiowas to paint murals in public buildings in Oklahoma and beyond. During 1934 Mopope and Hokeah jointly painted two murals at the Cherokee Female Seminary (now Northeastern State University) in Tahlequah, Oklahoma. In 1936 Mopope won a contract to decorate the lobby of the new post office building in Anadarko. The contract was for the amount of eighteen hundred dollars to be paid to Mopope "and a group of Indian painters working under him" on Mopope's designs. The authorization stated that, "Mr. Mopope will be in charge of the work but under the supervision of Prof. Jacobson."[31]

The Kiowas had previously worked primarily in watercolors. The new projects in oil and fresco required further training, and Jacobson set about organizing that as well. Olle Nordmark, another Swedish-born artist and fresco painter, had emigrated to the United States in 1924 and was "considered the best fresco worker in the country." During the summer of 1938, he was engaged by the Bureau of Indian Affairs to teach fresco painting to Indian students at Fort Sill for two months. By that time, the Kiowas had already done several fresco works, but the superintendent at the Kiowa Agency was asked to strongly encourage the artists to participate in Nordmark's classes. Willard Beatty, director of education, wrote to Superintendent McCowan to "please make an effort to get Mopope and Auchei [*sic*] interested in work. I believe that it will be very much to their advantage." Letters were dispatched to agents, teachers, and artists across the state to invite Indian artists to enroll as special students in Nordmark's art classes at Fort Sill Indian School. The presence of the original Kiowa artists in these classes was used to vouch for the attractiveness of this opportunity.[32]

Nordmark's engagement with the BIA occurred in conjunction with some large projects for the decoration of federal buildings, the largest of which was the new Department of the Interior building in Washington, DC. Nordmark was given a free hand to devise his course and to purchase necessary materials, to be paid for by a Carnegie grant. Secretary of the Interior Harold Ickes had decided already in 1933 that American Indian artists should be involved in the mural project. He had been advised to contact Oscar Jacobson, who recommended three artists, James Auchiah, Stephen Mopope, and Gerald Nailor. Not until early 1939 did the six final artists (Stephen Mopope and James Auchiah, Gerald Nailor, Velino

Herrera, Allan Houser, and Woody Crumbo) begin their work on the murals. Each artist received two thousand dollars in pay. This was equal to the salaries of white artists, but it was paid out in several increments, in keeping with the same racial prejudice expressed by d'Ucel—that Indians could not be trusted to manage their money well if given the entire amount at one time.[33]

James Auchiah described the work on the murals they did for the basement cafeteria in the DOI building. Mopope was exceedingly careful in his work and did not want anything to go wrong with the intricate designs. In the preparatory course Nordmark told them "that all murals should have texture." He wanted them to make very thin outlines with only a few texture lines. He also taught them very practical things such as how to preserve and economize with materials, like keeping tubes of watercolor in fruit jars with a vacuum lid on to keep them fresh. Auchiah appeared uncomfortable with the strictures of Nordmark's teaching, suggesting that he hampered "our Indian way of painting." Nordmark followed the artists to Washington, DC, and Auchiah noticed his privileged position. "He did not have to go through channels. He could talk direct to commissioner. We have to go through channels. He has order from higher ups that the local officials have to give him his way. He has absolute control over us." At the same time, Auchiah appreciated what he learned. Nordmark also took a special interest in the Kiowa artists. "For some reason Nor[d]mark kept close check on Mopope and I. He ran around with us. Off the record took us to dinner. Asked 100 questions about Indian art. Sometimes I thought he wanted to be a student himself and learn about Indian art from Mopope and I. He bought some pictures. He did wonderful job in teaching us the technique of secco painting." Jacobson, however, did not approve of the styles Nordmark taught and thought it took them "too far away from Indian style."[34]

Auchiah's description and memory expose the paternalism to which the Kiowas were subjected, and the privileged position of immigrants of Swedish descent in that system. Both Jacobson and Nordmark enjoyed standing as experts and authorities, and they could exercise "absolute control" over the Indians. The fact that it was a benevolent rule, aimed to improve the skills and opportunities for the Kiowa artists, should not be allowed to conceal the structural inequality of their positions and in their relationship.

In time, the murals painted by American Indian artists across the country constituted an impressive collection. Many of these publicly available works of art have since been destroyed, as buildings have decayed, been demolished, or deteriorated through regular wear and tear. In some cases, the production of a mural became a collective experience of sharing stories and affirming memories. The new post office building in Anadarko is one such example. In early 1935, the Public Works Branch sought the advice of the superintendent on the Kiowa Agency on how best to proceed with engaging the Kiowa artists to decorate the rather complicated spaces in the planned new building. Monroe Tsatoke was first approached and provided some preliminary sketches, but he was already severely hampered by tuberculosis, and he died early in 1937. Stephen Mopope's design eventually won the bid, but he had help from his friends Auchiah, Asah, and Hokeah. During the weeks that they worked on the murals, visitors crowded into the post office to watch the artists paint. The audience consisted to a large extent of knowledgeable older people who expected historical accuracy and did not hesitate to tell the men so. The sixteen panels, an unusually large collection, depict scenes from Kiowa history in the time before reservation life, and Vanessa Jennings emphasizes the importance of the murals as recordings of history. They show painted tipis, which were no longer in use, and shields that belonged to real Kiowa warriors. Jennings said that if her grandfather had not recorded it, it would have been forgotten. One panel shows a woman facing away from the viewer. She is shown carrying a fully beaded cradleboard, a tradition among Kiowas, Kiowa-Apaches, and Comanches that had been all but lost in the reservation period. The mural and other Mopope paintings became an important instrument in documenting the depth of the tradition, which Jennings, among others, has continued until this day. However, the process of construction also led to the imparting of valuable historical information, as curious spectators corrected Mopope along the way. In one panel a village scene shows meat hanging outside tipis, but some old women told him that there would never have been meat racks so close to the tents because of the smell and because it would attract flies. Mopope also faced harsh critics whose views clashed with his artistic requirements. One older woman told him that he should not paint a short skirt on a woman scraping a hide. Mopope tried telling her that he shortened the skirt to create the

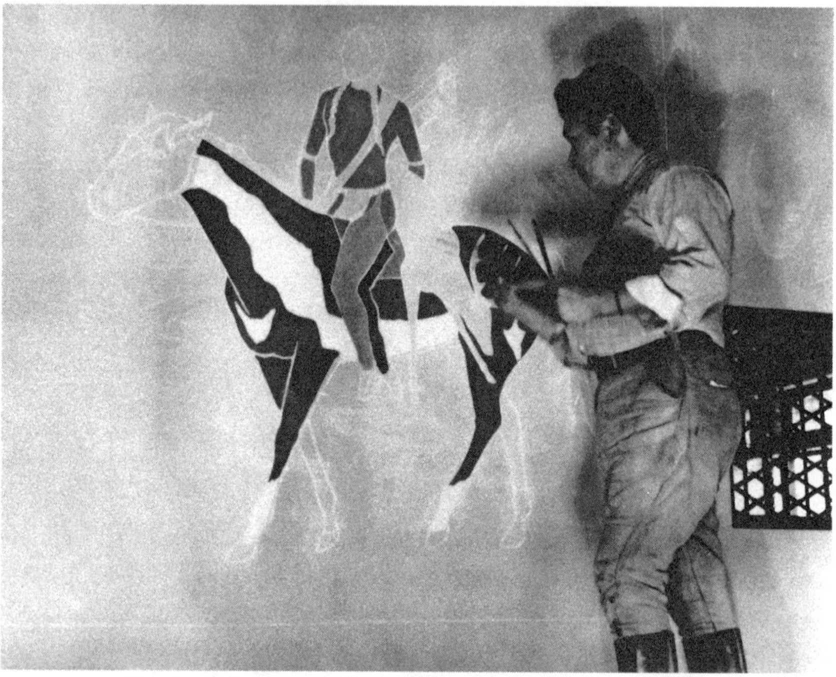

FIGURE 14. Stephen Mopope painting murals at the US Post Office in Anadarko, 1937. Mopope stood on scaffolding high up by the ceiling filling in sections of color in the outline drawn on the wall. The finished mural is seen in plate 8. Courtesy Vanessa Pukeigope Jennings.

best proportion for the image, but the old woman considered this a lie (see plate 9).[35]

At times the communal interest in the project clashed with the artist's need to focus. Mopope painted freehand, without the use of a prior projection on the wall. He began working during the day, but soon curious Kiowas appeared to watch him and the others work. They would "come and they would sit, and they would watch him, and out of respect . . . you have to stand there and you have to listen to someone until they're finished talking, you know, in our culture you can't just say, oh wait, I don't have time for that." To be able to work uninterrupted, he began working at night. This arrangement also had another reason. If he was working during the day, he would have been obliged to feed all the onlookers when he took his food breaks. Jennings explains: "you have all these different levels of society within the Kiowa tribe, and you're not supposed to be materialistic" and think that "I can't pay for that cause that's going to cut into my budget." So when it came to lunchtime "and Grandpa was hungry it was Grandpa's obligation whoever was sitting there" and so he had "to pay for their—and keep in mind this is during the Depression—so it was a financial burden."[36] Jennings's explanation surely puts the white notion that Indians could not be trusted to handle money wisely in perspective.

In an interview with C. Ross Hume, a judge in Anadarko, Mopope described the meaning behind the panels. The motifs included a ceremonial Sun Dance fan, depictions of different dances, recital of war deeds, the practice of placing children in beaded cradles, moving camp, hunting scenes, and shields. The article ends with an exhortation common for its time: "Anadarko is anxious in this dedication to pay tribute to this past before it becomes just a memory and a myth for all mankind." This contrasts sharply with Vanessa Jennings's assertion that the murals, in fact, laid a foundation for the continuation of Kiowa cultural practices and an active recording of history for posterity. Jenny Tone-Pah-Hote argues in her dissertation that the "past that Mopope, Auchiah, and Asah recreated implied a future narrative that countered the vanishing Indian myth that Hume spoke of so nostalgically." A central panel is one of a mother carrying a cradleboard. This "suggested a future through the image of the child. The mural presented a forward-looking view of the Kiowa as a nation."[37]

THE NATIONAL FOLK FESTIVAL, 1934

The courses in Norman turned out to be much more than just a flash in the pan both for Jacobson and for the Kiowa artists. Instead, they laid a foundation for a connection that lasted over decades and lifetimes. Jacobson continued from this beginning to teach, support, and befriend American Indian artists. The Kiowas, Stephen Mopope especially, continued developing their artistic skills and the contacts they had begun establishing while at the university and under the guidance of Jacobson. The National Folk Festival, in particular, became an opportunity for the Kiowas to use the public's fascination with Indian dancing and singing to showcase their art to a large audience.

The first National Folk Festival took place in St. Louis in 1934, propelled by the unquenchable energy of Sarah Gertrude Knott. Historical pageantry and folk festivals flourished in the early decades of the twentieth century, providing recreation and entertainment, as well as arenas for formulating historic heritage. Both drama productions and festivals could be either progressive or reactionary. Some openly glorified the Ku Klux Klan while others took up issues of labor conflicts and race relations. Immigrant groups, too, organized their own festivals and dramatized aspects of history they wished to claim as their heritage, like the pageant in Minneapolis that Jacobson participated in when he taught at Minnesota College. The National Folk Festival was born out of the imagination of Knott, who, as a drama teacher at a small North Carolina college, had worked with one of the leading proponents of the pageantry movement, Fredrick Koch. In contrast to most folk festivals, it encompassed multiculturalism from the start. Knott's ambition was to foster a festival that would gather "groups from the different sections of the country with their folk music, dances, and plays, to see what the story would tell of our people and our country?" The program involved American Indians, African Americans, and Spanish Americans, as well as different immigrant groups and groups representing various labor collectives, such as lumberjacks and sailors.[38]

Knott put together an impressive group of folklorists to serve on the festival's national committee. Among them were several who had particular interests in American Indian culture and music, including Frances Densmore, Martha Beckwith, and Stith Thompson. One of Knott's most trusted companions in the venture was OU folklorist Ben Botkin. It is likely that it was through Botkin that Oscar Jacobson was asked to provide Indian dancers for the event. Knott turned directly to Jacobson with a request, but the restricted status of Oklahoma Indians made it necessary to go via the Indian commissioner, who involved the superintendent on the reservation. Jacobson expressed delight at the opportunity to escort the Kiowas to St. Louis. According to Jeanne d'Ucel, "His Kiowas, among whom were the finest dancers in the country, took kindly to the idea." Jacobson asked his acquaintance Jasper Saunkeah to lead the group, and Saunkeah recommended that Mopope, Asah, Tsatoke, Auchiah, Justin Poolaw, Gregory Huampy, Joe Attocknie, and Timothy Berry be included as dancers. The agency promised three cars for their transportation, and with the $250 furnished by the festival, Jacobson believed expenses would be covered.[39]

D'Ucel's account of the adventures of the troupe naturally focuses on the perspective of the Jacobsons, but it also contains a valuable description of the scale and difficulties involved in organizing a major dance performance in the 1930s:

> The preparations involved a considerable amount of work and planning for Dad. To begin with, the small subsidy the Festival Foundation provided was totally inadequate to finance a group large enough for a worthy performance. Dad solved that by talking the Indian agency at Anadarko into providing transportation, 3 cars with drivers. A Kiowa chief, Sankeah, who was a good drummer, would, in addition, drive his own car. His two daughters, excellent dancers and beautiful, were attending Haskell Institute in Kansas. They would be picked up there on the way, with other students.[40]

On the eve of the expected departure from Norman, the phone rang in the Jacobson residence:

> We were not yet asleep when the telephone rang. Ah! These unmovable, unemotional Indians! Auchiah, so excited he was stuttering, informed Dad that one of the agency cars had some mechanical trouble. Therefore he, Auchiah, had arranged for another car whose owner would drive it for only $50. Auchiah did not take into account that the driver would have to be fed and housed too. "Wait" said Dad. We haven't enough money for that. If the agency car is not repaired in time, some of the people will have to go by bus. But what do the agency people say?" Auchiah did not know for he was in the country. . . . At 12.30 a call from the Indian agent puzzled because Auchiah had just told him that Dad didn't want the cars after all, and had bought bus tickets. True, he said, one car needed some repairs but another was available in its place. He promised to send them to Norman early. Dad called Auchiah as planned to reassure him. By now Auchiah was all up in the air because he could not get in touch with Tsa-to-ke, Mopope or Asah; all lived in the country and a terrific thunderstorm was raging, turning the unpaved roads of the Reservation into quagmires.[41]

As morning dawned, three agency cars arrived, but "hardly an Indian." Soon, however, "good, dependable Sankeah" arrived with three dancers, Auchiah "the mischief compounder" among them. "Poor Sankeah is tired, having spent most of the night trying to round up the crowd who were here and there, and nowhere." Finally, Mopope drove up together with Asah, three other dancers, and Jeanette and her sister who were to drive the car back to Redstone.[42]

Even today, almost a century later, inclement weather turns the roads at Redstone nearly impassable. Similar conditions existed all across the KCA Reservation. Assembling a group of dancers and singers who could be depended upon to turn up at any given time appears an overwhelming task. Fortunately, and probably necessarily, the dancers who traveled with Jacobson to St. Louis were all more or less related to the people living at Redstone.

Finally there, the participation of the Kiowas turned into a raging success. The Kiowas were asked to open the festival and when "they appeared, the beautiful maidens in their fringed and beaded doeskin dresses won all hearts." Mopope excelled. D'Ucel wrote, "Mopope outdid himself in his solo Eagle dance, a performance no other Indian of modern days ever equaled."[43]

The *St. Louis Post-Dispatch* ran a long article on April 30, 1934, under the headline "Tom-Toms and Negro Spirituals Mark Folk Festival Opening." It stated that tradition and preservation were paramount goals for the festival. "Traditions of the first Americans were emphasized yesterday as the throbbing tom toms of the Kiowas sounded through the Municipal Auditorium, marking the opening of the National Folk Festival and affording a forerunner of programs designed to preserve the legends and lore of peoples fused now in the national melting pot." The report continued with common tropes of Indians but also set up the juxtaposition between the wild life on the prairie and the modern-day artists. It extolled the tenacity the Indians showed in preserving tribal traditions, "illustrated yesterday as the Kiowas, attired in beaded buckskin and gorgeous head-dresses, sang and danced as their forefathers did when only the tepee loomed on western plains." The dancers, however, are "well-educated, several with college degrees, four of them artists whose paintings have hung in Paris and London, reside in modern Oklahoma homes but they cling to the secret of their rituals. Save for the terse explanation 'this is a dance in time of war' or 'this is a festive event,' even O. B. Jacobson, director of the school of art of the University of Oklahoma, who accompanies them, has not been informed of the symbolism which lies behind every note and movement."[44]

A new paragraph entitled "Indians Discuss Automobiles" brought out the contrasts even further: "Behind the scenes, the Indians discussed automobiles, baseball and other topics talked of by young men all over the country, but when their time came to dance they became grave, hastened on the stage with intent earnestness." Jasper Saunkeah, who led the troupe on this trip as on several others, attempted to counter the notion of the disappearance of Indians into the melting pot of assimilation. "Their chief, Saunkauh [*sic*], who is a United States Deputy Marshall, observed that 'the red man is not vanishing; we have 2300 in our tribe today—more than we had 50 years ago.'"[45]

The Kiowas (and one Comanche) performed in the program under the heading of "Indian Dances and Music." The text in the program leaflet proclaimed: "The Kiowas are well known by students of folklore for their careful preservation of their ancient art. The presentation of their singing and dancing is exactly as handed down from one generation of their tribe to the next, unsullied by white influences."[46] This has the imprint of Jacobson's influence, who strongly encouraged the Kiowas to paint from within their own culture and not allow themselves to be corrupted by white practices.

Exhibiting and selling their art was the prime interest of both Jacobson and the Kiowa artists, and the correspondence between Knott, her right-hand man, M. J. "Major" Pickering, and Jacobson, the superintendent, and the Kiowa artists demonstrate how adamant both Jacobson and the Kiowas were about their importance as artists. In 1936, in preparation for the third annual festival, Knott again desired the participation of the Kiowas. We believe, she wrote, "that we are working out a satisfactory arrangement by which we will again have the splendid dancers for the first two nights of our Festival." In addition to this they had "arranged as at previous festivals also for the boys to show their paintings for sale in our handicraft exhibition during the entire period of the Exposition, and Exposition officials have pointed out a way in which they might even stay with their paintings longer." However, in addition to this, the festival organizers wished to have "proper Indian representation" in a camp during the whole week and as participants in "the spectacle to be known as 'Cavalcade.'" This "Cavalcade" must have been just the kind of performance that Jacobson considered demeaning, as the letter ends with the following stipulation to the superintendent: "The boys in the group, consisting of Monroe Tsa-to-ke, Stephen Mopope, Spencer Asah, James Auchish [*sic*], Gregory Haumpy, Joe Attockie [*sic*], Justin Poolaw, and Timothy Berry are the only ones whom we do not want included in any of the Exposition or Cavalcade representation, as this is the wish of Professor Jacobson and the officials of the National Folk Festival."[47] Jacobson maintained that the Kiowas were artists, foremost, and not objects of entertainment. The dancers, too, balanced between their role as performers and their desire to educate the public of their existence and their belonging in modern America.

NA-GOEY, A SWEDISH KIOWA CHIEF

In the summer of 1928, newspapers reported that, "Prof. Oscar B. Jacobson . . . has been adopted as a member of the Kiowa tribe of Indians." Leading Kiowas on the KCA Business Committee had decided to show their appreciation for his work in support of the Kiowa artists by making him an honorary member of the tribe and gave him the name of Na-Goey. Clippings kept in Jacobson's scrapbook describe the event as a combination of interests from the local chamber of commerce and the tribal business committee. The ceremony occurred at the big powwow camp erected seven miles west of Anadarko, which also served as the location for the Anadarko Indian Exposition, and Ned Brace as chairman of the KCA Business Committee led the formal induction of Jacobson into the tribe. Present at the event was also a local Chickasha Republican, John Nichols, who headed the Chickasha Chamber of Commerce and spoke at the event in support of the Republican presidential nominee, Herbert Hoover, and his running mate, Charles Curtis, a Kaw from Kansas who would become the first American Indian to hold the office of vice president (between 1929 and 1933). Prior to the Kiowa ceremony, Jacobson attended a dinner as guest of the Anadarko Chamber of Commerce, and he "urged that support be given the Indian youths now studying . . . at the university and pointed to the value of their art work in perpetuating the tribal art and its relative value in years to come."[48]

All of the newspaper items made a point out of Jacobson being the second white man that Kiowas had honored with this distinction, the first being Oklahoma's first Republican senator, J. W. Herreld. The *Norman Transcript* also pointed out that he was the second OU man who had been made an Indian chief after Edward Everett Dale, who had been distinguished by the Blackfeet the previous summer.[49] Despite my best efforts, I have found it difficult to ascertain the nature of this "adoption." Newspaper reports and Jeanne d'Ucel's account of the ceremony, written more than thirty years later, are the only evidence of the occasion. Vanessa Jennings does not recall ever having been told about it, suggesting that the event was not as momentous to the Kiowas as it was to Jacobson and his family. None of the interviews Arthur Silberman conducted with Kiowas sheds any light on it. It appears most likely that the Kiowa students decided to thank Jacobson during the annual exposition, and that naming him chief was an honorary name reflecting his position as their professor and sponsor.

It is, however, also the possibility that this adoption signified an important political move for the Kiowas. David La Vere argues in a study of the KCA Business Committee that in the early decades of the twentieth century it lacked any real authority to decide over political and economic issues on the reservation, but it did exercise control over adoptions. He notes how debates over adoption and inclusion on tribal rolls had a particular urgency during the years of allotment, and the business committee sometimes voted to adopt non-Indigenous individuals "who could help the Indians navigate through the tempest of twentieth-century American Indian policy." To my knowledge, no records remain of such deliberations in the case of Jacobson, but this would offer a possible motivation for the Kiowa leadership to honor him and his work in a ceremonial fashion.[50]

What emerges in the record is a standard narrative of a white man being made an Indian chief. It is a story that meant much to the Jacobsons, and it served as a node around which Oscar could construct his reputation as an educator and promoter of Indian culture. D'Ucel's account is detailed, and in parts fanciful. When Lewis Ware telephoned them about the plans, the Jacobsons packed two tents and supplies and drove out to Anadarko together with their three children. They camped the night, and the next morning "we waited at a certain crossroad until a car, giving us the agreed password, led us in a roundabout way to the big encampment, in a wooded bend of the river. There were about 2000 Indians assembled there, mostly Kiowas, though a section was reserved for visiting Comanches, Arapahoes, Cheyennes, Apaches, and we the only whites." Newspaper accounts described the location of the event and put the number of people closer to one thousand and also made clear that there were several other white people attending the event. The secrecy d'Ucel describes may have been for show, or it had been exaggerated in her recollection. She continued with a lively and rather fanciful description, painting an image of camp life set in a distant past:

> It was a colorful place, full of joyous activity. War bonnets adorned the tent poles; strings of drying jerky hung like garlands from the trees. Here groups of women were tanning skins by old processes; there, men were making bows and flutes. Under the guidance of patriarchs some young fellows were practicing archery, in preparation for the buffalo hunt scheduled the next day, by government permission, in the nearby Game Preserve. Dancers and drummers were rehearsing farther away. On little Indian fires the various items for the big noon meal were cooking. Children, the smallest completely naked, romped with friendly dogs.

The pastoral scene and the jovial setting contrasted with how Indians appeared when among white people in the cities. D'Ucel described being drawn in by the "ambience and the sense of collectivity" and understood how this "cohesive element" had served as "a source of strength and survival for the Indians in their sorrowful days, after the whites took over their continent."[51]

After partaking in the meal, and initial dances and speeches, the actual "adoption ceremony" took place. Jacobson was called to the center of the dance ground and he was introduced to the assembled crowd:

> He was praised and thanked by the head chief, Ned Brace, and other chiefs in turn, and by his students who filed by to shake his hand. It was announced that the council wanted to adopt him as a warchief, this being the highest rank, and had decided to give him the name Nah-go-ey in memory of their great warriors of the past. They presented him with an ancient, treasured peace pipe and

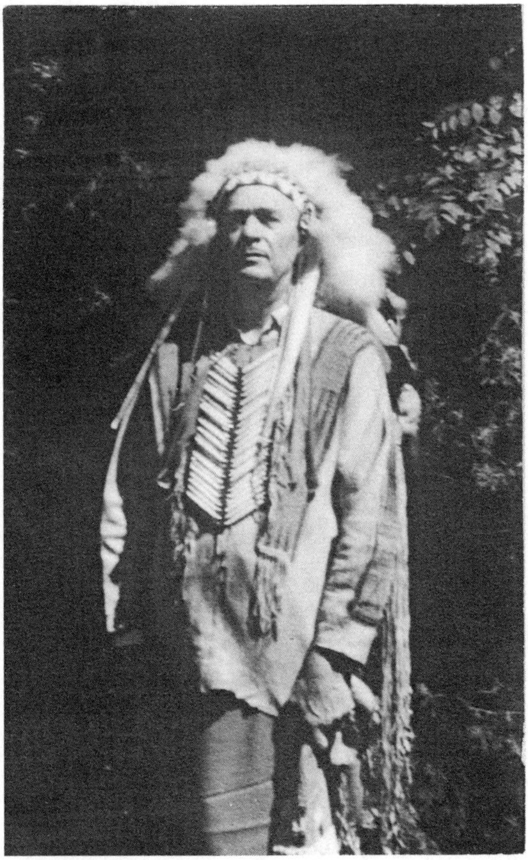

FIGURE 15. Oscar Jacobson in Kiowa regalia that he received at the ceremony when he was honored with the Kiowa name Nah-Goey. Photo taken in 1945. Courtesy Sophie Sheppard.

a tobacco pouch embroidered with porcupine quills, a beautiful piece of work, rare nowadays.

Of course Dad had to make a speech. Five interpreters assigned to the different linguistic groups, translated his words. What he told them about their Indian heritage and its value, not only to themselves, but to all America, and why it should be preserved, struck a responsive chord. They cheered and cheered; and a very old man advanced spontaneously to sing a song of triumph with an expression of ecstatic joy on his face.[52]

It is not surprising if d'Ucel many years later had forgotten or glossed over some details, such as that Jacobson participated in a dinner held by the Anadarko Chamber of Commerce on the eve of the adoption ceremony, or that other white attendants gave political stump speeches. It does not diminish the tremendous honor awarded to Jacobson, however. That Jacobson, in 1928, spoke to the assembled Kiowa nation on a reservation where their lands were held in trust, their movements restricted, and government officials in control of their income and resources—and told them that Kiowa traditions and culture held a significant value for the entire American nation—was momentous and a fitting pinnacle to the initial phase of educating American Indian artists in Oklahoma.

PART III

CONCURRENT CAREERS

CHAPTER 6
FRIENDSHIPS FORGED AND BROKEN

AN ODDLY DISTORTED PATTERN emerges when one studies the networks and interactions surrounding the art of the Kiowas. On the one hand, their reputation went worldwide, and they broke into an art scene already enamored with primitivism and abstract geometrical figures. On the other hand, the circle of people involved seems exceedingly small. A sharp contrast emerges between the freedom of movement of Euro-Americans and the detailed micromanagement of a few Kiowa individuals. While it is difficult to ascertain the whereabouts and continued links between the similarly small cohort of Swedish immigrants who came through Lindsborg (such as Jacobson, G. E. E. Lindquist, Victor O. Freeburg, and Harry Larson), the Kiowas are found in detailed government documents. White people, from tightly knit communities, had the freedom to move and choose their connections and circumstances, but American Indians became enmeshed in bureaucratic nets. Countless reformers, bureaucrats, teachers, and missionaries expressed their opinions on and deeply held concern for how Indians could be helped and eased into—as well as protected from—modern American society. Reputations were made based on access to and contacts with members of Indigenous nations.

Controversies flared up around the various roles of promoter and protégé in the relationship between the Kiowas and their white supporters, and these demonstrate the spaces available for maneuver. While becoming manifest in different ways, these clashes were really part of one major conflict winding its tentacles around both white and Kiowa societies. One such manifestation pitted Jacobson, Susie Peters, and others who had initially encouraged the Kiowa artists against one another, and it dragged on for years. Another clash involved Mopope as a key figure, embroiling white officials, supporters, and other Kiowas. The following exploration of how the Jacobsons perceived of their role begins with a look at these tensions and continues with a discussion of Jacobson's life and career after he launched the first contingent of American Indian artists into the limelight of the nation. The focus is primarily on the role of friendships in the life of the Jacobson family, particularly in their relationships with generations of American Indian artists.

FALLING OUT

Newspaper reports generally portrayed the arrival of the Kiowas in Norman as a happy collaboration between the energetic matron, Susie Peters, and the sympathetic expert on primitive art, Oscar Jacobson. But such a glossy picture obscures bitter conflicts. Rumors began to spread that Jacobson made a personal profit from his work with the Kiowas. These rumors came at a time when he was at a low ebb physically, having worked himself to the edge of collapse during the years of the Depression. D'Ucel in her memoir blamed Peters extensively (without revealing her full name), and she did not mince words: "The most avid spreader of ugly rumors was a woman who should have known better, and who did." She claimed to have "been the true discoverer of the Kiowa artists, on the ground that she had given them watercolor kits as Christmas presents once." In her narrative d'Ucel denied ever having met Peters nor did the Jacobsons, at first, understand her antagonism. "Then we learned that she had demanded a commission on everything the artists sold or Dad sold for them, enjoining them to keep this arrangement secret." Apparently, she had told the Kiowas "that they owed their 'painting power' to her, and that, if they failed to pay her, they would lose that power." Finally, she accused Jacobson of enriching himself through his work with the Kiowas. "I still have a letter Mrs. P wrote President Bizzell in violent protest against what she called the awful scandal of Dad's receiving a double salary. Of course, the president informed her that Dad received his one salary as a professor; and that neither the University nor anyone else paid him a cent for his labors with the Indians. Just the same she went on reviling Dad."[1]

The pain and frustration these denunciations caused the Jacobsons is evident from these lines. The Jacobsons' involvement with the Kiowas had been an all-consuming commitment for years. They had invested their time, their physical space, their networks, and their personal funds in realizing the vision borne out of the anger Jacobson had felt at seeing what he viewed as a cheapening of Indian culture at the market in Santa Fe in 1915, when Jeanne had challenged him to help Indians develop their own art.

But Susie Peters, too, was a woman with a mission to aid the Kiowas. In 1918 she had accepted a posting as field matron on the Kiowa Agency and as such the Redstone District fell under her province. A wisp of a woman, she fearlessly immersed herself in her commitment to assist the Kiowas in her charge and expended her own energy and resources in pursuit of improved conditions on the reservation. She was described as "a fine horsewoman; she knew and loved this Indian country, she knew and loved all that was fine in the Indian, having lived since a small girl in their country." She was determined, sometimes obstinate, and an outspoken critic of what she considered deplorable behaviors and practices. She took a firm stand against Indians living in tents and congregating in camps and opposed what she called "the customary sect dance," considering it a great risk to both their morals and their health. But she was also passionate about preserving and supporting Kiowa women's creative heritage. In May 1920 she reported that she had held the first of what she planned to be a series of meetings with Kiowa women, and more people came "than I could well take care of," and she "was greatly pleased at the interest shown."[2]

In 1921 Peters founded the Mau-Tame Lodge with financial support from the Indian Defense Association of Northern California, in order to encourage the preservation of traditional Kiowa beadwork and clothing. A focus on beadwork served several purposes. It would make financial sense, it would keep women and girls busy who, she said (misjudging Kiowa women's work), otherwise tended toward idleness, and, she concluded, "this work is fascinating and there is always a ready market, and no better means of employment." The lodge, or club, engaged some of the most prominent women on the reservation, such as Laura Pedrick, the sister of chief Ahpeahtone, who had been educated at Carlisle and herself served as a field matron. The connection between Peters and the women in the families of the Kiowa artists was particularly strong. Many of them participated in the Mau-Tame club, they worked together to preserve and can garden produce, and Peters tended them when they were ill and in childbirth and during the many devastating times when a child died. So close were the ties that in 1954, the Kiowas honored her by adopting her and giving her a Kiowa name, just as they had with Jacobson some two decades earlier.[3]

Peters also took the lead in organizing participation in various fairs, ceremonials, and other events at which both Kiowa men and women could display their arts and dances. For several years running during the early 1930s, she managed a contract for the young Kiowa artists to participate in the newly established Gallup Indian Ceremonial. The contract included a booth through which they could sell their paintings and participation in the Indian program in the evenings, plus free lodging. This was a good deal since in many other places participants had to pay for their own accommodations. The Gallup Ceremonial became an important venue for the Kiowa painters in utilizing the dance performances to attract attention to their artworks. Initially, sales were good and went through Mrs. Peters as middleman. The first couple of years were the most lucrative, and then sales went down. Increasingly, her managerial role in these tours became a source of irritation for the Kiowa artists, and in the early 1930s, Stephen Mopope took the step to break away from Susie Peters's influence and strike out on his own as a dancer and artist.[4]

His decision, later followed by Auchiah, may well have precipitated the acrimonious accusations between Peters and the Jacobsons. According to Auchiah, Peters "wanted to keep control over the boys," and she desired to "take the boys on a tour because the contract, program contracts, which various people wanted around the West Coast was very tempting to her." Increasingly, however, the artists began to feel that "she don't keep up her end of agreement," and they did not want sales and commissions to go through her. It came to a head during a trip to Seminole, on a private occasion when Peters claimed it was only through her contacts that the Kiowas had gotten this opportunity and insisted that letters and bookings would go through her. At that point "Mopope got fed up" and quit working with her. Auchiah continued with her a little longer, but he finally left her as well. To some extent, it appears as though the Kiowas had outgrown Susie Peters's direction. Auchiah expressed that "Jacobson had different and better ideas and better sponsorship than Mrs. Peters was providing." He had more art connections, while she did not really understand art and could not offer them constructive criticism. In addition, she did not participate in peyote meetings or ceremonial gatherings, which Jacobson apparently did.[5]

Auchiah credits her with helping the artists in the beginning. In doing so, he also revealed a discrepancy in Jeanne d'Ucel's account. "Dr. Jacobson found out about boys from submission of their paintings. He kept on encouraging Miss Peters . . . Miss Lane to keep training the boys. One of these days when OU would have scholarship fund he'd like to have boys over." Jacobson and Peters and Lewis Ware continued to be in contact until they "finally got to the point that Mrs. Peters and Jacobson broke off because Jacobson wanted to publish a book in France. Mrs. Peters had some manuscript started." According to Auchiah, then, Peters and Jacobson had indeed met (quite in contradiction to d'Ucel's statement) and had worked together until the publication of the *Kiowa Indian Art* portfolio. At that time, Peters had plans to publish her own account of the development of art education on the Kiowa reservation. Indeed, it makes more sense that these few white people who were so committed to supporting and developing the work of these young Kiowas knew about one another and met on several occasions.[6]

This fits with the timing of a letter by Peters, in which she defends herself against accusations that she had gained unreasonably from contracts. In a letter to Indian commissioner John Collier, written in 1934, she described her motives for taking the five Kiowa artists to the Gallup Ceremonial. "This was done as a means to find a sale for their pictures. At the time they were unable to make any sales, and becoming discouraged. Many of their pictures could be found in the local pawnshop." She had visited the ceremonial and was convinced that their art and participation in the dances would be valued "by artists and art lovers who visited there. I took them at a great sacrifice of strength and finances." She emphasized in the letter that she never made a profit from the venture. "What I have done was for a cause. I started these boys with about twelve others in a little studio at my field matron quarters. At my own expense, they were furnished meals, canvas, water colors and oil paints, when they would come and work."[7]

Her version of how the Kiowas came to the attention of the university is in direct contrast to Jeanne d'Ucel's. "Though Oscar B. Jacobson gives me little credit, he would never have heard of the Kiowa artists if it had not been for me taking them to the University." She helped them get clothes ready to go to Norman, mending and paying for cleaners and backing the purchases of new clothing. She helped them find a place to stay in Norman and then went to see Lew Wentz and talked the oil tycoon into financing their room and board "to the amount of $300 per month for the five of them. This with the sale of pictures made a fair amount of expense money." She felt that she had received very little but critique for her effort, and she accused Jacobson of enriching himself through his control of their paintings. "He did not lose financially. When they made a good picture he marked it sold, bought it for the price he fixed himself, until he had a fine collection." She showed deep frustration not only with Jacobson's success but also with what appeared as a lack of gratitude from the Indians. "As far as the Gallup trip, long ago I decided that I had done all I could there and would never go with them again. The last trip was very unpleasant, the boys fussing among themselves. Their personality has grown in their own minds that each one thinks they should be the manager." She ended her letter with a grief later echoed by d'Ucel, and which may have resonated with many frustrated white people: "I hope in your great desire to help the Indi[a]n that you will not forget that there are some white people who have given their lives for what they though[t] a great purpose, and there are those who are still giving. The Indian should be encouraged to appreciate this."[8]

In 1947 Charles Pond, the husband of Willie Baze Lane, the Chickasha artist who had taught oil painting on the reservation, stepped into the fray. In a letter to oilman and art collector Thomas Gilcrease, he described his wife's role as substantial in the success of the Kiowa artists. "She brought them up to the point where their work was internationally recognized, for they had been invited by the King of Spain to make their appearance and bring their paintings to his Court."[9] In 1951, when Lane had just died, Pond took up a correspondence with Gilcrease regarding her papers and art. In the process, he expressed grave concerns about Jacobson. Pond cautioned Gilcrease against allowing Jacobson any access to Lane's papers, since he did not trust him to return them, and added: "Rest assured that he will not give Willie much of a write up in his new book." Pond also recommended that Gilcrease should encourage Susie Peters to "write you the History of Arts of the Anadarko Reservation" and Lane's role in it before it was too late. Pond had in his possession letters from Susie Peters to his late wife, which staunchly dismissed Jacobson's work. Peters wrote Lane in June 1944: "Of course you were the one (*and* no other) when we were struggling along. Criticised and the Indians effort in Art Unappreciated. It was you who were sure they had something fine to give to the world. And you treated them Royally in your studio and in your home—and just because Jacobson is connected with the university he gets or takes all the praise. He really never was their instructor. Miss Edith Mahier had charge of that at the University."[10]

The honor and gratitude the Kiowas bestowed on Oscar Jacobson at the ceremony in Anadarko significantly colored his and his family's life in the years that followed. His "adoption as a Kiowa chief" became one of the nodes around which all his other achievements circled. It was frequently highlighted in both Swedish and American articles, providing a reference for his authority to speak about American Indian art and culture. Throughout his life, his actions and involvement with American Indian artists in general, and Kiowas in particular, demonstrates his deep respect for their recognition.[11]

For this reason, if no other, Susie Peters's accusation must have smarted. She, too, received an honorary adoption into the tribe, having devoted her life to the welfare and uplifting of the Kiowa Indians. She suffered the insult of the Kiowa artists who sided with Jacobson and accused her of withholding their earnings and taking credit for their achievements. Many others on the reservation, including Jeanette Berry, remained loyal in their friendship with her throughout their lives. Susie Peters and Oscar Jacobson both invested so heavily in their connection to the Kiowa Indians that the conflict over who initiated and who sustained the Indians' success embittered their lives for years to come. For both, the goal of improvement and recognition of American Indians gave their lives a primary commitment that may have aided them in managing their own sense of marginality in the American society, she as a woman and he as an immigrant. This is not to suggest that their situations were parallel. Jacobson was a university professor and had built a reputation far across the nation, he had the ear of the Indian commissioner, and he had his own career as an artist. Peters appeared ever more petulant in her letters and indicated to her friend Willie Baze Lane that there were both class and gender dimensions to her frustration, when she ended: "Mrs Pond that's the way I've found the world and I do not believe its worth our effort to try to do anything about it."[12]

She might have found an ally in Jeanne d'Ucel, a superbly talented woman who nonetheless had to accept living in the shadow of her more charismatic and illustrious husband. But this did not happen. D'Ucel denied ever meeting Peters and took her accusations as a personal affront, as she chose to support her husband and build his reputation with unwavering loyalty. In her writings, she did this by focusing on a feature of their life that formed a central and celebrated element for both of them, that of friendships. D'Ucel's writings chronicle the importance of friendships with people of all colors and origins and how they structured the Jacobsons' strategies of inclusion and separateness as immigrants in American society. It was in and through these friendships that the influence of the Kiowa artists, and successive generations of American Indian artists, can be seen most distinctly in Jeanne and Oscar Jacobson's lives.

WEBS OF FRIENDSHIPS

Weaving is the metaphor d'Ucel used in her writings to describe the most important relationships of her life together with Oscar Jacobson. "In the tapestry of our life some of the brightest threads represent our contacts with interesting people, whether for a brief hour, or for long, matured friendships." A short text entitled "Glimpses," written in the early 1960s, chronicles some of these relationships with people who visited the Jacobsons or whom they met on their travels. "We have been fortunate and blessed in our friendships," d'Ucel asserted, and only rarely did these meetings fail to produce mutual sympathy. Some people were already famous when the Jacobsons met them, some became well known later. The Jacobson home was not so much a castle as a gateway. Not only Kiowa artists passed through their doors but also a host of people famous for various exploits.[13]

Oscar Jacobson's scrapbooks record an extensive network developing over the years. In combination with d'Ucel's manuscripts, apparently written for their children and grandchildren, the scrapbooks are a testament to the Jacobsons' ambitions and their sense of social position, but also to their pathos and sheer delight in people. Both Oscar and Jeanne enjoyed entertaining. It is evident in Oscar's youthful antics with his circle of friends in Lindsborg and at Yale, and in the many Swedish and Swedish American visitors he hosted while in Minnesota, such as the prominent physicist Svante Arrhenius, president of the Swedish Nobel Institute. After they were married in 1912, Oscar and Jeanne continued to host parties

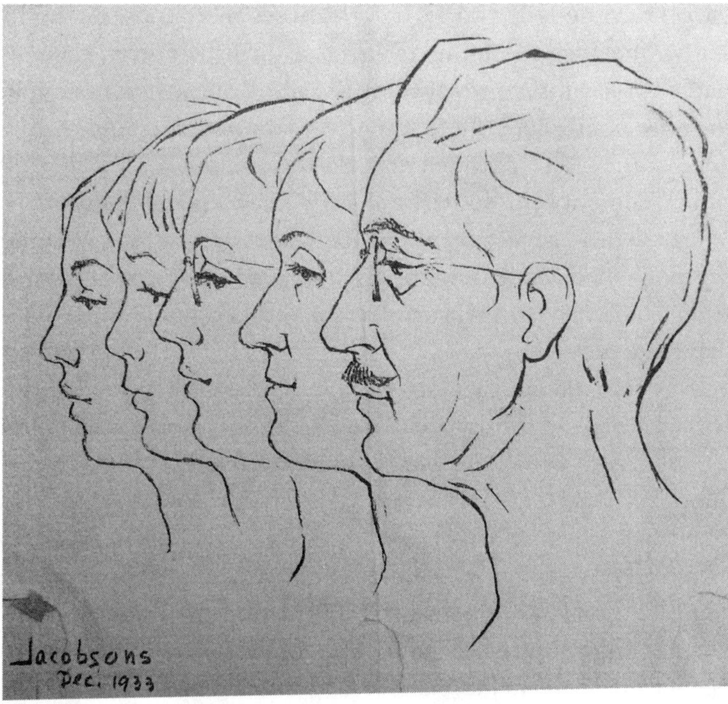

FIGURE 16. Sketch of the five Jacobsons, by Oscar Jacobson, 1933. Found in Jacobson's scrapbook for the years 1930–1947. Vol. 5, Box 5, Scrapbooks, OJC. Courtesy Oklahoma Historical Society.

and invite guests into their first home in Pullman. In November 1912, the young couple entertained a member of the Swedish nobility. The local paper reported:

> Professor and Mrs. Oscar Brousse-Jacobson of the State College of Washington entertained some 40 intimate friends Thursday evening in honor of Count Lage Posse of Almnaes, Sweden, who has been the guest of his old friend, Professor Brousse-Jacobson in Pullman a few days.
>
> Count Posse is the only son of the noted and wealthy count, Goran Posse, and a nephew of the famous court painter, Count Von Rosen. He is closely connected with members of the royal family, being an intimate friend of Prince Bernadotte, nephew of King Gustav V. The young nobleman is fond of America, its people and institutions, and has traveled across the continent five times.[14]

D'Ucel recorded the visit at the very outset of "Glimpses": "A polished gentleman, he gave the Pullman ladies a thrill by kissing their hands. We had planned a very small reception for him of our most intimate friends only; but we soon found out that many people would be mortally offended if they were not included. So the reception grew into a mob; even then, some whom we felt we hardly knew enough to invite, chose to feel insulted. I learned then how fond of titles Americans are."[15] This remark notwithstanding, scrapbooks and manuscripts suggest that the Jacobsons, too, enjoyed their links to famous people. To some extent, it may have aided them in becoming Americans, but it also served to place them apart and allowed them to criticize aspects of their new country.

The Jacobsons' curiosity about people and their willingness to open their home also fueled a deeper critique of prejudice and stratification in American society. Shortly after Count Posse's stay, they had another esteemed visitor, whose arrival did not elicit a note in the local newspapers. Booker T. Washington, the preeminent African American educator, visited Pullman on a tour across the country to raise funds for Tuskegee Institute. The Jacobsons' neighbor, the Reverend James Robinson, found out that the only hotel in Pullman refused to let a room to Washington and his secretary, so he offered his own apartment at Cliff House. Robinson moved to a cot in his chapel and borrowed a blanket from Jeanne, while asking her to host Washington and his aide for dinner. The Jacobsons did. "We ascertained that all who would sit at our table were sympathetic and everything went well; although one teacher, a Southern lady, absolutely refused to enter the dining room while the 'niggers' were there, and she wouldn't speak to us or the Reverend for months afterwards." Oscar and Jeanne "found Dr. Washington an interesting and charming man of great modesty, and a keen sense of humor."[16]

Critique of racism and racial segregation also emerged in an encounter the Jacobsons had on their way home from their year in North Africa. The meeting was framed in a cosmopolitan setting, which allowed for a specific form of criticism of the provincial nature of American racism. "Among interesting people we count also a black lady who was our fellow passenger on a transatlantic crossing. It was in 1926; we were returning from a sabbatical in Europe and Africa, sailing from Marseilles . . . and it turned into a delightful cruise, perfect for a convalescence. We stopped in Spain twice, once in Portugal and twice in the Azores." Over the course of the journey Jeanne befriended the woman, which "seemed to infuriate a Tennessee family aboard. They took great pains to make obvious detours around us. We were highly amused, as their contempt for us (nigger lovers, no doubt) was equaled by ours for them. Even before we became acquainted with Mrs. Hadley we had avoided them as we were repelled by their vulgarity." The rudeness of the Tennessee family (unmarked in any other way but undoubtedly white) contrasted sharply against the civility of Mrs. Hadley, the black woman they befriended. She was, it turned out, from Sierra Leone and introduced herself as the wife of a former attorney-general of the colony. Her grandfather had been an English officer who had married a woman from the colony and Mrs. Hadley had received a good education. "I would say that she had received a better than average education even for a white girl," d'Ucel concluded. She now devoted herself to furthering education for girls in Sierra Leone and hoped to interest Julius Rosenwald, the wealthy philanthropist who was deeply involved in supporting education efforts for African Americans and American Indians, in her project.[17]

Oscar expressed concern for what awaited her after her arrival in the United States and asked Jeanne to warn her about racial discrimination. "At once she laughed and told me that she knew about segregation, having made a short trip to the States two years before. She had cleverly found that, by using the native costume of Sierra Leone, she could avoid some of the unpleasantness of being black, as it set her apart from the American Negroes." In other ways, too, she set herself apart from African Americans. "She was very candid about an experience of hers in that previous journey, when she had been on a railroad train, in the South, on some sort of holiday. 'Frankly' she said 'I was glad for segregation as the behavior of the colored people was something to be ashamed of.'" She discussed racial attitudes in the different countries where she had lived and traveled, and noted a special affection for France. "'You know' she told me 'I can breathe freely in France; whether in shops, hotels, or anywhere, I have the feeling that I am a human being and that the color of my skin does not matter.'"[18]

Race in this account was intimately tied up with class and education. Taken together, the writings of d'Ucel indicate that for her, and presumably Oscar, sensitivity to class and a certain form of educated civility, superseded race. They abhorred what they viewed to be ignorance and narrow-mindedness, whether it was manifested in racism or in religious fanaticism. Theirs was a secular form of cosmopolitan intellectualism, with distinct traces of elitism, perhaps more evident in Jeanne than in Oscar. However, Jeanne felt more clearly than Oscar did the effects of a gender hierarchy that structured American society and that may have made it more urgent for her to affirm her place.[19]

"Distinguished and glamorous guests" continued to pass through their house. Norwegian polar explorer Roald Amundsen gave a talk that was "most interesting and a testimonial to his great modesty; he never used the pronoun I." Vilhjalmur Stefansson from Canada, an Arctic explorer of Icelandic descent, lacked Amundsen's "mystic depths" but was "engaging in his own way."[20] Novelist Sinclair Lewis, whom Oscar had known since Yale, visited them in Norman at "the peak of his renown." He had attached himself to the group of westerners of Swedish origin while at Yale. The Jacobsons remembered him as a prankster and enjoyed following his rising career with acclaimed novels such as *Main Street*, *Babbitt*, and *Elmer Gantry*. When Lewis visited them several years later, however, they found him a changed man. "He was melancholy and rather embittered," having found that fame and riches "was not what he had hoped." His famous red mane had faded, and he appeared tired. "We felt sad and terribly sorry for him."[21]

Another author, Rabindranath Tagore, found a place at the Jacobsons' table. In 1921, eight years after receiving the Nobel Prize in literature, he visited University of Oklahoma. Norman had little to offer in terms of accommodation for visitors and therefore Tagore had been put up in Oklahoma City, which would have forced him to take the train—"the accurately nicknamed Galloping Goose"—to and from his lecture at the university. When the Jacobsons found this out, they arranged to have Tagore stay in their house instead. They found him a charming and inquisitive guest, conversant on art and literature and on contemporary political issues in India. Both Oscar and Jeanne relished that he appreciated their countries of origin. "He was delighted to find that Dad was a native of Sweden; naturally he loved the nation that had awarded him the Nobel prize. He was equally fond of France where he had many friends and where his literary works had received their first recognition." His open lecture at the university had been well publicized and a large crowd attended, greeting Tagore with an ovation as he entered. However, d'Ucel noted, his lecture on mysticism and India's spiritual character proved too esoteric for this audience and "bewildered his listeners." The early 1920s was a time, she recalled, "when the West considered almost everything from a concrete, positivist, realist, yes, materialistic point of view. Before long the audience was baffled and interest waned. Tagore sensed it. But the more he tried to explain an intangible thing, the farther away they drew from him. They were bored and looked upon him as a visionary talking nonsense. It troubled him; it troubled us too. We wished that he had spoken as he did to us earlier about things of easier approach." The evening ended at an impasse. "It was painful to see the sad expression in Tagore's eyes, as if he had a sense of complete failure." Yet, even though d'Ucel berated the western audience for its lack of sophistication, she saved her greatest disdain for supercilious easterners. "A visitor from Boston—a Brahmin—remarked to Dad the next day that he would never have shaken hands with or listened to a man from India where they had castes. Dad only smiled. What was the use of saying anything to a Bostonian of that ilk?"[22] Again, they marked their distance from Americans, whether, in their view, positivistic westerners or elitist easterners.

Naturally, many of the Jacobsons' friends were artists and novelists. Already in their first year in Norman they became acquainted with the writer John Joseph Mathews, "Osage, with a dash of French blood," who later sat on the Osage Council. Mathews described Oscar as someone to emulate: "a man in whom 'virility and ruggedness' comingled happily with attributes of the 'classic gentleman,'" as noted by Mathews's biographer Michael Snyder. Mathews traveled to Algeria five years before the Jacobsons undertook their North African trip and met with Berbers—an experience that encouraged him to eventually write about his own Osage people.[23] Oscar established a long relationship with the sculptor Gutzon Borglum, the son of Danish immigrants, and he encouraged and mentored poet and playwright Lynn Riggs, who was of Cherokee descent. Riggs, who was studying at University of Oklahoma at the time and working to afford college fees in addition to writing, would drop by the Jacobsons for conversations and advice. He was on the brink of exhaustion and considered leaving the university. Oscar advised him to go to Santa Fe and arranged for him to meet with friends of his there. "In the relaxed atmosphere" there, Riggs "was able to blossom" and wrote his first drafts of what would later become his best known work *Green Grow the Lilacs* (subsequently turned into the lyrics for the musical *Oklahoma*). Santa Fe in the 1920s attracted a multitude of artists "of many dispositions, opinions and aims." The Jacobsons "were on friendly terms with just about all of them; we enjoyed their works however disparate they were. Dad, as he always did, helped them to get recognition by booking them in various exhibits here and elsewhere. For he was always catholic in his tastes and free from professional jealousy." Oscar arranged for exhibitions of several Mexican artists in Norman, and they encountered many Latin American artists and writers who attended the University. "We found them enjoyable in many different ways," wrote d'Ucel, "although we didn't always share in their politico-artistic fervour." Musicians from different corners of the globe also found their way into their acquaintance, including an Algerian musician, Edmond Yafil, who revitalized Arab and Moorish music. His compositions reminded them of their time in North Africa and their affinity for Moorish music and architecture. "That always tugged at our hearts," Jeanne d'Ucel explained.[24]

The d'Ucel manuscripts delight in a colorful mosaic of encounters and experiences, often framing her husband as a generous facilitator. Travels enriched their lives, expanded their circle of friends, and affirmed their connection to a world of culture. North Africa "tugged at" their hearts, not least d'Ucel's, whose book *Berber Art*, written after their return to Norman, had been published by the University of Oklahoma Press with Oscar's decorations on the jacket.[25]

Norman had become their home. They arrived there as pioneers in 1915. By 1925 the art department had four full-time teachers. Oscar described his experience as living "100 years in one decade."

> The struggle and the romance of it gave our lives a richness beyond computation and that we fully appreciated. For we had found Oklahoma a raw, Western land with an intoxicating atmosphere; the lacks and discomforts were compensated for by the color, the feeling of stupendous progress, the valiant optimism and the friendliness we found among whites and Indians. Dad likened this period to the age of chivalry in Europe. Like the knights of old, the cowboys were rough, but they had admirable qualities and a high code of honor. They might be unlettered in the accepted meaning of the term; yet they had culture of a kind. The world has finally come to value their epic or romantic tales and songs.[26]

The Jacobsons were at the heart of this development. Their Oklahoma friends and contacts included the oilman and entrepreneur Frank Phillips, Lew Wentz of Ponca City who once ranked as one of the five richest men in America, and M. Gordon Matzene, who had become enamored with oriental art and culture while staying in Beijing. Matzene came from an Anglo-Danish background, and d'Ucel described him as "by all odds one of the most fantastic among our friends." This friendship had momentous significance for the OU art museum as Matzene donated his entire collection to the university, with generous financial support from Wentz. Neither of the two men, however, wished to have their names made public, so Jacobson had to call it "merely an Oriental collection, and to fend off press questions. The mystery deepened and later was the cause of unpleasantness for Dad." The "unpleasantness" consisted of questions regarding the provenance and artistic value of the collection as it had to be kept under conditions of anonymity. However, relatively soon it became known as the Wentz-Matzene Collection and formed a substantial part of Jacobson's plans for the OU art museum.[27]

YEARS OF BOUNTY AND SORROW

The 1940s and early 1950s were years of harvest for the teacher, director, and artist Oscar Jacobson. In 1941 Bethany College bestowed on him an honorary doctorate of fine arts, to Birger Sandzén's great pleasure. The following year, he received the International Business Machine Corporation Medal for his contributions to the art world, and in 1949 he was inducted into the Oklahoma Hall of Fame. He exhibited frequently and showed both earlier and more recent works. He painted ferociously. In December 1948, for example, an exhibition of twenty-two paintings showed at the OU Museum of Art including twenty that he had painted during that summer, which they spent as usual in their Colorado cabin in Allen's Park. He resigned from the directorship of the school of art in the middle of 1945 at the age of sixty-three and was appointed as research professor and later David Ross Boyd Professor Emeritus. The art department had grown in size and in reputation and added several new faculty members. Some of them considered Jacobson's style old-fashioned and wanted to develop the program in a different direction.[28]

In the summer of 1947, devastation struck the family as Oscar and Jeanne's son Oscar André died after a car accident in the Colorado mountains. His ashes were placed in a niche high up in a granite ridge, close to the family's cabin. Jeanne told her neighbors how Oscar Sr. sat for two weeks on a simple wooden bench on top of a stone outcropping facing the ridge, returning only for meals and nightfall. When he came back to Norman after the summer he showed no outward signs of mourning and finally began to paint again.[29]

In 1952 after Jacobson's formal retirement, the university honored him by renaming the art museum building Jacobson Hall. "Dad was speechless with surprise, and I was elated," wrote d'Ucel, particularly grateful as this countered what many in the state considered to have been negative treatment of his work and person. Soon thereafter he was included in the *American Art Directory*. In 1957, Philbrook Art Center honored him with a solo exhibition, and in 1960 he received a citation from the US Department of the Interior, Bureau of Indian Arts and Crafts, honoring his efforts in support of Indian arts.[30]

Jacobson could look back on a life of success. His achievements and efforts as a teacher, an artist, and an innovator had met with recognition. He still retained connections with his country of birth, yet he was an immigrant who had carved out a respected place for himself and his family in the new country. A huge part of this had come about through his contacts with American Indigenous people (see plate 10).

JACOBSON AND FRIENDSHIPS WITH AMERICAN INDIANS

The warp and weft of friendships weaving together throughout Jeanne d'Ucel's narrative in "Memoirs" and "Glimpses" did not specifically include American Indian contacts—perhaps because another entire manuscript, entitled "About Indians," was devoted to them. But perhaps it is also indicative of the deep separation that divided the lives of American Indians and white Americans. Yet, those relationships too affirmed the joy of friendship. The manuscript opens with a sentence that proclaims: "Of his various lives, the Indian one has given Dad perhaps the greatest joy."[31] And, it might be added, his greatest recognition.

The friendships that developed between Jacobson and American Indian artists had such a profound significance for all their lives and work that without attempting to understand them it would be difficult to see what motivated him and the artists he worked with over such a sustained period of their lives. Special relationships between white settlers and Indigenous people forms a trope with deep roots in colonial history and has often been used as a euphemism and justification for colonial domination and land taking. It is difficult to find a language for talking about interracial friendships that does not reduce the distances or overstate the mutuality of the relationship or miss out on attempts made to bridge divides and establish communication despite inequalities and differences. A notion of "a special friendship" haunts much of the imagination accompanying the expansion of European settlement, not just in North America but across the globe. This idea of friendship takes shape in stories of special relationships to the Indigenous peoples of the area that set a colony apart from its competitors. Thus, colonial propaganda drew parallels between the English before the Anglo-Saxon invasion and the Indigenous Nations in Virginia so as to argue for a special affinity. Particularly strong and long-lasting narratives evoke a history of connections between Germans and American Indians. Surveying arguments for special connections between a range of European peoples and American Indians, Christian Feest concludes, "Whatever the key terms of the analogy, European nations have had no difficulty in finding a special bond with Indians in their own distinctive heritages." Sweden had its own set of powerful stories of friendly relations emerging from the aftermath of the Swedish colonial attempt along the Delaware River in the seventeenth century, stories repackaged and circulated among Swedish Americans in their arguments for belonging in America. The late 1920s and 1930s were marked by celebrations of the anniversary of the Swedish colony, and officials on both sides of the Atlantic lauded Swedish (and Finnish) values and comportment as a reason for peaceful interaction. The commemorations generally focused on the modern-day relations between three independent nations (Sweden, Finland, and the United States), but the friendly interactions in the seventeenth-century colony figured prominently as a starting point. Adam Hjorthén argues that "the inclusion of Indian representations resonated with, and functioned to strengthen, the contemporary 1930s image of Sweden as a modern, progressive, and humanitarian country."[32]

While previous scholarship thus confirms the self-serving (perhaps self-aggrandizing) nature of such protestations of special friendships, H. Glenn Penny argues for the need to move beyond aggregated entities such as states, colonies, and metropoles in assessing the "joint recognition of a common fate that emerged out of ongoing discussions of shared characteristics among members of these groups over a long period of time." It is not enough, he suggests, to view all such notions of affinity as projections of one-sided fantasies, and furthermore, "very few scholars entertain the possibility that some American Indians might sense similar affinities as well." Although skepticism is certainly justified when settlers claim friendly engagement with the Indigenous peoples they have dispossessed, there is reason to seek new ways to interpret and understand the entanglements, both individual and collective, that arise out of colonial contact. Indeed, immigrant-Indigenous encounters challenged philosophical and ethical interrogations into the nature of friendship that required of both a consideration of where and how to draw boundaries. It is perhaps significant, in this context, that when Jacobson wrote about Delaware people for *The American Swedish Monthly* in June 1938, during the heyday of celebrations of colonist-Indian friendship, he entirely avoided that kind of language.[33]

The friendships that the Jacobsons entered into with American Indians may be said to belong to a set of intercultural relationships characterized as circumscribed, tentative, always threatened, and dependent upon the mutual investment of real effort. How can one assess such individual bonds across ethnic and racial boundaries? In a study of British–East Indian connections in England at the turn of the twentieth century, literary scholar Elleke Boehmer metaphorically characterizes them as zigzagging and fuzzy, producing what she calls an indirection in their "generally halting, shy, tacit, hit-and-miss" quality. "Zigzag" signifies "changes of tack" and "fuzzy" refers to "the perpetual indeterminacy that is consequent on such indirection for commentators both at the time and in the present day." Boehmer and other scholars who venture into the territory of intercultural and interracial friendships "concede how complicated, difficult and tentative many of these connections were, and how challenging they remain to historical interpretation."[34]

A different way of framing such interactions is to view them as encounters between cultural mediators. Margaret Connell Szasz describes the work of culture brokers as translation, "literally and culturally—among the various sides of the cross-cultural equation." It is not a simple computation, however, as American Indian educator Janine Pease Pretty on Top (Crow) points out, in describing the stakes involved for Indigenous people: "we carry baggage wherever we go. It's not just me and you meeting, it's my grandma and her great-grandma and so on." Encounters impact the future and will therefore also affect coming generations. "It's a very loaded situation, very tense." Searching for a common language is vital, and spanning the distances between strangers must "start with visiting." Listening is "difficult for people whose values and spiritual commitments are so different. You think you're using the same language, and you really aren't."[35]

Without communication there can be no survival. Leela Gandhi, in *Affective Communities*, finds in the risky friendships between strangers an anticolonial possibility, a "language of self-estrangement." It is a language that does not offer self-determination to oppressed peoples, nor overthrow imperial governments, but it can "alter the genetic structure of the societies in which they eventuate, subtly varying for future use their ethical, epistemic, and political composition."[36]

For Oscar Jacobson, the honor bestowed on him by the Kiowas marked not the end of his involvement with American Indian artists but, rather, the beginning of a period of broadened contacts. In a biographical sketch written by Edna Nyquist and published in the *American Swedish Monthly* in 1938, Jacobson described his involvement with American Indian students as "only incidental" and a natural part of his work. "But," Nyquist commented, "no other part of his work with the exception of his own painting, has brought him so much fame." In the 1930s, the art department had a larger enrollment of American Indians than any other department at Oklahoma University, and Oklahoma was definitely the place to be for young American Indian artists. Describing Jacobson's "initiation into the Kiowa tribe," Nyquist continues, "observing Nah-goey walk across the campus or through his building where the Indians are likely to congregate, one cannot help noticing the respect they show in speaking to him."[37]

The initial contacts with the six Kiowa Indians soon swelled into a monumental undertaking. Word spread of Jacobson's support for American Indian art, and Indian artists from all across the country approached him to ask for help. "I found myself mentor—sometimes adopted father—to a great many of them." Over the years, Jacobson came to mentor more than one hundred artists "belonging to all tribes." Jacobson utilized the Public Works of Art Projects (PWAP) as a platform for engaging American

Indian artists, and he secured contracts and supervised the execution of murals across the state and beyond, which helped launch artists like Ernest Spybuck (Absentee Shawnee), Richard West (Cheyenne), Woody Crumbo (Cherokee), Blackbear Bosin (Comanche-Kiowa), Allan Houser (Chiricahua Apache), Archie Black Owl (Cheyenne), and Cecil Dick (Cherokee) on their artistic careers.[38]

Jeanne d'Ucel's manuscript details the evolution of a course focusing on the history of American Indian art, which attracted more and more "white and red students alike." Growing numbers of American Indians began to attend the university, although most of them, d'Ucel commented, "had some white blood." This younger cohort of students had qualified for university through previous studies and therefore joined the regular courses. While the first group of Kiowa students had come from a background of close ties to Kiowa ceremonies and cultural practices, the students who now arrived did not always have a connection to tribal cultures. "Dad chuckled," wrote d'Ucel, at the memory of how "he Indianised some of them."[39]

However well intentioned, this is a statement that reveals how specific notions of what it meant to be "Indian" underscored Jacobson's appreciation of Indigenous culture and how he had internalized an image of himself as an authority on those peoples. It also indicates that the friendships were not perceived as between equals but, rather, patterned on that between mentors and their disciples. In a few cases, that balance would be challenged but most often it remained the norm.[40]

Among the students who now crossed the Jacobson threshold were Acee Blue Eagle (Pawnee-Creek and Scottish), Franklin Gritts (Cherokee), Chief Saul (Choctaw), Cecil Murdock (Kickapoo), Saupity (Comanche), Kenneth Anquoh (Kiowa), and Richard "Dick" West (Southern Cheyenne). The last of these became a particularly close friend of the Jacobsons. He was the first American Indian to achieve a bachelor of fine arts degree from Oklahoma University; he later went on to earn a master of arts degree, and in 1963 he was awarded an honorary doctorate. West became director of the arts program at Bacone College in Muskogee, Oklahoma. He and Oscar remained in contact throughout their lives.[41]

In her memoirs, d'Ucel relates an amusing incident that demonstrates the easy communication between West and Jacobson. Once, on a trip to Oklahoma City, they were caught on different sides of a road right at the high tide of afternoon traffic. Dick West had traveled to the city with the Jacobsons in order to submit some sketches to the *Daily Oklahoman,* but when they met up again in the afternoon, West had lost his drawings. It was impossible to hear anything above the noise of the traffic, and so Jacobson resorted to Indian sign language and suggested to West a place where he might have forgotten them. A policeman saw them gesticulating and thought that Oscar was an escaped inmate from the nearby Central State Mental Hospital. Oscar replied that he was "only having a little social hour with my Indian friend over there." West had returned and signaled across the street and Oscar "took a wicked delight in signaling back." Relishing the story, West spread it back on campus and the "art students especially would greet one another with strange gestures. And, in the Follies of that year, the most applauded skit was one where a tall fellow, wearing an old, well smeared paint smock, (swiped from Dad's studio, to make identification unmistakable) conversed in 'sign' language with a real Indian."[42] Lisa K. Neuman, in her book on Bacone College, interviewed Dick West, and he confirms his friendship with Jacobson. According to West, Jacobson had a "refreshingly complex view of Indians" and did not "group all Indians together as did many 'Anglo-Saxons,'" something he attributed to Jacobson being Swedish American.[43]

Jacobson began planning an illustrated volume on North American Indian paintings. D'Ucel's description of this work shows how closely the couple collaborated. "To save his time I did research on the historical background and I helped him assemble the necessary biographical information. Many Indians do not like to write or answer letters. (One drove 100 miles rather than do that). So we had to travel much during the next several summers to secure data. The Second World War engulfed the United States just as the work was nearing completion; it had to be laid aside until 1946. Then it required review to bring it up to date." The two volumes entitled *Les Peintres Indiens de l'Amérique du Nord (American Indian Painters)* came out in 1950 with the same publisher as the book on Kiowa art. The volumes showcased artists from thirty-six American Indian nations.[44]

Another anecdote reveals how Oscar Jacobson related to American Indians but also how he mediated contacts between European visitors and American Indigenous peoples. In the summer of 1939, the German-born actress Hilde Wagener visited her brother, who happened to live near the Jacobsons in their Colorado cabin. Wagener greatly desired to "see Indians," and Oscar and her brother took her on a whirlwind trip across the Navajo reservation. At Kayenta, Oscar heard of a group of white men going to a dance and asked if he could come along. A missionary who headed the group warned him that the northern Navajo holding the dance rarely interacted with white people and might be hostile to their presence. D'Ucel described the event:

> Arriving at the scene of the ceremonial, Dad went to stand near some Navajos who appeared not to notice him. After some considerable time Dad offered his pack of cigarettes to his neighbor. The pack was passed around and emptied. All smoked in silence for at least 15 minutes. Finally the fellow asked offhand "Where' you from?" "Oklahoma" said Dad who knew his Indians and could be as laconic as any of them. Another long silence "Where' you going?" "Passing through" Silence. "Which way?" "Gallup" Silence. "For the ceremonial?" "No" Still more silence. "Why?," "No time" Silence. Then Dad asked "Are you going?" "Maybe" Silence. Again Dad asked "Do you dance?" "Some" Long silence. Dad remarked "Some Navajos are good dancers" A grunt of approval. He continued "So are the Kiowas." A noncommittal grunt. "Especially Mopope" The next grunt was surprised, and several Navajos drew nearer. One asked "Do you know him?" "Yes." Dad added "Hokeah is also a good dancer." There were nods of assent. The crowd was watching Dad with interest. He took his time letting their curiosity boil; then he said "How is Harrison Begay?" There was an explosion of surprise "You know him?" "Yes" said Dad "and Tahoma." They were excited now, wondering about this man who knew their artists. Beaming when they learned who he was, they surrounded him; soon some of the elder more reserved men came to shake hands with this new found friend.[45]

Their daughter Yolande described similarly her father's approach to American Indians as one of patience and sharing. He would take his time and share cigarettes, and he would not push or ask questions. He "was not condescending."[46] Undoubtedly appreciated for his reticence and generosity, his approach also led to results that baffled other white intermediaries.

These accounts seem to suggest that Jacobson's rapport with Indians was based on a direct and perhaps inborn quality of reserve. However, as she continued, D'Ucel demonstrated that his approach was part of a studied strategy: "Dad had them where he wanted and he could secure their cooperation." Abandoning his monosyllabic conversation style he now told the assembled men: "In my party there is a lady who comes from the other side of the ocean, who has never before seen Indians. She wants to take pictures. You know how it is; people like to have a souvenir from the places where they have been (grunts of understanding) Now I know, you people don't like to be photographed, but to be nice to this strange lady maybe you would let her take some pictures, in the morning, don't you think so?" Early the next morning four Navajos rode into the trading post calling Jacobson's name. To everyone's amazement, Hilde Wagener got her pictures, and "the old trader Weatherill shook his head at this unbelievable display of Navajo friendship."[47]

Such stories of easygoing relationships between Oscar and American Indians, remembered by family members and corroborated by colleagues, portray him as an unusual intercultural communicator. But they also completely erase the differences in power and influence that structured these interactions. Rarely is there in d'Ucel's writings and Jacobson's comments any hint of the political and social consequences of discrimination and government control in the lives of the Indians befriended by the couple. Considering Jacobson's early anger at the exploitation he witnessed at the Santa Fe market and his efforts to defeat the Bursum Bill, this lack of political involvement is noticeable.

Jacobson seems to have enjoyed these interactions for their own sake, but he also used them to fulfill the desires of curious visitors for exotic Indian displays. A visit from the famous Danish physicist Niels Bohr and his family in 1937 allowed Oscar Jacobson another opportunity to affirm his special connection to American Indians. The Bohrs' nineteen-year-old son, Hans, particularly wished to "see real Indians." Jacobson told some of his Indian students about the well-known scientist and his son, and they agreed to put on a performance for the visitors. D'Ucel reminisced about what may have been "the most exclusive Indian dance ever performed." Jacobson did not miss the opportunity for his students to display their art as well. The audience consisted of the three Bohrs and Jacobson's colleague the physicist J. Rud Nielsen and his wife, who were thrilled. Hans told Jeanne "that he had to pinch himself to make sure he was awake, seeing and talking to Red Indians that he had dreamed about all his life."[48] This was a rare event in another way as well. It brought together to two facets of friendship emphasized in D'Ucel's separate manuscripts, where "Glimpses" focused on their engagement with acquaintances, both famous and ordinary, who had enriched their lives, and "About Indians" dealt with specific contacts with American Indians.

Another aspect of Jacobson's friendships with American Indians emerges in his connection to Allan Houser, the eminent Apache sculptor and painter. Houser was the grandson of Geronimo and "one of the best Indian painters and one of Dad's protégés." As a young man Jacobson had met Geronimo, who was then a prisoner of war at Fort Sill, and according to D'Ucel, the "old Apache liked Dad well enough to give him his autographed photograph. After years of captivity he had mellowed; he even accepted some white things, sweets for instance on which he doted; and he had learned to write to the extent of printing his name."[49]

His grandson, Allan, had been one of the painters commissioned to paint a mural for the Department of Interior building in Washington together with Mopope and Auchiah, and he had done several other murals as well for public and private buildings. He often painted scenes from the Mescalero Apache "when their little band held the U.S. army at bay for years, terrorizing the country." D'Ucel described him and noted in his work "something of the superlative pride of the Apaches, that sometimes appears to border on arrogance." One day, a man writing a children's book about Geronimo approached Jacobson. The man's eastern publishers thought it would add to the book's appeal if it included illustrations "by the descendant of the Apache bandit" and wished for Jacobson to facilitate a contact:

> Dad said to him "I'll give you Allan Houser's address, but that's all. He venerates his grandfather who is a hero for the Apaches. I respect his feelings; in fact I sympathise with them. Therefore I will not give you an introduction, for I don't want to appear as sponsoring your book in case it is offensive to him." "Oh!" replied the writer "I am not uncomplimentary to the old fellow. Besides," he added, as if it were a convincing argument, "the illustrations

> would be extremely well paid." At that Dad laughed. "I'm afraid you don't know Indians. That wouldn't carry any weight with even the poorest of them." Allan did not illustrate the book.[50]

By the time D'Ucel wrote her memoirs, Geronimo and the struggle of the Apaches had been somewhat reevaluated in American society at large. She found it encouraging that in a recent Hollywood movie, "instead of picturing the Apaches as blood thirsty savages, the cruel circumstances that led them to the war path are shown with some sympathy. And, in the Arizona State Capitol, hangs a portrait of Geronimo, painted by Allan Houser at the request of the Arizona legislature."[51]

Importantly, these stories situate Jacobson as an insider to Indigenous culture, while other white people displayed ignorance of—and sometimes acted rather boorishly and insultingly toward—American Indians. He most certainly did have a much greater familiarity with Indigenous cultures than most white Americans, and he used it to broker contacts, sometimes facilitating them, as in the case of Hilde Wagener, while at other times denying support as in his response to the author from the East. Taken together with a lifetime of complex relations vis-à-vis the cultural and intellectual elite of the nation, this may have been, from his own horizon, Jacobson's assertive comeback to those Anglos and easterners who did not fully embrace him and his work. A mixed sense of inferiority and underdevelopment in comparison with East Coast institutions and culture offset by assertions of the superior nature and naturalness of the West suffuses much of the writings of both Jeanne and Oscar, beginning already in the letters between Oscar and Birger Sandzén.[52]

Turning the tables on these expectations became something of Jacobson's forte. In 1935, in preparation for the Southwest Education Conference that was to be held at the University of Oklahoma, President Bizzell informed Jacobson that all "the big guns from the East express the same wish, to see a real Indian." He and Jacobson both knew that the participants coming from the East Coast had specific expectations. Well-educated judges, lawyers, and doctors "would not satisfy the Easterners' dream of Indians, because they would be almost indistinguishable from the guests." Jacobson had an idea. He approached Acee Blue Eagle and asked him to put on a "proper display" while delivering a speech at the main banquet. Blue Eagle "appeared in tribal garb" and was properly

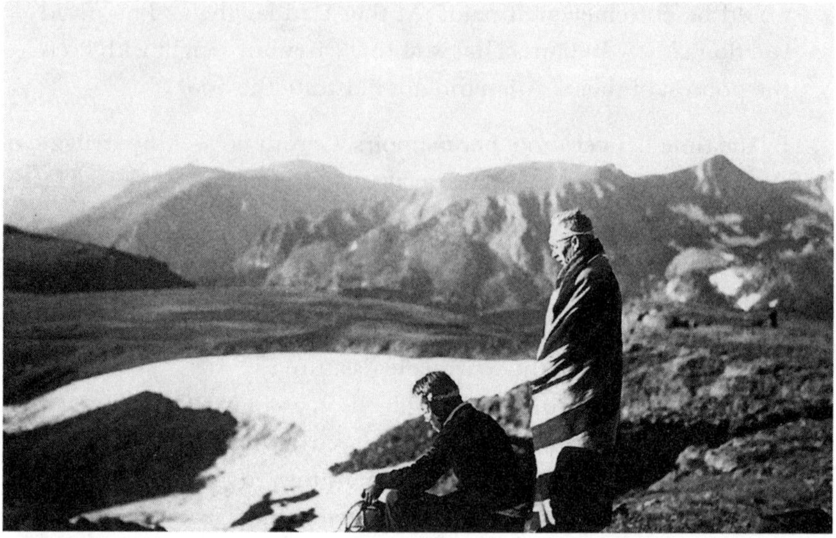

FIGURE 17. Saying a prayer. Jacobson together with Garcia at Iceberg Lake, Colorado, 1941. Oscar had been asked by Jemez artist Jose Toledo to perform a ceremony by the lake on his wedding day. Toledo sent sacred pollen and eagle feathers including detailed instructions to Jacobson in a registered mail package. Together with Garcia, also from Jemez Pueblo, Jacobson offered a prayer for the newlyweds. Courtesy Sophie Sheppard.

gawked at. A "famous professor from Harvard—or was it Yale?" tried speaking to him in pidgin English, and Blue Eagle responded with grunts. The climax came at the end of the dinner. "One can imagine the surprise of the Harvard man and others when Acee delivered an excellent talk in perfect English. All Oklahomans also enjoyed the show."[53] As so often in d'Ucel's recollections, the joke was on the easterners, poking a hole in their presumed superiority, while eschewing class, race, or gender hierarchies at play within communities in Oklahoma and the West.[54]

It is difficult to assess, based on these reminiscences, the precise depth of Jacobson's knowledge of Indigenous people and their cultures. Most of his contacts appear to have been premised on a teacher-student model and carried out within the setting of the university. Some of these students became lifelong friends, but it did not necessarily mean that Jacobson was immersed in their communities. His contacts with the Kiowa Nation remained the closest, and he visited his friends on the reservation regularly over the years and took part in ceremonies. This indicates that over the years he acquired a deeper understanding of Kiowa society. He and his wife also appear to have become close to Jemez Pueblo artist Jose Toledo and his family, a relationship that touched both families in a very personal way. Jacobson helped Toledo on the way with his painting career and they became close friends. Since the Jacobsons were unable to travel to Jemez on the occasion of Toledo's marriage, he asked Jacobson to perform a special prayer for the couple up by a mountain lake in Colorado and for that purpose sent "by registered airmail some sacred pollen and eagle feathers."[55]

REVERSED ROLES

Over the years Jacobson's role as promoter and mentor of Indians changed, and although he more than likely remained friends also with younger generations of American Indian artists, more and more they broke away from the vision of traditional American Indian painting that he had promoted. Dick West and Oscar Howe were examples of this. Both men stayed close friends of the Jacobsons, but they diverged from his teaching. They developed in more abstract directions under the tutelage of a later generation of painting faculty in the 1940s, and with inspiration from the controversial US State Department exhibition *Advancing American Art,* which showcased contemporary American works. Many of the works were nonrepresentational, and several of the included artists were charged with left-leaning sympathies. In the Cold War climate of the late 1940s this engendered massive criticism against the exhibition. West argued that abstraction constituted "a part of the Indians [*sic*] artistic thinking" from long before European influences, and they sought to wed motives and styles that could be recognized as simultaneously both Indigenous and modern. The "traditional type of Indian painting" had been produced so many times "to the point of being hackneyed." Howe, whom Jacobson initially hired to illustrate his volume on *North American Indian Costumes,* similarly found inspiration in patterns and motives in quill work and tipi paintings and combined these with cubist and surrealist forms and techniques.[56]

Jacobson may not have been so averse to these changes as his younger colleagues assumed. He was instrumental in bringing the exhibition of contemporary paintings to the university and assisted in the museum's bid when the works were auctioned off, securing the largest number of any bidder, including works of Edward Hopper and Georgia O'Keefe. He nonetheless considered the postwar style of painting too pessimistic and lacking the "buoyancy of spirit he believed that the visual arts should express." Yet, he also confessed to his daughter Yolande that "Indian painting of that style perfectly flat had gone about as far as it could have got without becoming repetitive." He told her he believed it would have to "evolve into something else . . . there would be a time when you couldn't tell it was Indian painting and yet it would have hopefully elements that it started out with Indian art." For this reason, he was keen to publish the book about North American Indian painting before it was too late.[57]

Two events toward the end of his life demonstrate how the world the Jacobsons had helped shape had now altered almost beyond their recognition. In 1963 Oscar Jacobson received an invitation to Hollywood from Vincent Price, to appear as a guest on the popular TV show *This Is Your Life* devoted to the life of Lakota artist Oscar Howe. Jacobson's brief appearance as an important but supportive influence in Howe's life represented a curious reversal in the relationship between Native artists and their Swedish patron. In this instance, Howe was the star and shared some of his magic with Jacobson. D'Ucel described the fallout of the show:

> After the making of the tape, in Hollywood I had written 2–3 people in Norman alerting them to see the program on its release the following week. They told others who told still others. There were also some who just happened on the program. For days Dad was hailed by people, sometimes complete strangers, calling "I saw you on TV." I finally said to him "What's the need of working for serious purposes? Just say a few words on TV, and you are famous—for a week anyway." A pile of mail was waiting for us; several letters from friends scattered over the country who had chanced on the program; one came from a college classmate of Dad's with whom he had lost contact for 40 years.[58]

The brief moment of Jacobson's appearance on the show staged him as a supporting actor; to the Americans watching, the roles between promoter and protégé had been reversed with Oscar Howe now the celebrity. D'Ucel's reference to post-show mail had a corollary in the Howe household, which reinforces this change in balance. Letters arrived to Howe from near and far including letters from leading politicians and prominent people in the media industry. In reply to one, his wife commented that they "had been receiving mail from all over the country, [and] I am answering about ten to twenty every day."[59]

That same year Oscar and Jeanne again reconnected with his first Kiowa students. James Auchiah had strived for many years to have his grandfather, the famous war chief Satanta, recognized and honored with a reburial at the Fort Sill army post. The Jacobsons received an invitation from the Fort Sill commander and the Kiowa tribal council to attend the ceremony. Jeanne's description of Satanta is much less flattering than the one she gave of Geronimo: "Satanta, a fierce Kiowa warrior of a century ago, was a Nemesis of the whites. Even some of his own people considered him unnecessarily cruel and ruthless."[60]

Oscar Jacobson was now in his early eighties; he had suffered a severe stroke and had trouble with his heart. The trip down to Fort Sill in the middle of summer appeared overwhelming. However, an acquaintance from Pennsylvania who was curious about Indians offered to drive them. D'Ucel recollected: "we found ourselves in the midst of many people we knew, Kiowas, and Indians of all tribes, come from all over the state, also whites. Auchiah beaming, rushed to thank us for coming and proceeded to introduce many more persons. Everybody seemed pleased that the artist's teacher and friend was on hand." Jeanne found the ceremony ludicrous. Both whites and Indians offered speeches which "helped paint an image of a great hero without fear or blemish of any kind. Not one word was uttered about the butchery of children that had been Satanta's trade mark. Even the director of the Texas prisons who had come with a large delegation from that state, added his praise to the towering panegyric. Such is the world!"[61] Again, d'Ucel's portrayal of Kiowas did not question the frontier mythology that cast them as savages, and her description of Satanta suggests that she accepted a common American portrayal of Indians as particularly brutal in the history of Kiowa–US relations. These relations had not yet been reappraised in scholarship or in popular culture, as had begun to happen with the perception of the Apache struggle against American domination.[62]

In terms of the politics of American Indian relations to the United States and to the state of Oklahoma, the world may have moved away from and ahead of the Jacobsons. The struggle to have Satanta reburied at Fort

Sill and honored for his leadership during one of the darkest periods in Kiowa history shows James Auchiah and his relatives' determination. For Auchiah and for his fellow Kiowa artists, their respect for Kiowa ways and their dedication to preserving and adapting Kiowa traditions and practices to the contemporary world always came first. It was their primary motivation as artists and as citizens of the Kiowa Nation. Auchiah "illustrated the Indian notion that an art form touches the life of everybody in his tribe, including the dominions and powers that are gifts from all forms of life," writes J'Nell Pate. "Auchiah was the embodiment of the Indian belief that man must yield back that which the tribe and the living environment required for their own fulfillment."[63]

Yet, despite being out of step with contemporary developments in Indian-white relations, Jacobson did not leave the event without recognition. "Next came the presentation of gifts by the tribal council. The General received a war bonnet and seemed genuinely surprised. Various other things were handed to the ranking guests. To Dad's and my astonishment he was given something; to his delight this was a peyote fan, the one article that he lacked and had tried in vain for years to buy." The Kiowa artists remained loyal to the end, recognizing the significance of Jacobson's support and, yes, even friendship over the many decades of a long life. D'Ucel, however, saw mostly losses. "Dances completed the ceremony. Auchiah led the principal one with an exclusive group of Kiowas. Unfortunately the costume of these warriors comprised a long back cloak of turkey red cloth. Many of the bonnets and sub disks with feathers died in indigo, pink or lavender, made us shudder. Alas! now even the Indians find these delightfully colorful, giving proof that taste can be corrupted."[64]

The dancers sporting red capes most likely belonged to the Black Legs Society, which had been revived following the Second World War based on the knowledge of elders who had learned the ceremonies and songs before the society ceased to function in 1927. Members of the Anquoe and Palmer families initiated the revival, among them brothers of Lyndreth Palmer, Stephen Mopope's nephew, who had been killed in Germany in 1944. The colorful adornments on bonnets and bustles were outgrowths of the experimentation and performances honed by the Kiowa art students. In spite of everything, Jeanne d'Ucel and Oscar Jacobson had been part of the movement that shaped changing manifestations of Indianness, modern yet unsevered from pre-reservation traditions partly because of the sponsorship and encouragement of people such as themselves. The Kiowas continued to honor that support in ceremonies such as the one commemorating Satanta's life. In 1952 the Anadarko chapter of the MacDowell Club invited Oscar Jacobson to give a lecture on Indian art, and Mr. and Mrs. Stephen Mopope received an invitation as special guests. No wonder they kept the invitation! Inextricably entwined but not always attuned to one another's needs and desires, the Kiowas and the Swedish American couple remained connected for life.[65]

CHAPTER 7

Dancer, Artist, and Teacher

AFTER LEAVING NORMAN, Stephen Mopope forged a career as a painter and a leader of dance troupes. Unique among early American Indian artists, he was able to continue painting and make this the basis of his living until his death in 1974. He applied his own considerable artistic skills, but he also benefited from his connections to leading networks on the reservation through his membership in the Ohoma Society and through his father-in-law and uncle on the tribal KCA Business Committee. Finally, the education in Norman and the support from Jacobson gave him leverage in the otherwise closed world of art galleries and shows. His abundant notes and sketches show how much ingenuity, adaptability, and determination were required for the creation of this career, in the space that seems to end when the Kiowa artists left Norman after their studies. Kiowa life beyond the purview of white patrons contained wide and varied paths and challenges, obligations and restrictions. Following the trails of Stephen Mopope and his closest family circle allows us a glimpse of concurrent worlds that structured and inspired his life and work, and in a similar manner that of other Indian artists as well. This was a sphere distinctly Indian and Kiowa but also personal and private. His story shows his adherence to traditions yet also his ability to turn both to the past and to the future for inspiration. Mopope continued, as Kiowas had for centuries, a life of mobility, but now with the aid of the most modern modes of transportation, the car and the train. The home he shared with Jeanette Berry served as a gateway as much as the Jacobsons' house, but it was also the starting node and the point of return that kept him firmly connected to the Redstone Valley. Stephen Mopope continued painting—and dancing—throughout his life. These were his main occupations, but he also farmed and took other jobs to supplement the family's income, such as working as a policeman on the reservation. His remaining personal papers enable us to chronicle how he strove tirelessly to make this possible by forever being alert to contacts who might be interested in purchasing art and by writing to galleries and collectors. They show how he came to function as a chief organizer for dance troupes, as individuals and organizations contacted him to ask Indians to participate in private events and local and national exhibitions long after the end of his stay with Jacobson in Norman. Mopope and Berry wove their lives sometimes in conjunction with white contacts but always in relation to the world of the KCA Reservation, striving to carry Kiowa traditions into a new and stressful future.

Both James Auchiah and Stephen Mopope began asserting themselves as leaders in the wake of their experiences in Norman. This does not seem surprising, considering their background in families with strong links to the historical leadership of the tribe, their close involvement in warrior societies and ceremonies, their familiarity with white society, and their personal capacities. Of the six original Kiowa artists, these were the two most likely to take on roles as mediators between artists and dancers on the reservation and the surrounding world. Susie Peters described Auchiah as "a grandson of the famous war chief St-tan-ta, paints deep historical pictures of his tribe," and Mopope as "probably the most progressive of the group." Bougetah Smoky returned to the reservation after only one term in Norman and put her energies into beadwork and became prominent in the community of women beadworkers. Spencer Asah was commissioned to teach art at Fort Sill Indian School and also stayed primarily on the reservation. Monroe Tsatoke died from tuberculosis already in 1937, cutting short what could have been a successful artist's career as many considered him exceptionally talented. Jack Hokeah, the brilliant dancer with a hearing impairment, developed an alcohol problem, drifted westward, and eventually found a home with Maria Martinez, the famous potter, in Santa Fe. James Auchiah soon stopped painting, and in 1940 he was offered a post as art instructor from fourth grade and up at Riverside Indian School, a job he performed well. In 1930 Auchiah had become secretary of the local Native American Lions chapter and involved himself in developing club activities on the reservation.[1]

When Mopope left Peters it was with the expressed purpose of independently managing his own affairs. This helped trigger the controversy between Peters and Jacobson, which had major ramifications for Mopope and the other artists and started the process by which Mopope asserted his independence from Peters and other white promoters. He was a grown man, already well into his thirties, who lived in a world that both infantilized him and his colleagues and desired the avenue the Indians provided to a world of mystic primitivism. He straddled two worlds as he sought to negotiate an alien marketplace that was his resource to continue his life as an artist, with the demands and requirements of a life as a Kiowa traditionalist.

NEGOTIATING EXPECTATIONS ON INDIAN DANCING

In the spring of 1934, James Auchiah wrote to the commissioner of Indian affairs asking to be appointed the leader of the Kiowa artists' delegation to the Gallup Ceremonial. The other artists did not want Auchiah to lead them, and the reason seems to be that they each desired freedom from guardianship. A flurry of letters between the commissioners and Superintendent McCowan at Kiowa Agency clarified that the Kiowas (Mopope prominent among them) who had previously been in the charge of Susie Peters now wished to manage their own affairs. Susie Peters understood his choice. "Steven [*sic*] is standing in with Jacobson and that is wise—as it gets him places."[2] It would be wrong, however, to assume that Mopope simply went from one promoter to another. When he left the guardianship of Susie Peters, it was not in order to submit to another leader but to take on that role himself.

Concurrently with their engagements in Norman, the artists were building their reputation at art fairs and Indian fairs across the Southwest. Scholars have noted that the various fairs, local celebrations, and expositions that took shape during the first decades of the new century became sites for negotiations and contests over control of this particular form of entertainment and also over the understandings and images of what it meant to be "Indian."[3] It is no coincidence that tensions emerged between white promoters such as Susie Peters and American Indian performers such as Mopope and Auchiah, over dancing engagements. Peters aided the Kiowas in participating in the newly established Gallup Ceremonial, but it quickly became a venue that the Kiowa artists molded in their own ways. Jenny Tone-Pah-Hote argues that at the "Gallup Ceremonial and other locales, the Kiowa painters utilized dance performances as a way of selling their works, but performance also became a way that they 'authenticated' the images in their paintings and demonstrated the

Kiowa were indeed a contemporary tribal nation." Composing a group of dancers and a program of dances and music was intimately linked with their artwork and in their dance performances "they brought their art to life in ways that emphasized the contemporary nature of the paintings they produced, and allowed them to demonstrate a contemporary image of Kiowa nationhood, which they emphasized in both mediums." Tone-Pah-Hote underlines that this image was clearly gendered and focused on the plains warrior imagery that dominated their paintings as well as their dancing.[4] Fancy war dancing and paintings of dancing warriors thus reinforced one another to the detriment of other possible configurations of "Indianness" and catered to a market with a particular taste for that kind of imagery. This enabled the Kiowas to create a niche for their art but carried within it seeds of tension and specific limitations.

A trip to Ramona Indian Village in Hollywood in 1931 demonstrates these impositions, tensions, and creative adaptations. While attending the Gallup Ceremonial, Susie Peters received an invitation for "the Kiowa boys" by the "Ramona Supper Club" in Los Angeles. After the trip Peters reported to Agent Buntin that the Kiowas had been treated as celebrities. "Their pictures are on display at the Biltmore Hotel Salon. The most exclusive art showing in the City." They appeared on a radio broadcast from Warner Bros. radio station, and they "entertained the Los Angeles Breakfast Club." They also danced at the brand new Olympic Stadium in Los Angeles before a crowd of forty thousand people in conjunction with the crowning of the LaFiesta queen.[5]

In her letter, Peters focused on the exposure of the Kiowas' art. A vividly enticing poster for the Hopi Snake Dance held in Ramona Indian Village in Mopope's possession also demonstrates their attraction as dancers and representatives of exotic Indigenous peoples. It proclaimed to (presumably) non-Indian visitors that it was an opportunity to observe the "Kiowa Indians" (quotation marks in poster original) "in Their $10,000 Costumes." The list of Kiowa dancers included Auchiah, Asah, Gilbert and Stephen Mopope, Hokeah, and Charlie Tsoodle, each introduced as a descendant of famous warriors and orators. Spectators were promised "gorgeous costumes, brilliant feathers, fantastic masks, bright beads and elaborate regalia; a portrayal of strange ceremonies. . . . It is a rare opportunity to see the perpetuation of real Indian tribal dances, and to see and meet the most noted full-blooded Indian dancers, singers

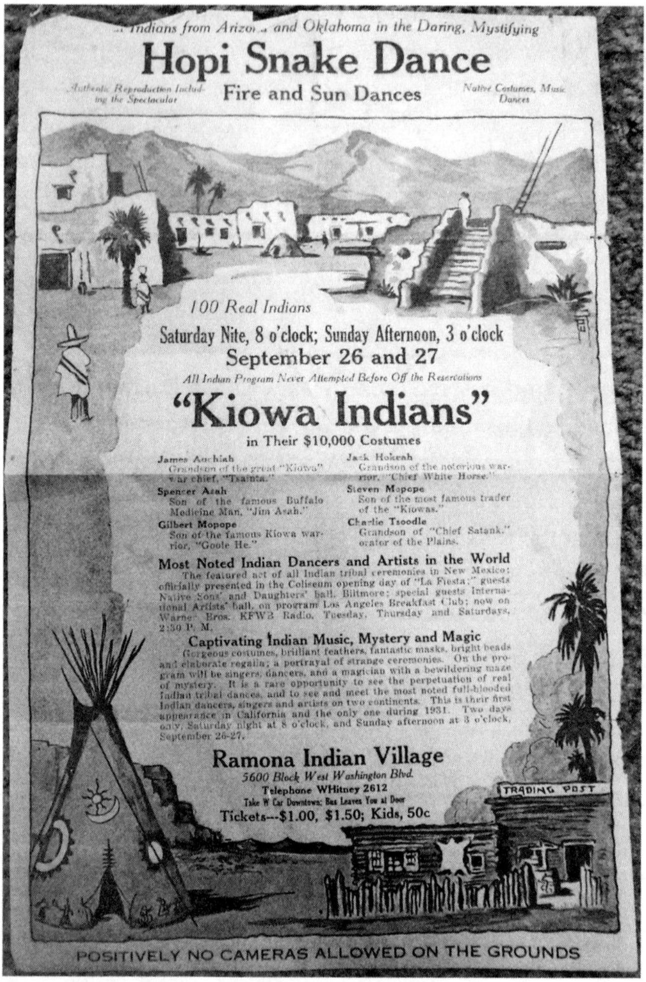

FIGURE 18. Poster for Ramona Indian Village, 1931, featuring "Kiowa Indians, in Their $10,000 Costumes." Stephen Mopope Papers. Courtesy Vanessa Paukeigope Jennings. Photo by author.

and artists on two continents." The poster's promotional text shows some of the negotiations facing the Kiowas as they performed as dancers. They were performers and artists, their creative sensibilities visible in their "gorgeous costumes" and "brilliant feathers." Their dance styles and decorations were innovations, not replicas of a frozen culture; yet spectators expected to view "the many traditional ceremonies of the 'Kiowas' . . . upholding traditions handed down for centuries."[6]

One evening the Kiowas participated in the program at the Los Angeles Art Ball, an event where the famous silent movie star Mary Pickford was crowned queen. James Auchiah related an account of the banquet that demonstrates creative adaptations of ceremonies for white audiences—adaptations that displayed a distinctly modern character. Pickford told the Kiowas that she wished for an Indian name, and Mopope took charge of arranging a ceremony. First they wired home to Kiowa elder and flute player Belo Cozad to ask if they might give away one of the Cozad names. He replied in the affirmative and added his greetings to the Hollywood actress. They then took eagle feathers from their war bonnets and "pulled this elaborate naming ceremony," at which they presented her with a couple of feathers and a name.[7]

The trip to Hollywood further stretched the already strained relations between Susie Peters and the Kiowas. According to Auchiah, Peters "wanted to take the boys on a tour because the contract, program contracts, which various people wanted around the West Coast was very tempting to her." Auchiah recalled that several parties vied for control over the Kiowa group during their more-than-five-week stay in Los Angeles. Peters signed contracts on their behalf with different parties without letting them know the details and kept their checks from the various engagements. It rankled Mopope and Auchiah that she controlled what they could do and what they earned. They brought it up with an independent "public relations man," seeking his opinion on what to do, similarly to what they did in Norman when they went to Jacobson to ask his advice regarding invitations and contracts. Peters did not like that they challenged her leadership and "put the clamp down on everything that we tried to do and she watched the boys like a hawk." She tried to limit their independent contacts with interested parties. The "naming ceremony" for Mary Pickford aggravated matters further. Auchiah suggested that this was "where Mopope fouled up with her." He thought Peters wanted to come along and be introduced to Pickford but Mopope chose "one of the boys to accompany him instead."[8] This was a clear demonstration that Mopope wanted to be in charge of the Kiowa artists. Subsequently, Mopope organized participation in the Gallup Ceremonial with a group that competed directly with another under the guidance of Peters. This caused tension and competition among dancers on the reservation.[9]

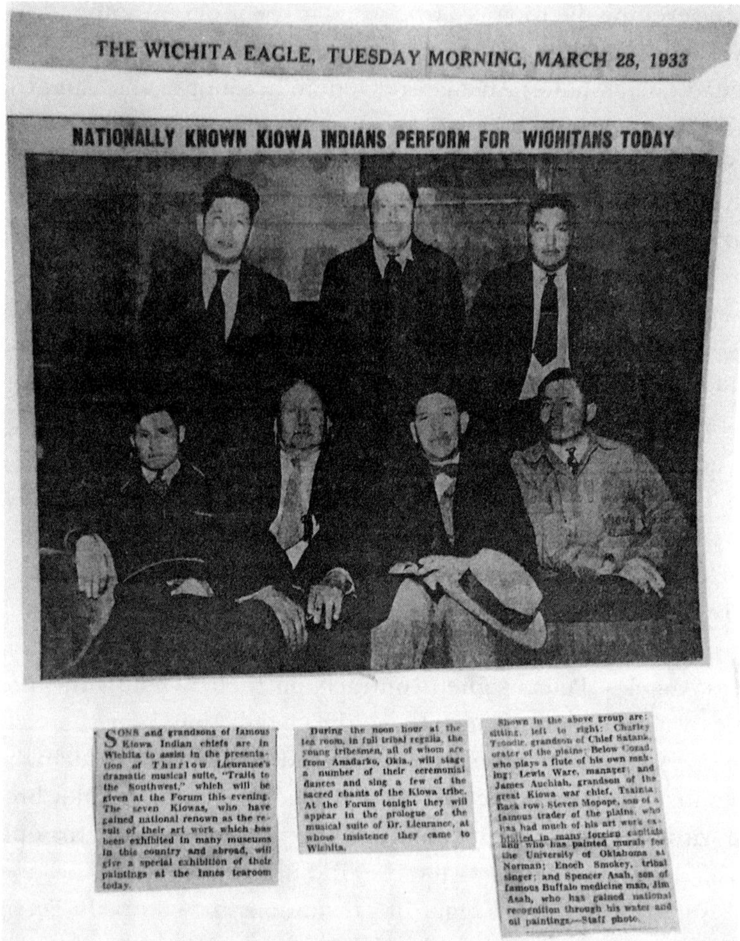

THE WICHITA EAGLE, TUESDAY MORNING, MARCH 28, 1933

NATIONALLY KNOWN KIOWA INDIANS PERFORM FOR WICHITANS TODAY

SONS and grandsons of famous Kiowa Indian chiefs are in Wichita to assist in the presentation of Thurlow Lieurance's dramatic musical suite, "Trails to the Southwest," which will be given at the Forum this evening. The seven Kiowas, who have gained national renown as the result of their art work which has been exhibited in many museums in this country and abroad, will give a special exhibition of their paintings at the Innes tearoom today.

During the noon hour at the tea room, in full tribal regalia, the young tribesmen, all of whom are from Anadarko, Okla., will stage a number of their ceremonial dances and sing a few of the sacred chants of the Kiowa tribe. At the Forum tonight they will appear in the prologue of the musical suite of Dr. Lieurance, at whose insistence they came to Wichita.

Shown in the above group are: sitting, left to right: Charley Tsoodle, grandson of Chief Satank, orator of the plains; Below Cozad, who plays a flute of his own making; Lewis Ware, manager; and James Auchiah, grandson of the great Kiowa war chief, Tsainta; Back row: Steven Mopope, son of a famous trader of the plains, who has had much of his art work exhibited in many foreign capitals and who has painted murals for the University of Oklahoma at Norman; Enoch Smokey, tribal singer; and Spencer Asah, son of famous Buffalo medicine man, Jim Asah, who has gained national recognition through his water and oil paintings.—Staff photo.

FIGURE 19. "Nationally Known Kiowa Indians Perform for Wichitans Today." From *Wichita Eagle*, March 28, 1933. Mopope standing at left, Asah at right, Auchiah seated at far right. Courtesy Vanessa Paukeigope Jennings Collection.

PERFORMING AND SUBVERTING INDIANNESS

Breaking free from white organizers only liberated the Kiowas from one level of expectations on how to perform as Indians. Another trip that Stephen Mopope participated in demonstrates how Kiowas struggled to subvert these meanings. As performers they had to skirt a fine line between the public's nostalgia for the vanishing wilderness of the West and the need to present a proper appearance that signaled their belonging in modern American society. An article in the *Wichita Eagle* from March 1933 ran a headline "Nationally Known Kiowa Indians Perform for Wichitans Today," above a photograph of a group of seven well-dressed men in suits and ties. The text declares that "sons and grandsons of famous Kiowa Indian chiefs are in Wichita," and during the noon hour they will "in full tribal regalia . . . stage a number of their ceremonial dances and sing a few of the sacred chants of the Kiowa tribe." The seven included Charley Tsoodle, Below (Belo) Cozad, Lewis Ware, James Auchiah, Stephen Mopope, Enoch Smoky, and Spencer Asah. The men were introduced as heirs of great warriors, and their performance described as "ceremonial" and "sacred," thus offering spectators a glimpse into an otherwise different world anchored in traditions. The photograph of the men, of whom at least six sported short haircuts, with James Auchiah wearing a stylish jacket and Lewis Ware holding a straw hat, contrasted effectively with the representation of Indians as frozen in time.[10]

The Kiowas were in Wichita to "add color" to the performance of *Trails Southwest*, a symphony by Thurlow Lieurance, a well-known Wichita composer of popular music who acted as a promoter of Indian music and musicians. Lieurance and his wife had met the Kiowas while they were traveling in the Southwest gathering inspiration for the symphony. According to the newspaper, the Lieurances "visited with them in their lodges. The Indians danced and sang for the Wichitans, furnishing inspirations for Indian themes in the symphony." Contrary to the photograph on the front page, the text of another piece in the same edition of the newspaper stated that during the morning, the Indian visitors were expected to "look over Wichita, covered in Indian blankets," and later in the afternoon they would "be at the Forum chanting their songs and giving their weird dances." The Kiowa men—probably traveling on passes like the one issued by the Caddo County Judge in 1931, which declared that "these boys are good citizens and are well worthy of the respect and cooperation of the good people of the Southwest"—had to balance good behavior against white audiences' expectations of a wild and titillating show. While the men certainly owned blankets, and their families regularly put up camp, the reference to "lodges" and "blankets" were aimed at a predominantly white audience who wished to think of Indian life as a romantic remnant of a past that no longer existed but that could be re-created for them through chants and strange dances.[11]

Who made the decision about the arrangement of the photo of the visiting Kiowas? There is such an abundance of newspaper photographs of Indians in dance regalia, that it prompts the question of intention behind this particular one. Blankets and lodges conjured up fears of stilted development and hostility toward civilization. Still in the 1930s school officials feared that Indian children would "return to the blanket" once they had left the protective and corrective environment of boarding schools. For the Kiowas, it may have seemed particularly important to adhere to notions of civilized comportment. While it was important for agents and matrons to emphasize the progress made, perceptions of Kiowas as violent and alien to American society continued well into the twentieth century. Suits and ties no doubt served to dispel such fears and emphasize that blankets and ceremonial dances were only for show. A similar contrast, deployed to demonstrate the difference between contemporaneous Indian life and their performance of inherited tradition, emerges in articles from the first performances held in Norman and Oklahoma City after the Kiowa students had entered art school at University of Oklahoma. In one of the first articles to introduce the Kiowa artists, readers were informed that many western Oklahoma Indians "still adhere to blankets, the long hair and the moccasin." For this reason, it was not "contrary to custom that the four boys should be pictured here in tribal costume." However, the article pointed out that they "attend school in conventional attire and might pass an [*sic*] ordinary collegians upon casual notice."[12]

In the case of the article from Norman, it is likely that Oscar Jacobson prompted the writer to make the clarification. Throughout his promotion of the Kiowa artists, Jacobson showed astute awareness of the importance of image and presentation. However, in the Wichita instance it may well have been Lewis Ware who stood behind the arrangement. Increasingly from the 1930s onward, Ware emerged as a leader of Indian initiatives in managing cultural and social events and as a capable liaison between Kiowas and whites. In 1938 he took over as president of the American Indian Exposition, held annually in Anadarko. He frequently served as the link between the Jacobsons and the Kiowa artists, and they apparently held him in high regard.[13]

Lewis Ware exemplifies a shift in the power dynamics structuring the performance and exhibition of Indian dances. Initially run by Anglo entrepreneurs, events like Wild West shows and seasonal fairs such as the one held at Craterville near Cache, Oklahoma, began to stir dissatisfaction among participating Indians that benefits accrued to white impresarios and not to the main performers. The Southwestern Indian Fair Association was born as an Indian-run alternative in 1932, and the association sponsored the event characterized by many as "the powwow's golden era on the Southern Plains."[14] By 1935 it changed its name to the American Indian Exposition, and as such it flourished into the present century, although its heyday may be located in the 1950s and 1960s. The representatives on the fair's board, coming from the Kiowa, Comanche, Apache, Cheyenne, Arapahoe, Caddo, Wichita, and Delaware tribes, asserted "the necessity of depending upon ourselves in any line of endeavor in our contact with the white people to be successful and fully enjoy the benefits resulting therefrom." They resolved to take control over this event and to petition the governor of Oklahoma to "give the fair board for the western Oklahoma Indians a fair and impartial consideration when any appropriations are made for this purpose."[15] Clyde Ellis describes the resolution as a "dramatic . . . determination of Indian people to claim overt control" over dancing and argues that this "shift in agency is important, for it heralded a decisive turn in the battle to protect, promote, and maintain dance culture."[16] In this perspective, Mopope's assertion of independence vis-à-vis Susie Peters was representative of a larger phenomenon, as Indians increasingly took control of their own dance performances.

Whether done tongue-in-cheek, as the Mary Pickford naming ceremony appears to have been, in Auchiah's telling, or in expressions of gratitude as in the ceremony in 1928 bestowing chiefly honor and a name on Oscar Jacobson, American Indians participated in creating a specific form of identification for white people—with great ramifications. White people desired these ceremonies to appear rooted in age-old traditions, and regardless of how the Indian people forged them, they became clothed in a desired aura of authenticity. For all its seeming connection to ancient and static Indian civilizations, the ceremony the Kiowas "pulled" in Hollywood appears distinctly modern. They used the telegraph to consult regarding the name, and the Kiowa "boys" celebrated movie stars along with a whole generation of contemporaries.

The Kiowas in effect became cocreators of the modern version of traditional Indians. Philip Deloria argues that the "mutually constitutive nature of modern/antimodern practices . . . typified the many touristic escapes that defined modern life."[17] In the early decades of the twentieth century, "Indian people participated in the making of Indian Others as never before." The American (and European) fascination with "the authentic Indian" enabled a space for creative adaptations, which Native people such as Stephen Mopope appeared both eager and capable of occupying. However, as Deloria points out, "the fact that native people turned to playing Indian—miming Indianness back at Americans in order to redefine it—indicates how little cultural capital Indian people possessed at the time. Such exercises were fraught not only with ambiguity, but with danger."[18] One risk lay in the fact that, even though Indians attempted to alter stereotypes by using modern technology and materials to construct new ceremonies and images, ingrained ideas of Indians "proved almost impervious to assault." As a consequence, Native people performing Indianness risked reasserting stereotypes "for a stubborn white audience, making Indianness an even more powerful construct and creating a circular, reinforcing catch-22 of meaning that would prove difficult to circumvent."[19]

CREATING A NEW STYLE

Mopope's influence on the development of a new form of artistic performance can be approached from two directions. On the one hand, he participated in remodeling the dance performance and its accouterments, and on the other, he developed its entrepreneurial context by shaping programs, managing contacts, negotiating contracts and organizing events. Several accounts agree that Mopope was a formidable dancer—and innovator. When newspapers and festival programs promised spectators a view of Indian culture exactly as it had been handed down for centuries, they denied the creative innovation and thoughtful consideration that went into creating this publicly visible form of culture. The *St. Louis Star Times* hinted at this when it wrote about the Kiowa opening of the National Folk Festival in 1934: "The striking splendor of their costumes, aglow with color, was enough to cause the audience to gasp. The costumes varied only in minor details from those used in the tribal dances. They were a trifle showier, largely through the use of bells instead of gourds and beads instead of porcupine quills. The costumes were made by the Indians themselves."[20]

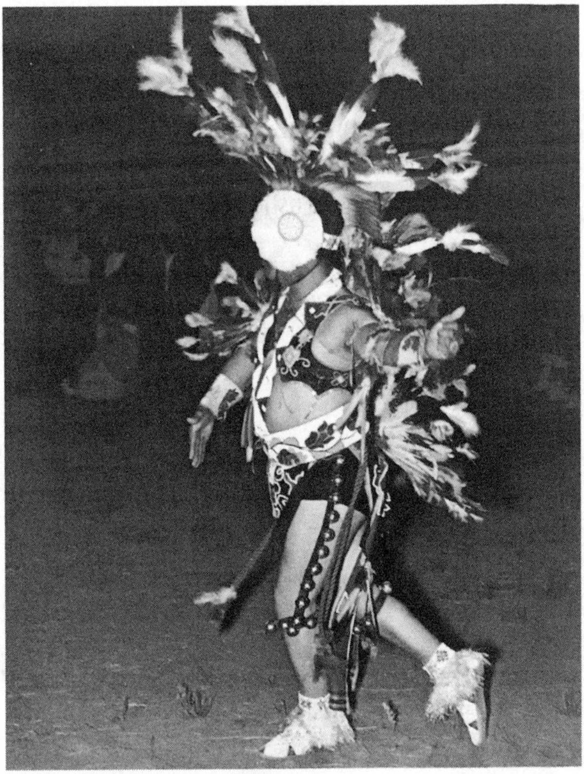

FIGURE 20. Stephen Mopope dancing. George Palmer describes him: "He was kind of heavy and when he danced when you were anywhere near where he was stomping you could kind of feel the ground vibrating. . . . He just looked fierce and danced in a very robust hard way. . . . Everybody else just kind of tinkered around but he meant business when he went out." Courtesy Vanessa Paukeigope Jennings.

In the 1930s Mopope and the others were already seasoned performers, with experience from powwow dancing and exhibitions for commercial purposes. It suited his flair, his persona on the dance ground was commanding, and he reveled in designing new aspects of his dance regalia that attracted attention from all audiences. Mopope brought back materials and decorations from his travels and incorporated them in his outfits. According to his daughter, he was the first to attach hackles (long, slender feathers) that he had bought in the East, later to become a standard feature of fancy dance regalia. These were the same kind of hackles that well-dressed women wore in their hats and around their necks and cuffs. Mopope's extant papers attest to his wide array of influences in constructing costumes. He stood in contact with traders to get bells and feathers, he noted outstanding bonnet makers in the Far West (Nevada), and he sold roaches (powwow head dresses) to dancers up north, all the way to Saskatchewan.[21]

Gus Palmer, himself an accomplished dancer, describes that as boy he was awed by Mopope's appearance:

> I kind of grew up out of diapers into tailfeathers and bells but I was frightened absolutely petrified of Steven when he war danced because he wear [*sic*] at that time it was a very strange combination of gear, dancing gear. It had kind of a combination of Crow Indian and Kiowa dancing outfit and lots of different Northern design beadwork and he painted his face up kind of fierce looking and he was you know he was a big fellow. He was kind of heavy and when he danced when you were anywhere near where he was stomping you could kind of feel the ground vibrating and so I would sit there with my stuff on and I was absolutely afraid of the guy. He just looked fierce and danced in a very robust hard way and I was kind of scared. Everybody else just kind of tinkered around but he meant business when he went out.[22]

The Eagle Dance for which Mopope was famous was actually an adaptation to influences from the Northern Plains, a connection that appeared in his dancing, his regalia, and in his paintings. "Mopope always had this feeling about the Northern Indian tribes such as Sioux, Cheyenne, North Plains Indian," Auchiah told Silberman. He explained that, while the Kiowas did have eagle dancers, they traditionally wore a bustle and held the eagle wing in hand as a fan. According to Auchiah, Mopope's Eagle Dance grew out of his connection with the Crows and with the Southern Cheyennes.[23]

On tiny scraps of paper, the back of receipts, torn-out newspaper pages, and corners of envelopes, Mopope kept record of his business contacts. Innumerable little pieces attest to his tireless labor to keep track of interested buyers, exhibitors, and impresarios of dance events. In the beginning, during the 1930s, Oscar Jacobson helped launch Mopope's career as an artist, astutely attaching it to his considerable fame as a dancer. A letter from Jacobson, dated in 1939, sheds light on this parallel process. Jacobson wanted Mopope to fill in some blanks in descriptions of him and his work. Jacobson wrote: "I know most of the things that you have done and the places where you have exhibited your paintings, the mural painting jobs I secured for you and the dance concerts to which we went together in Texas and Missouri." He ended by encouraging him: "Don't forget to mention in the questionaire [*sic*] the prizes you have won in dancing and painting as that is important."[24] By the 1940s Mopope was widely recognized by both Indian and white audiences as an outstanding dancer, respected artist, and a reliable organizer of events. But he was also a cocreator of a particular construction of contemporary Indianness, which built its modern allure on presumed connections to an authentic and often mythic past. Coping with disparate requirements—such as outside expectations on how Indians were envisaged as fitting into American society, acquiring an income to feed a family, and ritual and ceremonial obligations—indeed required a fancy dance step. And Stephen Mopope had several.

THE NATIONAL FOLK FESTIVAL AND THE KATY RAILROAD

Mopope's involvement in three particular dancing spheres sheds light on the interwoven strands shaping and preserving dancing as a vital American Indian expression. These were engagements with the National Folk Festival, with the Missouri-Kansas-Texas (Katy) Railroad, and with intratribal and intertribal celebrations and ceremonies. Each in its own way points to aspects of Mopope's dancing career that have wider significance for understanding how Indians molded, used, and sustained dance as a central performance of tribal culture as well as an important foundation for economic subsistence. The Folk Festival highlights entanglements with a multiethnic, but primarily white, world of entertainment and culture, the Katy Railroad engagements represent Indian-controlled tourist ventures, and the private and tribal ceremonials at which he participated demonstrate his role as teacher and elder.

After the initial success in St. Louis in the spring of 1934, the Kiowa dancers became a mainstay of the National Folk Festival, traditionally opening the festival on the first night. Letters between the main organizers of the festival, the Indian agent, and Jacobson show how Jacobson increasingly deferred requests to Mopope, whose requirements directly influenced the context of the Kiowas' participation. In the summer of 1934, just following the success in St. Louis, Knott again wished to engage the Kiowas for an event. Two of them, in all likelihood Stephen Mopope and Monroe Tsatoke, went to the superintendent and inquired about the possibilities for them to leave the reservation to take part in the "Century of Progress," the World's Fair Exhibition organized in Chicago in August that year. Jacobson was spending the summer in his Colorado home and could not step in as director, but the Kiowas knew what they wanted. They wished to know what they were expected to do at the fair and demanded to be paid in addition to being allowed to exhibit their paintings.[25] They were willing to dance, but not without a space for them to show their artwork as well.

In addition to their becoming a set item on the program, a personal acquaintance developed between the festival's main organizer, Sarah Gertrude Knott, and Stephen Mopope. A postcard from 1937 sent to him from the Ambassador Hotel in Washington, DC, informed him that Knott was there "working on plans. Hope all goes well with you." In 1941 Knott wrote and thanked Mopope and the other Kiowas for their "fine cooperation with us" on the programs. She continued: "We count you our real friends and absolutely know that we can depend on you. You always do a good job for us and we expect to have you as long as we have a National Folk Festival." The tone grew ever more personal, and in 1947, when St. Louis once again was the venue for the festival, Knott wrote Mopope already in the planning stage and requested his input. A handwritten note on the letter urged: "Please bring as many as you can, Steve—and as good! We want to knock' em cold—Don't we Kids?" The organizers expected Mopope to participate not only as a dancer but also as an artist. In 1957 Knott writes in her own hand on the form letter containing the planned events: "Steve—space is free. You can sell. We want you!"[26]

This apparent amity notwithstanding, Mopope's insistence on determining the rules for his participation frustrated Knott and Pickering. In 1937, a letter marked "Personal" to the superintendent launched a complaint against him. "Frankly, we are not pleased at the attitude being taken by Steve Mopope." Pickering found it hard to get in touch with Mopope and his group to make arrangements and they never quite knew "how many were coming and other details." At the same time, they were "very fond of Steve and all the other boys and we would like to have them on our program again, but we wonder if they are not beginning to think they are sort of indispensable to the program." This apparently irked the organizers, and they noted that extensive media coverage, "with many illustrations," had influenced Stephen's and the other Kiowas' attitude. A solution might be to hire another Kiowa group. "A number of our good friends who know the work of other Kiowas, feel that you have members of that tribe who would be just as good."[27]

Clearly, Mopope and the other Kiowas were expected to be grateful for the publicity they had gotten from the festival, and for having their expenses paid during previous participation. That Mopope's group now expected such treatment in order to contribute their expertise rankled the organizers who, like so many of the white people who felt that they made space for Indians, expected gratitude (and often subservience) in return. But Mopope and his group were seasoned and professional performers. The idea that artistic ability and the desire to express themselves in dance and music ran in their blood was a convenient notion that allowed white people, however sympathetic to Indians, to exploit these expressions and downplay both the skills and the hard work it took to develop and maintain quality—and the fact that both art and performances constituted much needed opportunities for the Kiowas to support themselves. Yet, even in his irritation, Pickering recognized Mopope's skill. "With Steve's group we figure that seven would be enough, because they are all highly experienced" while with a new group ten might be needed so that the less skillful could "form more or less of a background."[28]

Despite these rumblings, Stephen Mopope again participated with a group that year, and in every festival until 1943. That year he had more important things to do. The war effort involved the Mopope family; Stephen was volunteering in different ways and did not have time to attend the National Folk Festival. Pickering wrote to the superintendent that the news "gave us a great blow," and he asked if other Kiowas could come and dance. He had also heard that Susie Peters had presented a group of younger dancers at events in the Southwest, and the festival organizers were eager to have younger dancers with the stamina to dance fast war dances. That year, and again in 1944, the superintendent sent another group under Jasper Saunkeah. Pickering's letter in 1937 had made reference to possible contention among the Kiowas, and letters from 1944 again reveal strain over who should represent the Kiowas at the festival. Mopope wrote the organizers to offer his group's participation but refused to come under Saunkeah's leadership. Pickering found himself in a predicament, explaining to McCowan that they had "grown very fond of these men and there is no doubt as to their outstanding ability in presenting the best balanced Indian program we have ever had, and in all we have had representatives of about twelve tribes. Steve plays the drum for all the dances and, of course, himself dances the Eagle Dance remarkably well. Also he can play the flute and it is always a great novelty for the audiences to hear that. He sees to it that all of the group are properly instructed and dressed. In addition to that, his display of paintings always brings great additional credit to the Indian and particularly the Kiowas."[29]

Between 1934 and 1961, Kiowas led by Stephen Mopope participated in at least ten of the national festivals. Mopope, in dance regalia, even adorned an advertisement leaflet for the second festival in Chattanooga in 1935. It was a mark of their long-term connection that Knott received a Kiowa dress and posed in it for a photograph.[30] Undoubtedly, such extensive exposure to audiences and participants all over the country served Mopope and the Kiowa dancers well in developing contacts and engagements, and in furthering national recognition. Leonora Barrett from Anson, Texas, the town famous for hosting "the Cowboys' Christmas Ball," had seen the Kiowas dance at the Folk Festival and noted Jacobson's involvement. She wrote to him in 1938, requesting his help to engage the Kiowas. Jacobson immediately forwarded the letter to Mopope from his summer home in Colorado, adding a handwritten note on the top: "Dear Mopope. I answered—told her to get in touch with you direct. How are you? Greetings." Hattie Hill, superintendent for a home for orphaned children and youths located in Clarksburg, West Virginia, wrote in 1942 hoping to have the Kiowas participate in their annual town festival as they "all enjoyed your splendid group so much at the National Folk Festival."[31]

It would be tempting to attribute the launching of Mopope's career as a dance manager to Jacobson's intervention in 1934, but Mopope had additional contacts. His father-in-law, Tennyson Berry, had returned to the reservation from Carlisle with education, leadership skills, and the determination to remain an Apache Indian. Along with Mopope's uncle Jim Waldo, Berry's classmate at Carlisle, he let his hair grow long again, performed at dances and ceremonials, and never ceased being a practicing member of the Native American Church. At Carlisle, Berry had played alto saxophone in the school's marching band, and led by John Phillip Sousa they had performed at President McKinley's inauguration in 1897. Berry and Waldo both sat on the KCA Business Committee for the reservation, together with Comanche leader Quanah Parker. Parker was an astute businessman, and the committee settled on who would be allowed to lease the right-of-way for railroads across reservation land. Through their contacts, Mopope was engaged to provide entertainment for tourists on the Missouri-Kansas-Texas Line as it passed through Indian country. During the 1940s and 1950s, Stephen and Jeanette involved their whole family, packed up their grandchildren and engaged a dance troupe that would travel on the railroad dancing and singing for tourists and selling beadwork and paintings. These trips could be quite extensive, and they went all the way to Chicago and New York. While it allowed the Mopope family a measure of control over their own affairs, racism circumscribed railroad travel. At least one year, the group had to endure transport in the back of a cattle truck.[32]

By the 1940s Mopope increasingly received direct appeals for dance troupes and performances, sometimes through the most modern of means. A telegram on May 27, 1946, arrived with the urgent message: "YOU AND PARTY TO DANCE AT COUNTRY CLUB TUESDAY NIGHT MAY 28 FOR GOVERNOR'S CONFERENCE." He had dance engagements all around Oklahoma, Texas, Kansas, Missouri, and as far away as California and the East Coast. Mopope stood in contact with rodeos, Indian clubs, arts festivals, and ceremonies. He brought dancers to powwows, and events at Lion's Club, Junior Chamber of Commerce, fraternities, colleges, insurance conventions, and different town celebrations.[33]

FAMILY AFFAIRS AND TRIBAL RESPONSIBILITY

In the 1940s there were still prominent people on the reservation who did not approve of any kind of dancing. LaQuinta Mopope remembered how a preacher came to talk to Mopope to convince him to give up his dancing. Her father refused, arguing that "I earn a living for my family by traveling and we dance and we get paid for our dancing. . . . [I]t's just like any show people in this world they get paid for dancing . . . I get paid for my dancing and so does the people that I take."[34] Mopope did provide for people in his vicinity through his labors as a dance organizer. On a list of participants at Cameron College in Lawton, Oklahoma, from April 1953, Mopope noted that the sixteen dancers and drummers should get paid $5.00 each to appear on stage at 8 P.M. on Monday night, April 14. In addition, the eight drivers were reimbursed with $2.25 each. The dancers and drummers included eleven men and five women, among them Mopope's father-in-law, Tennyson Berry, James Auchiah, and Jeanette Mopope. A 1947 list of participants for the Insurance Convention in Oklahoma City, organized by Jasper Saunkeah, shows an even more impressive roster of Kiowa dancers. Mopope assembled nineteen men and ten women, with seven tipis. The names demonstrate the significance of family ties in these ventures. They included the Wares, Palmers, and Berrys, Silver Horn, as well as Spencer and Ida Asah. Jeanette brought her tipi and so did their daughter Vanette.[35] Planning and executing dance events required logistical support and business acumen. Mopope's papers reveal how he struggled to organize and provide for the dancers he engaged. Despite the hardships of the Depression, the Kiowas had several dance engagements during the 1930s. Yet, Mopope noticed the effects of the downturn with cancellations and bounced checks. Thirty years later, costs and remunerations had gone up considerably. A trip to Medicine Lodge for the special Kansas Centennial involved contracting two other men, Louie Toyebo and Frank Sovo, to organize ten cars and one truck each to haul tipi poles. Each driver received $15.00 for the round trip while the truck cost $60.00. In addition to this, beef and rations had to be provided.[36]

While Mopope and his fellow dancers cultivated a public presence that played upon notions—and expectations—of Indian Otherness and served their commercial interests, their dancing remained firmly lodged within communities deeply invested in dance as a foundational cultural expression. Dancing was not only for wages, not even primarily. Among Mopope's papers there are many notes to private events to which Stephen and Jeanette were invited and expected as friends. They also organized dances at their place, and Vanessa Jennings describes some of these ordinary, familial events:

> Grandpa Steve, with the help of Charlie and Laura Whitehorse, John and Matilda Emhoolah, Mark and Eva Keahbone, Spencer and Laura Asah, Willie and Helen Horse and their son, Roland and others, would set up a drum either in the front room or on the front lawn. . . . All of the children would come running from the

> bedrooms, the fields and other places to dance. . . . There were no spectators. We were all participants. Grandma Jeanette had several sets of wings made from chicken feathers to use for the "Eagle Dance." There were also several sets of home-made hoops for Hoop Dancing. We danced to War Dance songs, Buffalo Dance, Snake Dance and Round Dance songs. It was great fun.
>
> The only shortage was boys. We were all little girls, with the exception of "Old Man" who was our little cousin. As youngsters, our Grandpa Steve dressed us in fancy feathered war dance bustles. We danced at the American Indian Exposition in Anadarko, Oklahoma, the Inter-tribal Indian Ceremonial, Gallup, New Mexico and at the various dance presentations he had contracts for. The only time we were not allowed to dress in feathers, was at the O-Ho-mah Lodge Society Ceremonials. All his girls had the opportunity to strut their stuff. LaQuinta Mopope, my mother, Vanette Mopope, Donna Jean Mopope, Dorothy Whitehorse Delaune, "Kiowa Girl" Asah, Lula Jean "Cheyenne Girl" Blackowl, my aunts, took their turn. Later, my sister, Stevette and I danced in feathers. In my family other women who danced were Arlis Geikaunmah, Georgette (Gigi) Palmer and Frankie Ware. Dancing was fun. It gave us a little extra money and it taught us the importance of preparing and taking care of our dance clothes. We learned to appreciate the beauty and joy of dancing and at the same time the proper respect and serious nature of what you are doing.[37]

In Vanessa Jennings's account, dancing emerges as a multilayered expression and vehicle for learning. It was fun—an exercise that brought generations and friends together. It served to teach young people discipline and respect. It taught skills in making outfits and paraphernalia connected to dancing, and it provided an income. It blurred gender lines in preference for passing on and performing traditions, and it contained deeply religious aspects that distinguished it from entertainment. In the years following his sojourn in Norman, Mopope increasingly devoted his time to mentoring younger generations of Kiowas. In a short biographical piece, Oscar Jacobson wrote in the early 1950s: "Because of his intense love for the traditions of his race, Mopope has undertaken the task voluntary labor of teaching his young Kiowa friends how to dance. He is also determined to perpetuate the knowledge of the sign language in which he excels." As Ellis has noted, dancing "emerged as a kind of permeable boundary in search for stability and cultural continuity. It proved resilient and adaptable, and was capable of reinforcing important ideals and values even as the context and expression of these things shifted."[38]

The Mopope-Berry household sponsored frequent dances at their place. An undated flyer in Jennings's collection announces: "Indian Pow Wow, August 2–3–4, At the Mopope Place 2 miles west and 1–2 north of Apache Y. ALL KINDS OF DANCING EACH AFTERNOON & NIGHT, EVERYBODY WELCOME. Plenty of Camping Space—Plenty of Water." These events were open to all kinds of participants and ranged from private to public events. In this family of women, it appears that women frequently stood behind the organization of dances. Jeanette's grandfather was a captive Mescalero Apache. To honor him, she would give a dance on his birthday and send for dancers from Mescalero who would come and perform the Apache Fire Dance. A letter to Jeanette from a friend informed her about negotiations to get dancers from Arizona to the Mopope powwow. The writer also wished to know what format the dance would have, would there be a performance of the Apache Blackfoot Club, or "just war and round dancing—or open drum"? The dances took place on Jeanette Berry's land, where she and Steve had built an arbor and planted elm trees. Her white house, with a wide sun porch, fronted a dance ground "to which many Kiowas would come to pray and dance."[39]

Particularly powerful and laden with meaning were the dances held in honor of Indian soldiers killed in action or returned safely from war. The Kiowas danced not only for their own warriors. During the 1940s, in a striking example of cross-cultural brokerage, American Indians performed dances for German prisoners of war held in POW camps across Oklahoma. Mopope and his troupe offered shows to prisoners at a camp in Oklahoma City. Some people expressed reservations about these engagements, but Mopope argued that all soldiers faced similar conditions. He said about the German POW that "they were probably just like our boys . . . they're probably in the same boat as ours. So I hope if somewhere they'll treat our boys like that." They also danced at army bases and visited hospitals. LaQuinta Mopope recalled her father going to a ward with amputees. "They were dancing and this young man asked dad to come over and He said well I can't see you dance but he said you dance for me too cause I can't get up and dance no more." The meeting was profoundly emotional for Mopope who lost his nephew in the war. To those who criticized him for dancing for soldiers he said: "That's the only thing we can do for them. . . . We can't ever repay them for what all they've done for us." Dancing for combat soldiers and POWs was voluntary work, and he would ask "all those who want to go and donate their time."[40]

OVERLAPPING ACTIVITIES

Often the engagements as dancer and artist overlapped, although it appears as though (and quite naturally) the balance shifted over the years. The younger Mopope had frequent dance appointments, but with his advancing age the artist took over. Yet, dancing and painting grew out of the same fountain of inspiration throughout most of his life. At Pawnee Bill's Historic Wild West Show in 1939, held in Pawnee, Oklahoma, Mopope led the Kiowas in the "Hummingbird Dance." This and other programs demonstrate the close linkages between the various forms of artistic creativity of the Kiowas. The artists painted what they did, what they had seen, and what they had heard from elders. In *Kiowa Indian Art*, the portfolio of porchoir reproductions of their early work that Jacobson had published in France in 1929, several plates visualize in vivid color and frozen movement the grace and accomplishments of the artists as dancers. Jack Hokeah represented the "Hummingbird dance," a fancy dancer in bright purple with feather bustles on his upper arms and back, a feathered train, and bells around his ankles. Spencer Asah portrayed himself in a kneeling movement in *Asah Dancing*. Mopope painted *Eagle Dance* shown from the back (see plate 6), displaying the spectacular wings spread wide, and a gorgeously decorated *Flute Player* dancing with an eagle dance fan, beaded flute adorned with feathers, and the Morningstar of the Feather Dance (Ghost Dance) on his shoulder.

The Committee on Indian Arts and Crafts, a result of John Collier's appointment as commissioner of Indian affairs, issued a report in 1934 on how best to support and encourage Native arts and crafts. Among its conclusions were that the only viable markets for Indian artistic output were to be found in the fine arts and tourist souvenir markets, but it failed to note the close connection between arts and crafts and ceremonial practices.[41] The work of Stephen Mopope and his colleagues demonstrates precisely this connection, even as it supports the commission's findings of the significance of fine arts and tourist markets. Several of the early works of the Kiowas depicted ceremonies and prayers. The works contained in the *Kiowa Art* portfolio included Jack Hokeah's *Kiowa Priest at Prayer, Chasing Evil Spirits,* and *Greeting of the Moon God*; Monroe Tsatoke's *Dance of the Dog Soldiers,* and *Medicine Dance*; and Mopope's *Kiowa Singers, Osage Piote Man,* and *Making Medicine.*

The controversy surrounding the Ghost Dance, or Feather Dance as the Kiowas referred to it, had fractured the reservation community along different fault lines. One of the leading opponents to the dance, Ahpeahtone, was a peyote man. His resistance to the Feather Dance may well have been connected to his peyote beliefs, just as was the case with Quanah Parker who viewed the Ghost Dance with suspicion and saw it as a competing belief. However, some people combined the practices, and this seems to have been the case with some of Mopope's relatives. In one painting, Mopope portrayed the Feather Dance vividly (see plate 11). In it, a man and a woman cloaked in pale shirts decorated with the crescent moon and the Morning Star stand between two tipis and in front of a line of people sitting on the ground. They all wear similarly adorned shirts. In the middle, between the tipis but behind the standing couple is a green tree, the cedar, always green and alive. He painted, Vanessa Jennings asserts, what he had seen, thus preserving its history. In many of his early paintings and murals, the crescent moon and the Morning Star of the Feather Dance adorn dancers and decorations, lending them a sacred character.[42]

In 1934, while in St. Louis for the Folk Festival, Jacobson took the Kiowas sightseeing in the city. They asked to be taken to the zoo and standing before the cage displaying a cormorant, they began speaking among themselves in Kiowa, apparently excited. The next day at the performance the men outdid themselves, and Jacobson complimented them. Monroe Tsatoke spoke for the group when he showed the professor a small silver charm he wore under his breast-plate. "This," he told Jacobson, "is a cormorant, our totem. We wanted to see the real one at the zoo and ask him to stand by us. He is a good totem. I'm glad I know him; we had never seen a live one before."[43] The cormorant is a central symbol for the Native American church, and the young men all included peyote symbols in their early paintings. Seeing a cormorant live for the first time must have given them all courage before their opening performance. Dance and art lived entwined together in the lives of the Kiowa artists. Much of their work was art for sale, tailored to the tastes of primarily non-Indian customers, but they also painted to recount histories and ceremonial events, which they either had heard of or had experienced themselves.

MAKING A LIVING AS AN ARTIST

Indian New Deal reformers operated according to the 1928 Meriam Report, which observed that the government must enable American Indians to manage their own affairs, while providing them with adequate levels of health care and education. According to the report, American Indians who wished "to merge into the social and economic life of the prevailing civilization of this country should be given all practicable aid and advice in making the necessary adjustments," while those who desired to "remain an Indian and live according to his old culture should be aided in doing so." The new administration under John Collier viewed artistic expressions and the continuation of traditional crafts as key components in a policy that would allow Indigenous peoples to maintain distinct cultures while participating in a market economy. The formation of the Committee on Indian Arts and Crafts in 1934 served to implement new policies for marketing Indigenous arts and crafts production. While self-sufficiency was the goal of these policies, they took for granted that American Indian artists and artisans would require continued counsel and supervision from white benefactors. Mopope's career, however, demonstrates considerable self-direction in determining what he produced and to whom he sold.[44]

Alvin O. Turner characterizes the Oklahoma art scene as weak and particularly hard hit by the Depression, which made it exceedingly difficult for the Kiowas and other American Indian artists to make art their living. In fact, he suggests that, "income from painting never supported any of the Kiowa Five for more than a few years."[45] This concurs with the observations made in Washington that the art market was a volatile place for Native artists. While this may be true on an aggregated level, and financial success in general bypassed the Kiowas, this study finds that Stephen Mopope ardently built on the start he had received through his association with Jacobson to maintain a lifelong career as an artist. His papers attest to a diligent maintenance of contacts and, as was the case with his engagement as dance troupe organizer, a vast correspondence connecting him to buyers and exhibitors.

On innumerable small scraps of paper, he noted information about possible purchases. Notations included private individuals with addresses and phone numbers, and contact information for curio shops, department stores, banks, restaurants, galleries, and Indian trading stores. There were names of visitors to the Anadarko Indian Expo, and recommendations coming from friends and colleagues, such as Woody Big Bow or his sister Clara. Some names belonged to other Indians who wanted to buy paintings or items connected to dance regalia. Although most names were local to Oklahoma and the surrounding states, there were also contacts as far away as Pennsylvania and Canada. On the torn off corner of an envelope, he had scribbled in pencil: "Vincent Price. Collecting Ind. Art for Sears Roebuck travelling Art Show. Buy paintings." Several notes also recorded sales, such as one from December of 1944: "completed *135 Xmas Cards.* Sold @ 35 each—which brought $47,25. Due—30 cards." Tiny notebooks, half the size of a one-dollar bill, contained addresses, accounts of accidents, notes of potential buyers, tasks, shopping lists, etc. One such entry demonstrates that Mopope tried to keep control of his sales, and that this could lead to conflicts. "INDIAN HOSPITAL, LAWTON MARCH 10TH 1963. Showed me Reproduce or Reprint of a BUFFALO HUNT by Mopope—this painting not supposed to be on sale—without Mopopes CONSENT—Dick Pengelton—Release Contract—Not to Handle the Mopope Art."[46]

It is, of course, impossible to calculate his income from sales of artwork during these years. The persistent effort to find customers, attested by letters offering paintings for sale to art galleries and other buyers, demonstrates that it was, then as now, difficult for an artist to make a living. However, judging from sales slips, information about checks contained in letters he saved, and notations, he did receive a steady stream of payment for his paintings. In addition, the checks for dances, prize money for competition victories, and income from leases on his land, all suggest that Stephen Mopope was indeed making a living, primarily as an artist and a dancer, well into the 1960s. For example, sales at Gallup Indian Fair during the late 1920s and early 1930s could be impressive, and Mopope and the others often netted one thousand dollars (Mopope always coming out best, according to James Auchiah, peaking one year at fourteen hundred dollars). In today's monetary value—measured as "historic standard of living"—this equaled nearly twenty thousand dollars. In 1950 he sold artwork for nearly the equivalent of two thousand dollars to Texas galleries, and in 1969 a request to redo the murals in the Anadarko post office would have netted in excess of fifty thousand dollars in 2017 value.[47]

The connections and networks visible through the letters that Mopope kept paint a picture of a vast web spreading primarily across Oklahoma and adjacent states, but with tentacles stretching far beyond. While Jacobson is represented in this pattern, he was far from alone, and with time Mopope built his own network, just as he did with his dance undertakings. Some of it was a direct outcome of his time in Norman, such as when a fellow student and artist, Derald Swineford, wrote him in 1938. Swineford now lived in Dallas where he kept a bookshop and had met a woman at the Dallas Art Carnival who wished to buy two Mopope originals after seeing them in the Kiowa Art portfolio. The university remained a source of sales contacts, and in 1946, the wife of Erich Eichholz, professor of modern languages, wrote Mopope on the recommendation of Don Whistler, principal chief of the Sac and Fox Nation and also an OU alumnus, to request "paintings of individual Indian dancers."[48]

Closeness to Fort Sill in Lawton also offered Mopope many opportunities to exhibit and sell his work. Mary Mathis, the Service Club librarian, wrote in 1945 of plans for "getting together a collection of original Indian paintings for exhibition and possible sale. I should like very much to include some of your work." Mathis continued: "Most of the boys in training here have never seen any real Indian art since they are from the East and North, so I feel sure there would be a great deal of enthusiasm." Good publicity could be promised, and Mathis concluded with a request for "names and addresses of other Indian artists, who might be interested in cooperating," which enabled Mopope to become a conduit for the work of his colleagues as well. Correspondence with regular exhibitors and fair organizers most likely formed the mainstay of Mopope's entrepreneurial activity. He wrote to galleries and museums and offered paintings, and sometimes he received requests from them. He kept in touch with Indian traders in different places, for both sales and purchases, as Mopope required supplies for his production of both paintings and dance regalia.[49]

More prestigious and necessary for maintaining his reputation as an artist were his contacts with the Philbrook Art Center and the Gilcrease Museum, both in Tulsa. As Alvin O. Turner points out, both institutions were vital in establishing Oklahoma as a national center for American Indian art. Already in 1936 the Tulsa Arts Association had begun hosting an annual Indian week, to be replaced ten years later by the Philbrook Museum of Art. This institution had been founded in 1938 with an endowment from oil magnate Waite Phillips and his wife, Genevieve. The National Exhibition of American Indian Painting became an instant success and continued to draw students and artists into the late 1970s. Mopope's correspondence contains letters from the museum consistently expressing respect and admiration for his contributions. In 1950 the director Bernard Frazier, the initiator of the Indian Annual as it was known, congratulated Mopope on having a painting chosen for an exhibition of Indian paintings on loan to the Smithsonian. In 1962 Mopope's presence was requested as a juror in the Indian painting competition, and in 1966 the museum planned a special event to honor him and the other Kiowa artists.[50]

Another oilman, Thomas Gilcrease, had also begun collecting western and Native American art in the 1940s, and Mopope's artist colleague Woody Big Bow informed him that Gilcrease particularly wished for his paintings. One list of potential buyers from August 1959 noted "Mr. Gilcrease. Wanted to buy paintings for his New Art Museum. He is soon leaving for abroad—see him in October? He wanted to buy Mopope's paintings." This contact was no doubt useful to his career but did not guarantee sales. Mopope's offer to paint murals in the museum met with a kind but firm refusal. Gilcrease became a formidable figure in Oklahoma and western art circles, and Mopope's exchange with him included personal Christmas cards. Mopope's correspondence with other art institutions included the Museum of New Mexico Art Gallery in Santa Fe, the Dallas Fine Arts Museum, the Texas Memorial Museum in Austin, and the Pennsylvania Academy of the Fine Arts. Stanley Marcus, heir to the Neiman-Marcus Department Store in Dallas, wrote a personal letter to regret that plans had changed so that he was no longer "in the market for murals."[51]

Mopope's correspondence shows him nurturing advantageous connections. One connection that stands out linked him with the powerful Oklahoma oil and gas company, the Kerr-McGee (Kermac) Corporation. In 1964 he entered a bid to paint murals for the Kermac Building in Oklahoma City. While he did not win the bid, his design received much praise and requests for sales ensued. This was not his first contact with the corporation, as he had already approached Robert S. Kerr, then governor of Oklahoma, in 1946. A letter Mopope kept described the nature of their involvement in a most friendly tone, referring to Mopope's proposal for new car tag designs.[52] Apart from demonstrating Mopope's keen sense for establishing and maintaining valuable business connections, the letter also indicates the range of his artistic production. He made designs of various kinds; he drew insignia, illustrated phone books, catalogs, leaflets, and signs, and decorated peyote boxes. His granddaughter describes how he "fixed up circus and carnival signs, he fixed up so that you could put your head through. And he had prices set." For such and other more commercial decorations he cut out pictures of nudes from 1930s and 1940s artist's sketchbooks and painted them as Indians. Jennings remembers him always sketching: "And he was 'quick, quick, hand me a paper, I've got an idea.'"[53]

MOPOPE AND THE NATIVE AMERICAN CHURCH

Paintings portraying the peyote ceremonies of the Native American Church grew out of a central component of Mopope's life and beliefs, up until a dramatic change in 1944. Peyotism spread from the Southern to the Northern Plains and throughout the Midwest in the early decades of the twentieth century, and Stephen Mopope and his relatives took an active part. They were practicing members of the church, and Vanessa Jennings has written an account of the trips they made on behalf of "Chief Peyote":

> Between the years of 1919 and early 1944, Stephen Mopope, my grandfather, made numerous travel adventures to the Crow Indian Reservation in Montana to attend Peyote Ceremonies and other cultural events. He traveled with "Crooked Neck Charlie" Anquoe, Charlie Whitehorse, Mark Keahbone, Bert Geikaunmah, Charlie Apekaum, James Auchiah and other family members. All were relatives. All lived in the Kiowa community known as Redstone, with the exception of James Auchiah. Also, part of the traveling Peyote men were Tennyson "Ah-Ko-Bah" Berry, Stephen Mopope's Carlisle Indian school educated father-in-law, Clayton Bitseedy and Apache Ben. The men were from the Kiowa-Apache community known as Gawky Creek.

> The Crow have had a documented close friendship with the Kiowa for generations. Their friendship was so strong that [there] were inter-marriages and family adoptions. The formal exchange of important tribal rituals, such as the "Kado" or Sun Dance, ceremonial objects and medicines further strengthened this important relationship. This is the basis for my story.
>
> My grandfather had a Model-T Ford that served as transportation. On this particular trip, "Crooked Neck Charlie" was [at] a Peyote meeting at the home of the Big Day Family in Pryor, Montana. The evening preparation for the ceremony had come to a sudden halt because of an unexpected visitor. That visitor was the very powerful and respected Crow Chief, Plenty Coups. He rode up on his horse. His demeanor showed his anger. The women of the family stayed inside the small frame home and watched with curious faces pressed against the glass window panes. The man of the house stepped out of the tipi to meet the important visitor. He requested the Kiowas to continue drinking their coffee and the preparation of the sacred altar for the Peyote ceremony. Outside words of greetings were exchanged as a matter of formality. However, there was no question that this was going to be a confrontation. Chief Plenty Coups commanded that "the Peyote staff, the gourds, fans, the Peyote drum and its drumstick be thrown in the water IMMEDIATELY. This is not our way! Get rid of it now! THIS BELONGS TO THE KIOWA. THIS IS NOT CROW!"
>
> The Big Day family politely listened. When Chief Plenty Coups finished his angry litany, he left. Later that night the Peyote meeting was led by "Crooked Neck Charlie" and the intrepid Kiowa and Kiowa-Apache men. After it was completed, they began their long trek back to Oklahoma. . . . What I am telling you is the truth according to my grandfather, Stephen Mopope's words.[54]

Jennings's account does not specify when these trips to Crow country took place. In interviews Omer Stewart made with Crows they reported visits from Kiowas bringing peyote meetings from 1916 to 1928, but dates are uncertain.[55] It is therefore quite possible that they occurred while Mopope and Auchiah pursued art studies in Norman. Jeanne d'Ucel's lamentation that as soon as summer came the Kiowas left town and went back to the reservation signaled that other concerns now held priority, and ritual obligations loomed large among these. Their concurrent worlds were at cross-purposes.

Mopope put his skill to the service of his faith. LaQuinta Mopope described how he drew sacred images on a drum hide to be used for the singing during peyote meetings, and he designed peyote boxes. Peyote boxes held the ritual instruments of the ceremony, and they have been described as both "a cornucopia of potential power," and "works of art." Mopope's boxes went to people he visited in Montana as well as to local people. He carved designs that he used in decorating the boxes. He also painted ceremonies. Laura E. Smith discusses his painting *Peyote Healing Ceremony* (n.d.), emphasizing how Mopope foregrounded lived experience, and she argues that his art, "in its challenge to critics who believed peyotism to be dangerous to mind and body, was modern."[56]

Mopope's and Berry's involvement in the Peyote Church came to an abrupt halt in 1944. That year they planned and prepared rituals and ceremonies to protect Kiowa warriors going into battle during the Second World War, among them Mopope's nephew Lyndreth Palmer. Vanessa Jennings describes being told how the meeting revealed impending disaster. It all seemed to go well. Jeanette met the men in the morning after the ceremony "excited and happy," but the young man "looked at her with the saddest expression." He took her arm and told her, "I won't be back, not alive! They will be carrying my body! I saw it in the fire last night. I won't make it. That's why I am telling you now how grateful I am for all that you and my uncle have done for me!" Later Jeanette found Stephen sitting alone. After some time he spoke, "Last night everything was going so well. The prayers were powerful and the songs came one after another. Then, that medicine man spoke to me. 'You and your boy, make your hearts strong! I am going to show you something. Look into my fire.'" Stephen looked and "saw our boy's coffin draped with our American flag. It was horrible. This is my vow. I will never attend another peyote meeting as long as I live! I am not strong enough for that medicine to show me things!"[57]

Corporal Lyndreth Palmer, Mopope's nephew, was killed in action in France, near Mars-la-Tour, on December 5, 1944. Vanessa Jennings continues her story: "My grandfather, Stephen Mopope, died in 1974. He was a man of his word. He never participated in another peyote meeting during his lifetime. At his funeral service, the President of the Kiowa chapter of Native American Church spoke of my grandfather in a good way. He and the other men wore their red and blue Peyote blankets when they came to pay their respects. It was a dignified farewell to my grandfather."[58]

SUSTAINING AN ARTIST—JEANETTE'S SUPPORT

Stephen Mopope loved coffee. "If I was starving, if they gave me a cup of coffee I could live for a year," his daughter remembered him saying.[59] Daily routines in the Mopope-Berry household included an early morning breakfast with coffee, after which Stephen would retire to his studio in the back of the house and paint all morning. Of all the original Kiowa artists who came to Norman in the 1920s, Mopope was the only one who continued painting throughout his life. Spencer Asah stopped painting fairly soon after classes in Norman, because, according to Jeanne d'Ucel, religious obligations took up a great deal of his time. James Auchiah, too, ended his career as an artist as a consequence of religious influences. Both men continued teaching art to young students at the Fort Sill and Riverside Indian Schools. Even after experiencing a spiritual crisis, Mopope did not give up painting. Why was that so? There are only secondhand sources to the reasons why Asah and Auchiah discontinued their artistic careers, and there may be reasons to question this information. In speaking to Arthur Silberman in the 1970s, James Auchiah expressed a clear and abiding interest in art and in reminiscing about his work and collaboration with Mopope. The difference between their careers may lie as much in different opportunities and determination to continue, as in the influences of religious beliefs. Mopope's letters to his mother testify to his all-consuming desire to paint as well as to the support he received from his wife. Mopope's engagement as both dancer and artist subsequently enabled a steady income, which he could augment with money from leases and from part-time employment as a deputy police officer on the reservation.[60]

From the 1920s to the late 1960s, Stephen Mopope served as a special officer deputized to work on Indian land under the jurisdiction of the Anadarko Indian Agency and the Pawnee Indian Agency. Federal and state police officers could not exercise authority on restricted Indian land and therefore required the assistance of Indian deputy officers. The deputy sheriff on the agency, Hoyt Shelby, was a friend, and it was through this connection that Mopope got the assignment. His responsibilities were to represent the law on Indian land, often in connection with abuses against

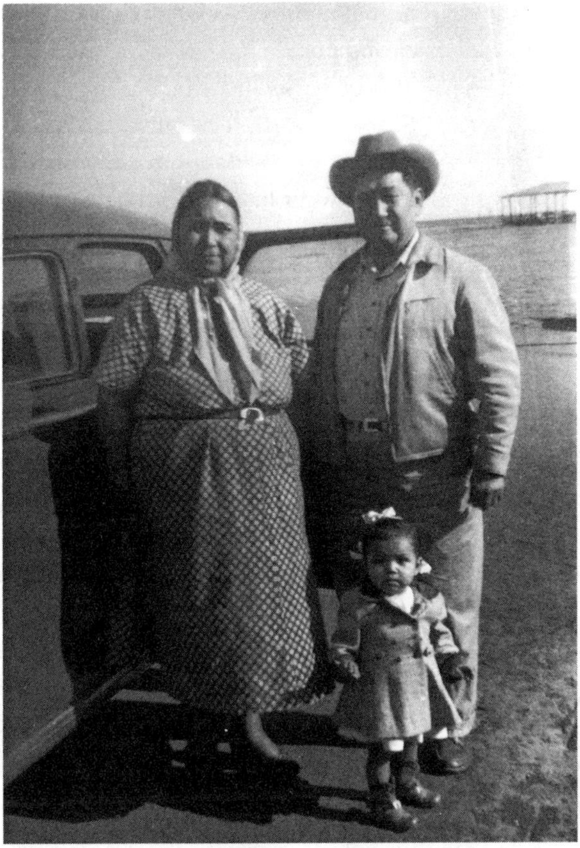

FIGURE 21. Stephen, Jeanette, and granddaughter Vanessa, mid-1950s. From Vanessa and Carl Jennings Neg. Coll. They are on their way to "Agency Day" in Anadarko. Whenever they traveled to the Indian Agency, Jeanette would dress her grandchildren in their best clothes and fix their hair. Jennings recalls: "She and Grandpa Steve said that when you conduct business at the Anadarko Indian Agency or in town, you must dress your best and be on your best proper behavior." Courtesy Oklahoma Historical Society.

the laws prohibiting the sale of alcohol to Indians. Bootlegging whisky joints were common along the Washita River. Steve and Jeanette had a lifelong aversion to alcohol as they had seen much misery among their family members resulting from intoxication. One young woman had been forced to drink by her husband, and when she passed out her husband would share her body with his drinking buddies. A nephew was killed in a car accident involving a drunk driver. Another boy was murdered by another

Kiowa youth. Vanessa Jennings writes: "Alcohol had ruined the lives of many of my grandfather's loved ones. That is why he was against it."[61]

Until the late 1940s Mopope was involved in farming his land, but when his grandmother Keintaddle died he gave up farming and sold his tools and cattle. According to his daughter, he "just more or less retired from farming. Then he went back to his painting and traveling." Income from leases on this land did not make him a wealthy man, but it was still an important source of income to supplement art sales and dance engagements. That he was able to give up farming is a testament to the backing he received from Jeanette Berry. Her unwavering support enabled him to focus on art and make that a viable route forward. Her life represented a parallel course, one that intersected with Stephen's at certain times, but otherwise with its own demands and focus. They shared some labors such as raising a family and the burden of the harrowing loss of children. Two of their daughters grew to adulthood, but they buried eight babies who died of consumption, influenza, diarrhea, and other infections.[62]

The couple had separate finances and separate jurisdictions within the household. They managed both their leases and their income from their arts and crafts separately. "His money that he made from his lease and from his sales was *his* money. And my grandmother had *her* money," Jennings notes.[63] Jeanette managed her own land, and that is where the family lived. She regularly carried out farm chores, including taking care of Stephen's cattle when he was traveling. In 1939, while he stayed in Washington to complete murals in the Department of the Interior Building, the family ran out of meat. Jeanette called Stephen with her concern, asking him which cow he wanted her to slaughter, and he responded, "kill one of 'em young bulls." She got out her rifle, stalked into the pasture and shot his prize bull through the head, one that he had paid twelve hundred dollars for. On another occasion, she gave away his racehorse at a powwow giveaway. Perhaps she did these things to make a point about his long absences from the family and their needs. However, she remained loyal to his commitment to art. Vanessa Jennings remembers her as a strong woman who gathered the family together. "My grandmother stayed here. And she ran the farm. And she took care of everything, and she was, she was just this incredible woman. . . . I couldn't keep up with her. Man, she's out there, she's got an axe whack, whack, whack. We got this big amount of wood, split and ready, and you know we were expected to do the same. And my grandma used to say: 'You don't count your work, you don't complain, and you don't brag about your work.'"[64]

Jeanette had clear ideas about the different ways in which she and her husband thought about their land. "Men don't think about a home the way a woman does. Look at us!" she would tell her granddaughter, "'Look at all the land your grandpa's got, he's the one, he's got land that sits on the north side of the Washita and then the balance is on the south side. He's got his mamma, and his daddy's land, and his brothers', he's got land that's all the way down to ah, ah, down by the Red River. . . . Look at all the land your grandpa has,' she said, 'where are we living?' She said, 'we're living on *my* land.'"[65] Despite Mopope's wealth in land, Jeanette's home was the heart of the family. She was an accomplished beadworker, and sales from her work contributed to the family economy, even though it was clear that whatever she earned was her money, just as the land was her land. She was active in the community and a noted presence in the women's Mau-Tame beadwork club and in the civic life of Anadarko. In the 1950s she was president of the Inter-Tribal Service Club, and in 1952 she was in charge of organizing a memorial service dinner for Sgt. Luke Taimpeah, killed in action in Korea in 1951. For this purpose, she solicited contributions from businesses all over Anadarko.[66]

Several of Vanessa Jennings's recollections attest to this independence, and to the struggle and fierce pride required to maintain one's place and reputation. Conflicts developed within the confines of the reservation community as well as in relation to the world outside its boundaries. On one occasion, Jeanette decorated a pouch set for a Comanche woman who had ordered it for her daughter. Jeanette and Stephen left to go to the grocery store and to buy some fabric, and the couple's small granddaughters were alone when the Comanche woman arrived to ask for the set. The girls asked the woman to wait, but she said she had no time and took the pouch set with her and left the girls with some money. When their grandparents returned, Jeanette immediately noticed that her beadwork was gone, and in its place lay a ten-dollar bill. The girls could tell that something was wrong, when their grandmother told them to get their grandfather to take them all to Fort Cobb that very moment. "The next few miles were filled with a stern lecture from their grandmother about several important points about truth and integrity. She ended with an admonishment of no one was allowed to handle her business transactions concerning her work or her money while she was absent." They reached their destination, and Jeanette, with her granddaughters in tow, knocked on the front door. The ensuing confrontation ended with Jeanette cutting all of the cut beads off the pouch set, leaving the bags unbeaded with the comment that now they were worth only the ten dollars that the woman had left with her granddaugthers. They then left the house driving back to Lawton in silence. Finally, Berry spoke: "no one will look out for you except Grandma and Grandpa. There will be times when drastic measures must be taken when someone cheats you and *expects you to say nothing*! Life is not for the weak. You have to be brave enough to stand up and defend yourself. Do you understand?"[67]

In the eyes of her granddaughter, Jeanette Berry was a formidable woman and perhaps at times unforgiving. In a tightly knit community, existing under conditions of prolonged pressure and competing for meager resources, it is not surprising that the success and prominence of some individuals caused jealousies and resentment. Relationships with the white community on and beyond the reservation also had their complications. The conditions structuring all relations with authorities had to go through the Indian agency and placed Kiowas in an inferior position in their interaction with agency officials, and in all matters relating to health, government checks, or purchase orders. Kiowa women were consistently regarded as backward and subject to derogatory treatment. Jeanette Berry would not accept this. Vanessa Jennings recalls: "My grandmother took care of her own lease. You didn't send a backup, you didn't send the farmer's wife, that farmer had to come and talk to her in person. And if she went to his house and we had to go to the back door, forget it, that lease, that lease was not his. My grandmother was not going to the back door for nobody. And she said it just, just that way. 'You don't let anybody send you to the back door.' I never knew what the back door was, but boy it sounded scary."[68]

EXPANDING HORIZONS

Mopope's success as an artist and dancer expanded his horizons and extended his movements. He loved traveling. Accounts from the early days of the Kiowa students' contacts with white patrons suggest that the latter brought the Kiowas along for extended trips to expose their work to buyers, and to promote them as dancers, giving the impression that well-traveled white people brought stationary and inexperienced Indians into the world. Nothing could be farther from the truth. The Kiowas never ceased to be mobile, despite the authorities' best efforts. In fact, the struggle over mobility, which is evident in the reports of government officials from the first decades of the twentieth century, demonstrates the government's desire to take control over the scope, manner, and direction of Indian mobility. Several factors contributed to impede the Kiowas' desire to travel, but it never curbed it entirely, despite racism, poverty, and injunctions against leaving the reservation without permission.

Stephen Mopope and Jeanette Berry maintained regular contacts with Indian communities further west, frequently attending festivals in New Mexico and Arizona, and in Montana and even western Canada. Still in the 1930s, roads on the Navajo Reservation were mostly gravel, turning muddy after rains, and going out to participate in powwows involved traveling by horses and wagons. In later years, when he no longer felt capable of making extensive trips, his daughter remembered that he liked to propose outings. He would ask her to go with him on short trips around the reservation. He had a favorite place a little off the trading post at Cache and he liked to drive through the Wichita Mountains. "He said well let's just look at the buffalos and the prairie dogs and stuff like that." Traveling had meant much more than leisure in his life. He used to travel, his daughter remembered, to maintain links with buyers and traders. The Wichita Mountains Wildlife Refuge with its managed herd of buffalos and chattering towns of prairie dogs was also a place where he found needed supplies. A letter from the refuge manager, Ernest Greenwalt, informed him in 1944 that whenever they had six buffalo hides available he could buy them for $2.50 a piece. The ending of the letter testifies to more than just a business relationship. "I enjoyed your visit yesterday, and hope that you can visit the Wichita again. If at any time we can be of help to you in your work, please advise."[69]

Sometimes he traveled together with Oscar Jacobson, long after he stopped being a student at the university. LaQuinta Mopope remembers Jacobson's visits. "Long time ago and then he'd used to come up and see us and everytime he'd drove up you know we always expected candy, apples and oranges cause he'd just bring a whole bunch of stuff for us kids." Then they would go off in different directions. Mopope brought his paintings and accompanied Jacobson to different universities where he lectured and Mopope showed his art. As mentioned earlier, there were parts of the country where Mopope "couldn't get into unless we were with Jacobson."[70]

In 1965 LaQuinta Mopope sponsored a dance at their home in honor of her father. The article in the *Anadarko Daily News* provided a summary of his life achievements:

> Mopope whose Indian name is Wood-coy, meaning Painted Robe, is recognized as one of the founder and leading exponents of contemporary plains Indian painting.
>
> He is one of the five original Kiowas taken to the University of Oklahoma in 1927 by Dr. Oscar B. Jacobson and tutored in the art department. In 1928, he achieved his first artistic success when his paintings were shown at the First International Art Exposition, Prague, Czechoslovakia.
>
> One of the original members of the Oho-mo Lodge, he was taken into it as a small boy at the White Buffalo place, located two miles south of Washita.
>
> Mopope, who is also a famous fancy war dance champion, has continued to participate in art exhibitions throughout the United States and abroad.
>
> He is represented in museum collections in Tulsa at the Philbrook Art Center and the Gilcrease Institute as well as the private collections of William and Leslie Van Ness Denman, of California, and Dr. Jacobson, in Norman.
>
> The designer of the official seal of Indian City, U.S.A., his paintings hang in the Department of the Interior, Washington, D.C.
>
> Other Mopope paintings decorate federal buildings in Muskogee and Fort Sill and colleges at Tahlequah and Weatherford.[71]

The brief piece in the newspaper reveals Mopope as an innovative artist and dancer, steeped in tradition but wide-ranging in his contacts and travels. In summary, based on his own extant papers, we can see that he built this career through diligent efforts to create and maintain networks and links crisscrossing the reservation, spanning Oklahoma, and extending in larger circles including Native people and whites across the United States and Canada. His art and his dancing displayed deep connections with his background in the Kiowa community and with his curiosity in other Native traditions, such as those of the Northern Plains. While traditional in some respects he creatively reshaped other practices. He fashioned regalia to suit new dances and incorporated novel materials. He experimented with different materials in his paintings as well, and a large collection of art magazines and postcards testify to his enduring pleasure in the European and American worlds of art. The range of his activities fits well with the observation by the Committee on Indian Arts and Crafts that Indian artists and artisans primarily found an outlet by catering to a tourist market and to the fine arts scene.

This was not all, however. Mopope's production included items made for other Native people who used them for ceremonies and social occasions. It took tenacity and passion to sustain his commitment to art. Jeanette Berry's steadfast support and his deep involvement in the Redstone community made such commitment possible. Jacobson's intervention provided Mopope and the other artists with the necessary skills and created a platform for sales, but the art circles that began in Norman were never the center of their world. Rather, it all formed a concurrent experience, which had to be balanced against the requirements, hopes, and restraints of the KCA Reservation. Stephen and Jeanette Berry Mopope never forgot that they were Indians. "If you think the Indian wars are over—you're mistaken," they repeatedly told their grandchildren. Even though Stephen himself stopped participating in peyote ceremonies in 1944, he kept informed of the pressures against these beliefs and practices. A note saved among his papers shows that in 1967 he took down information on efforts to stop Bill 32, introduced to the Oklahoma House of Representatives to declare peyote a drug. He also kept flyers informing of the goals and activities of the American Indian Movement (AIM) in Oklahoma.[72]

The interlinking of the concurrent worlds of Kiowas and white Americans caused possibilities but also friction and in this tension the Kiowas, as other American Indians, were at a distinct disadvantage. Philip Deloria describes the first decades of the twentieth century as a period of paradox for Native people. On the one hand, poverty, violence, and devastation colored the conditions in every Indian community, and the American nation appeared to all but forget the existence of Indigenous populations. Yet, on the other hand, the period offered opportunities for both Indians, like the Kiowa students who came to Norman, and whites like Oscar Jacobson, to "challenge the old script—and maybe even write a new one." Even if the role left available for Indian people to fill was limited, and often placed them in an impossible bind as cocreators of a stereotypical "Indianness," they were also cocreators of modernity.[73]

Conclusion

PAINTING NATURE, PAINTING CULTURE

ON A BLUSTERY DAY in early March 2015 I sauntered across the University of Oklahoma campus in Norman. On the North Oval stood a new statue that had not been there when I was a student in the 1980s: a tall bronze statue, signed Allan Houser, of an Apache warrior saluting with his gun turned toward the horizon. In Oklahoma City, outside the Oklahoma History Center across from the capitol another of Allan Houser's large bronze sculptures greets the visitors. Enoch Kelly Haney's massive Indian scout adorns the top of the capitol building. American Indians and their artistic creations are a visible and tangible presence in the state of the red earth. Oscar and Jeanne Jacobson's house in Norman is now a Native American art center. Nearly a century after five Kiowa men and one woman began to perfect their painting skills in a special studio at University of Oklahoma, American Indian arts and crafts in some form or other can be found in virtually every gift shop and art gallery in the western United States. American Indian artists are represented in major art galleries and their art held in private collections across the nation and the world. Who would have imagined that in 1915, watching the poverty-ridden conditions of the KCA Reservation about the same time that the Jacobsons arrived at the humble college town of Norman? In what art historian Bill Anthes calls a "remarkable renaissance of Native North American cultural production," men and women across the Southwest defied the devastating circumstances of allotment and assimilation policies to assert cultural and physical continuity between past and present through producing objects and practices of beauty and adapting them to novel contexts.[1]

The focus of this book is on one particular example of this remarkable resurgence, configured around Kiowa artists and their engagement with University of Oklahoma fine arts professor Oscar B. Jacobson. I have argued that it was the confluence of concurrent histories of American Indians and European immigrants that generated this development. Emerging from two hugely different forms of diaspora, the Swedish immigrant and the Kiowas reestablished and reshaped home in Oklahoma through their passion for art.

Jacobson certainly wished to emphasize his role in this occurrence. In 1958, the *Oklahoma Almanac* published an article by Jacobson entitled "Indian Artists of Oklahoma," which consisted of a recapitulation of his work with American Indian artists. The lion's share of the text was devoted to the first six Kiowa artists and their work, and Jacobson formulated his own part in the development of a national and international recognition for Indian art: "When I first came to Oklahoma in 1915, it was the policy of the Government and the churches to change Indians into Whites as quickly as and completely as possible. I was a voice crying in the wilderness; sometimes people looked on me as a queer person, because I insisted that 'heathen' Indian pottery, beadwork, paintings, etc., also music, myths and ritual dances, were as beautiful and precious as their primitive Greek counterparts lovingly preserved in museums."[2]

Scholars have exposed the contradictory character of federal Indian policy in the early decades of the twentieth century, and how various organizations and interest groups that involved themselves in aiding the Indians adopted different approaches to assimilation and formed volatile and changing coalitions in response to issues such as the dance ban controversy in the 1920s, the policies of allotment, the alienation of tribal land, federal guardianship, and educational policies. Jacobson, like many other white promoters of Indian art, allied himself with the position perhaps most visibly championed by John Collier, believing that Indian art and culture must be protected and preserved and that American Indians offered a special contribution to the nation as a whole. Likening Indigenous cultural expressions to "their primitive Greek counterparts," Jacobson established American Indian culture outside and prior to modern development. He valued it as such, but the reference to primitivism cannot be understood beyond the prevailing racial theories of the early twentieth century, which inscribed an indelible difference and unquestioned hierarchy on the racial characterizations of peoples. Yet, to Jacobson and to many of his contemporaries supporting Indigenous art, racial traits could also be a source of strength. "The Indian artists find their most sympathetic and stimulating subjects in their racial culture and tradition," he wrote. "It was their culture and tradition, deeply rooted in their spiritual nature, that nourished their nature and enabled them to survive the years and years of maltreatment by the Whites, also the well-intentioned good treatment sometimes as harmful as the bad because it was lacking in understanding."[3]

His retrospective breathed a note of triumph. "Now, in Oklahoma, at least, where the Indians are integrated, where they engage in all modern pursuits as well and efficiently as Whites, the culture and the tradition remain as a cherished inheritance; it is to be hoped that they will never be completely lost." While overstating the level of integration and acceptance that Indigenous peoples experienced in the state in the 1950s, he was correct in stressing that remarkable changes had taken place. "The tide has turned. The Indian has been discovered, with such enthusiasm in fact, that hardly a month passes, without a book on Indians rolling off the presses of the nation. It is my pride and joy that I had a part in this re-appraisal."[4]

It may be easy to interpret Jacobson's description of a voice crying in the wilderness as casting himself as the Indians' savior, but it is just as possible to understand him as assuming the prophetic role of a messenger. Countless evenings in the Jacobson home—when the Kiowas brought out the drum and sang songs and told stories from their own people's history—must have made an impression on both Oscar and Jeanne. Recurring visits to the reservation, socializing on the front porches of his students' family homes, and participating in peyote ceremonies, allowed Oscar to learn about conditions, traditions, and emotions that undergirded the actions and ambitions of his students and friends. He had the platform from which to announce the value of Indigenous art, and he used it exceedingly well, but the message itself was a joint creation in which the Kiowa artists were equally invested.[5]

In 1966 Oscar Jacobson's heart gave up the battle, and he died in his home. He was eighty-four years old. Stephen Mopope was hit by a car in 1974 and after a few weeks he succumbed to a ruptured spleen and other internal injuries at the age of seventy-six. James Auchiah was heartbroken at hearing of the death of his friend and followed him later in the same year. By then most of the group of people who formed such an unexpected but energetic alliance in the 1920s, and the people near them, had passed on. They left a cultural landscape irrevocably altered because of their actions and involvement. Their concurrent trajectories had intertwined to vitally contribute to what Anthes characterizes as "a remarkable and unexpected outpouring of creativity," in the midst of assault of assimilation policies, land loss, and government and missionary attacks on Indian culture at the beginning of the twentieth century. They did so not by deliberate design, but it grew out of their separate desires, needs, and histories.[6]

DIASPORA IDENTITIES

In the ceiling of the Jacobsons' cabin in Allens Park sat a small replica of a Viking ship. About one foot long, outfitted with tiny oars, a sail, and a sea monster bow, it adorned a central crossbeam, testifying to the world of Jacobson's claim and dual (at least) belonging. He had made it himself, including sewing the sail, and the symbol of Jacobson as a Viking and his family as colonists in the New World adorned bookplates and greeting cards (see plate 12).[7]

The symbol was not accidental. Of all his guises, I suspect the Viking appeared the closest image of how Oscar Jacobson—born by the Baltic seaside, incessant traveler who rooted himself in the plains and mountains of the American West—wished to represent himself. He had come of age in an America obsessed with Vikings, where formidable efforts were made to establish the early Norsemen as the "first" explorers of the continent, a landscape Jacobson strove tirelessly to portray in all its majesty, "unconquered by man." Despite his love for the arid desert and mountain ranges, it was the Viking crossing of the ocean that set his life in motion and animated his creation of structures of belonging. Art was the medium of expression through which he manifested his immersion in the new land while never letting go of the links to the region of the world where he had first encountered life. And it was through his connections to Indigenous America that he forged his special place as of the West but also external to the nation that had colonized it.[8]

A 1955 article by O. R. Landelius in the magazine *Utlandssvenskarna* (Swedes in foreign lands) illustrates these tensions in his life. According to d'Ucel, Oscar never met Landelius, but the article was "without a doubt, the shrewdest and most understanding criticism of Dad's paintings ever written." Landelius stressed that, in addition to his own painting, Jacobson's fame derived from "the extraordinarily great and valuable pedagogic and organizational contributions he has made towards the preservation of the original Indian art through revitalization and renewal, primarily among tribes living in and around Oklahoma." Landelius further emphasized the significance of his efforts to put together traveling exhibits that showcased the works of the American Indian artists across the United States and overseas. One such exhibition appeared in Gothenburg and in Helsinki in 1955 and inspired Landelius's article. Yet all of Jacobson's activities in the service of Indian art, as organizer of federal works projects during the Depression, and as a guest lecturer at an impressive number of universities and museums all across the United States, had not curbed his own artistic outpouring. He "loves the monumental depiction of nature—the boundless expanse of the prairies and tablelands, the desolate wilderness of the Rocky Mountain formations, the wholeness and mighty intensity of the deserts, the piercing clarity of the sky, the timeless floating of the clouds—and with congenial empathy he poeticizes this on his canvases into an eternally shifting drama, loaded with nature's internal lyrical epos. Grand lines, whole surfaces, strong brush strokes and coloristic intensity characterize the bulk of this painting."[9]

The article in *Utlandssvenskarna* neatly summarizes the convergent threads that knitted together Jacobson's life and endeavors: the labor to support and encourage American Indian artistic talent, his own engagement as an artist, and his connections to Sweden and to Swedish America. This trinity helps to explain why he did not engage in debates over Indian policy, nor link up other than momentarily with the host of other reformers and artists' collectives that actively involved themselves in preserving, improving, or altering conditions on behalf of American Indians. Jacobson remained first and foremost, as Landelius expressed it, a teacher and an artist. His activism was an outgrowth of those commitments and passions. His desire to stand independent from parties, religions, and organizations may have stemmed from his identity as an artist but also from his conscious identification with the West and with Sweden.

Ruth B. Phillips argues similarly in her article on three "stranger-artists" and their contacts with Indigenous art. In his "painterly recreations of a raw and unsettled land" Jacobson "seems also to have been clearing a space in which he could root himself in America." The Viking ship, placed prominently in his primary location for painting, affirmed both his voyage and his arrival. She identifies, in the "shocks and reterritorialisations produced by immigration, exile and diaspora," an opening toward "fresh acts of seeing" that enabled the stranger-artist to question the myths of Indigenous disappearance and challenge institutional separations of folk art, ethnography, and craft. This, she argues, allowed them to position the Indigenous artist within modern art and push "to admit indigenous work to venues of fine art rather than ethnography."[10]

The diasporic condition, which I have argued inflected the lives of both this particular immigrant and the American Indians he tutored, sustained within it a search for new roots, always shaded by the ambivalent meanings of belonging and against a backdrop of things lost. Oscar Jacobson never fully assimilated, I suggest. He chose to become a westerner and to remain a Swede—although naturalized in 1915, his identification as an American appears more complicated. His granddaughter remembers him as being intensely patriotic for his chosen country: responding to the gold crisis in 1933, he turned in his whole collection of antique gold coins despite the fact that coins were exempt. But he also kept traits that noticeably set him apart from Anglo-America. The parallel, but apparently never transecting, trajectory of his contemporary G. E. E. Lindquist from Lindsborg may illustrate this point.[11]

Gustavus Elmer Emanuel Lindquist was born in 1886 to Swedish parents who had settled in Lindsborg. After graduating from Bethany College in 1908 he longed to become a missionary. A chance encounter with the Reformed Church missionaries Walter and Mary Roe convinced him to focus on internal missions to American Indigenous people. He became close friends with the Roe's ward, Henry Roe Cloud (Winnebago), who would become one of the most public American Indian voices of his time. Between 1912 and 1915 Lindquist worked as secretary of the YMCA at Haskell Indian Institute and spent summers with the Mescalero Apaches in southern New Mexico. Together Roe Cloud and Lindquist cofounded the Roe Indian Institute, a nondenominational academy for Indian students, located near Wichita in Kansas, and they collaborated on Lindquist's book *Red Man in the United States* (1923), which was the first book detailing socioeconomic conditions among American Indian communities. While initially critical of assimilationist policies, Lindquist would eventually change his position, and he became the most ardent of John Collier's critics, arguing forcefully that the commissioner's policies for tribal self-government would condemn American Indians to ghettoized conditions of isolation and impoverishment and would subject them to continued racial hatred.[12]

David W. Daily describes Lindquist's evolution from a Swedish-speaking youth "in a world where assimilation did not force a choice between ethnic and national loyalties" to a man whose "speech bore little trace of a Swedish accent," and whose church affiliation had changed from a small sectarian free church to the mainstream Congregational Christian Church, a descendant of Puritanism. For Lindquist, who experienced scathing prejudice against Swedish immigrants from his future mother-in-law, assimilation turned into "a very personal project to fight social bias and prove—in himself and in his work among the Indians—the universal human capacity for advancement and self-improvement." Like Jacobson, he maintained lifelong connections to Sweden, but his assimilation as an American allowed him to define himself "through self-discipline, moral rectitude, and increased prosperity." He applied the same goals in his advocacy for American Indians.[13]

It is somewhat surprising that two men who so passionately involved themselves in work to improve the conditions and perceptions of American Indians, and who must have known about one another from the small town on the Kansas plains, appear to have had nothing to do with one another. Not least as Lindquist was also familiar with the KCA Reservation and in his photographic collection were pictures of the Redstone Baptist Church and parsonage. Part of the distance between Lindquist and Jacobson could have sprung from Jacobson's rejection of organized religion. But it is also possible that their different approaches to assimilation and to the place of the American Indians within the nation placed them in entirely separate circles. It was in the monumental nature of the West that Jacobson found solace and belonging, not in the national project of the United States. It was in nature and in the West that he encountered American Indians, not as objects for his canvases but as collaborators in the search for the soul or essence of nature. Nor was he, like Lindquist, a man of words. He expressed himself through his art and only incidentally (or instrumentally) through writing.[14]

The Kiowa artists also lived with the tension between past and present colored by the diasporic desire for return and intense efforts to adapt Kiowa concepts of kinship, spirituality, and self-representation to a new psychological, economic, social, and political landscape through their art and other cultural expressions. Auchiah's and Asah's efforts to have their forefathers recognized as American heroes, Auchiah's long-standing commitment to recording Kiowa history, and Asah's responsibilities for a sacred medicine bundle all reflect the substantial effort that went into establishing the Kiowas as a significant presence in Oklahoma. Mopope accomplished this primarily through his artwork and dancing. If there was an element of nostalgia in these activities, this is something they shared with Jacobson. Mopope confessed to Scott Fulton, whom he frequently met toward the end of his life at a gallery in Oklahoma City, that he admired "the old Indian ways and wanted to keep them and wished he'd been part of them." He wished that he could have known buffalo hunting the way it was done before the Kiowas were forced onto the reservation. He "wanted to kill that buffalo with a spear and he wanted to jump off his horse, and to skin the buffalo. He wanted to be as much Indian as he could. He wanted to have that experience." He knew "he wasn't going to have it but he really wanted to have it" (see plate 13).[15]

Yet, it was more than nostalgia that colored the work of Mopope, Auchiah, and their colleagues. The struggle for survivance lay at the heart of their endeavors, and through their efforts to visualize ceremonies and social life, they documented the past and present of the Kiowa people and reveled in the beauty of their aesthetic expressions. Jacobson helped the artists to achieve some fame, but this did not mean they could leave behind reservation conditions and stereotypical representations and expectations of American Indians. Mopope did not only paint the works of art he longed to do, he also painted to order to pay his bills, often reproducing conventional images of Plains warriors to meet the desires of white buyers. Auchiah described how they were offered money to paint "forbidden drawings," to illustrate "love magazines," presumably asking for explicit sexual content. Within the reservation, too, other Kiowas questioned their choice of pictorial content and this probably limited what they were able to do. Jealousies relating to his relative success as an artist marred the later years of Mopope's life and, when he died, led to divisive conflicts over his estate, resulting in the loss of several of his original paintings. Despite such tragedies, his work had an enduring meaning for the transmission and retention of Kiowa culture. "Grandpa never realized what the importance of his work had been," Jennings says.

But if it had not been for him and the other artists, the record of painted tipis, decorated shields, cradleboards, and dances may well have faded into oblivion and not remained as a vibrant part of contemporary Kiowa culture.[16]

PAINTING NATURE, PAINTING CULTURE

Both Jacobson and Mopope recognized that it was possible to be modern in many different ways. Nostalgia formed a characteristically modern phenomenon, one that bound Indigenous people and immigrants to one another and that also resonated among the population at large. They both expressed nostalgic sentiments in their desire for a past that in different ways sharply diverged from their present, and this influenced their art. In Mopope's case, it referred to a time when he perceived that his people independently fashioned their lives and when the ceremonies and material practices that he attempted to document in his paintings took shape and flourished. For Jacobson, the past was a time when nature was untainted by human presence. At one showing of his paintings, he posted a handwritten placard with a quote from Will Rogers: "A place looks better before it gets houses on it than it does afterward." It would appear that their paintings foregrounded utterly different things, rather neatly reversing the conventional binary of Indigenous connections to nature and white associations with culture. Jacobson painted landscapes devoid of the demoralizing, destructive influence of man, and Mopope painted history and culture. But both of them lived firmly in the present. They utilized cameras to capture images of families and friends and to aid them in painting, they worked with colors and pigment produced by the best manufacturers, and they both loved their T-Fords and the freedom of movement these provided.[17]

In discussing Mopope's oeuvre, it seems important to delineate between the paintings produced on order, for the market, and those that he painted expressing and creating a visual record of Kiowa history and culture. The first category consisted mostly of dancing figures, and these he produced using his box of templates. The other paintings were shaped with minute attention and deliberation. Fulton conveyed Mopope's determination to paint the past as it had been passed down to him and as he, himself, had seen it: "You know he'd thought about these paintings when he painted them, and he didn't just paint them off the top of his hat.

He'd thought about them and in his opinion they were very authentic he wouldn't have painted them if it wasn't in his opinion they were perfect in authenticity."[18]

Mopope's art grew from an environment of constant storytelling. Stories were passed between generations, and through those stories the Kiowas inhabited the landscape. Mopope liked to tell stories himself, and Fulton liked to hear them. "I'd say almost 100 percent that the stories he told were folklore stories and he'd liked to tell me that because I liked to listen to that sort of thing and he liked to tell me Indian things, and things in the past and Indian things and how it was that is what he talked about most of the time."[19] Mopope manifested his vision of a western and Oklahoma landscape inhabited by Indian people, working, hunting, loving, dancing, singing, and praying. The cedar pole of the Feather Dancers, the tipi and sacred fire of the Native American Church, the campsites filled with painted tipis, drying racks of buffalo meat, children's cradles, couples courting, and medicine men praying and performing healing rituals, all manifested that Kiowas belonged to this land. In addition to Kiowas, his images showed Osage road men, Apache and Hopi dancers, and so on.

Mopope's style was described by Robert G. Donnelley as "a more generalized image of the Kiowa world, a nostalgic evocation of traditional tribal life centered on the horse culture of the mounted Plains warrior." Although tied to stories, this was not a vision of stagnation, of a timeless past in which Indian people reveled. His attention to detail showed changes in apparel and objects that hinted at a persistent and changing culture. In *Indian Gathering*, for example, metal pots in the foreground hold the food provided for the assembled people (see plate 14). He also re-created a landscape peopled by a variety of nations and practices. His daughter described his joy in Kiowa continuity: "He said he was proud to see his people doing so well for themselves . . . trying to keep it like it was. [He said], 'It just does something to you in here. It makes you feel good.'"[20]

His painting process thrived from sustained conversations with other artists and their constructive criticism. Fulton recalled Woody Crumbo and Mopope entering the gallery and putting up one of Mopope's paintings on the easel, discussing it in detail. Crumbo criticized it to Mopope's appreciation. This practice, Fulton thought, had originated with the training they received with Jacobson, and Mopope in his old age regretted

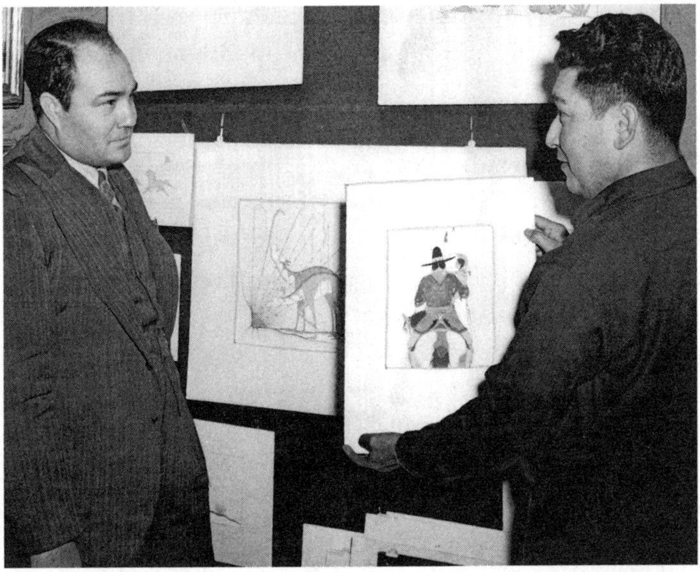

FIGURE 22. Acee Blue Eagle and Stephen Mopope. In *Daily Oklahoman*, November 26, 1940. Mopope liked to discuss paintings with his colleagues, a practice they had begun while students with Jacobson at the University of Oklahoma. Photograph by Bill Johnson. Courtesy Oklahoma Historical Society.

the fact that younger artists no longer sought each other's counseling or critiqued each other's work. Mopope was critical of a younger generation of American Indian artists for not paying attention to detail and authenticity and would say "these young bucks, they don't know what they're painting."[21]

In contrast, although Jacobson began his career as a portrait painter, he increasingly painted landscapes, particularly of the West, devoid of people. It would be easy to interpret this as a colonialist vision of land empty for the taking, a projection space for masculine virtue and domination. Maybe there was a touch of that. Toward the end of his life, when his heart condition made it too strenuous for him to enjoy the Colorado altitude, he expressed in an interview his pleasure in Oklahoma, which still had places left to explore (see plate 15). Yet, in Jacobson's vision of the pristine landscape of the West there seemed to be less a desire for the glory of conquest than sadness over capitalist exploitation of the land. It seems not too far-fetched to assume that both Jacobson and his Swedish compatriots and Mopope and the other Kiowas painted in ways influenced by powerful tropes that were diametrically opposed to one another. The narrative of the settling of Lindsborg reiterated that the land was empty when the Swedes took shelter in their first dugouts, even as they mentioned a previous Native American presence. They saw vast stretches, unbounded by humans, and they were awed by its magnificence, its colors, and its promise. In contrast, the Kiowas saw a landscape where people moved, danced, hunted, cooked, courted, and prayed. The trope that characterized the Kiowas' paintings in the early twentieth century was one of loss, but not one of emptiness.[22]

Like Mopope, Jacobson combined lofty ideals of "art for art's sake" with a pragmatic approach to quotidian requirements. To pay one's bills it was necessary to know the public's tastes. Both artists became somewhat ungenerous toward innovations of younger generations, losing themselves, perhaps, in nostalgic reminiscences, yet their role in reshaping the sentiments, appreciation, and understanding of Indigenous art is undeniable. Both Oscar Jacobson and Stephen Mopope looked backward as they painted. Jacobson expressed his longing for the past in paintings devoid of human influence. In this he joined with scores of other artists who portrayed an uncorrupted natural world. Mopope, on the other hand, painted the history of his people, a past of independence and with the rich texture of deeply held values and traditions. Yet both of them reached across the gulf dividing Indians and whites in Oklahoma to forge something new. Certainly, there was self-serving interest informing these contacts but also a mutual respect and appreciation that went beyond instrumental connections.

SERENDIPITOUS FRIENDSHIPS

Were they friends? Over the years, several people have asked the question with earnestness, and I certainly approached this project with that in mind. The question of friendship was central not only to d'Ucel, Peters, and others who invested much of their time in aiding the Indians. Scholars who have wished to understand these events and relationships share this concern.

In retrospect, the paternalism of the conditions in Norman is palpable. Legal structures of inequality framed the interactions between Kiowas and white people, but so did social and cultural practices and expectations. The emphasis on "helping" the Kiowas, on the kind and supportive environment nurtured around their painting, and on the efforts involved in smoothing their adaptation to the complex and uninformed American society underscored the agency of the helpers and promoters, not that of the American Indians. Jeanne d'Ucel stressed the tireless labor Jacobson performed on behalf of the Kiowas, but it was not a thankless task. The Kiowas honored him, and he, with the dedicated help of his wife, became an authority on "primitive" art and carved out an academic position of national repute. He could afford to keep his charming Swedish lilt until the end of his days, because he had proved himself a real westerner with a unique channel to the original Americans. This does not deny the very real concern and sympathy that the Jacobson couple exhibited for American Indians, nor the sincerity of their actions.[23]

The fact that the majority of the sources, letters, diaries, articles, and so on, were written by the Euro-American counterparts in these interactions, and that white people controlled much of the conditions for Kiowa people throughout most of Mopope's life does not mean that the Kiowas could not use these interactions for their own purposes. Mopope skillfully maintained advantageous contacts over decades, and he was able to gain benefits for his kin and friends in securing contracts and engagements. But did these contacts develop into relations that went beyond instrumentality?

The answer seems to be yes. Arthur Silberman, an art collector who amassed information regarding the Kiowa Indian artists and their relationships to white patrons such as Oscar Jacobson, often returned to this question. In an interview with LaQuinta Santos, Stephen Mopope's daughter, he asked, "So your dad I gather had only warm feelings for Jacobson?" LaQuinta responded: "really, really warm feeling. He and he'd drive all the way to out to the old home place up to my granddad Mopope's house you know to visit us because that's where we lived." In her answer, she connected the tight bonds between Jacobson and her father with the former's effort in driving to their house, located at some distance from Norman along poor and treacherous roads. Scott Fulton answered Silberman's question in a similar way: "I know he had a really fond admiration for Jacobson. He liked him a lot." When I—unable to let go of the same question—asked Mopope's granddaughter, she responded similarly and added: "What makes it so impressive is that their work was going on in the midst of rampant racism. Jacobson risked his reputation by his association with Indians." She continued to underline that the Kiowas risked jail by continuing to dance, and to uphold the ceremonies that they did. Jacobson must have known the hazards involved, and why it was important to them to paint as and what they did.[24]

Historic legacies of inequality are never easy to accept. It is human to wish to ignore them, to imagine that time has removed us from the injuries. Building bridges across vast stretches of pain is hard work, demanding humility, dedication, a willingness to listen, and not least, generosity. It appears that both Oscar and Stephen offered one another that. Oscar Jacobson's grandson, Sim Sheppard, remembers once in the early 1970s visiting a powwow and introducing himself to Stephen Mopope after hearing his name announced over the loudspeaker. Sheppard was astonished and humbled by the great warmth in Mopope's response when he learned of Sim's relationship to Oscar.[25]

MEANINGS

Regarding this book as a whole, admittedly important aspects of the lives of both men and the communities of which they were a part, as well as contemporaneous events and developments in the United States, have been glossed over in the attempt to highlight the specific limitations and possibilities structuring the lives of *both* the Kiowa artist and the successful immigrant. Attempting to view events from two different vantage points—concurrent in time but incongruent—challenges the cohesion of a narrative. This approach was borne out of the conviction that any biography of one alone would fail to illuminate the significance and consequences of their encounter. Ultimately, of course, it is up to each reader to determine to what extent the book has succeeded in fulfilling this ambition.

American Indians and white immigrants live to this day in concurrent worlds, but present in the same time and place. I have attempted to respect the nature of different experiences while pointing out the meaning of their entanglement. Envisioning the concurrence of Mopope's and Jacobson's lives required maintaining different frames of reference. Jacobson's world always tended to take over as a consequence of the wealth of material relating directly to the Swedish-French couple. Their words were strong and evocative and the possibilities of making exhilarating connections ubiquitous. In contrast, Mopope's world often appeared accessible only through white commentators. Valuable interviews provided a counterbalance, but the problem remains that sources allow unequal access to the worlds of Indigenous peoples and immigrants in early twentieth-century America. Another difficulty lay in the temptation in the material I found to treat the Kiowas as a collective and a representative of a people while Jacobson emerged as a unique individual. To counter this tendency, I chose to focus on Stephen Mopope and to build a distinctive portrait of his life.[26]

But this story is also something more than descriptions of individual contexts and choices. What is significant is how the courageous actions of a handful of young Kiowas and an immigrant couple searching for moorings in a new land contributed layers of change to the world they shared, altering it forever. The Apache Mexica philosopher Viola F. Cordova describes American Indian perceptions of historical change as the sum total of myriad human actions, incrementally building foundations for future generations. Imagine, she writes, "a ball to which one slowly adds a layer; each layer is a 'present' that is laid over a steadily growing 'past' that supports the present. There is no preexistent 'future' into which one moves." This makes people "'cocreators' with a natural process in constructing the future. The future is not 'there'—we are creating it through our present actions." Our actions "bring the 'future' universe into existence." She equates present actions to "layers of snow added to a snowball—the shape of the present outer layer determines the future shape of the whole."[27]

Hindsight makes it easy to see the racial stereotypes and the sexism suffusing the period. It is much more difficult to catch sight of the preconceived notions of one's own time. But given those strictures, what did they make of it? It is evident that Jacobson viewed Indians as constituted of a certain nature and that he both romanticized and judged them. It is as unlikely that he would transcend this view as it is to expect Mopope to become a champion of women's rights or show an understanding of Susie Peters's circumstances in a world dominated by men. Still, I believe both artists moved the fence posts. Both of them and the people around them challenged conventions in their own societies and reached out courageously to strangers and unfamiliar situations, thus enabling new perceptions and possibilities to take shape. Jacobson identified a potential in the talent and skills of the young Kiowas that, despite his conventional descriptions of them, liberated them from being viewed only as representatives of their racial natures. Oklahoma and the United States today recognizes that American Indians can be artists, and their creative presence is irrefutable. Mopope painted pictures and told stories that not only preserved Kiowa culture but also showed it is constantly emerging and as modern as any other.

Oscar Jacobson and Stephen Mopope's actions and their friendship mattered, had consequences, and enabled others to think of Oklahoma as a place for both Indigenous and immigrant communities to engage one another and to look past loss in order to forge something new and beautiful. Stephen Mopope and his Redstone friends opened the door for Allan Houser, Dick West, Archie Blackhawk, and Oscar Howe, then followed a long line of distinguished, creative, and provocative American Indian artists, many of whom looked to Oscar Jacobson as their mentor and supporter. The young Kiowas displayed discipline and commitment in using their talent and opportunity to adapt what they had heard and learned to new mediums, and they proved willing to share cultural elements with Oscar and Jeanne Jacobson, who in their turn opened their home to his extracurricular students. Oscar, inspired by his contacts with Birger Sandzén at Bethany, saw the value of the art and culture of his surroundings rather than judging them by the dominant conventions of his time.[28] Serendipitous encounters brought about by the intervention of a field matron, a mission school teacher, tribal elders, and a reservation agent solidified into mutual respect and even friendship as they went about negotiating boundaries of history, aesthetics, and community in ways that had a lasting influence on art and on intercultural relations in America.

Notes

INTRODUCTION

1. "Real Thing in These Costumes," *New Haven Union*, December 2, 1908, in Box 2, Scrapbook 1902–1918, Oscar B. Jacobson Collection, Oklahoma Historical Society Research Division, Oklahoma Historical Society, Oklahoma City (hereafter cited as OJC).

2. Fur, "Concurrences as Methodology." My thinking on concurrent histories and claims aligns with postcolonial work challenging the universality of historical claims such as Chakrabarty, *Provincializing Europe*; Seth, "Once Was Blind."

3. Cooper and Stoler, *Tensions of Empire*, 6.

4. Phillips, "Turn of the Primitive," 48. Her examples include Jacobson, George Swinton (an Austrian exile), and Joseph Weinstein (a diasporic Jew).

5. Hansen, "Entangled Encounters," 183.

6. Hutchinson, *Indian Craze*, 6. See also Gandhi, *Affective Communities*; Boehmer, "Zigzag Lines"; Reese, *Women of Oklahoma.*

7. Fur, "Indians and Immigrants." The scholarship on Swedish emigration/immigration is extensive but rarely mentions American Indians. See, for example, Lars Ljungmark, *For Sale—Minnesota: Organized Promotion of Scandinavian Immigration, 1866–1873* (PhD dissertation, Göteborg, 1971. (Note: all Swedish dissertations are published by the relevant universities, which have their own noncommercial presses.) See also Robert C. Ostergren, *A Community Transplanted: The Trans-Atlantic Experience of a Swedish Immigrant Settlement in the Upper Middle West, 1835–1915* (Uppsala: Studia Multiethnica Upsaliensia, 1988); Beijbom, *Mot löftets land*; Jimmy Engren, *Railroading and Labor Migration*; H. Arnold Barton, *The Old Country and the New: Essays on Swedes and America* (Carbondale: Southern Illinois University Press, 2007).

8. In *Women Who Pioneered Oklahoma*, Baker and Henshaw refer to all non-Indian women as "Anglos." Although fine-tuned to indigenous differences, neither Blackhawk, in *Violence over the Land*, nor Tate, in *Indians and Emigrants*, identifies migrants according to origin. See also Spickard, *Almost All Aliens*, 23, 25.

9. Deloria, *Indians in Unexpected Places*, 6, 231, 238.

10. Deloria, *Playing Indian*; Øverland, *Immigrant Minds*; Attebery, *Up in the Rocky Mountains.*

11. Reese, *Women of Oklahoma*, xvi; Jensen, *Calling This Place Home*, xiii–xiv, 449; Hansen, *Encounter*, 17–19, 56, 235–43.

12. Sackman, *Wild Men*, 142.

13. The well-known Swedish feminist Fredrika Bremer traveled across America in the mid-nineteenth century and described Indian Territory as a bright clearing in the otherwise primeval wilderness, "settled by a peaceful, flourishing Indian society, which one day may enter the great Union as an independent, Christian Indian state." Bremer, *Hemmen*, 130.

14. Franklin, "Black Oklahomans," 36–51.

15. Baird and Goble, *Oklahoma: A History*.

16. Reese, *Women of Oklahoma*, xv.

17. Debo, *Oklahoma: Footloose and Fancy-Free*, vii.

18. Debo, *And Still the Waters Run*, x.

19. The state flag depicting an Osage warrior shield was adopted in 1925. "The Oklahoma State Flag," online at http://netstate.com/states/symb/flags/ok_flag.htm; Jim Campbell, "Indian Statue Placed Atop Okla. Capitol," *UPI*, June 7, 2002, www.upi.com/Top_News/2002/06/07/Indian-statue-placed-atop-Okla-capitol/UPI-84551023484200/ (both accessed October 10, 2015).

20. Madigan, *Tulsa Burning*; Haley, *Buffalo War*; Lookingbill, *War Dance*; Hagan, *Taking Indian Lands*.

21. Comaroff and Comaroff, *Ethnography and the Historical Imagination*, 34; Stoler, "Colonial Archives," 99; Mbembe, "The Power of the Archive," 25. What I refer to as "silent archives" are described as "intangible" in Hägerdal, "Oral Tradition."

22. Jennings, "Why I Make Cradles," 95.

23. D'Ucel, "Memoir," 37.

24. Jensen, *Calling This Place Home*, xiii; Newman, *On Records*, 9. On contesting Western history and on importance of family histories, see Smith, *Decolonizing Methodologies*, 28–35, and 144–45.

25. Jimerson, *Archives Power*, 193.

26. Berlo and Phillips, *Native North American Art*; McLerran, *New Deal*; Hutchinson, *Indian Craze*; Smith, *Horace Poolaw*.

27. Szabo, *Art from Fort Marion*; Earenfight, *A Kiowa's Odyssey*; Rand, *Kiowa Humanity*; Tone-Pah-Hote, "Envisioning Nationhood"; Allbright, Berlo, and White, *A World Unconquered*; Tall Chief, "Jacobson and the Kiowa Five."

28. Kidwell and Velie, *Native American Studies*, 14; Swanson, "Tangled Web," ch. 1, 1–3.

29. Ellis, *Dancing People*, 8; Williams, *Staging Tradition*, 18.

CHAPTER 1. DIASPORAS, 1860S–1910S

1. Clifford, *Routes*, 247.

2. Spickard, *Almost All Aliens*, 32, also 115–17; Smithers, "What Is an Indian?," 3–5. For Sweden, see for example, Beijbom, *Mot löftets land*.

3. Haig-Brown, "Decolonizing Diaspora," 10.

4. Werbner and Fumanti, "Aesthetics," 156–57; Werbner, "Materiality of Diaspora," 17.

5. Palmer, *Telling Stories*, 57.

6. Account of origin stories, told to and published in Parsons, *Kiowa Tales*, 15.

7. Levy, "Kiowa," 907; Tone-Pah-Hote, "Envisioning Nationhood," 50.

8. Momaday, *Way to Rainy Mountain*, 5. See also Wright, *Guide*, 169–70.

9. Fowler, "Great Plains," 10–11; Levy, "Kiowa," 907.

10. Hämäläinen, *Comanche Empire*, 168; also 161–62, 172.

11. Mary Buffalo in La Vere, *Life among Texas Indians*, 216.

12. "Kiowas Created the Tornado," Vanessa Paukeigope Jennings Collection, in the author's possession (hereafter cited as VPJC).

13. Rand, *Kiowa Humanity*, 11–33; Meadows, *Kiowa Military Societies*, 4–9; Levy, "Kiowa," 910–12.

14. Vanessa Paukeigope Jennings (VPJ), interview, November 14, 2011 (transcripts of all interviews are currently in the author's possession but will eventually be placed in the collections at the Oklahoma History Center); "Po-Kei-Tay's Name," VPJC. One of his war deeds was commemorated in the Black Legs warrior society. During a battle with Mexican soldiers, Ghou-Lay-ee killed one of them and pushed his hands across the man's head and removed his red cape as a trophy. A Mopope descendant who serves as one of the society's two "special boys" wears a black hand painted on his face. See also Meadows, *Kiowa Military Societies*, 50–52. I have elected to spell all Kiowa names without hyphens, or in the manner in which individuals themselves wrote them.

15. VPJ, interview, November 14, 2011. See also Levy, "Kiowa," 917; Parsons, *Kiowa Tales*, xix; Mooney, *Calendar History*, 155–56.

16. VPJ, interview, June 9, 2012; Parsons, *Kiowa Tales*, 17–18.

17. Hämäläinen, *Comanche Empire*, 165, 172–73.

18. Prucha, *American Indian Treaties*, 281. See also Wright, *Guide*, 171–72; Fowler, "Great Plains," 32–40.

19. Rand, *Kiowa Humanity*, 58–63. Rand argues that Kiowas had already become dependent on rations to some degree and their economy destroyed before 1867, while Hämäläinen finds that Comanches and their Kiowa allies continued to support themselves through hunting, raiding, and trading into the 1870s. Hämäläinen, *Comanche Empire*, 330–33.

20. Lookingbill, *War Dance*, 33. See also Haley, *Buffalo War*, 21–31.

21. Lookingbill, *War Dance*, 22–30; Haley, *Buffalo War*, 169–83; Rand, *Kiowa Humanity*, 58–92.

22. Sundbärg, *Emigrationsutredningen, bilaga XIII*, 7. It should be noted that Sweden and Norway formed a union from 1815 to 1905. In the history of emigration, however, the records and statistics are kept by each nation separately. Among immigrants, identification by and large followed local origins and with few exceptions did not develop into a joint Swedish Norwegian identity. See Anderson and Blanck, *Norwegians and Swedes*.

23. Wohlin, *Emigrationsutredningen*, 85–93; Larsson, Johansson, and Larsson, *Smålands historia*, 222–27. My father relayed to me how his grandmother remembered that in her childhood her mother scraped the cutting board when there was no longer any food in the house.

24. Larsson, Johansson, and Larsson, *Smålands historia*, 227; Norman and Runblom, *Amerika-emigrationen*, 225–27. The average population of the three counties did not exceed six hundred thousand in the period between 1870 and 1900. Wohlin, *Emigrationsutredningen*, 86.

25. Larsson, Johansson, and Larsson, *Smålands historia*, 221–22.

26. Pleijel, *Hustavlans värld*.

27. Johansson, *Ur Minnet*; Andersson, *Svenska Missionsförbundet*; Hallingberg, *Läsarna*; Fur, "Robert Fur," 8.

28. "Eknö," 4, 8.

29. Jacobson and Jacobson, *Jacobson Family*, 235–36.

30. D'Ucel, "Memoir," 34.

31. D'Ucel, "Memoir," 35.

32. D'Ucel, "Memoir," 35–36. See also "Eknö," 8; Johannesson, *Den läsande familjen*.

33. Jacobson and Jacobson, *Jacobson Family*, 236.

34. D'Ucel, "Memoir," 36.

35. Sundbärg, *Emigrationsutredningen, bilaga VII*, 144–45.

36. Sundbärg, *Emigrationsutredningen, bilaga VII*, 150. See also letters on pp. 153, 156, 165–66 that level similar criticisms at Swedish society. For a general overview of the history of Swedish migration to North America, see Runblom and Norman, *From Sweden to America*; Norman and Runblom, *Transatlantic Connections*.

37. Lookingbill, *War Dance*, 26–28.

38. Lookingbill, *War Dance*; Earenfight, *A Kiowa's Odyssey*.

39. Szabo, *Art from Fort Marion*; Greene, *Silver Horn*; the author's observation from visit to Fort Marion, April 2014.

40. Rasmussen, "New Literary History," 266. See also Rand, *Kiowa Humanity*, 65–67.

41. Old Lady Horse, n.d., in Marriott and Rachlin, *American Indian Mythologies*, 169–70.

42. Evidence of the past can be read in the pictorial calendars constructed by Kiowa historians, such as Dohasan's calendar, which stretches from 1832 to 1892. The calendar records wars and massacres, recurring epidemics (in 1839–40, 1849, 1861–62, and 1892), as well as ceremonies and celestial events. Calloway, *First Peoples*, 303–6.

43. VPJ, interview, November 14, 2011.

44. Item 1137, Box J-2, Manuscripts 1890–1913, Mrs. W. C. Jarboe Collection, Western History Collections, University of Oklahoma Libraries, Norman (hereafter cited as WHC).

45. VPJ, interview, November 14, 2011; P. B. Hunt, report 1882, "Extracts from Reports of the Earlier Agents of Kiowa Reservation," Box 618, Kiowa, Comanche, Apache Nation Records, Oklahoma History Center, Oklahoma Historical Society, Oklahoma City (hereafter cited as KCAR); Campbell quoted from Reese, *Women of Oklahoma*, 131; Frank D. Baldwin, report 1896, "Reports, Agents 1893–1901," Box 618, KCAR. See also Rand, *Kiowa Humanity*, 48–57, 88–92, 128–30.

46. Ernest Blecker, report 1910, Box 618, KCAR. See also Reese, *Women of Oklahoma*, 122.

47. VPJ, interview, November 14, 2011; "Letters of Indian Agent at KCA," 1891, Kiowa Agency Letter Press Book, microfilm 1256, reel 19, Bizzell Memorial Library, University of Oklahoma; Herman Clouse, "Christmas letter (1914) and brochure describing Rainy Mt. Mission," Item 245, Box S-2, Hedwig Schaefer Collection, WHC. See also Wright, *Guide*, 249–51; Rand, *Kiowa Humanity*, 81.

48. Hagan, *Taking Indian Lands*, 184. For a detailed treatment of the Jerome Commission's work with Kiowa allotment, see Hagan, *Taking Indian Lands*, 181–207. "The records of the Indian Claims Commission, together with the journals recording the negotiations of the Cherokee Commission document the cavalier manner—unbecoming to a great nation—by which the United States acquired fifteen million acres from its wards in Oklahoma between 1889 and 1893." Hagan, *Taking Indian Lands*, 240.

49. Hagan, *Taking Indian Lands*; see also Hoxie, *Final Promise*, 154–56; Wilkins and Lomawaima, *Uneven Ground*, 110–13.

50. Kracht, "Kiowa-Comanche-Apache Opening."

51. There were most likely more. Swedes constituted 2.5 percent of the foreign-born white population in Oklahoma in 1910, numbering 1,020 persons. Goins and Goble, *Historical Atlas*, 140.

52. Letter from "P. A. J.," in Sundbärg, *Emigrationsutredningen, bilaga VII*, 135–37; Johnson and Peterson, *Svenskarne i Illinois*, xi–xii. See also Merrill, "Art of Birger Sandzén," 3; Brøndal, "The Fairest"; Blanck, "Mixture of People."

53. Brøndal, "The Fairest," 28. See also Blanck, *Becoming Swedish-American*, 32–35; Attebery, *Up in the Rocky Mountains*. For an exhaustive treatment of Swedish settlements in North America, see Nelson, *The Swedes*; Hansen, *Encounter*; Memoir of Erick P. Erickson, Emigranters självbiografier efter person A–H, Albin Widén Collection, 15:7:10, Svenska emigrantinstitutet (Swedish Emigrant Institute), Utvandrarnas hus (House of Emigrants), Växjö, Småland, Sweden (hereafter cited as SE). The ultimate description of the darkness of emigration experience in a Swedish context (although set on the Canadian prairie) is Grove, *Settlers of the Marsh*.

54. Jacobson and Jacobson, *Jacobson Family*, 138–46, 237.

55. National Central Bureau of Statistics, *Historical Statistics*, 96.

56. Jacobson and Jacobson, *Jacobson Family*, 236–37. On arrival regimes, see Kraut, "Doing as Americans."

57. Blanck, "A Mixture of People," 41, 49–50; Hansen, *Encounter*, 207–8. See also Spickard, *Almost All Aliens*, 204–6, 279–81; Brøndal, "The Fairest."

58. Zilliacus, *Amerika-Boken*, 94–95; Bergin, *Lindsborg: Bidrag*, 3, 22.

59. Nelson, *The Swedes*, 273–80.

60. Kiowa leaders to the President of the United States, June 30, 1876; J. D. Cameron, letter, August 5, 1876 (copy), both in Box 274, KCAR.

61. Rand, *Kiowa Humanity*, 49.

62. Porter, "Progressivism," 272–73.

63. Rand, *Kiowa Humanity*, 133. See also Gibson, *Oklahoma*, 193–202; Levy, "Kiowa," 918–19.

64. Greene, *Silver Horn*, 3, 13, 26; Calloway, *First Peoples*, 303.

65. James Mooney to Agent Charles E. Adams, April 3, 1891, Box 274, KCAR. See also H. R. Clum, Interior Department, Office of Indian Affairs (OIA), to Indian Agent at Wichita Agency, requesting Indian objects, January 28, 1873; Thomas Donaldson to Agent Charles E. Adams, July 20, 1890; Superintendent Stinchecum to Perry Gotham, February 20, 1917, all in Box 274, KCAR; Rand, *Kiowa Humanity*, 114–17, 134, 140–43.

66. H. Caruthers to P. B. Hunt, July 18, 1884; Commissioner Atkins to Jesse Lee Hall, March 26, 1887, Box 274, KCAR; also Joshua Ross to Agent Richards, July 30, 1875, Box 274, KCAR; Moses, *Wild West Shows.*

67. Vizenor, *Native Liberty*, 45.

68. Widén, *Svenskar*, 12, also 9–21; Williams, *Skribent.*

69. Widén, *Svenskar*, 121–41; Blanck, *Becoming Swedish-American.*

70. Pihl from Holm, *God's People*, 3; Bergin, *Lindsborg efter femtio år*, 16, also 46. See also Lindquist, *Smoky Valley People*, 40, 77; Nelson, *The Swedes*, 274.

71. Pihl from Holm, *God's People*, 45–46; Olsson from Lindquist, *Smoky Valley People*, 15–16.

72. Widén, *Svenskar*, 89–90. In a 1916 poem dedicated to the founder of the Augustana Church, T. N. Hasselquist, the Swedish American journalist Jakob Bonggren described Swedes as pilgrims who "made prairies into parks." Williams, *Skribent*, 166.

73. Norelius, in *Hemlandet*, September 3, 1862, 3.

74. *Läsebok för folkskolan*, 484. This section remained unabridged and unaltered in later revised and illustrated editions.

75. "Bak' indianens björkkanot/ Propellerbåten trafvar/ Och byggnadstomter läggas ut/ På indianska grafvar." Widén, *Svenskar*, 78. See also Björk, "Stories of America"; Pålsson, *I Skinnstrumpas spår*, 54, 56–57; Fur, "Colonial Fantasies."

76. Widén, *Svenskar*, 78. See also Johannesson, *Den läsande familjen*; Fur, "Indians and Immigrants."

77. Fowler, "Great Plains," 22–27; Wright, *Guide.*

78. Pihl from Holm, *God's People*, 44; Bergin, *Lindsborg: Bidrag*, 23.

79. Bergin, *Lindsborg: Bidrag*, 97–98. I thank Angela Hoffman for pointing out the contrast between stories about Spillman Creek and Lindsborg.

80. Bergin, *Lindsborg: Bidrag*, 42–43.

81. Lindquist, *Smoky Valley People*, 1.

82. Bergin, *Lindsborg efter femtio år*, 16.

83. For example, see Gjerde, *Minds of the West.*

CHAPTER 2. A WESTERNER AT YALE, AN EASTERNER IN PULLMAN, AND A SWEDE IN BETWEEN, 1890–1920S

1. Jacobson and Jacobson, *Jacobson Family*, 531–32.

2. D'Ucel, "Memoir," 37.

3. Jacobson and Jacobson, *Jacobson Family*, 467–68; d'Ucel, "Memoir," 37–38.

4. Jacobson and Jacobson, *Jacobson Family*, 467–68; Chronology, organized by Greg Pickett, Oscar Jacobson File, Birger Sandzén Memorial Gallery Archives, Lindsborg, Kansas (hereafter cited as SGA); Ron Michael, oral communication.

5. There is some confusion as to the details of his education at Bethany College. Greg Pickett, in a detailed chronology of Jacobson's life, notes that he graduated with a Bachelor of Painting degree in 1903 and comments that "many sources suggest 1908, but Bethany records—though not conclusive—indicate 1903." Delbert Jacobson, in his family history, cites the painting degree but places it in 1908. Jacobson and Jacobson, *Jacobson Family*, 468. D'Ucel writes: "It is always

a source or amusement to friends that he took his first degree in Business and Accounting, at Bethany College." ("Memoir," 38–39).

6. D'Ucel, "Memoir," 39. See also Lindquist, *Birger Sandzén.*

7. *Lindsborg News-Record,* July 2–3, 1902, Box 2, Scrapbooks 1902–1918, OJC.

8. *Lindsborg Record* and *Lindsborg News,* October 16, 1903, Box 2, Scrapbooks 1902–1918, OJC. Another of his nicknames was "Eat-Em-Up Jake" (*Bethany Messenger,* January 1905, Box 2, Scrapbooks 1902–1918, OJC). See also d'Ucel, "Memoir," 37.

9. Truettner, *The West as America;* Dorsey and Harlow, "We Want Americans"; Øverland, *Immigrant Minds,* 37–39.

10. *Lindsborg Record,* October 30, 1903, Box 2, Scrapbooks 1902–1918, OJC. The news clipping reports that it was thanks to Senator Barton, Col. Culp, and Dr. Swensson that Oscar secured the appointment. D'Ucel, "Memoir," 40; Jacobson and Jacobson, *Jacobson Family,* 468.

11. *Bethany Messenger,* October 19, 1904, Box 2, Scrapbooks 1902–1918, OJC.

12. "Klockan 5 'startade' vi att promenera på Broadway kledda i våra alraheligaste Cowboy kostymer. Vi höll på att stanna trafiken för tillfället. Sen tog vi 'dinner' på ett af de finaste hotellen. Uppköp gjorde vi men det såg ut som afferna i de stora departmentstoren voro vid mycken 'low ebb' medan vi voro inne. Frälsningsarmeen var ute och sjöng och väsnades på 6th gatan. Vi stannade at lyssna 'at respectable distance' men det dröja inte länge förän vi drog den mindre finkänsliga publiken ifrån pridikanterna och der var ju icke som sig borde. Så vi lemnade för Utstellningen Mycket nöjda med oss sjelfva och att folket 'appreciatade' oss. . . . Ja vi togo 'in' 6 shows i den natten men betalde si det gjorde vi då rakt inte. Nä! hä! Vi gick in fritt vid hvarenda plats och ingen ens nös åt oss. Ja det var roligt så det förslog. Det var den första galenskap jag har varit med om på lenge och nu får 'felle' jag 'behäva' mig igen" (Jacobson to Sandzén, May 15, 1904, SGA).

13. D'Ucel, "Memoir," 40.

14. Jacobson to Sandzén, April 15, 1904, SGA.

15. Jacobson to Sandzén, April 15, 1904; also May 15, 1904, SGA.

16. Jacobson to Sandzén, April 15, 1904, SGA. The translation of the Swedish is "It's so beautiful, it makes you sick."

17. Oskar Jakobson, "Swedish Art at the World's Fair," *Lindsborg Record,* September 2, 1904, Box 2, Scrapbooks 1902–1918, OJC. (At this point in time, he was still spelling his name this way.)

18. Jacobson to Sandzén, April 5, 1904, SGA.

19. D'Ucel, "Memoir," 39–40; Jacobson to Sandzén, April 5, 1904, SGA. See also d'Ucel, "About Indians," 37.

20. Rydell, *All the World's a Fair,* 177 (also 160, 178); Breitbart, *World on Display,* 70; Parezo and Fowler, *Anthropology.*

21. Efland, *History of Art Education,* 66–67. *Bethany Messenger,* in January 1905, noted that Jacobson would continue art studies at Yale "where so many Bethany graduates have already achieved honors" (Box 2, Scrapbooks 1902–1918, OJC). See also "Student roll, Yale University, 1905," Scrapbook, Folder 14, Victor Oscar Freeburg Papers, Yale University Libraries Manuscript and Archives; d'Ucel, "Memoir," 41–42; for awards see Box 2, Scrapbooks 1902–1918, OJC.

22. *New Haven Leader,* January 27, 1905, Box 2, Scrapbooks 1902–1918, OJC. See also D'Ucel, "Memoir," 43.

23. "Not Bottle Night in Library Street," *New Haven Union,* June 20, 1905, Box 2, Scrapbooks 1902–1918, OJC.

24. *New Haven Leader,* January 27, 1905; "Society," *New Haven Register,* February 9, 1906, Box 2, Scrapbooks 1902–1918, OJC.

25. "Play of 'Sunset' Well Produced," *New Haven Union,* August 14, 1907; "Yale Men in Western Play," *Saturday Chronicle,* December 14, 1907, Box 2, Scrapbooks 1902–1918, OJC.

26. *New Haven Leader,* January 2, 1908; "Real Indian Togs," *Saturday Chronicle,* January 27, 1908, Box 2, Scrapbooks 1902–1918, OJC.

27. Poster for *Sunset,* Folder 14, Scrapbook, Victor Oscar Freeburg Papers, Yale University Libraries Manuscript and Archives; Deloria, *Playing Indian,* 101–2. See also "Live Indian in 'Sunset' Play," *New Haven Union,* n.d., Scrapbook, Folder 14, Victor Oscar Freeburg Papers; Parezo and Fowler, *Anthropology.*

28. Freeburg, "Sunset." See also Weaver, "The Colonial Context of Violence."

29. Deloria, *Playing Indian,* 101.

30. Freeburg, "Sunset."

31. Freeburg, "Sunset"; "'Sunset' Goes Well at Y.M.C.A.," *New Haven Register,* December 21, 1907; "'Sunset' Very Successful," *Saturday Chronicle,* March 7, 1908, Scrapbook, Folder 14, Victor Oscar Freeburg Papers. On frontier plays, see Wattenberg, *Frontier Dramas;* on stereotypes see Green, "Pocahontas Perplex."

32. Attebery, *Up in the Rocky Mountains,* 114–15. See also Deloria, *Playing Indian;* Øverland, *Immigrant Minds.*

33. "Unique 'Kawraw Kiotes' Den,'" *Saturday Chronicle,* June 2, 1906, Box 2, Scrapbooks 1902–1918, OJC.

34. "Unique 'Kawraw Kiotes' Den,'" *Saturday Chronicle,* June 2, 1906, Scrapbook; *New Haven Register,* July 14, 1907, Box 2, Scrapbooks 1902–1918, OJC.

35. Hutchinson, *Indian Craze,* 26, 31, 50.

36. Phillips, "Turn of the Primitive," 48. See also Hutchinson, *Indian Craze,* 24–25.

37. *Lindsborg Record,* June 7, 1906. See also "School of Fine Arts," *New Haven Palladium,* June 2, 1906; "Yale School of Fine Arts," *New Haven Journal Courier,* June 2, 1906, all in Box 2, Scrapbooks 1902–1918, OJC.

38. Swanson, "Tangled Web," ch.1, 1; ch.4, 20. For Sandzén, see Swanson, "Tangled Web," ch. 4, 3-4; for OBJ, see ch. 4, 18. See also Swanson, "Pictures from a New Home."

39. *Svenska Tribunen,* February 25, 1908; Victor Oscar Freeburg, "En framstående svensk-amerikansk konstnär," *Ungdomsvännen,* June 1, 1910, Box 2, Scrapbooks 1902–1918, OJC. Similarities in the wording of these two articles suggest that Freeburg may have been the author of the piece in *Svenska Tribunen,* or at least had it at hand when writing his text.

40. *Nya Idun,* October 1, 1910. See also *Nya Idun,* November 1, 1910; *Minnesota Stats Tidning,* November 27, 1910. All in Box 2, Scrapbooks 1902–1918, OJC.

41. "Beauties of Fatherland Swedish Artist's Theme," *Minneapolis Sunday Tribune,* November 20, 1910, Box 2, Scrapbooks 1902–1918, OJC.

42. "The Modern Art in Sweden," *Nya Idun,* December 1910, 282, Box 2, Scrapbooks 1902–1918, OJC.

43. Øverland, in *Immigrant Minds* provides an analysis of such strategies and argues that ethnic leaders among various immigrant communities asserted their claims to Americanness in three strategies. They claimed that they had a connection to the earliest settlements on the continent, they argued that they had shed their blood to defend American unity, and they asserted that they contributed essential American values. The ethnic press and commemorative celebrations and publications were essential vehicles for such "homemaking myths." See Blanck, *Becoming Swedish-American,* who stresses the importance of the Augustana Synod, centered in Rock Island, Illinois, in establishing a Swedish American identity through its curriculum at Augustana College and through extensive publications, and in the promotion of the Swedish legacy in America.

44. *Nya Idun,* December 25, 1910, Box 2, Scrapbooks 1902–1918, OJC; Williams, *Skribent,* 170.

45. *Minnesota Journal,* January 25, 1909; "Prof. Arrhenius Is Honored," *Minneapolis Tribune,* May 11, 1911; *Minneapolis Journal,* February 15, 1911; *Picayune* (Minneapolis), February 1909. All in Box 2, Scrapbooks 1902–1918, OJC.

46. Blanck, *Becoming Swedish-American,* 186–94. Of course, it was not only Scandinavians who celebrated the Viking connection. Norse sagas became hugely popular among English-speaking Americans in the United States in the early nineteenth century, and the fascination with Vikings has remained, not least in Minnesota. See Kolodny, *In Search of First Contact.*

47. "Big Pageant Planned," February 10, 1911, *Pioneer Press, St. Paul*; "Pageant of Minnesota History," program, May 4–5, 1911, Box 2, Scrapbooks 1902–1918, OJC.

48. "Indians Play Big Part in Pageant," *Pioneer Press, St. Paul,* Box 2, Scrapbooks 1902–1918, OJC; O'Brien, *Firsting and Lasting,* xxiii.

49. "No Pajamas for Indians; Pageant Costumes a Mystery," Box 2, Scrapbooks 1902–1918, OJC.

50. Oscar Jacobson, "How the Scandinavians Have Made Good in America," *The Evergreen,* May 21, 1913, 3, Box 2, Scrapbooks 1902–1918, OJC.

51. Jacobson and d'Ucel, "Art in Oklahoma," 263, 267.

52. "I Förgrunden—Lovande ung svensk-amerikansk konstnär," *Svenska Tribunen,* February 25, 1908. See also *Minneapolis Journal,* February 15, 1911; *Svenska Tribunen,* August 11, 1911; Victor Oscar Freeburg, "En framstående svensk-amerikansk konstnär," *Ungdomsvännen,* June 1, 1910. All in Box 2, Scrapbooks 1902–1918, OJC.

53. Cunningham, "The Art of Oscar Brousse Jacobson," 28, clipping, SGA.

54. White, "Artist in the Wilderness," 40, 51; Bentley, "Oscar Brousse Jacobson."

55. Oskar Jakobson, "Swedish Art at the World's Fair," *Lindsborg Record,* September 2, 1904, Box 2, Scrapbooks 1902–1918, OJC.

56. White, "Artist in the Wilderness," 40; Sandzén to Jacobson, January 15, 1920, March 20, 1942, August 10, 1944, July 31, 1947, SGA. Sandzén constantly emphasized to his students the importance of color. See Lindquist, *Birger Sandzén,*

23–24, 40; also North, "Forty Years of the Prairie Water Color Painters." Phillips, argues that Jacobson's "post-impressionist style and his mature focus on landscape continued to reflect Sandzen's foundational influence" (Phillips, "Turn of the Primitive," 51).

57. Oscar Jacobson, "Pullman, Washington," *Lindsborg Record,* November 1, 1911, Box 2, Scrapbooks 1902–1918, OJC. Considering Jacobson's attention to form and color, he may have meant "opaline" when describing the mountains.

58. D'Ucel, "Memoir," 49.

59. "A Christmas in the Wilderness," *Lindsborg Record,* January 10, 1912, Box 2, Scrapbooks 1902–1918, OJC.

60. "A Christmas in the Wilderness," *Lindsborg Record,* January 10, 1912, Box 2, Scrapbooks 1902–1918, OJC.

61. "A Christmas in the Wilderness," *Lindsborg Record,* January 10, 1912, Box 2, Scrapbooks 1902–1918, OJC.

62. For a discussion of masculinity and Swedes in the West, see Attebery, *Up in the Rocky Mountains,* 111–18, 132–33, 160–61.

63. See also Øverland, *Immigrant Minds*; Williams, *Skribent.*

64. Jacobson and Jacobson, *Jacobson Family,* 469.

65. D'Ucel, "Memoir," 49–50. Later, Oscar played the ghost in *Hamlet,* with a costume he constructed out of silvered cardboard. D'Ucel, "Memoir," 51.

66. D'Ucel, "Memoir," 48; "Beginning of the Great War Described by an Eye Witness," *Pullman Herald,* September 18, 1914, Box 2, Scrapbooks 1902–1918, OJC. See also McCormick, "Oscar Brousse Jacobson," 16.

67. D'Ucel, "Memoir," 76.

68. D'Ucel, "Memoir," 75. See also *Lindsborg News,* September 3, 1915, Box 2, Scrapbooks 1902–1918, OJC. Sandzén had also recommended Sam Holmberg for the job in 1908; see Samuel Holmberg to Oscar Thorsén, September 1, 1908, SGA.

69. Sandzén to Jacobson, January 12, 1916; October 14, 1915; May 5, 1920, all in SGA.

70. Sandzén to Jacobson, March 21, May 5, March 21, 1920, also November 14, 1915, and April 26, 1916. All in SGA. Regarding their demanding work schedule, see also d'Ucel, "Memoir," 52.

71. "Western Artists Displaying Pictures," *Oklahoma Daily,* January 14, 1916, Box 2, Scrapbooks 1902–1918, OJC. See also clippings in OJC Scrapbooks; "Indian Association Basis of Pictures," *Oklahoma Daily,* February 9, 1923, Box 3, Scrapbooks 1918–1926, OJC; Swanson, "Tangled Web."

72. Mary Mauk, "Oklahoma to Relive Her Past," *Oklahoma Magazine,* April 1917, Box 2, Scrapbooks 1902–1918, OJC. Huhndorf identifies this as "imperialist nostalgia," which conceals "both the facts of conquest and the complicity of colonial culture (past and present)" in ruthless dominance (*Going Native,* 76).

73. "Spirit of Oklahoma like Beautiful Piece of Marble with Artists Still at Work," *Daily Oklahoman,* May 19, 1919, Box 3, Scrapbooks 1918–1926, OJC.

74. Allbright and White, "Jacobson, Culture Broker," 18–23; Allbright, "Jacobson: A Swedish Immigrant," 53–58.

75. Jacobson, "Fording Algeria," 5. See also Phillips, "Turn of the Primitive," 51–52.

76. White, "Artist in the Wilderness," 60.

77. Lecture brochures, Box 3, Scrapbooks 1918–1926, OJC.

78. Phillips, "Turn of the Primitive," 54.

CHAPTER 3. DANCING IN PLACE, 1900–1920S

1. "Census, June 30, 1901," Box 125, KCAR; VPJ, personal communication, February 10, 2016.

2. Linda Reese offers a vivid description of Kiowa poverty at the turn of the century, and of the web of white officials and missionaries surrounding them. See Reese, *Women of Oklahoma*, 107–43.

3. Mooney quoted in Reese, *Women of Oklahoma*, 115. See also Turner, "Native American Art." Oklahoma Indians were excluded in the Indian Reorganization Act of 1934, precisely because many had assimilated to the extent that they viewed the act a backward step. See McLerran, *New Deal*, 77; Nisbeth, "Indianerna i Nord-Amerika"; Zilliacus, *Amerikas förenta stater.*

4. Kracht, "Kiowa Religion," 25; Smith, *Horace Poolaw*, 10.

5. "Report Concerning Indians in Oklahoma, Oregon and Pennsylvania," 1907, Box 618, KCAR.

6. Katherine Ellis Treat, Field Matron's report, Kiowa Agency, June 30, 1911, Box 192, KCAR; Ida M. Schofield to Agent Stecker, September 25, 1908, Box 191, KCAR; Request from Superintendent Stecker to Commissioner of Indian Affairs, to authorize checks for Stephen Mopope, November 11, 1912 and May 23, 1913, Box 324, KCAR. See also Request for Clyde Mopope, February 11, 1913, April 28, 1914; Gilbert Mopope, March 3, 1913; Donald Mopope, April 17, 1913, Box 324, KCAR. For farming conditions and health issues see also Katherine Ellis Treat, Field Matron's report, March 1–April 1, 1911; March 31, September 30, 1913; September 30, 1914, Box 192, KCAR; Susie Peters, Field Matron's report, Kiowa Agency, January 22, 1921, April 12, 1924, Boxes 195–196, KCAR. The official name was the Kiowa Indian Agency, but on typewritten forms and letters, matrons and agents referred to it as the Kiowa Agency.

7. List of account with Hugh Graham, from September 1905 to September 1909, Box 618, KCAR.

8. Smith, *Horace Poolaw*, 38; Rand, *Kiowa Humanity*, 150. See also Tone-Pah-Hote, "We Worked."

9. Hoxie, *Final Promise*, 174; List of land apportioned to Indians in the Kiowa, Comanche, Apache, and Wichita Reservations in Oklahoma, 1900, Box 89, KCAR; Mopope agricultural leases, Box 65, KCAR. See also Smith, *Horace Poolaw*, 37; Hoxie, *Final Promise*, 158–59.

10. Katherine Ellis Treat, Field Matron's report, Kiowa Agency, December 31, 1912, Box 192, KCAR.

11. "Report Concerning Indians in Oklahoma, Oregon and Pennsylvania," 1907, Box 618, KCAR.

12. VPJ, interview, November 14, 2011.

13. "Keintaddle and St. Patrick's," VPJC.

14. "Grape Robbers," VPJC.

15. "Grape Robbers," VPJC.

16. Annual School Census Report, n.d.; Attendance of Indian pupils, February 21, 1912, Box 752, KCAR.

17. Katherine Ellis Treat, Field Matron's report, Kiowa Agency, February 8 (numbers) and June 19, 1911 (quote), Box 192, KCAR; Resolutions adopted by Field Matrons, May 16, 1912, see also December 31, Box 192, KCAR.

18. "Academic Course of Study for Kiowa Schools. Kiowa Agency, Oklahoma," n.d., Box 742, KCAR.

19. Trafzer, Keller, and Sisquoc, *Boarding School Blues*, 26. See also Adams, *Education for Extinction*, 145–49.

20. Hoxie, *Final Promise*, 195, 198, 202, 210. See also Adams, *Education for Extinction*; VPJ, interview, November 14, 2011.

21. Rhoades, "Keintaddle," 91; Lauretta Ballew, Field Matron's report, Anadarko District, April 1–June 30, 1908, Box 192, KCAR; Meadows, *Kiowa Military Societies*, 54–60, 274.

22. Assimilation constituted the main thrust of US Indian policy after the end of open warfare and until the change of direction in policy after the 1920s. A focus on domesticity saturated the Dawes Act, which stipulated that monogamous marriages, patronyms, education, and agricultural labor should be combined with individual property. See Hoxie, *Final Promise;* Simonsen, *Making Home Work*; Wall, "Gender and the 'Citizen Indian.'"

23. T. J. Morgan, Circular from Commissioner of Indian Affairs, March 19, 1890; Addendum to Circular from Commissioner of Indian Affairs, April 4, 1890; Letter from Commissioner to Indian Agents, August 26, 1890, Box 274, KCAR; Simonsen, *Making Home Work*, 38, 112.

24. Commissioner to Indian Agent, Anadarko, July 3, 1908, Box 267, KCAR.

25. Katherine Ellis Treat, Field Matron's report, Redstone Mission, January 1–April 1, 1911; see also December 31, 1913 with supplement; both in Box 192, KCAR. Charles B. Rogers, an attorney for the Shawnee and Delaware tribes in Oklahoma commented in 1937 that changing "Native customs of marriage and divorce to fit into the legal demands of the United States Government" constituted in his experience the most difficult adjustment. "Interview with Charles B. Rogers, November 4, 1937," Indian-Pioneer History, vol. 42, Box 243, Foreman Collection, Oklahoma History Center, Oklahoma Historical Society, Oklahoma City (hereafter cited as OHC).

26. List of land apportioned to Indians in the Kiowa, Comanche, Apache, and Wichita Reservations in Oklahoma, 1900, Box 89, KCAR; "Census, June 30, 1901," Box 125, KCAR.

27. Resolution adopted by Field Matrons, May 16, 1912, Box 192, KCAR; Agent C. V. Stinchecum to Farmers and Field Matrons, November 7, 1916, Box 193, KCAR; Susie Peters, Field Matron's report, Kiowa Agency, December 27, 1919, Box 195, KCAR; Jenny Gray, Field Matron's report, Kiowa Agency, October 14, 1916, Box 193, KCAR; Susie Peters, Field Matron's report, Kiowa Agency, May 13, 1922, September 1, December 1, 1923, Box 195, KCAR. See also Lauretta Ballew, Field Matron's report, Anadarko District, February 15–28, 1908, Box 192, KCAR; Susie C. Peters to Superintendent Stinchecum, April 8, 1918; Superintendent Stinchecum to Susie C. Peters, April 12, 1918.

28. Hansen, *Encounter,* 92.

29. Agent Stecker to Commissioner of Indian Affairs, July 25, 1913, reproduction from the National Archives in VPJC.

30. Katherine Ellis Treat, Field matron's report, Kiowa Agency, June 30, 1913, with supplement, Box 192, KCAR.

31. Katherine Ellis Treat, Field Matron's report, Kiowa Agency, September 30, 1913, with supplement, Box 192, KCAR. See also September 30, 1914, Box 192, KCAR; Susie Peters, Field Matron's report, Kiowa Agency, December 27, 1919, Box 195, KCAR; Reese, *Women of Oklahoma,* 122–23; Hansen, *Encounter,* 115–16.

32. Katherine Ellis Treat, Field Matron's report, Kiowa Agency, June 30, 1914, with supplement, Box 192, KCAR.

33. Superintendent Stinchecum to the Commissioner, November 2, July 13, 1921, Folder 5, Box 109, SC. See also Circular by Superintendent L. S. Bonnin, August 3, 1923, Folder 5, Box 109, Arthur and Shifra Silberman Native American Art Collection, Dickinson Research Center, National Cowboy and Western Heritage Museum, Oklahoma City (hereafter cited as SC).

34. "Mopope and the Battle Tipi," VPJC. For Kiowa propriety, see also "Grandpa's Feather Dancers," "No Time for Mourning," "A Marriage Proposal," "The Kiowa-Apaches Visit," VPJC; Meadows, *Kiowa Military Societies,* 57, 293–95.

35. "Mopope and the Battle Tipi," VPJC.

36. Lauretta Ballew, Field Matron's report, Anadarko District, July and September 1908, Box 192, KCAR.

37. Kracht, "Kiowa Ghost Dance."

38. Commissioner Morgan to W. D. Myers, August 9, 1889; Commissioner Morgan to C. Adams, July 10, 1890, Box 266, KCAR. See also letter Morgan to Adams from July 24, 1890; Commissioner Morgan to Indian Agents, October 22, 1891; Acting Indian Commissioner to US Indian Agent, Kiowa Agency, November 22, 1890, Box 266, KCAR.

39. Kracht, "Kiowa Ghost Dance," 459; George Hunt to Agent Blackmon, July 12, 1907, Box 266, KCAR. See also Commissioner Morgan to George D. Day, January 2, 1892; Note from Big Tree, Chaddlekaungky, Lone Wolf, and Comalty to Frank Baldwin, May 29, 1896; Big Tree to Baldwin, August 10, 1895, April 19, 1896; Report of Delos Lonewolf, July 1, 1898; Lucius Aitson to Walker, October 31, 1898, all in Box 266, KCAR. For a thorough treatment of the conflicts surrounding dances on the Kiowa Agency, see also Ellis, "There Is No Doubt"; Crawford, *Kiowa;* Brant, "Indian-White," 433–37.

40. Maryetta Reeside to Frank Baldwin, November 18, 1895, Box 266, KCAR. See also Ellis, "There Is No Doubt," 561.

41. See Kracht, "Kiowa Ghost Dance," 463–69.

42. Agent Stecker to Commissioner of Indian Affairs, July 25, 1913, reproduction from the National Archives in VPJC; Assistant Commissioner E. B. Merritt to James Ahtone, June 27, 1916, Box 266, KCAR.

43. VPJ, interview, November 14, 2011.

44. VPJ, interview, November 14, 2011; Meadows, *Kiowa Military Societies,* 253, 270, 275.

45. Stewart, *Peyote Religion*, 3.

46. Stewart, *Peyote Religion*, 82, 86; see also 53–67, 85, 123, 138–40; Kracht, "Kiowa Ghost Dance," 468.

47. Superintendent to James Tong ko am ha, June 22, 1917, Box 266, KCAR. See also Jasper Saunkeah to Superintendent Stinchecum, October 17, 1917, Box 185, KCAR. There is some disagreement as to the relationship between the Ghost Dance and the Ohoma society. Benjamin Kracht argues that the Ghost Dance segued into the Ohoma dances, while older Kiowas, whom William Meadows interviewed, maintained that there was no overlap between the ceremonies. See Kracht, "Kiowa Ghost Dance," 465–66; Meadows, *Kiowa Military Societies*, 273.

48. Kracht, "Kiowa Powwows," 327.

49. VPJ and Dorothy Whitehorse, interview, June 13, 2012.

50. Superintendent Stinchecum to Commissioner of Indian Affairs, January 2, June 4, 1917; List of Indians whose shares were returned to the Treasury, July 12, 1917, reproduction from the National Archives in VPJC. Meadows cites Francis Tsonetokoy and Parker McKenzie saying that "many of the Kiowa who signed affidavits simply collected their money and headed for dances in Cheyenne country, where the 'heat was off' at the time" (*Kiowa Military Societies*, 274).

51. Edgar Keahbone to Hugh Scott (copy), December 5, 1927, Folder 5, Box 109, SC.

52. Scott quoted from McDowell to Commissioner, December 5, 1927; Lewis Ware and Edgar Keahbone to Commissioner, March 14, 1930; J. A. Buntin to Commissioner, March 25, 1930; Commissioner to Ware, June 5, 1930, Folder 5, Box 109, SC .

53. Meadows, *Kiowa Military Societies*, 65–67; Kracht, "Kiowa Ghost Dance," 467. Animosities were at their greatest in the period up until the Second World War, as Meadows points out. Boundaries were never definite between groups identified as Christian and Traditionalists, and on many issues they united. Nevertheless, a certain tension persists and is identifiable in the interviews with Jennings.

54. VPJ, interview, November 14, 2011.

55. Missionary records, "Redstone Mission School," Folder 8, Box 7, SC.

56. VPJ, interviews, November 14, 2011, and June 13, 2012.

57. Parsons, *Kiowa Tales*, x; Smith, *Horace Poolaw*, 32; "Steve, Mark and the Cow," VPJC.

58. Meadows, *Kiowa Military Societies*, 275, also 253, 270.

59. Ellis, "Sound of the Drum," 13. See also Ellis, *Dancing People*, chapters 3 and 4.

60. Kracht, "Kiowa Powwows," 321–23; Ellis and Lassiter, "Introduction," viii–xi; Ellis, "Sound of the Drum," 9–11.

61. Ellis, "Sound of the Drum," 16; Ellis, *Dancing People*, 112; Meadows, *Kiowa Military Societies*, 281–82.

62. Ellis, *Dancing People*, 21–25; Parsons, *Kiowa Tales*, ix, 125; "List of Kiowa Indians between ages 18 and 45 years who have not registered in 1st or 2nd draft," and "List of names of persons whose registration cards are in the possession of this local Board," KCAR, Box 795.

63. Rhoades, "Keintaddle," 89–93; Green, *Silver Horn*.

64. "Mopope and the Battle Tipi," VPJC.

65. Greene, *Silver Horn,* 51. See also Smith, *Horace Poolaw,* 123–24; Greene, *Silver Horn,* 51–85.

66. "Mopope and the Battle Tipi," VPJC. See also Greene, *Silver Horn,* 204–7. Greene dates the event to sometime around 1916, but Jennings places it in 1913.

67. Lois Smoky, interview by Arthur Silberman, August 27, 1979, SC. See also Reyhner and Eder, *American Indian Education,* 101.

68. "Woman Responsible for Kiowa Indian Artists Relates How They Began in 1917," WPA story no. 7, Folder 5, Box 7, SC. Varied spelling of Stephen/Steven in source. The text for the WPA story was taken from a manuscript written by Peters but retold in the third person.

69. James Auchiah, interview by Arthur Silberman, June 5, 26, 1971, SC; VPJ, interview, June 9, 2012. Records at St. Patrick's Mission show that Sister Olivia taught Stephen Mopope (1912–16), Jack Hokeah (1915–20), Lois Smoky (1919–22), and Spencer Asah (1920–22). "Binder—transcripts of interviews with Auchiah, 1971–72," Folder 1, Box 137, SC.

70. Lois Smoky, interview by Arthur Silberman, August 27, 1979, SC; Willie Baze Lane Papers, 1921–51, 11–13, Folder 12, Box 10, SC.

71. I find this highly unlikely. I have listened and read through WPA interviews with Delaware elders in Anadarko and none of them remembered or recognized Swedes, although several mentioned being the first Indian tribe to meet Europeans. I suspect that awareness of the Swedish connection through New Sweden emerged only in the 1960s, in conjunction with an invitation to Delawares from Oklahoma to visit Sweden, engineered by Olof Norbeck at the celebration of the 325th anniversary of the founding of the colony.

CHAPTER 4. ENCOUNTERS IN NORMAN, 1926–1930S

1. "Indian Art in Oklahoma," *My Oklahoma,* May 1927; "Kiowa Indian Boys Study Art to Preserve Tribal Lore," *Oklahoma News,* June 3, 1927, Box 4, Scrapbooks 1926–1932, OJC. Bougetah spent the spring semester of 1928 in Norman, and Auchiah arrived in the fall of 1928; see James Auchiah, interview by Arthur Silberman, June 26, 1971, SC.

2. Laura Pedrick to Superintendent McCowan, August 5, 1936, Folder 20, Box 3, SC; James Auchiah, interview by Arthur Silberman, June 5, 1971, SC; Lois Smoky, interview by Arthur Silberman, 5 February 1980, SC.

3. D'Ucel, "About Indians," 27, 28. See also "Jacobson Lectures on Indian Art Thursday," *Daily Oklahoman,* March 7, 1916, Box 2, Scrapbooks 1902–1918, OJC; White, "Artist in the Wilderness," 58; Roberts and Roberts, *New Mexico,* 165–66. It is uncertain whether Jacobson meant *White Shadows* as a political statement, as there are no documents other than d'Ucel's memoir to support such a conclusion.

4. D'Ucel, "About Indians," 17; Jacobs, *Engendered Encounters;* Daily, *Battle for the BIA.*

5. One anonymous reviewer called her text "frankly and obviously propagandistic." While I do not agree, I am most grateful to the reviewer for pointing out the necessity for discussing her text as a source. Sources that corraborate her evaluations include Good, "Art Pioneer"; Joe Taylor, interview by Arthur

Silberman, SC; and Scott Fulton, interview by Arthur Silberman, March 13, 1980, SC. See also Phillips, "Turn of the Primitive."

6. D'Ucel, "About Indians," 28.

7. "Interesting Oklahomans," *Oklahoma Magazine*, April 1927, Box 3, Scrapbooks 1918–1926, OJC.

8. "Interesting Oklahomans," *Oklahoma Magazine*, April 1927, Box 3, Scrapbooks 1918–1926, OJC.

9. Expressed, for example, in Jacobson's article "East and West," which will be discussed below.

10. D'Ucel, "About Indians," 5–6, 24.

11. "A Kiowa Art Exhibit," *My Oklahoma*, August 1927; "Kiowa Indian Boys Study Art to Preserve Tribal Lore," *Oklahoma News*, June 3, 1927, Box 4, Scrapbooks 1926–1932, OJC.

12. "Indian Art in Oklahoma," *My Oklahoma*, May 1927, Box 4, Scrapbooks 1926–1932, OJC. See also Jacobs, *Engendered Encounters*, 149–80.

13. Jacobson, "Steve Mopope (Painted Robe)."

14. D'Ucel, "Indian Painters."

15. In the 1920s and 1930s primitive art became fashionable in symbiosis with modern art, and anthropology discovered the primitive as well. See Perry, "Primitivism and the Modern"; Goldwater, *Primitivism*; Fabian, *Time and the Other*; Deloria, *Playing Indian*.

16. James Auchiah, interview by Arthur Silberman, June 5, 1971, SC.

17. James Auchiah, interview by Arthur Silberman, August 29, 1972, SC. See also Lois Smoky, interview by Arthur Silberman, May 19, 1980, SC.

18. "A Letter to Mother," [n.d.] VPJC.

19. "A Letter to Mother," [n.d.] VPJC.

20. Mopope to Pau-kei-gope, 8 February 1934, VPJC.

21. Lois Smoky, interview by Arthur Silberman, August 27, 1979, SC. See also Levy, "University of Oklahoma"; Hubbell, "Desegregation"; Snyder, *John Joseph Mathews*, 24–25; James Auchiah, interview by Arthur Silberman, June 5, 1971, SC.

22. Olinka Hrdy, interview by Arthur Silberman, Folder 1, Box 10, SC; Lois Smoky, interview by Arthur Silberman, August 27, 1979, SC; James Auchiah, interview by Arthur Silberman, June 5, 1971, SC; credit book, Stephen Mopope Papers (hereafter cited as SMP), currently in the author's possession but to be placed at the OHC.

23. James Auchiah, interview by Arthur Silberman, June 5, 26, 1971, SC. See also "Meeting with Stephen Mopope, December 2, 1972," Folder 1, Box 137, SC.

24. James Auchiah, interview by Arthur Silberman, June 26, 1971, SC. One of the anonymous reviewers for this book commented that, despite Jacobson's dislike, the artists continued to use both metallic paints and colored background paper and they rarely used brown paper. However, the majority of the paintings included in the Kiowa Art portfolio were painted on brown or brownish gray background paper.

25. James Auchiah, interview by Arthur Silberman, June 26, 1971, SC.

26. Scott Fulton, interview by Arthur Silberman, March 13, 1980, SC.

27. D'Ucel, "Indian Painters," 2, 4; d'Ucel, "On Indian Art," 279–80.

28. D'Ucel, "Indian Painters," 7.

29. James Auchiah, interview by Arthur Silberman, June 5, 26, 1971, SC; Joe Taylor, interview by Arthur Silberman, SC; d'Ucel writes that this was a conscious strategy on Jacobson's part: "fearing that unearned money might have an undesirable effect, Dad persuaded Mr. Wentz to buy paintings instead of giving the funds outright" ("About Indians," 7).

30. Greene, *Silver Horn*, 63, 80.

31. D'Ucel, "About Indians," 6. On Jacobson's ideas of Indian racial characteristics, see Jacobson, *Kiowa Indian Art*, 7–10; for an interpretation, see Phillips, "Turn of the Primitive," 52–55; d'Ucel, "On Indian Art," 280.

32. Turner, "Native American Art," 158; Neuman, "Painting Culture," 178. See also Bernstein and Rushing, *Modern by Tradition*, 31–38.

33. James Auchiah, interview by Arthur Silberman, June 5, 1971, SC; SMP. While most of the cards and magazines were acquired later, such as *Art Anatomy and Figure Drawing*, by George Hirsch from the 1940s, and *The Art Digest*, from the 1930s, it is likely that he was introduced to such publications and to the use of postcards at OU.

34. D'Ucel, "Indian Painters," 3, 5, 6, 8, 9–10.

35. Mann, "Kiowa Indian Art," 64.

36. "OU Boxing Team Try-Outs," VPJC.

37. James Auchiah, interview by Arthur Silberman, June 5, 1971, SC; Lois Smoky, interview by Arthur Silberman, August 27, 1979, SC. It seems incongruous that the Kiowas should have been party to the creation of the mascot "Little Red." However, the "tradition of having a band member appear in Indian dress began in the early 1930s when the Sequoyah Club powwow became part of football ceremonialism." The *Sooner Yearbook* from 1935 mentioned that the "Sequoyah Club" had existed for at least two decades. The club organized both students and faculty "who have in their veins the blood of the American Indian" and aimed to "foster racial pride among the descendants of the original Americans, to preserve tribal traditions and legends, and to further the cause of the education of Indian Youth." Kidwell, "American Indian Studies," 30–31, 32. See also Snyder, *John Joseph Mathews*, 23–25.

38. Olinka Hrdy, interview by Arthur Silberman, SC.

39. White, *Oklahoma Moderne*. I thank an anonymous reader for pointing this out to me.

40. James Auchiah, interview by Arthur Silberman, August 29, 1972, SC; D'Ucel, "Indian Painters," 2, 5, 6; d'Ucel, "On Indian Art," 278.

41. Olinka Hrdy, interview by Arthur Silberman, SC.

42. "Kiowa Indians to Present Program of Native Music," *Oklahoma Daily*, March 11, 1928; Ed Capers, "Indian Dances, Music Intrigue City Audience," *Daily Oklahoman*, November 23, 1928; also "Oklahoma City Clubs Will Give Benefit Program for Kiowas," *Norman Transcript*, November 21, 1928, Box 4, Scrapbooks 1926–1932, OJC. The flute player was most likely Belo Cozad who was a friend of Mopope's. Articles mention a similar program the previous year, so the Kiowas began almost immediately upon their arrival in Norman to perform dances and singing.

43. Jacobson, *Kiowa Indian Art*, 6. See also D'Ucel, "About Indians," 7; "Colorful Dances Given by Kiowas Using Heirlooms," newspaper clipping, undated 1928, Box 4, Scrapbooks 1926–1932, OJC.

44. Jeanne d'Ucel, "The Indian Artists Step Forward with a Cultural Gift for America," *Kansas City Star*, June 5, 1938, Box 6, Scrapbooks 1946–1953, OJC. Jacobson gave frequent lectures on the topic of "The Indian's Contribution to Art," Box 5, Scrapbooks 1930–1947, OJC; Berlo, "From Indigenous America," 108.

45. Allbright, "Jacobson: A Swedish Immigrant," 26–38; Jacobson, "East and West," 26.

46. Sandzén to Jacobson, May 5, 1920, SGA; D'Ucel, "Memoir," 78. See also "Exhibit at Art Institute," *Kansas City Times*, May 10, 1921, Box 3, Scrapbooks 1918–1926, OJC; Sandzén to Jacobson, January 12, 1916, SGA; "Western Artists Displaying Pictures," *Oklahoma Daily*, January 14, 1916, Box 2, Scrapbooks 1902–1918, OJC.

47. D'Ucel, "Memoir," 94. See also Sandzén to Frida and Greta [Sandzén], June 15, 1924, Sandzén to Carl Smalley, June 24, 1924, Sandzén to Gustaf Sandzén, July 23, 1924, SGA.

48. "Oklahoma City Clubs Will Give Benefit Program for Kiowas," *Norman Transcript*, November 21, 1928; "Kiowa Artists Score Hit," *Kansas City Star*, April 27, 1929, Box 4, Scrapbooks 1926–1932, OJC.

49. "Paintings by Kiowas a Unique Art Form," *Minneapolis Journal*, March 31, 1929; "Kiowa Artists Score Hit," *Kansas City Star*, April 27, 1929, Box 4, Scrapbooks 1926–1932, OJC.

50. D'Ucel, "About Indians," 8, 10. See also Jeanne d'Ucel, "An International Sensation," *Sooner Magazine*, January 1930, Box 4, Scrapbooks 1926–1932, OJC. On primitivism and indigenous art, see Kirschenblatt-Gimblett, "Objects of Ethnography"; Clifford, *Predicament of Culture*.

51. Berlo, "From Indigenous America," 108, 112–13. See also Perry, "Primitivism and the Modern"; Goldwater, *Primitivism*; Jacobson, "Meaning of Modernism."

52. Jacobson, "Introduction," *Kiowa Indian Art*, 3, 4, 10, 11.

53. D'Ucel, "About Indians," 17; OBJ to Superintendent Buntin, June 26, 1931; "Exposition of Indian Tribal Arts", Letter detailing exposition, Folder 4, Box 109, SC.

CHAPTER 5. NEGOTIATING CONFLICTING CULTURES

1. Vrdoljak, *International Law*, 126–27.

2. D'Ucel, "About Indians," 9; Jacobson and d'Ucel, *American Indian Painters*, 14; James Auchiah, interview by Arthur Silberman, June 5, 1971, SC.

3. Joe Taylor, interview by Arthur Silberman, November 18, 1981, SC; Nyquist, "Artist and Educator."

4. Superintendent Buntin to OBJ, January 13, 1934, Folder 4, Box 109, SC; Hoxie, *Final Promise*, 213.

5. D'Ucel, "About Indians," 7. See also Superintendent Buntin to OBJ, January 13, 1934, Folder 4, Box 109, SC.

6. See Fur, "Earrings."

7. "Indian Art in Oklahoma," *My Oklahoma,* May 1927; "A Kiowa Art Exhibit," *My Oklahoma,* August 1927, Box 4, Scrapbooks 1926–1932, OJC.

8. Ruth Robinson, "Kiowa Indian Artists Record Tribal History and Traditions in State Murals," *Oklahoma News,* February 21, 1937, Box 5, Scrapbooks 1930–1947, OJC.

9. Chang, *Color of the Land,* 199; VPJ, interview, June 9, 2012. See also Wattley, *A Step Toward*; Snyder, *John Joseph Mathews,* 38. Jennings recalled the revelation in the 1960s of a secret room adjoining a café in Apache, Oklahoma, containing Klan capes and hoods. Tone-Pah-Hote cites a poster found among Weston LaBarre's papers, which had been posted on a Kiowa home in Mountain View, Oklahoma, in the 1930s. The poster warned "all Indians addicted to the use of peyota [*sic*] and Other forms of heathen or pagan forms of worship . . . TAKE DUE WARNING! The Clan in Your Community Will Look After You." Tone-Pah-Hote, "Envisioning Nationhood," 105–6.

10. VPJ, interview, November 14, 2011.

11. LaQuinta Mopope Santos, interview by Arthur Silberman, January 31, 1982, Folder 8, Box 11, SC.

12. Deloria, *Indians in Unexpected Places,* 120, see also 225.

13. James Auchiah, interviews by Arthur Silberman, June 5, 26, 1971, SC.

14. Lois Smoky, interview by Arthur Silberman, August 27, 1979, SC; d'Ucel, "About Indians," 14; Lois Smoky, interview by Arthur Silberman, May 2, 1980, SC.

15. VPJ, interview, June 9, 2012; Tone-Pah-Hote, "Envisioning Nationhood," 185, 186, 187, 187. See also Greene, *Silver Horn,* 123; Smith, *Horace Poolaw,* 169.

16. James Auchiah, interviews by Arthur Silberman, June 5, 1971, and August 29, 1972, SC. See also Smith, *Horace Poolaw,* 132.

17. D'Ucel, "Memoir," 80.

18. Whitney, "Historic Jacobson House," 8–9. Recent scholarship on diaspora is increasingly focused on the constructions of homes and architecture in the old and new homelands. See for example, Banerjee, McGuinness, and McKay, *New Routes.*

19. Yolanda Sheppard, interview by Arthur Silberman, November 14, 1981, SC.

20. VPJ, interview, November 14, 2011. I have spoken also to Clara Sue Kidwell in 2006 and Cricket Rhoades-Connewerdy in 2011 when each one was director of the Jacobson House, and they have both corroborated what Jennings told me in the interview. In a comment to a friend d'Ucel noted that during those years "she had never cooked so much food . . . with . . . my basement full of hungry young Indian students," quoted in Dowling, "The Meltons," 31.

21. D'Ucel, "About Indians," 8.

22. D'Ucel, "About Indians," 8; LaQuinta Mopope Santos, interview by Arthur Silberman, January 31, 1982, SC; d'Ucel, "Indian Painters," 7.

23. D'Ucel, "About Indians," 8–9.

24. D'Ucel, "About Indians," 9; Lois Smoky, interview by Arthur Silberman, August 27, 1979, SC; Copy of Susie Peters's field matron record of George Mopope, including photo of house, in VPJC. Jennings comments in email to author (August 18, 2018): "It was mandatory to have the Field Matron come out

and make a physical site inspection, complete with notes and photographs. The Field Matrons, like Susie Peters, had incredible amounts of power and the discretionary use of that fearful power."

25. Jennings, personal communication. N. Scott Momaday describes the abiding and sacred bond between Kiowas and the land, in *The Man Made of Words*, 30–49. See also Parham, "All Go to the Hop Fields," 318–19.

26. D'Ucel, "Memoir," 186–88; Jacobson and Jacobson, *Jacobson Family*, 380.

27. McLerran, *New Deal*, 66.

28. D'Ucel, "About Indians," 16; Hutchinson, *Indian Craze*, 35–47.

29. D'Ucel, "About Indians," 16–17; d'Ucel, "Memoir," 189. See chapter 7 below for Jacobson's comments on his career. Phillips notes a distinct difference between the approach of Jacobson (and other "stranger-artists") and that of other educators of Indian artists, such as Dorothy Dunn, who came from "established settler background" ("Turn of the Primitive," 66). See also Jacobson and Jacobson, *Jacobson Family*, 482.

30. D'Ucel, "Memoir," 189. See also d'Ucel, "About Indians," 23; Superintendent McCowan to John S. Ankeney, January 10, 1934; Superintendent McCowan to John Woolery, May 28, 1935, Folder 4, Box 109, SC; McLerran, *New Deal*, 166–67.

31. "Kiowa's Chapel Murals Attract Wide Attention," *Daily Oklahoman*, undated 1930, Scrapbook, Box 4, vol. 4, OJC; Insell A. Hopper to Superintendent McCowan, July 10, 1936; Acting Director of Procurement to Mopope, December 1, 1937, Folder 4, Box 109, SC; McLerran, *New Deal*, 265n64.

32. Geo. C. Wells to Della Ryan, June 29, 1938; Willard Beatty to J. B. McCowan, June 28, 1938, both in Folder 4, Box 109, SC. See also Swanson, "Tangled Web," Appendix C, 10; Geo. C. Wells to Frank Gritts, June 29, 1938, Folder 4, Box 109, SC.

33. McLerran, *New Deal*, 168–92; Willard Beatty to Superintendent McCowan, April 18, 1938; Willard Beatty to Olle Nordmark, June 28, 1938, Folder 4, Box 109, SC.

34. James Auchiah, interview by Arthur Silberman, June 5, 1971, SC.

35. Olin Dows to McCowan, March 30, 1935, McCowan to Monroe Tsatoke, April 4, 1935, McCowan to Olin Dows, April 9, 1935, Folder 5, Box 109, SC; "Meeting with Stephen Mopope, December 2, 1972," Folder 1, Box 137, SC; VPJ, interviews, November 14, 2011 and June 9, 2012; Tone-Pah-Hote, "Envisioning Nationhood," 254–55.

36. VPJ, interview, November 14, 2011. The mural contract caused some tension between the Kiowas as well. When Monroe Tsatoke passed away, his wife accused Mopope of stealing his work, suggesting that the designs behind the paintings in the post office would have been his. VPJ, interview, April 3, 2014.

37. "Meaning of Mural Paintings on Post Office Walls Given," *Anadarko Daily News*, December 5, 1937, Box 5, Scrapbooks, OJC; Tone-Pah-Hote, "Envisioning Nationhood," 253–54.

38. Williams, *Staging Tradition*, 18. On Swedish festivals, see Blanck, *Becoming Swedish-American*, 184–203.

39. D'Ucel, "About Indians," 17. See also Williams, *Staging Tradition*, 16–38;

Sarah Gertrude Knott to John Collier, March 19, 1934; John Collier to Superintendent McCowan, April 6, 1934; John Collier to Sarah Gertrude Knott, April 6, 1934; OBJ to McCowan, April 11, 1934, Folder 4, Box 109, SC.

40. D'Ucel, "About Indians," 17–18.

41. D'Ucel, "About Indians," 18–19.

42. D'Ucel, "About Indians," 20.

43. D'Ucel, "About Indians," 21.

44. *St. Louis Post-Dispatch,* April 30, 1934, Box 5, Scrapbooks, OJC. The *Norman Transcript,* April 23, 1934, also ran a notice of Jacobson's role in taking the Kiowas to the Festival, Box 5, Scrapbooks 1930–1947, OJC.

45. *St. Louis Post-Dispatch,* April 30, 1934, Box 5, Scrapbooks 1930–1947, OJC.

46. Program in Box 4, Scrapbooks 1926–1932, OJC. The *St. Louis Post-Dispatch* also published a photo of Mopope in dance regalia on April 29, 1934.

47. Sarah Gertrude Knott to McCowan, May 4, 1936, Folder 5, Box 109, SC.

48. "Indian Tribe Adopts Artist as Member," *Christian Science Monitor,* August 20, 1928; "Professor Jacobson Named Chief of Kiowa Tribe at Ceremony near Anadarko Friday," *Chickasha Daily Express,* July 28, 1928, Box 4, Scrapbooks 1926–1932, OJC.

49. "Jacobson Adopted by Kiowa Indians," *Daily Oklahoman,* August 16, 1928; "Oscar B. Jacobson Made Kiowa Chief," *Norman Transcript,* July 31, 1928, Box 4, Scrapbooks 1926–1932, OJC.

50. La Vere, "Minding Their Own Business," 63.

51. D'Ucel, "About Indians," 11–12.

52. D'Ucel, "About Indians," 12–13.

CHAPTER 6. FRIENDSHIPS FORGED AND BROKEN

1. D'Ucel, "About Indians," 26.

2. "Woman Responsible for Kiowa Indian Artists Relates How They Began in 1917," 25–26, Folder 5, Box 7, SC; Susie Peters, Field Matron's report, August 20, 1921, and May 8, 1920, Box 195, KCAR.

3. Susie Peters, Field Matron's report, August 3, 1921, Box 195, KCAR. See also Letter to Agent Stinchecum, April 8, 1918, Box 195, KCAR; Alice L. Marriott, "Summary of the Work of the Indian Arts and Crafts Board in Oklahoma, 1937" (unpublished manuscript), and Laura Pedrick to Superintendent McCowan, August 5, 1936, Folder 20, Box 3, SC; "Indians Adopt White Woman in Rare Rites," *Oklahoma City Times,* November 12, 1954, Folder 15, Box 11, SC. I have not been able to ascertain whether this was a similar ceremony to the one that honored Jacobson, but in a tribute to her, photos, newspaper clippings, and a narration of her work have been compiled and hang in a picture frame at the Indian Hall of Fame in Anadarko.

4. James Auchiah, interview by Arthur Silberman, June 5, 1971, SC. Jenny Tone-Pah-Hote observes that Peters's "relationship with the painters was more than that of a field matron," and that her role as promoter and spokesperson for them "sometimes masked the fact that by the time the Kiowa Six attended the University of Oklahoma, they had all reached adulthood and were in their twenties." Tone-Pah-Hote, "Envisioning Nationhood," 173.

5. James Auchiah, interview by Arthur Silberman, June 5, 1971, August 29, 1972, SC. In the transcript of the interview with Auchiah, Jacobson is consistently misspelled as "Jacobsen." I have elected to correct the spelling, as it in no way alters the meaning. See also VPJ, interview, April 3, 2014.

6. James Auchiah, interview by Arthur Silberman, August 29, 197, SC. Vanessa Jennings recalls that her grandfather told her it was Susie Peters who contacted Jacobson. VPJ, interview, June 9, 2012. See also Susie Peters to Rt. Rev. Msgr. William Hughes, November 29, 1930, "Documents from St. Patrick's Mission, Marquette University Archives," Folder 17, Box 7, SC.

7. Susie Peters to John Collier, July 5, 1934, Folder 4, Box 109, SC.

8. Susie Peters to John Collier, July 5, 1934, Folder 4, Box 109, SC. Collier responded briefly that he had not heard anything untoward about her and that he was convinced she had done her utmost for Kiowa art. Superintendent McCowan echoed this but commented that he thought the Kiowas should be allowed to decide for themselves if they wished to keep her as manager or not. John Collier to Susie Peters, August 1, 1934; Superintendent McCowan to John Collier, August 7, 1934, Folder 4, Box 109, SC. See also Susie Peters to Nettie Wheeler, December 5, 1962, Folder 15, Box 11, SC. About expectations of gratitude and colonialism, see Martin, "Good Fortune Obligates," 69–72.

9. Charles Pond to Thomas Gilcrease, September 17, 1947, Folder 12, Box 10, SC.

10. Charles Pond to Thomas Gilcrease, April 22, 1951; Susie Peters to Willie Baze Lane, June 12, 1944. See also OBJ to Charles Pond, March 14, 1951; Charles Pond to Thomas Gilcrease, June 3, September 1, 1948. All in Folder 12, Box 10, SC.

11. Nyquist, "Artist and Educator," 12. See also "Oklahoma to Honor Five with Induction into Hall of Fame," *Daily Oklahoman*, November 11, 1949; Landelius, "Oscar B. Jacobson"; Nordfelt, "Bondpojke." In a curriculum vitae that Oscar Jacobson himself prepared for O. R. Landelius, he listed "Honorary Chief, Kiowa Indians," among the honors he had received for his own art, Utlandssvenska arkivet, SE.

12. Susie Peters to Willie Baze Lane, June 12, 1944, Folder 12, Box 10, SC.

13. D'Ucel, "Glimpses," 1.

14. "Count Posse Visits Member of College Faculty," *Spokesman Review*, November 25, 1912, Box 2, Scrapbooks 1902–1918, OJC. See also "Prof. Arrhenius Is Honored," *Minneapolis Tribune*, May 11, 1911; "Arrhenius Hyllas," *Minnesota Stats Tidning*, May 17, 1911, Box 2, Scrapbooks 1902–1918, OJC.

15. D'Ucel, "Glimpses," 2.

16. D'Ucel, "Glimpses," 2.

17. D'Ucel, "Glimpses," 2, 3, 4.

18. D'Ucel, "Glimpses," 4–5.

19. I discuss gender more explicitly in Fur, "Earrings."

20. D'Ucel, "Glimpses," 5, 6.

21. D'Ucel, "Glimpses," 16, 17.

22. D'Ucel, "Glimpses," 17, 18, 19. See also "Tagore Will Discuss Mystic East Tonight," *Oklahoma Daily*, February 11, 1921, Box 3, Scrapbooks 1918–1926, OJC. D'Ucel in her manuscript apparently mistakenly placed his visit in 1919.

23. D'Ucel, "About Indians," 34; Snyder, *John Joseph Mathews*, 30.

24. D'Ucel, "Glimpses," 20, 42, 43, 47. See also 34–38, 38, 42–43, 45–47, 48.

25. D'Ucel, *Berber Art*.

26. D'Ucel, "Glimpses," 49.

27. D'Ucel, "Glimpses," 58, 62. See also Allbright and White, "Jacobson, Culture Broker," 25; *Oklahoma Daily*, May 31, 1936, Box 5, Scrapbooks 1930–1947, OJC.

28. Allbright and White, "Jacobson, Culture Broker," 26–27; Sandzén to Jacobson, June 8, 1941, SGA; White, "A Modernist Moment," 53–54. White suggests that Jacobson was "asked to step down," but Leonard Good, Jacobson's colleague and friend, wrote that he had already announced in 1944 that he wanted to resign as director. Good, "Art Pioneer"; "Jacobson, 4 Others Selected for Hall of Fame Induction by Oklahoma Memorial Group," *Norman Transcript*, November 13, 1949, Box 6, Scrapbooks 1946–1953, OJC; Allbright, "Jacobson: A Swedish Immigrant," 95–96.

29. Dowling, "The Meltons," 36. During these years their daughter Yolande and her husband, Craig, also lost a son, Anders, to leukemia. D'Ucel, "Memoir," 278, 281, 287.

30. D'Ucel, "Memoir," 310; Allbright, "Jacobson: A Swedish Immigrant," 100–101.

31. D'Ucel, "About Indians," 1.

32. Feest, "Europe's Indians," 325; Hjorthén, *Border-Crossing Commemorations*, 300, also 130–43. See also Galloway, Gemünden and Zantop, *Germans and Indians*; Fur, "Romantic Relations," 145–49; Fur, "Fabrications of Friendship," 105–19; Blanck, *Becoming Swedish-American*, 187–91.

33. Penny, *Kindred by Choice*, 14, 22–23; Oscar B. Jacobson, "The Delawares."

34. Boehmer, "Zigzag Lines," 15. See also Sackman, *Wild Men*, 289–92, 306–9.

35. Szasz, *Scottish Highlanders*, 23; Pease, "The Quality of Listening," 108–9.

36. Gandhi, *Affective Communities*, 188–89.

37. Nyquist, "Artist and Educator." See also Landelius, "Oscar B. Jacobson."

38. Oscar B. Jacobson, "Indian Artists," 126–27.

39. D'Ucel, "About Indians," 28.

40. There is similarity between Jacobson's paternalism and Susie Peters's in their belief that they could teach Indians to be more properly "Indian." Reformers encouraging the Indian arts and crafts movement likewise relied on ideas of superior knowledge concerning what was genuine and authentic. See Jacobs, *Engendered Encounters*, 149–72.

41. D'Ucel, "About Indians," 28–29.

42. D'Ucel, "About Indians," 29–30. See also Yolanda [*sic*] Sheppard, interview by Arthur Silberman, November 14, 1981, SC. (Her name was Yolande, but Silberman or his assistant spelled it Yolanda.)

43. Neuman, *Indian Play*, 194.

44. D'Ucel, "About Indians," 31–32; Jacobson and d'Ucel, *Les Peintres Indiens*. See also OBJ to Mopope, December 12, 1939, and Form letter from OBJ, April 30, 1947, SMP.

45. D'Ucel, "About Indians," 32–33.

46. Yolanda [*sic*] Sheppard, interview by Arthur Silberman, November 14, 1981, SC.

47. D'Ucel, "About Indians," 32–33. Jacobson did try to learn Navajo, as attested by a letter requesting a reader in Navajo language. Jacobson to Phoenix Indian School, November 7, 1940, J-18, no. 8, OBJC.

48. D'Ucel, "Glimpses," 33–34.

49. D'Ucel, "About Indians," 37. Geronimo sold his autographed photograph for one dollar at the St. Louis World's Fair, which is probably where Jacobson acquired one. Owning one did not in itself mean that the two were acquainted.

50. D'Ucel, "About Indians," 37.

51. D'Ucel, "About Indians," 38. The movie referred to is likely *Broken Arrow* (1950), which differed from the previous pattern in western movies and aspired to a more accurate representation of Apache culture in an effort to address issues of tolerance and racial equality. Manchel, "Cultural Confusion."

52. "Interesting Oklahomans," *Oklahoma Magazine*, April 1927, Box 3, Scrapbooks 1918–1926, OJC. Similarly, Jacobs writes about feminists in the Southwest who measured "their own status within their subculture by who best 'knew' the Pueblos and who wrote most authentically about them" (*Engendered Encounters*, 102–3).

53. D'Ucel, "About Indians," 47–48.

54. Roxanne Dunbar-Ortiz describes the constrictions and consequences of class differences and racism in her autobiographical account: Dunbar-Ortiz, *Red Dirt*. For aspects of class, race, and gender, see also Chang, *Color of the Land*; Reese and Loughlin, *Mainstreet Oklahoma*; Joyce, *Alternative Oklahoma*; Debo, *And Still the Waters Run*.

55. D'Ucel, "About Indians," 43, also 44–46.

56. West quoted from White, "A Modernist Moment," 62.

57. Allbright and White, "Jacobson, Culture Broker," 27; Yolanda [*sic*] Sheppard, interview by Arthur Silberman, November 14, 1981, SC.

58. D'Ucel, "Memoir," 344. See also Welch, "This Is Your Life."

59. Quoted in Welch, "This Is Your Life," 259.

60. D'Ucel, "About Indians," 52.

61. D'Ucel, "About Indians," 52–53.

62. In the mid-1980s, in the Kiowa exhibit case at the Smithsonian Natural History Museum in Washington, DC, a plaque proclaimed that the Kiowas had killed more white people in relation to their own population numbers than any other American Indian people (author's observation, 1986).

63. Pate, "Kiowa Art," 199. See also "Kiowas to Honor Memory of Famed Warrior Satanta," *Wichita Falls Times*, September 20, 1963, p. 7B, Folder 4, Box 69, SC.

64. D'Ucel, "About Indians," 53.

65. Meadows, *Kiowa Military Societies*, 60–65; card in SMP; "Chief Satanta Historical Celebration," program in Box 6, Scrapbooks 1946–1953, OJC.

CHAPTER 7. DANCER, ARTIST, AND TEACHER

1. Susie Peters to Muriel Wright, October 23, 1936, Folder 5, Box 7, SC. See also Service rating form for James Auchiah, DOI, 1941, James Auchiah to Willard W. Beatty, with note from Superintendent, February 26, 1942, Idena Powell to John Collier, July 17, 1937, all in Folder 5, Box 109, SC; James Auchiah, interview by Arthur Silberman, June 5, 1971, SC; Auchiah to Willie Baze Lane, June 18, 1930, Folder 12, Box 10, SC.

2. Susie Peters to Willie Baze Lane, March 26, 1942, Folder 12, Box 10, SC. See also John Collier to James Auchiah, May 22, McCown to Collier, June 23, 28, Collier to Auchiah, July 10, 1934, all in Folder 4, Box 109, SC.

3. Smith, *Horace Poolaw*, 47–69; McNelly, *Native Performers*, 84–85, 124–25.

4. Tone-Pah-Hote, "Envisioning Nationhood," 150, 174.

5. Susie Peters to John Buntin, September 18, 1931, Folder 4, Box 109, SC.

6. Hopi Snake Dance Poster, September 26–28, 1931, SMP.

7. James Auchiah, interview by Arthur Silberman, August 29, 1972, SC. See also Susie Peters to John Buntin, September 18, 1931, Folder 4, Box 109, SC. On Belo Cozad, see Tone-Pah-Hote, "Envisioning Nationhood," 67–68. Despite substantial efforts I have not been able to find confirmation of this naming ceremony in Mary Pickford's papers, nor do I have information regarding what name she was given. However, she acted the part of Indian women in several of her Biograph films. In 1937 she also received a poem from R. Hand, "the Tribal Poet of California," as a tribute. The column in the *Los Angeles Times*, February 22, 1937, described how a "stolid, silent Indian appeared with a package in his hand. Entering the house quietly he handed the package to a servant and, without a word, silently departed." I thank Susan Oka, acquisition librarian at Academy of Motion Pictures Arts and Sciences, for finding this information.

8. James Auchiah, interview by Arthur Silberman, August 29, 1972, SC.

9. Scott Tonemah, interview by Arthur Silberman, April 14, 1982, Folder 6, Box 12, SC; Charles Tsoodle, interview by Arthur Silberman, December 10, 1989, Folder 8, Box 12, SC.

10. "Nationally Known Kiowa Indians Perform for Wichitans Today," *Wichita Eagle*, Tuesday morning, March 28, 1933, clipping in VPJC.

11. "Seven Nationally Known Indians Arrive for 'Trails-Southwest,'" *Wichita Eagle*, Tuesday morning, March 28, 1933, VPJC; Letter from Caddo County Judge, VPJC. See also Deloria, *Indians in Unexpected Places*, 187, 205–6.

12. "A Kiowa Art Exhibit," *My Oklahoma*, May 1927, Box 4, Scrapbooks 1926–1932, OJC. See also Adams, *Education for Extinction*, 273–306. On progress, see Buntin, "History of the Kiowa."

13. "Lewis Ware, Kiowa Indian Is President," *The Tribesmen* 1, no. 2–3 (September–October 1938), SMP; d'Ucel, "About Indians," 11.

14. Ellis, *Dancing People*, 142.

15. Ellis, *Dancing People*, 142, 143.

16. Ellis, *Dancing People*, 143, 120.

17. Deloria, *Playing Indian*, 115.

18. Deloria, *Playing Indian*, 125.

19. Deloria, *Playing Indian*, 126. On modernity see also Smith, *Horace Poolaw*; Hutchinson, *Indian Craze*.

20. *St. Louis Star Times*, April 30, 1934, Box 5, Scrapbooks 1930–1947, OJC.

21. LaQuinta Mopope, interview by Arthur Silberman, January 31, 1982, 20, SC; notes in SMP.

22. Gus Palmer, interview by Arthur Silberman, September 22, 1982, SC.

23. James Auchiah, interview by Arthur Silberman, June 5, 1971, SC.

24. OBJ to Mopope, December 12, 1939, SMP.

25. McCowan to Gertrude Knott, June 19, 1934, Folder 4, Box 109, SC. Since Mopope's name is at the top of the list on the reverse side of letter, it can be assumed he was one of the two who approached the superintendent.

26. Knott to Mopope, postcard dated December 29, 1937, Knott to Mopope, May 6, 1941, March 31, 1947, and Form letter detailing plans for festival with no day date, 1957. All in SMP. See also Williams, *Staging Tradition*, 35–37, 66, 95.

27. M. J. Pickering to Superintendent McCowan, April 26, 1937, Folder 5, Box 109, SC.

28. M. J. Pickering to Superintendent McCowan, April 26, 1937, Folder 5, Box 109, SC.

29. Pickering to McCowan, April 1, 1943, March 22, 1944, Folder 5, Box 109, SC. See also Pickering to Mopope, March 13, 1944, Jasper Saunkeah to McCowan, March 20, 1944, Pickering to McCowan, May 25, 1944, all in Folder 5, Box 109, SC. Contentions among different groups for the opportunity to represent Kiowas at various fairs appear in other interviews that Arthur Silberman collected, expressing discordant views on Mopope's leadership and influence. See Scott Tonemah, interview by Arthur Silberman, April 14, 1982, and Charles Tsoodle, interview by Arthur Silberman, December 10, 1989, SC.

30. Williams, *Staging Tradition;* VPJC.

31. Leonora Barrett to Oscar Jacobson, June 10, 1938, Hattie C. Hill to Mopope, February 23, 1942, in SMP.

32. VPJ, interviews, November 14, 2011 and June 9, 2012. Similar programs for tourists occurred on the Santa Fe Railroad. "When Tennyson was removed and taken to Carlisle Institute one of the things they were taught was not to participate in anything Indian. The first thing he did when he came back was to grow his hair long. My grandpa's uncle, Jim Waldo, was at Carlisle. And he did the same thing. He wore a black white man's jacket, but he wore leggings and moccasins" (VPJ, interview, June 9, 2012). See also Hagan, *Quanah Parker*; program from "Katy Week Indian War Dances," SMP; VPJ email to author, May 8, 2018.

33. Telegram from Roy Griffin, May 27, 1946, SMP. See also letters from Les Winget, February 22, 1946, and The Thunderbird Club, Oklahoma A&M, Okmulgee, March 19, 1951; Invitation to celebration of Caddo Town, November 12, 1948; Program for Ada's eleventh Annual Rodeo, August 15, 1946; letter from J. M. Cooper to Mopope, May 14, 1954; Program for Palo Duro Indian Ceremonial, with Mopope illustration on cover, September 15, 1956; Invitation to war dance at Tulsa Pow-Wow Club, n.d., all in SMP.

34. LaQuinta Santos Mopope, interview by Arthur Silberman, January 31, 1982, SC. Ellis discusses the economics of dancing and argues that show dancing "put money in the performers' pockets when the alternatives were limited and the chances of making it on their own at the reservations were stark" (*Dancing People*, 100).

35. Lists in SMP. The Lawton event included, apart from the Mopopes themselves, Mark Keahbone, Ernie Keahbone, Wilson Ware, George Palmer, Roy Neister, Tennyson Berry, James Auchiah, Nathan Doyebi, James Salar, Mack Whitehorse, Frances Shoulder Blade, Eva Keahbone, Ruby Doyebi, and Vanette Williams.

36. Letters from Mrs. John W. Charles (?), November 29, 1931, from Norman Beard, June 4, 1935, SMP. Bounced checks appeared at other times as well, for example the letter from Victor Alessandro, for the Symphony Society of San Antonio, August 13, 1951, SMP.

37. "Grandpa's Feather Dancers," VPJC. LaQuinta Mopope remembered doing war dancing until she was fourteen years old, when her mother suggested that it was no longer lady-like to continue. LaQuinta Santos Mopope, interview by Arthur Silberman, January 31, 1982, SC. See also Ellis, *Dancing People*, 152–53.

38. Jacobson, "Steve Mopope (Painted Robe)"; Ellis, *Dancing People*, 18.

39. Flyer in VPJC; Letter to Jeanette Berry, July 13, 1965, SMP; VPJ, interview, June 9, 2012. See also LaQuinta Santos Mopope, interviews by Arthur Silberman, April 13, 1974, and January 31, 1982, SC.

40. LaQuinta Santos Mopope, interview by Arthur Silberman, January 31, 1982, SC.

41. Jennifer McLerran points out that the report lacked any "recognition of the culturally significant relationship of native arts and crafts production to traditional ceremonial and religious practices" (*New Deal*, 84).

42. Stewart, *Peyote Religion*, 65–67, 80–81; VPJ, interview, June 6, 2012. See for example mural in Oklahoma Supreme Court Building, formerly Oklahoma Historical Society.

43. D'Ucel, "About Indians," 22.

44. McLerran, *New Deal*, 66.

45. Turner, "Native American Art," 159.

46. Loose papers in SMP.

47. James Auchiah, interview by Arthur Silberman, June 26, 1971, SC; "Seven Ways to Compute the Relative Value of a U.S. Dollar Amount—1774 to Present," http://measuringworth.com/uscompare (accessed December 7, 2018). Amounts calculated conservatively.

48. Letters from Derald Swineford, May 16, 1938, and Mrs. Erich Eichholz, January 13, 1946, SMP.

49. Letter from Mary Mathis, June 5, 1945, SMP. Another Fort Sill contact had come across Mopope's paintings at the 1944 Craterville Fair, and sent one to her university in Utah, to great acclaim. Letter from Gladys L. Kotter, August 7, 1944, SMP. See also letters to Frances Quarles (undated), from Ernest J. Greenwalt, November 10, 1944, from Pawnee Bill's Indian Trading Post, November 5, 1946, from Reese Queenan, April 2, 1951, from C.A. Dill, September 15, 1952, all in SMP.

50. Turner, "Native American Art"; letters from Bernard Frazier, August 29, 1950, Jeanne Snodgrass, January 15, 1962, Donald G. Humphrey, April 27, 1966, SMP.

51. Note regarding Gilcrease, SMP; Stanley Marcus to Mopope, October 3, 1950, SMP. See also Letters from E. Teenor, November 4, 1949, Dallas Museum of Fine Arts, April 25, 1950, Sue C. James, January 10, 1951, Anne M. Smith, April 13, 1959, Thomas Gilcrease (undated), all in SMP.

52. Letter from Robert S. Kerr, January 30, 1946, SMP. See also letters from D. A. McGee to Mr. and Mrs. Mopope, November 20, 1964, Porter Wharton Jr., December 4, 1964, Jack W. Roach, February 19, 1965, all in SMP.

53. VPJ, interview, June 9, 2012. Scott Fulton described how Mopope worked from templates when making paintings on order. He kept 7–8 templates in a box, all cardboard outlines of people, from which he derived the desired figure. Scott M. Fulton, interview by Arthur Silberman, June 13, 1979, SC.

54. "Chief Peyote Takes a Trip," VPJC. Omer Stewart relates similar information from interviews with Crows, attesting to the close relationship between Kiowas and Crows, and naming Charlie Anquoe and James Auchiah among Kiowas who brought peyote to the Crows. Stewart, *Peyote Religion*, 186–88.

55. Stewart, *Peyote Religion*, 186–88.

56. Maroukis, *Peyote Road*, 155; Smith, *Horace Poolaw*, 131. Maroukis includes a Mopope illustration of a peyote design made in the 1930s (*Peyote Road*, 169). See also LaQuinta Santos Mopope, interview by Arthur Silberman, January 31, 1982, SC.

57. "His Last Peyote Meeting," VPJC.

58. "His Last Peyote Meeting," VPJC.

59. LaQuinta Santos Mopope, interview by Arthur Silberman, January 31, 1982, SC.

60. Jacobson's description of the artists, Folders 42, 43, Box J13, OBJC; d'Ucel, "About Indians," 15; Turner, "Native American Art"; James Auchiah, interview by Arthur Silberman, June 5, 1971, SC.

61. "Mopope and the Badge," VPJC. See also LaQuinta Santos Mopope, interview by Arthur Silberman, January 31, 1982, SC.

62. LaQuinta Santos Mopope, interview by Arthur Silberman, January 31, 1982, SC. See also VPJ, interview, November 14, 2011.

63. VPJ, interview, November 14, 2011.

64. VPJ, interview, November 14, 2011. See also LaQuinta Santos Mopope, interview by Arthur Silberman, January 31, 1982, SC. Tall Chief, in *Jacobson and the Kiowa Five*, makes Jeanette and Stephen's relationship a recurrent theme in the play.

65. VPJ, interview, November 14, 2011.

66. Note card from March 29, 1956, and letter from John Gamble, November 2, 1950, SMP. Both communications refer to moccasins. John Gamble wrote from St. Louis, MO: "I received the moccasins in fine condition. Thanks so much. You certainly did a beautiful job on them." See also letter of reference from the Anadarko Chamber of Commerce, March 19, 1952, SMP.

67. "The Pouch Set," VPJC.

68. VPJ, interview, November 14, 2011. See also Reese, *Women of Oklahoma*, 108–43.

69. LaQuinta Santos Mopope, interview by Arthur Silberman, January 31, 1982, SC; Letter from Ernest J. Greenwalt, November 10, 1944, SMP.

70. LaQuinta Santos Mopope, interview by Arthur Silberman, January 31, 1982, SC.

71. "Dance Honoring Mopope to Be Held at His Home Aug. 8," *Anadarko Daily News*, August 1, 1965, 1, 3, SMP.

72. VPJ, interview, November 14, 2011.

73. Deloria, *Indians in Unexpected Places*, 226.

CONCLUSION

1. Anthes, "'Why Injun Artist Me,'" 418.

2. Jacobson, "Indian Artists," 126.

3. Jacobson, "Indian Artists," 127; Hoxie, *Final Promise*; Jacobs, *Engendered Encounters*; Ellis, "There Is No Doubt"; Simonsen, *Making Home Work*; Reyhner and Eder, *American Indian Education*.

4. Jacobson, "Indian Artists," 126–27. See also Baird and Goble, *Oklahoma: A History*, 267–68.

5. The Kiowas sang songs, Jeanne d'Ucel wrote, that no other white people got to hear. "About Indians," 8. See also James Auchiah, interview by Arthur Silberman, August 29, 1972, SC. Tone-Pah-Hote's dissertation makes the argument that the Kiowas consciously utilized expressive culture to define their nation as both historical and changing ("Envisioning Nationhood").

6. Anthes, "'Why Injun Artist Me,'" 418.

7. Dowling, "The Meltons," 40; Jacobson and Jacobson, *Jacobson Family*, 498.

8. For immigrants and landscapes, see Casteel, *Second Arrivals*, 5–16.

9. D'Ucel, "Memoir," 326; Landelius, "Oscar B. Jacobson."

10. Phillips, "Turn of the Primitive," 49, 54–55, 66.

11. Kolodny, *In Search of First Contact*, 213–55; Blanck, *Becoming Swedish-American*, 191–93; Blanck, "A Mixture of People"; Sophie Sheppard, email to author, November 21, 2016.

12. Daily, *Battle for the BIA*.

13. Daily, *Battle for the BIA*, 16, 18, 19, 21.

14. Dowling, "The Meltons," mentions that the Jacobsons were not religious, 36; Good, "Art Pioneer."

15. Scott M. Fulton, interview by Arthur Silberman, June 13, 1979, SC. See also Pate, "Kiowa Art"; Gerber, "Moving Backward."

16. James Auchiah, interview by Arthur Silberman, June 26, 1971, SC; VPJ, interview, November 14, 2011. See also Stephen Mopope court papers, Box 70, Folder 5, SC.

17. "Oklahoma Favorite Model For Jacobson Landscapes," *Oklahoma Daily*, December 10, 1949, Box 6, Scrapbooks 1946–1953, OJC. Boym, *Future of Nostalgia*, makes the argument that nostalgia is connected both to dislocation in space

and to a sense of disjuncture in time; for an article complicating the issue of nostalgia for Indigenous communities, see Orr, "The Nostalgic Native?"

18. Scott M. Fulton, interview by Arthur Silberman, June 13, 1979.

19. Scott M. Fulton, interview by Arthur Silberman, June 13, 1979.

20. Donnelley, *Transforming Images*, 192; LaQuinta Mopope Santos, interview by Arthur Silberman, January 31, 1982, SC.

21. Scott M. Fulton, interview by Arthur Silberman, June 13, 1979, SC.

22. Anderson, "The Kiss of Enterprise," and Nemerov, "Doing the Old America," in Truettner, *The West as America*; Mary Goddard, "Building Marked by Artist," *Daily Oklahoman*, January 19, 1953; Landelius, "Oscar B. Jacobson"; White, "Artist in the Wilderness," 37–39, 71.

23. On his keeping a Swedish accent, see his grandchildren Bob Harris and Sim Sheppard, in Jacobson and Jacobson, *Jacobson Family*, 482, 497; Joe Taylor, interview by Arthur Silberman, SC.

24. LaQuinta Mopope, Interview by Arthur Silberman, April 13, 1974, SC; Scott M. Fulton, interview by Arthur Silberman, June 13, 1979, SC; Author's notes from visit to Anadarko, June 9, 2012, in author's possession. Sophie Sheppard relates her great respect for her grandfather for his "radical act of support" for the Kiowas, "painting their ceremonies and rituals during a time when it was against the law for Native Americans to practice any of their religion" (email, November 21, 2016).

25. Sim Sheppard, email to author, March 4, 2015.

26. Sackman offers valuable comments on this dilemma in his afterword (*Wild Men*, 303–20).

27. Cordova, *How It Is*, 118–19, 175.

28. Phillips, "Turn of the Primitive," 51–55. She writes: "Neither Jacobson's mentoring nor Collier's policies created Native North American modernisms. Rather, they opened a door which artists walked through" (55).

Bibliography

ARCHIVAL MATERIALS

Birger Sandzén Memorial Gallery Archives, Lindsborg, Kansas (SGA).

National Cowboy and Western Heritage Museum, Oklahoma City, OK. Dickinson Research Center:

Arthur and Shifra Silberman Native American Art Collection (SC)

Oklahoma Historical Society Research Division, Oklahoma City, OK (OHC):
- Grant Foreman Collection
- Indian Archives Collection
- Kiowa, Comanche, Apache Nation Records (KCAR)
- Oscar B. Jacobson Collection (OJC)

Stephen Mopope Papers (SMP), in the author's possession

Svenska Emigrantinstitutet (Swedish Emigrant Institute), Växjö, Sweden (SE):
- Albin Widén Collection
- Utlandssvenska arkivet (Archive of Overseas Swedes)
  - Oscar Brousse Jacobson

University of Oklahoma Libraries, Western History Collections, Norman, OK (WHC):
- Hedwig Schaefer Collection
- Oscar Brousse Jacobson Collection (OBJC)
- Mrs. W. C. Jarboe Collection

Vanessa Paukeigope Jennings Collection (VPJC), in the author's possession

Yale University Libraries Manuscripts and Archives, New Haven, Connecticut:
- Victor Oscar Freeburg Papers

UNPUBLISHED MANUSCRIPTS

D'Ucel, Jeanne. "About Indians." Folder 5, Box 1, OJC.

———. "Glimpses." Folder 6, Box 1, OJC.

———. "Indian Painters of Oklahoma." N.d. Folder 10, J18, OBJC.

———. "Memoir and Biographical Writing." Folder 1–4, Box 1, OJC.

Freeburg, Victor Oscar. "Sunset: A Romantic Tragi-Comedy in Four Acts." 1908. Folder 4, Box 1, Victor Oscar Freeburg Papers, Yale University Libraries Manuscripts and Archives.

Fur, Gunnar. "Robert Fur—Folkbildare, förkunnare, far." In author's possession.

Good, Leonard. "Oscar Brousse Jacobson: Art Pioneer 1882–1966." Folder 17, J1, OBJC.

Jacobson, Oscar B. "Steve Mopope (Painted Robe) Kiowa." N.d. Folder 42, J13, OBJC.

Whitney, Carol. "The Historic Jacobson House." 1998. Folder 17, J1, OBJC.

PUBLISHED WORKS

Adams, David Wallace. *Education for Extinction: American Indians and the Boarding School Experience, 1875–1928.* Lawrence: University Press of Kansas, 1995.

Allbright, Anne. "Oscar Brousse Jacobson: A Swedish Immigrant Who Dramatically Changed Art Perception in Oklahoma." Master's thesis, University of Central Oklahoma, 2006.

Allbright, Anne, Janet Catherine Berlo, and Mark White. *A World Unconquered: The Art of Oscar Brousse Jacobson.* Norman: Fred Jones Jr. Museum of Art, University of Oklahoma, 2015.

Allbright, Anne, and Mark Andrew White. "Oscar Brousse Jacobson, Culture Broker." In Allbright, Berlo, and White, *A World Unconquered,* 7–32.

Anderson, Nancy K. "'The Kiss of Enterprise': The Western Landscape as Symbol and Resistance." In Truettner, *The West as America,* 237–83.

Anderson, Philip J., and Dag Blanck, eds. *Norwegians and Swedes in the United States. Friends and Neighbors.* St. Paul: Minnesota Historical Society Press, 2012.

Andersson, Axel. *Svenska Missionsförbundet.* Stockholm: Svenska Missionsförbundets förlag, 1928.

Anthes, Bill. "'Why Injun Artist Me': Acee Blue Eagle's Diasporic Performative." In *Native Diasporas: Indigenous Identities and Settler Colonialism in the Americas,* edited by Gregory D. Smithers and Brooke N. Newman, 411–41. Lincoln: University of Nebraska Press, 2014.

Attebery, Jennifer Eastman. *Up in the Rocky Mountains: Writing the Swedish Immigrant Experience.* Minneapolis: University of Minnesota Press, 2007.

Baird, W. David, and Danney Goble. *Oklahoma: A History.* Norman: University of Oklahoma Press, 2008.

Baker, Terri M., and Connie Oliver Henshaw, eds. *Women Who Pioneered Oklahoma: Stories from the WPA Narratives.* Norman: University of Oklahoma Press, 2007.

Banerjee, Sukanya, Aims McGuinness, and Steven C. McKay, eds. *New Routes for Diaspora Studies.* Bloomington: Indiana University Press, 2012.

Beijbom, Ulf. *Mot löftets land: den svenska utvandringen.* Stockholm: LT, 1995.

Bentley, Mayrene. "Oscar Brousse Jacobson." In "Oscar Brousse Jacobson: Western Light," Exhibition pamphlet, SGA. [n.d.]

Bergin, Alfred. *Lindsborg: Bidrag till svenskarnas och den lutherska kyrkans historia i Smoky Hill River dalen.* Rock Island: Augustana Book Concerns Tryckeri och Bokbinderi, 1909.

———. *Lindsborg efter femtio år: Bidrag till vår lutherska historia och svenskarnas historia i Kansas och sydvästern.* Rock Island: Augustana Book Concern, 1919.

Berlo, Janet Catherine. "From Indigenous America to North Africa: The

Cosmopolitan World of Oscar Jacobson and Jeanne d'Ucel." In Allbright, Berlo, and White, *A World Unconquered*, 103–33.

Berlo, Janet Catherine, and Ruth B. Phillips. *Native North American Art*. New York: Oxford University Press, 1998.

Bernstein, Bruce, and W. Jackson Rushing. *Modern by Tradition: American Indian Painting in the Studio Style*. Santa Fe: Museum of New Mexico Press, 1995.

Björk, Ulf Jonas. "Stories of America: The Rise of the 'Indian Book' in Sweden, 1862–1895." *Scandinavian Studies* 75 (2003): 509–26.

Blackhawk, Ned. *Violence over the Land: Indians and Empire in the Early American West*. Cambridge, Mass.: Harvard University Press, 2006.

Blanck, Dag. *Becoming Swedish-American: The Construction of an Ethnic Identity in the Augustana Synod, 1860–1917*. Dissertation, Uppsala University, 1997.

———. "'A Mixture of People with Different Roots': Swedish Immigrants in the American Ethno-racial Hierarchies." *Journal of American Ethnic History* 33, no. 3 (Spring 2014): 37–54.

Boehmer, Elleke. "The Zigzag Lines of Tentative Connection: Indian-British Contacts in the Late Nineteenth Century." In *India in Britain: South Asian Networks and Connections, 1858–1950*, edited by Susheila Nasta, 12–27. Basingstoke: Palgrave Macmillan, 2013.

Boym, Svetlana. *The Future of Nostalgia*. New York: Basic, 2001.

Brant, Charles S. "Indian-White Cultural Relations in Southwestern Oklahoma." *Chronicles of Oklahoma* 37 (1959): 433–39.

Breitbart, Eric. *A World on Display: Photographs from the St. Louis World's Fair 1904*. Albuquerque: University of New Mexico Press, 1997.

Bremer, Fredrika. *Hemmen i den Nya Verlden*, vol. 2B. Stockholm: Norstedts, 1853.

Brøndal, Jørn. "'The Fairest among the So-Called White Races': Portrayals of Scandinavian Americans in the Filiopietistic and Nativist Literature of the Late Nineteenth and Early Twentieth Centuries." *Journal of American Ethnic History* 33, no. 3 (Spring 2014): 5–36.

Buntin, Martha Leota. "History of the Kiowa, Comanche, and Wichita Indian Agency." Master's thesis, University of Oklahoma, 1931.

Calloway, Colin G. *First Peoples: A Documentary Survey of American Indian History*. Boston: Bedford/St. Martin's, 1999.

Casteel, Sarah Phillips. *Second Arrivals: Landscape and Belonging in Contemporary Writing of the Americas*. Charlottesville: University of Virginia Press, 2007.

Chakrabarty, Dipesh. *Provincializing Europe: Postcolonial Thought and Historical Difference*. Princeton, N.J.: Princeton University Press, 2000.

Chang, David A. *The Color of the Land: Race, Nation, and the Politics of Landownership in Oklahoma, 1832–1929*. Chapel Hill: University of North Carolina Press, 2010.

Clifford, James. *The Predicament of Culture*. Cambridge, Mass.: Harvard University Press, 1988.

———. *Routes: Travel and Translation in the Late Twentieth Century*. Cambridge, Mass.: Harvard University Press, 1997.

Comaroff, John L., and Jean Comaroff. *Ethnography and the Historical Imagination*. Boulder, Colo.: Westview Press, 1992.

Cooper, Frederick, and Ann Laura Stoler, eds. *Tensions of Empire: Colonial Cultures in a Bourgeois World.* Berkeley: University of California Press, 1997.

Cordova, V. F. *How It Is: The Native American Philosophy of V. F. Cordova.* Edited by Kathleen Dean Moore, Kurt Peters, Ted Jojola, and Amber Lacy. Tucson: University of Arizona Press, 2007.

Crawford, Isabel. *Kiowa: A Woman Missionary in Indian Territory.* Lincoln: University of Nebraska Press, 1998.

Cunningham, William. "The Art of Oscar Brousse Jacobson." *Haldeman-Julius Quarterly* 1, no. 1 (January 1927): 28–29.

Daily, David W. *Battle for the BIA: G. E. E. Lindquist and the Missionary Crusade against John Collier.* Tucson: University of Arizona Press, 2004.

Debo, Angie. *And Still the Waters Run: The Betrayal of the Five Civilized Tribes.* Princeton, N.J.: Princeton University Press, 1940.

———. *Oklahoma: Footloose and Fancy-Free.* Norman: University of Oklahoma Press, 1949.

Deloria, Philip. *Indians in Unexpected Places.* Lawrence: University of Kansas Press, 2004.

———. *Playing Indian.* New Haven: Yale University Press, 1998.

Donnelley, Robert G., ed. *Transforming Images: The Art of Silver Horn and His Successors.* Chicago: David and Alfred Smart Museum of Art, University of Chicago, 2000.

Dorsey, Leroy G., and Rachel M. Harlow. "'We Want Americans Pure and Simple': Theodore Roosevelt and the Myth of Americanism." *Rhetoric and Public Affairs* 6, no. 1 (2003): 55–78.

Dowling, Phyllis Aldridge Melton. "The Meltons and the Jacobsons: Two Families of Friends." *Crosstimbers: A Multicultural, Interdisciplinary Journal* (Spring 2002): 31–40.

D'Ucel, Jeanne. *Berber Art.* Norman: University of Oklahoma Press, 1932.

———. "On Indian Art." *The University Review* (University of Kansas City) (Summer 1938): 274–80.

Dunbar-Ortiz, Roxanne. *Red Dirt: Growing Up Okie.* Norman: University of Oklahoma Press, 2006.

Earenfight, Phillip, ed. *A Kiowa's Odyssey: A Sketchbook from Fort Marion.* Seattle: University of Washington Press, 2007.

Efland, Arthur D. *A History of Art Education: Intellectual and Social Currents in Teaching the Visual Arts.* New York: Teachers College Press, Columbia University, 1990.

"Eknö." Skärgårdsprojektet, Kalmar läns museum, Länsstyrelsen Kalmar län. https://kalmarlansmuseum.se/museet/rapporter/ekno (accessed August 26, 2018).

Ellis, Clyde. *A Dancing People: Powwow Culture on the Southern Plains.* Lawrence: University Press of Kansas, 2003.

———. "The Sound of the Drum Will Revive Them and Make Them Happy." In Ellis, Lassiter, and Dunham, *Powwow,* 3–25.

———. "'There Is No Doubt . . . the Dances Should Be Curtailed': Indian Dances and Federal Policy on the Southern Plains, 1880–1930." *Pacific Historical Review* 70, no. 4 (2001): 543–69.

Ellis, Clyde, and Luke Eric Lassiter. "Introduction." In Ellis, Lassiter, and Dunham, *Powwow*, vii–xv.

Ellis, Clyde, Luke Eric Lassiter, and Gary H. Dunham, eds. *Powwow*. Lincoln: University of Nebraska Press, 2005.

Engren, Jimmy. *Railroading and Labor Migration: Class and Ethnicity in Expanding Capitalism in Northern Minnesota, the 1880s to the Mid 1920s*. Dissertation, Växjö University, 2007.

Fabian, Johannes. *Time and the Other: How Anthropology Makes Its Object*. New York: Columbia University Press, 2014.

Feest, Christian F. "Europe's Indians," In *The Invented Indian: Cultural Fictions and Government Policies*, edited by James A. Clifton, 313–32. New Brunswick: Transaction Publishers, 1990.

Fenton, William N. "Structure, Continuity, and Change in the Process of Iroquois Treaty Making." In *The History and Culture of Iroquois Diplomacy*, edited by Francis Jennings, 3–36. Syracuse: Syracuse University Press, 1995.

Forsey, Leroy G., and Rachel M. Harlow. "'We Want Americans Pure and Simple': Theodore Roosevelt and the Myth of Americanism." *Rhetoric & Public Affairs* 6, no. 1 (2003): 55–78.

Fowler, Loretta. "The Great Plains from the Arrival of the Horse to 1885." In *The Cambridge History of the Native Peoples of the Americas*, edited by Bruce G. Trigger and Wilcomb E. Washburn. Vol. 1, *North America*, part 2, 1–55. Cambridge: Cambridge University Press, 1996.

Franklin, Jimmie Lewis. "Black Oklahomans: An Essay on the Quest for Freedom." In *Alternative Oklahoma: Contrarian Views of the Sooner State*, edited by Davis D. Joyce, 36–51. Norman: University of Oklahoma Press, 2007.

Fur, Gunlög. "Colonial Fantasies—American Indians, Indigenous Peoples, and a Swedish *Discourse of Innocence*." *National Identities* 18, no. 1 (2016): 11–33.

———. "Concurrences as Methodology for Discerning Concurrent Histories." In *Concurrent Imaginaries in Postcolonial Worlds*, edited by Diana Brydon, Peter Forsgren, and Gunlög Fur, 33–57. Leiden: Brill Rodopi, 2017.

———. "'The Earrings': Friendship across Ethnic and Gendered Boundaries in the American West." *Women's History Review* (2017). Online at DOI:10.108%96 12025.2017.1333946.

———. "Fabrications of Friendship? The Historiography of European-Indian Friendship in the Delaware Valley." In *Notions of America: Swedish Perspectives*, edited by Kerstin W. Shands, Rolf Lundén, and Dag Blanck, 105–19. Stockholm: Södertörns högskola, 2004.

———. "Indians and Immigrants—Entangled Histories." *Journal of American Ethnic History* 33, no. 3 (Spring 2014): 55–76.

———. "Romantic Relations: Swedish Attitudes towards Indians during the Twentieth Century." *Swedish-American Historical Quarterly* LV:3 (July 2004): 145–64.

Galloway, Colin G., Gerd Gemünden, and Susanne Zantop. *Germans and Indians: Fantasies, Encounters, Projections*. Lincoln: University of Nebraska Press, 2002.

Gandhi, Leela. *Affective Communities: Anticolonial Thought, Fin-de-Siècle Radicalism, and the Politics of Friendship.* Durham: Duke University Press, 2006.

Gerber, David A. "Moving Backward and Moving On: Nostalgia, Significant Others, and Social Reintegration in 19th Century British Immigrant Personal Correspondence." *The History of the Family* (2015): 1–24.

Gibson, Arrell M. *Oklahoma: A History of Five Centuries.* 2nd ed. Norman: University of Oklahoma Press, 1981.

Gjerde, Jon. *Minds of the West: Ethnocultural Evolution in the Rural Middle West, 1830–1917.* Chapel Hill: University of North Carolina Press, 1997.

Goins, Charles Robert, and Danney Goble. *Historical Atlas of Oklahoma.* 4th ed. Norman: University of Oklahoma Press, 2006.

Goldwater, Robert. *Primitivism in Modern Art.* Cambridge: Cambridge University Press, 1986.

Green, Rayna. "The Pocahontas Perplex: The Image of Indian Women in American Culture." *Massachusetts Review* 16 (Autumn 1975): 698–714.

Greene, Candace S. *Silver Horn: Master Illustrator of the Kiowas.* Norman: University of Oklahoma Press, 2001.

Grove, Frederick Philip. *Settlers of the Marsh.* Toronto: Ryerson Press, 1925.

Hagan, William T. *Quanah Parker.* Norman: University of Oklahoma Press, 1995.

———. *Taking Indian Lands: The Cherokee (Jerome) Commission, 1889–1893.* Norman: University of Oklahoma Press, 2003.

Hägerdal, Hans. "Oral Tradition and the Postcolonial Challenge: The Historiographical Autonomy of Non-Lettered Societies." In *Concurrent Imaginaries in Postcolonial Worlds,* edited by Diana Brydon, Peter Forsgren, and Gunlög Fur, 145–65. Leiden: Brill Rodopi, 2017.

Haig-Brown, Celia. "Decolonizing Diaspora: Whose Traditional Land Are We On?" *Cultural and Pedagogical Inquiry* 1, no. 1 (2009): 4–21.

Haley, James L. *The Buffalo War: The History of the Red River Uprising of 1874.* Austin: State House Press, 1976.

Hallingberg, Gunnar. *Läsarna. 1800-talets folkväckelse och det moderna genombrottet.* Stockholm: Atlantis, 2010.

Hämäläinen, Pekka. *Comanche Empire.* New Haven: Yale University Press, 2008.

Hansen, Karen V. *Encounter on the Great Plains: Scandinavian Settlers and the Dispossession of Dakota Indians, 1890–1930.* Oxford: Oxford University Press, 2013.

———. "Entangled Encounters, Land Taking, and the Oral Archive." In *Concurrent Imaginaries in Postcolonial Worlds,* edited by Diana Brydon, Peter Forsgren, and Gunlög Fur, 167–85. Leiden: Brill Rodopi, 2017.

Hemlandet, Det Gamla och det Nya, 3 September, 1862. https://newspapers3.mnhs.org/jsp/viewer.jsp?doc_id=mnhi0011%2F1FUNGP56%2F62090301&init_width=600&recoffset=0&collection_filter=All&collection_name=213eae36-842e-49d8-80fe-5d15ad15e075&sort_col=title&CurSearchNum=-1&recOffset=0 (accessed August 26, 2018).

Hjorthén, Adam. *Border-Crossing Commemorations: Entangled Histories of Swedish Settling in America.* Dissertation, Stockholm University, 2015.

Holm, Vernon C. F., ed. and trans. *God's People in a New Land: Memorial Volume of*

Manuscripts by Johan Augustin Pihl, A Swedish Immigrant (1831–1914). Lindsborg: Smoky Valley Historical Publications, 1984.

Hoxie, Frederick E. *A Final Promise: The Campaign to Assimilate the Indians, 1880–1920*. Lincoln: University of Nebraska Press, 2001.

Hubbell, John T. "The Desegregation of the University of Oklahoma." *Journal of Negro History* 57, no. 4 (October 1972): 370–84.

Huhndorf, Shari M. *Going Native: Indians in the American Cultural Imagination*. Ithaca: Cornell University Press, 2001.

Hutchinson, Elizabeth. *The Indian Craze: Primitivism, Modernism, and Transculturation in American Art, 1890–1915*. Durham, NC: Duke University Press, 2009.

Jacobs, Margaret D. *Engendered Encounters: Feminism and Pueblo Cultures, 1879–1934*. Lincoln: University of Nebraska Press, 1999.

Jacobson, Delbert, and Alice Jacobson. *The Jacobson Family: Ancestors and Descendants of Nils Petter Jacobsson and Anna Lena Olofsdotter*. Yorba Linda, Calif.: Shumway Family History Services, 1996.

Jacobson, Oscar B. "The Delawares." *American Swedish Monthly* 32 (June 1938): 73, 136–37.

———. "East and West." *American Magazine of Art* 11, no. 1 (November 1919): 22–26.

———. "Fording Algeria." *University of Oklahoma Magazine* 15, no. 3 (1927).

———. "Indian Artists of Oklahoma." *Oklahoma Almanac* 7, no. 5 (1964): 126–28.

———. *Kiowa Indian Art: Watercolor Paintings in Color by the Indians of Oklahoma, Monroe Tsatoke, Oscar Brousse Jacobson, Stephen Mopope, Jack Hokeah, Spencer Asah, and Lois Smoky*. Nice, France: C. Szwedzicki, 1929.

———. "The Meaning of Modernism in Art." *American Magazine of Art* 15, no.1 (January 1924): 697–702.

Jacobson, Oscar B., and Jeanne d'Ucel. *American Indian Painters/Les Peintres indiens d'Amérique du Nord*. Nice, France: C. Szwedzicki, 1950.

Jacobson, Oscar B., and Jeanne d'Ucel. "Art in Oklahoma." *Chronicles of Oklahoma* 32, no. 3 (1954): 263–77.

Jacobson, Oscar B., and Oscar Howe. *North American Indian Costumes (1564–1950)*. Nice, France: C. Szwedzicki, 1952.

Jennings, Vanessa Paukeigope. "Why I Make Cradles." In *Gifts of Pride and Love: Kiowa and Comanche Cradles*, edited by Barbara A. Hail, 95–101. Norman: University of Oklahoma Press, 2000.

Jensen, Joan M. *Calling This Place Home: Women on the Wisconsin Frontier, 1850–1925*. St. Paul: Minnesota Historical Society Press, 2006.

Jimerson, Randall C. *Archives Power: Memory, Accountability, and Social Justice*. Chicago: Society of American Archivists, 2009.

Johannesson, Erik. *Den läsande familjen: Familjetidskriften i Sverige 1850–1880*. Uddevalla, Sweden: Nordiska muséets handlingar 96 (1980).

Johansson, Sam. A. *Ur Minnet. Skildringar och Erfarenheter från den Andliga Brytningstiden i Vårt Land under Midten och Senare Hälften af Förra Århundradet*. Eksjö, Sweden: Smålands-Tidningens Förlag, 1911.

Johnson, E., and C. F. Peterson. *Svenskarne i Illinois. Historiska anteckningar*. Chicago: Williamson & Clark, 1880.

Joyce, Davis D., ed. *Alternative Oklahoma: Contrarian Views of the Sooner State.* Norman: University of Oklahoma Press, 2007.

Kidwell, Clara Sue. "American Indian Studies at the University of Oklahoma." In *Native American Studies in Higher Education: Models for Collaboration between Universities and Indigenous Nations,* edited by Duane Champagne and Jay Stauss, 29–42. Walnut Creek, Calif.: AltaMira Press, 2002.

Kidwell, Clara Sue, and Alan Velie. *Native American Studies.* Lincoln: University of Nebraska Press, 2005.

Kirschenblatt-Gimblett, Barbara. "Objects of Ethnography." In *Exhibiting Cultures: The Poetics and Politics of Museum Display,* edited by Ivan Karp and Stephen Lavine, 386–443. Washington, DC: Smithsonian Institution Press, 1991.

Kolodny, Annette. *In Search of First Contact: The Vikings of Vinland, the Peoples of the Dawnland, and the Anglo-American Anxiety of Discovery.* Durham, NC: Duke University Press, 2012.

Kracht, Benjamin R. "Kiowa-Comanche-Apache Opening." *Encyclopedia of Oklahoma History and Culture.* http://okhistory.org (accessed March 18, 2016).

———. "The Kiowa Ghost Dance, 1894–1916: An Unheralded Revitalization Movement." *Ethnohistory* 39, no. 4 (Fall 1992): 452–77.

———. "Kiowa Powwows: Continuity in Ritual Practice." *American Indian Quarterly* 18, no. 3 (Summer 1994): 321–48.

———. "Kiowa Religion in Historical Perspective." *American Indian Quarterly* 21, no. 1 (Winter 1997): 15–33.

Kraut, Alan. "Doing as Americans Do: The Post-migration Negotiation of Identity in the United States." *Journal of American History* 101, no. 3 (December 2014): 707–25.

Landelius, O. R. "Oscar B. Jacobson, pedagog och konstnär." *Utlandssvenskarna* 11 (1955): n.p.

Larsson, Olle, Lennart Johansson, and Lars-Olof Larsson. *Smålands historia.* Lund, Sweden: Historiska Media, 2006.

Läsebok för folkskolan: Första upplagan. Facsimile after the first edition 1868. Avesta, Sweden: Gidlunds, 1979.

La Vere, David. *Life among the Texas Indians: The WPA Narratives.* College Station: Texas A&M University Press, 1998.

———. "Minding Their Own Business: The Kiowa-Comanche-Apache Business Committee in the Early 1900s." In *Native Pathways: American Indian Culture and Economic Development in the Twentieth Century,* edited by Brian Hosmer and Colleen O'Neill, 52–65. Boulder: University Press of Colorado, 2004.

Levy, David W. "The University of Oklahoma." *Encyclopedia of Oklahoma History and Culture.* http://okhistoryorg (accessed March 29, 2016).

Levy, Jerry E. "Kiowa." In *Handbook of North American Indians: Plains,* 13:907–25. Washington, DC: Smithsonian Institution, 2001.

Lindquist, Emory Kempton. *Birger Sandzén: An Illustrated Biography.* Lawrence: Published for The Birger Sandzén Memorial Foundation by the University of Kansas Press, 1993.

———. *Smoky Valley People: A History of Lindsborg, Kansas.* Lindsborg, Kans.: Augustana Historical Society Publications, vol. 13, Bethany College, 1953.

Lookingbill, Brad D. *War Dance at Fort Marion: Plains Indian War Prisoners.* Norman: University of Oklahoma Press, 2006.

Madigan, Tim. *Tulsa Burning: Massacre, Destruction, and the Tulsa Race Riot of 1921.* New York: Thomas Dunne Books of St. Martin's Press, 2001.

Manchel, Frank. "Cultural Confusion." In *Hollywood's Indian: The Portrayal of the Native American in Film,* edited by Peter C. Rollins and John E. O'Connor, 91–106. Lexington: University Press of Kentucky, 1998.

Mann, Maybelle. "Kiowa Indian Art: A Pochoir Portfolio." *American Art & Antiques* (January–February 1979): 58–65.

Maroukis, Thomas C. *The Peyote Road: Religious Freedom and the Native American Church.* Norman: University of Oklahoma Press, 2010.

Marriott, Alice. *Kiowa Years: A Study in Culture Impact.* New York: Macmillan, 1968.

Marriott, Alice, and Carol K. Rachlin. *American Indian Mythologies.* New York: Harper and Row, 1968.

Martin, Mike W. "Good Fortune Obligates: Gratitude, Philanthropy, and Colonialism." *Southern Journal of Philosophy* 27 (1999): 57–74.

Mayhall, Mildred P. *The Kiowas.* Norman: University of Oklahoma Press, 1962.

Mbembe, Achille. "The Power of the Archive and Its Limits." In *Refiguring the Archive,* edited by Carolyn Hamilton, Verne Harris, Jane Taylor, Michele Pickover, Graeme Reid, and Razia Saleh, 19–27. London: Kluwer Academic Publishers, 2002.

McCormick, James C., and Monique Laxalt. "Oscar Brousse Jacobson." In *An Elegant Line: The Art of the Sheppard Family,* 13–27. Reno: Nevada Museum of Art, 2000.

McLerran, Jennifer. *A New Deal for Native Art: Indian Arts and Federal Policy, 1933–1943.* Tucson: University of Arizona Press, 2009.

McNelly, Linda S. *Native Performers in Wild West Shows.* Norman: University of Oklahoma Press, 2015.

Meadows, William C. *Kiowa Military Societies: Ethnohistory and Ritual.* Norman: University of Oklahoma Press, 2010.

Merrill, Elizabeth Jane. "The Art of Birger Sandzén." *American Magazine of Art* 17 (January 1927): 3–9.

Momaday, N. Scott. *The Man Made of Words.* New York: St. Martin's Griffin, 1997.

———. "Personal Reflections." In *The American Indian and the Problem of History,* edited by Calvin Martin, 156–61. New York: Oxford University Press, 1987.

———. *The Way to Rainy Mountain.* Albuquerque: University of New Mexico Press, 1969.

Mooney, James. *Calendar History of the Kiowa Indians.* Washington, DC: US Government Printing Office, 1898.

Moses, L. G. *Wild West Shows and the Images of American Indians, 1883–1933.* Albuquerque: University of New Mexico Press, 1996.

National Central Bureau of Statistics. *Historical Statistics of Sweden. Part 1. Population.* 1720–1967. 2nd ed. Stockholm: AB Allmänna förlaget, 1967.

Nelson, Helge. *The Swedes and the Swedish Settlements in North America.* Lund, Sweden: C. W. K. Gleerup, 1943.

Nemerov, Alex. "Doing the 'Old America.' The Image of the American West, 1880–1920." In Truettner, *The West as America,* 285–343.

Neuman, Lisa K. *Indian Play: Indigenous Identities at Bacone College.* Lincoln: University of Nebraska Press, 2013.

———. "Painting Culture: Art and Ethnography at a School for Native Americans." *Ethnology* 45, no. 3 (Summer 2006): 173–92.

Newman, Andrew. *On Records: Delaware Indians, Colonists, and the Media of History and Memory.* Lincoln: University of Nebraska Press, 2012.

Nisbeth, Hugo. "Indianerna i Nord-Amerika." *NU. Månadstidskrift* 2 (April 1876): 135–43.

Nordfelt, Eva. "Bondpojke från Småland Kiowa-indianernas hedershövding." *Kulturens Värld* 12, no. 1 (2002): 34–39.

Norman, Hans, and Harald Runblom. *Amerika-emigrationen.* Uddevalla, Sweden: Bokförlaget Cikada AB, 1980.

———. *Transatlantic Connections: Nordic Migration to the New World after 1800.* New York: Oxford University Press, 1988.

North, Cori Sherman. "Forty Years of the Prairie Water Color Painters." Pamphlet, SGA, 2015.

Nyquist, Edna. "Artist and Educator." *American Swedish Monthly* 32 (December 1938): 11–12, 43.

O'Brien, Jean M. *Firsting and Lasting: Writing Indians Out of Existence in New England.* Minneapolis: University of Minnesota Press, 2010.

Orr, Raymond. "The Nostalgic Native? The Politics and Terms of Heritage and Remembrance in Two Communities." *International Journal of Heritage Studies* 23, no. 7 (2017): 643–53.

Øverland, Orm. *Immigrant Minds, American Identities: Making the United States Home, 1870–1930.* Urbana: University of Illinois Press, 2000.

Palmer, Gus Jr. *Telling Stories the Kiowa Way.* Tucson: University of Arizona Press, 2003.

Parsons, Elsie Clews. *Kiowa Tales.* New York: American Folk-Lore Society, 1929.

Pålsson, Yvonne. *I Skinnstrumpas spår: Svenska barn- och ungdomsböcker om indianer, 1860–2008.* Umeå, Sweden: Institutionen för kultur- och medievetenskaper, 2013.

Parezo, Nancy J., and Don D. Fowler. *Anthropology Goes to the Fair: The 1904 Louisiana Purchase Exposition.* Lincoln: University of Nebraska Press, 2007.

Parham, Vera. "'All Go to the Hop Fields': The Role of Migratory and Wage Labor in the Preservation of Indigenous Pacific Northwest Culture." In *Native Diasporas: Indigenous Identities and Settler Colonialism in the Americas,* edited by Gregory D. Smithers and Brooke N. Newman, 317–46. Lincoln: University of Nebraska Press, 2014.

Pate, J'Nell. "Kiowa Art from Rainy Mountain: The Story of James Auchiah." *American Indian Quarterly* 1, no. 3 (1974): 193–200.

Penny, H. Glenn. *Kindred by Choice: Germans and American Indians since 1800.* Chapel Hill: University of North Carolina Press, 2013.

Perry, Gill. "Primitivism and the Modern." In *Primitivism, Cubism, Abstraction, The Early Twentieth Century*, edited by Charles Harrison, Francis Frascina, and Gillian Perry, 62–81. New Haven: Yale University Press, 1993.

Phillips, Ruth B. "The Turn of the Primitive: Modernism, the Stranger and the Indigenous Artist." In *Exiles, Diasporas & Strangers*, edited by Kobena Mercer, 46–71. London: MIT Press, 2008.

Pleijel, Hilding. *Hustavlans värld*. Lund, Sweden: Verbum, 1970.

Porter, Joy. "Progressivism and Native American Self-Expression in the Late Nineteenth and Early Twentieth Century." In *Native Diasporas: Indigenous Identities and Settler Colonialism in the Americas*, edited by Gregory D. Smithers and Brooke N. Newman, 273–95. Lincoln: University of Nebraska Press, 2014.

Pease, Janine Pretty on Top. "The Quality of Listening." In *Surviving in Two Worlds. Contemporary Native American Voices*, edited by Jay Leibold, 101–9. Austin: University of Texas Press, 1997.

Prucha, Francis P. *American Indian Treaties: The History of a Political Anomaly*. Berkeley: University of California Press, 1994.

Rand, Jacki T. *Kiowa Humanity and the Invasion of the State*. Lincoln: University of Nebraska Press, 2008.

Rasmussen, Birgit Brander. "Toward a New Literary History of the West: Etahdleuh Doanmoe's Captivity Narrative." In *Contested Spaces of Early America*, edited by Juliana Barr and Edward Countryman, 257–75. Philadelphia: University of Pennsylvania Press, 2014.

Reese, Linda Williams. *Women of Oklahoma, 1890–1920*. Norman: University of Oklahoma Press, 1997.

Reese, Linda Williams, and Patricia Loughlin, eds. *Main Street Oklahoma: Stories of Twentieth-Century America*. Norman: University of Oklahoma Press, 2013.

Reyhner, Jon, and Jeanne Eder. *American Indian Education: A History*. Norman: University of Oklahoma Press, 2004.

Rhoades, Bernadine Herwona Toyebo. "Keintaddle." In *Gifts of Pride and Love: Kiowa and Comanche Cradles*, edited by Barbara A. Hail, 89–93. Norman: University of Oklahoma Press, 2000.

Roberts, Calvin A., and Susan A. Roberts. *New Mexico*. Rev. ed. Albuquerque: University of New Mexico Press, 2006.

Runblom, Harald, and Hans Norman, eds. *From Sweden to America: A History of the Migration*. Minneapolis: University of Minnesota Press, 1976.

Rydell, Robert W. *All the World's a Fair: Visions of Empire at American International Expositions, 1876–1916*. Chicago: University of Chicago Press, 1984.

Sackman, Douglas Cazaux. *Wild Men: Ishi and Kroeber in the Wilderness of Modern America*. New York: Oxford University Press, 2011.

Seth, Sanjay. "'Once Was Blind but Now Can See': Modernity and the Social Sciences." *International Political Sociology* 7 (2013): 136–51.

Simonsen, Jane E. *Making Home Work: Domesticity and Native American Assimilation in the American West, 1860–1919*. Chapel Hill: University of North Carolina Press, 2006.

Smith, Linda E. *Horace Poolaw: Photographer of American Indian Modernity*. Lincoln: University of Nebraska Press, 2016.

Smith, Linda Tuhiwai. *Decolonizing Methodologies: Research and Indigenous Peoples.* London: Zed Books, 1999.

Smithers, Gregory D. "'What Is an Indian?'—The Enduring Question of American Indian Identity." In *Native Diaspora: Indigenous Identities and Settler Colonialism in the Americas,* edited by Gregory D. Smithers and Brooke N. Newman, 1–27. Lincoln: University of Nebraska Press, 2014.

Snyder, Michael. *John Joseph Mathews: Life of an Osage Writer.* Norman: University of Oklahoma Press, 2017.

Spickard, Paul. *Almost All Aliens: Immigration, Race, and Colonialism in American History and Identity.* New York: Routledge, 2007.

Stewart, Omer C. *Peyote Religion: A History.* Norman: University of Oklahoma, 1987.

Stoler, Anna Laura. "Colonial Archives and the Arts of Governance: On the Content in the Form." In *Refiguring the Archive,* edited by Carolyn Hamilton, Verne Harris, Jane Taylor, Michele Pickover, Graeme Reid, and Razia Saleh, 83–100. London: Kluwer Academic Publishers, 2002.

Sundbärg, Gustav, ed. *Emigrationsutredningen, bilaga VII: Utvandrarnes Egna Uppgifter.* Stockholm: P. A. Norstedts, 1918.

———. *Emigrationsutredningen, bilaga XIII: Allmänna ekonomiska data rörande Sverige.* Stockholm: P. A. Norstedt and Söner, 1912.

Swanson, Mary Towley. "Pictures from a New Home: Minnesota's Swedish American Artists." In *Swedes in the Twin Cities: Immigrant Life and Minnesota's Urban Frontier,* edited by Philip J. Anderson and Dag Blanck, 137–48. St. Paul: Minnesota Historical Society, 2001.

———. "A Tangled Web: Swedish Immigrant Artists' Patronage Systems, 1880–1940." *Art History Faculty Publications,* Paper 9 (2004). http://ir.stthomas.edu/arthistory_pub/9 (accessed August 26, 2018).

Szabo, Joyce M. *Art from Fort Marion: The Silberman Collection.* Norman: University of Oklahoma Press, 2007.

Szasz, Margaret Connell. *Scottish Highlanders and Native Americans: Indigenous Education in the Eighteenth-Century Atlantic World.* Norman: University of Oklahoma Press, 2007.

Tall Chief, Russ. "Jacobson and the Kiowa Five: A Play." In *The Native American New Play Festival: A Four Year Celebration,* edited by Sarah dAngelo and Regina McManigell Grijalva, 242–369. South Gate, Calif.: New Passport Press, 2016.

Tate, Michael L. *Indians and Emigrants: Encounters on the Overland Trail.* Norman: University of Oklahoma Press, 2006.

Tone-Pah-Hote, Jenny. *Crafting an Indigenous Nation: Kiowa Expressive Culture in the Progressive Era.* Chapel Hill: University of North Carolina Press, 2019.

———. "Envisioning Nationhood: Kiowa Expressive Culture, 1875–1939." PhD dissertation, University of Minnesota, 2009.

———. "We Worked and Made Beautiful Things: Kiowa Women, Material Culture, and Peoplehood, 1900–1939." In *Tribal Worlds: Critical Studies in American Indian Nation Building,* edited by Brian Hosmer and Larry Nesper, 253–72. Albany: State University of New York Press, 2015.

Trafzer, Clifford E., Jean A. Keller, and Lorene Sisquoc, eds. *Boarding School Blues: Revisiting American Indian Educational Experiences.* Lincoln: University of Nebraska Press, 2006.

Truettner, William H., ed. *The West as America: Reinterpreting Images of the Frontier, 1820–1920.* Washington, DC: Smithsonian Institution Press, 1991.

Turner, Alvin O. "Native American Art in Oklahoma: An Interpretation." In *Main Street Oklahoma: Stories of Twentieth-Century Oklahoma,* edited by Linda Reese and Patricia Loughlin, 154–74. Norman: University of Oklahoma Press, 2013.

Vizenor, Gerald. *Native Liberty: Natural Reason and Cultural Survivance.* Lincoln: University of Nebraska Press, 2009.

Vrdoljak, Ana Filipa. *International Law, Museums and the Return of Cultural Objects.* Cambridge: Cambridge University Press, 2006.

Wall, Wendy L. "Gender and the 'Citizen Indian.'" In *Writing the Range. Race, Class, and Culture in the Women's West,* edited by Elizabeth Jameson and Susan Armitage, 202–29. Norman: University of Oklahoma Press, 1997.

Waters, Anne. "Language Matters: Nondiscrete Nonbinary Dualism." In *American Indian Thought,* edited by Anne Waters, 97–115. Malden, Mass.: Blackwell Publishing, 2004.

Wattenberg, Richard. *Early-Twentieth-Century Frontier Dramas on Broadway. Situating the Western Experience in Performing Arts.* New York: Palgrave Macmillan, 2011.

Wattley, Cheryl Elizabeth Brown. *A Step toward Brown v. Board of Education: Ada Lois Sipuel Fisher and Her Fight to End Segregation.* Norman: University of Oklahoma Press, 2014.

Weaver, Hilary N. "The Colonial Context of Violence: Reflections on Violence in the Lives of Native American Women." *Journal of Interpersonal Violence* 24, no. 9 (2009): 1552–63.

Welch, Edward K. "This Is Your Life, Oscar Howe." *Journal of Popular Culture* 47, no. 2 (2014): 247–61.

Werbner, Pnina. "The Materiality of Diaspora—Between Aesthetic and 'Real' Politics." *Diaspora—A Journal of Transnational Studies* 1 (2000): 3–20.

Werbner, Pnina, and Mattia Fumanti. "The Aesthetics of Diaspora: Ownership and Appropriation." *Ethnos: Journal of Anthropology* 78, no. 2 (2013): 149–74.

White, Mark Andrew. "An Artist in the Wilderness: Oscar Brousse Jacobson and Worlds Unconquered." In Allbright, Berlo, and White, *A World Unconquered,* 37–98.

———. "A Modernist Moment: Native Art and Surrealism at the University of Oklahoma." *Journal of Surrealism and the Americas* 7, no. 2 (2013): 52–70.

———. *Oklahoma Moderne: The Art and Design of Olinka Hrdy.* Norman, Okla.: Fred Jones Jr. Museum of Art, University of Oklahoma, 2007.

Widén, Albin. *Svenskar som erövrat Amerika.* Stockholm: Nordisk Rotogravyr, 1937.

Wilkins, David E., and K. Tsianina Lomawaima. *Uneven Ground: American Indian Sovereignty and Federal Law.* Norman: University of Oklahoma Press, 2001.

Williams, Anna. *Skribent i Svensk-Amerika. Jakob Bonggren, journalist och poet.* Dissertation, Uppsala University, 1991.

Williams, Michael Ann. *Staging Tradition: John Lair and Sarah Gertrude Knott.* Urbana: University of Illinois Press, 2006.

Wohlin, Nils. *Emigrationsutredningen, bilaga IX: Den jordbruksidkande befolkningen i Sverige 1751–1900.* Stockholm: Nordiska bokh., 1909.

Wright, Muriel H. *A Guide to the Indian Tribes of Oklahoma.* Norman: University of Oklahoma Press, 1951, 1986.

Zilliacus, Konni. *Amerika-Boken: Hjälpreda för utvandrare.* Stockholm: Albert Bonniers förlag, 1893.

———. *Amerikas förenta stater.* New York: G. A. Grönlunds tryckeri, 1893.

Index

Page references in *italic* type refer to illustrations.